Picoeconomics (Micro-microeconomics) examines an elementary human paradox: that we are endangered by our own wishes, or, as Oscar Wilde put it, "When the gods want to punish us they answer our prayers." Even though this observation is ancient and has been confirmed by wide experience, none of the disciplines that deal with decision making have explained it.

Dr. Ainslie uses findings from behavioral experiments to show that there is a basic tendency for both lower animals and human beings to form temporary preferences for the poorer but earlier of two goals when the poorer goal is close at hand. People compensate for this tendency by strategically adjusting behavior in anticipation of their own future motivational states. Unlike theories that have accounted for irrationalities on the basis of repression or conditioning of motives, this book proposes that temporary preferences for objectively inferior goals arise inevitably from the way both animals and human beings perceive delay.

The implications of this change in viewpoint help provide a rationale for hitherto puzzling behavior, from Freud's defense mechanism to the force of willpower, as well as conspicuous failures of willpower in addictions and other psychiatric disorders. This approach also sheds light on subjects that have been controversial in moral philosophy: weakness of will, self-deception, freedom, and responsibility.

PICOECONOMICS

STUDIES IN RATIONALITY
AND SOCIAL CHANGE

STUDIES IN RATIONALITY AND SOCIAL CHANGE

Editors: Jon Elster and Michael S. McPherson

Editorial Board:
Fredrik Barth
Amartya Sen
Arthur Stinchcombe
Amos Tversky
Bernard Williams

George Ainslie

PICOECONOMICS

The Strategic Interaction of Successive
Motivational States within the Person

CAMBRIDGE
UNIVERSITY PRESS

Published by the Press Syndicate of the University of Cambridge
The Pitt Building, Trumpington Street, Cambridge CB2 1RP
40 West 20th Street, New York, NY 10011-4211, USA
10 Stamford Road, Oakleigh, Victoria 3166, Australia

© Cambridge University Press 1992

First published 1992

Printed in the United States of America

Library of Congress Cataloging-in-Publication Data
Ainslie, George, 1944–
Picoeconomics : the strategic interaction of successive motivational states
within the person / George Ainslie.
p.   cm. – (Studies in rationality and social change)
Includes bibliographical references and index.
ISBN 0-521-26093-0
1. Motivation (Psychology)   2. Choice (Psychology)   3. Reward (Psychology)
I. Title.   II. Series.
BF503.A46   1992
153.8 – dc20   91–24450
                                                                    CIP

A catalog record for this book is available from the British Library.

ISBN 0-521-26093-0 hardback

Contents

Preface

When the gods want to punish us they answer our prayers.
—Oscar Wilde, *An Ideal Husband* (1895/1989)

[We are] too often cursed with the granting of our prayer.
—Emerson, *Conduct of Life* (Bartlett, 1955)

We, ignorant of ourselves, beg often our own harms, which the wise powers deny us for our good.
—Shakespeare, *Antony and Cleopatra* (Stevenson, 1967)

We prayed for the rising of the Nile. The Nile came, and we were drowned.
—Arab proverb (Burckhardt, 1988)

Don't pray for what you will wish you hadn't got.
—Seneca, *Ad Lucilium* (Stevenson, 1967)

We have met the enemy, and he is us.
—Walt Kelley's *Pogo*

This book examines an elementary human paradox – perhaps *the* elementary human paradox – that we are endangered by our own wishes. Even though this observation is ancient and has been confirmed by wide experience, none of the disciplines that deal with decision making have explained it. One – economics – has barely recognized it at all, and only recently has economics ascribed it to anything beyond inadequate forethought. Each of the others – behavioral, cognitive, and psychoanalytic psychology and moral philosophy – has proposed at least one mechanism for it, but as the philosophers have demonstrated better than anyone, such mechanisms have served mainly to name the phenomenon and exempt it from further analysis, rather than to reconcile it with any basic concept of the nature of motivation. It has remained an anomaly, an apparent contradiction of most people's beliefs about how choices are evaluated.

This anomaly represents more than a philosophical conundrum. As our power to shape our world increases, so does our dangerousness. The profits of science are eaten up by our own perversity in the form of addictions, obsessions, aberrations of character, and self-imprisonment in life-styles of our own making. We need to understand the elementary properties of our motivation, not just to fill in a blank spot in basic science, but to save ourselves from our own theories of what will make us happy.

I shall review what has been said about this tendency to defeat ourselves, and then propose a comprehensive explanation. I do not claim that this explanation is unique – that there can be no other models that will be systematic and consistent with the facts currently known about motivation. However, I do argue that this is the first such explanation. By the same token, I cannot show that the many behavior patterns predicted by this mechanism actually do depend on it; but they do fit with such a theory, and this fit offers the first coherent explanation of many familiar but heretofore unaccountable behaviors. I hope that this work will lead others to formulate alternative explanations and find ways to test them, and that such a process will finally yield a model that can be uniquely supported by observation.

I have chosen an economic title in light of convincing evidence that even seemingly irrational and "unwanted" behaviors are goal-directed. Economics is the original theory of goal-directed choice. I shall argue that self-defeating behavior is best understood in terms of an economic marketplace within the individual. Both the psychoanalysts' libido theory and the behaviorists' reinforcement theory are economic in nature, and the recent burgeoning of "behavioral economics" has shown how nearly congruent reinforcement theory is with economics.

However, behavioral economics does not necessarily deal with the case in which one part of an individual seems to undermine the efforts of another part; a more specific title seemed necessary. Earlier I had proposed, with tongue in cheek, that the discipline that studies this case could be called "picoeconomics," that is, micro-micro-economics (Ainslie, 1986a); on reflection, that does seem to be the most appropriate term for it. Just as classical economics describes negotiation for limited resources among institutions, and microeconomics describes such negotiation among individuals, so picoeconomics describes interactions that resemble negotiation among parts that can be defined within the individual for control of that individual's finite behavioral capacity.

Such a process is not easy to observe. The economists themselves have done almost no empirical work that bears on self-defeating behaviors – just some field surveys of purchases and a few recent parametric self-report studies of hypothetical preferences. Most of the controlled experiments have been carried out in the area of behavioral psychology, and that is where the roots of this book are deepest. However, this method has a limited sensitivity, and the behaviorists' unnecessary philosophical bias (Day, 1969; Lieberman, 1979) against either obtaining experiential reports or theorizing about internal motivational processes has restrained their exploration of this problem.

The field that has most concerned itself with internal motivational conflict is psychoanalysis; I shall repeatedly trace the origin of the motivational concepts I use to Freud's work. His method of observation, though largely unable to discriminate causative factors from merely correlated ones, is highly sensitive to subtleties of motivation and can track them over long periods of time. The main drawback of psychoanalytic psychology is not its supposed fancifulness, but rather its abandonment of early attempts to relate its constructs to those of other behavioral disciplines, a development that has left its terminology quaintly fixated, as it were, on late Victorian science. The result has been a division of psychiatry into a group of schoolmen and a larger body of practitioners who have given up the attempt to examine motivation in any rigorous way.

The third major source of my approach is bargaining theory, particularly the ideas of Thomas Schelling. I shall argue that the study of bargaining supplies the concepts needed for adapting behavioral psychology to apply to intrapsychic conflict, an adaptation that will in turn create an adequate language for much of psychoanalytic theory. Bargaining games also represent a valuable experimental opportunity to test some hypotheses about internal conflict.

On the centenary of William James's *Principles of Psychology* it seems wise to recall his approach. Modern research relevant to motivation has become increasingly specialized, in the hope of getting sharper photographs of particular phenomena. James did experiments when they seemed necessary, but his primary data were "phenomenally given thoughts," the conscious experience that he had in common with his readers (James, 1890, p. vi). He did not despair of finding undiscovered order in everyday observations, and so he did not feel a need to throw the greater part of his energy into collecting new data. This is not to say that he accepted popular explanations for these observations; what could not be deduced from the observations themselves was metaphysics, something quite apart from the "natural science" he saw psychology to be:

> In this strictly positivistic point of view consists the only feature of [*Principles of Psychology*] for which I feel tempted to claim originality. [1890, p. vi]

Of course, positivism was to become stricter than James could have imagined, out of what he might have identified as a morbid fear of being deceived (1896/1967b); but that quest for certainty so reduced the sensitivity of positivism that it became itself something akin to metaphysics. During the great positivistic leap forward, only linguistics among the behavioral sciences kept its assurance that one could base explanation on an appeal to the ear of a native speaker. Now the thought experiment has reappeared in other fields, and we are again becoming free to use whatever sources of information are at hand, as James did.

It would be nice to be able to say, with another author who found undiscovered order in the obvious, that

> partly because there is less chance of misapprehending the sense of phenomena that are familiar to all men, the data employed to illustrate or enforce the argument have by preference been drawn from everyday life, by direct observation or through common no-

toriety, rather than from more recondite sources at a farther remove. [Veblen, 1899/1931, pp. vii–viii]

However, the modern writer has access to a wealth of "recondite
sources" as well as familiar experiences, and here and there the
former have suggested an indispensable key with which to reinterpret
the latter. In the spirit of William James, I shall attempt to balance
the ordinary and the technical, always hoping to at least illustrate the
resulting theory with examples that no one will be unable to relate
to his[1] own experience.

Many other fields have dealt with self-defeating behavior from time
to time. I shall refer to observations and ideas from cognitive psychology, which unfortunately has been limited by its disregard of
motivation, as well as ideas from sociology, ethology, moral philosophy, ethics, history, and the lore reported in both clinical and literary
works. Even theological concepts have been helpful – after all, the
priests of various religions were the main observers of motivational
conflict until the current century. I have also tried a variety of techniques to make my own observations of conflictual behavior. I shall
report on behavioral experiments with pigeons and with people, self-
report questionnaires, clinical and structured Piagetian interviews,
actual two-person bargaining games, and computer simulations. However, the available methods have been largely inadequate to observe
the choice-making process without disturbing it. Despite the absence
of data that would be more than suggestive, I have proceeded with
this book out of a belief that the main feature limiting our knowledge
of self-contradiction has not been the lack of data, but the inadequacy
of our concepts.

This work had its origins in an undergraduate project at Yale College;
the interdisciplinary approach derives from seminars attended in pursuing my major in culture and behavior, encounters for which I have

---

[1] Having read many earnest attempts to remove any connotation of gender from
the conventional third-person singular pronoun for someone of unspecified sex, I have
to agree with the editors of *Writing from A to Z*, who find "the repeated use of 'he
or she' or the newer contractions awkward and distracting" (Polking, 1990, preface).
The *con*notation that arises from using "he" for both male and unspecified genders is
unfortunate, but is not likely to be taken as *de*notation and thus is not of great
significance. I shall forbear experimenting with improvements.

repeatedly been thankful over the past quarter-century. The reward value functions I first used were those of my teacher, Frank Logan. I was fortunate in being referred soon afterward to Richard Herrnstein, at the Harvard Laboratories for Experimental Psychology, whose "matching law" fit the needs of my theory even better, and whose advice, comments, and encouragement have been invaluable down to the present. Howard Rachlin helped me translate my ideas into Skinner box experiments and published my first findings in his textbook before they were ready for a journal (Rachlin, 1970). In the meantime, Leston Havens, who supervised my psychiatric residency at Massachusetts Mental Health Center, gave me valuable ideas on the strategic nature of psychotherapies.

Preliminary sketches of this book have appeared as chapters of books edited by Jon Elster (Ainslie, 1986a) and by Michael Commons, James Mazur, Anthony Nevin, and Howard Rachlin (Ainslie, 1987b). Earlier versions of some parts appeared in *Social Science Information* (Ainslie, 1982, 1984, 1985) and in the *American Economic Review* (Ainslie, 1991).

Many people lent a helping hand to this book. Jon Elster suggested it almost a decade ago and has offered patient and valuable advice while waiting for it, meanwhile arranging provocative annual conferences among the few people in psychology, philosophy, and economics interested in intertemporal conflict. I am particularly indebted to a long line of undergraduate and graduate assistants, among whom Marci Klein, Andrea Bloomgarden, Michele Batter, and Nick Haslam stand out, and to other people who have offered comments on the manuscript, particularly Bill Whipple, Jon Baron, Drazen Prelec, Dick Herrnstein, Dick Thaler, and my wife Elizabeth, who is a far clearer writer than I. Margo Schaefer gave me valuable advice about the demon model in chapter 8, and Robin Ashmore helped to get it actually working on a computer. Finally, I thank the people in the Coatesville Department of Veterans Affairs Medical Center who supported me in this unorthodox undertaking, especially Jim Carson and Jim Harris in the administration, graphic artist Lynn Debiak (whose work was completed by Michele Batter), photographer Richard Sama, librarians Mary Lou Burton, Mary Walters, and Julia Canonica, and typists Gale McHenry and Ginny Domblesky.

This work was supported in its entirety by the Department of Veteran's Affairs.

1. The paradox of addiction

Modern industrial societies are rich by any historical standard, but we do not enjoy our riches well. The more we are able to buy freedom from hunger, disease, and drudgery, the more we are afflicted by an unaccountable malaise. As the old problems have been solved, activities that once were considered the rewards of success have come to pose new problems. Traditional pleasures like food, drink, and sport have become abundant, and new ones like cinema, flying, and automated games are invented in profusion; but as pleasure becomes easy, its enjoyment is increasingly described as "compulsive," meaning that it is strongly motivated, but fails to give satisfaction:

> Each day witnesses the birth of some new, wonderful invention, destined to make the world pleasanter to live in, the adversities of life more endurable, and to increase the variety and intensity of the enjoyments possible to humanity. But yet, notwithstanding the growth and increase of all conditions to promote comfort, the human race is today more discontented, more irritated and more restless than ever before.

The idea of a disease of civilization that oppresses paradoxically as material problems are solved is not new. The foregoing passage is from a Victorian book called *The Conventional Lies of Our Civilization* (Nordau, 1886). At almost the same time, George Beard (1881) was describing a similar malaise, "neurasthenia," which he blamed on the increased pace of life. Thorstein Veblen was soon to remind the world that monetary gain usually does not lead to lasting hedonic gain:

> As fast as a person makes new acquisitions, and becomes accustomed to the resulting new standard of wealth, the new standard

forthwith ceases to afford appreciably greater satisfaction than the earlier standard did. [Veblen, 1899/1931, p. 31]

Worse, he said that surplus wealth tends to be expended on the basically hostile activity of raising invidious comparisons between oneself and one's neighbors. From the nineteenth century to the present, many authors have described variants of a syndrome in which people indulge freely in some newly plentiful good, then suffer an insidious side effect that saps their enjoyment, not only of that good but of life generally (Adams, 1896; Bellah et al., 1985; Hendin, 1975; Henry, 1963; Kerr, 1962; Lasch, 1979; Linder, 1970; Scitovsky, 1976). The condition bears some similarity to the psychological state that Arnold Toynbee (1946, Vol. 1, pp. 275–532) claimed to see in the leadership of civilizations past the peak of their success, a mixture of sensual "abandon" and a loss of "creativity" that mark the beginning of a civilization's disintegration. These authors seem to be suggesting something more than the ancient complaint that the younger generation does not respect convention. Starting at the beginning of the industrial revolution, perhaps with Kierkegaard, some have specifically said that we should not trust conventional ideas of progress – indeed, that progress might be a blight.

However, such authors have never specified the pathogen for this malaise with any precision. It is said to involve an increase in subjects' ranges of available choices and, usually, the speed with which subjects can obtain their chosen goods. The subjects typically are free from drudgery and from domination by other people. Perhaps they are best described as being at leisure, at least in comparison with people who do not suffer from the syndrome. Most strikingly, its sufferers seem unable to stop doing the things that bring it on, even when they have clear indications as to what those things are. They are seduced, rather than attacked, by the destructive process.

If leisure is an important factor in the development of this syndrome, there is good reason for concern about it. In the past, leisure classes lived on relatively small islands of tranquillity in the midst of toil and danger. Never before the industrial revolution had leisure been the ordinary condition of life. In developed societies, even the very poor now come within a reasonable definition of leisure: When they lack the skills and work habits for which an employer will pay, they forgo amenities, but do not have to struggle long hours to avoid hunger and cold (Eisenberger, 1989, pp. 59–77). If universal leisure means the epidemic spread of an attendant pathology, that must call into question many of our assumptions about the basic nature of wealth.

1.1 Addictions provide a model for participatory disease

Of course, there have always been concrete examples of urgent pleasures with destructive effects that might serve as models for the more insidious disease. They usually are called "addictions" and are characterized by the sufferer's ambivalence about them. One feels imprisoned by them, "wants," in some sense of the word, to be rid of them, but keeps choosing them freely when given the chance.[1]

However, in recent years the number of activities recognized to have this puzzling, unwanted seductive quality has mushroomed (Hatterer, 1980). To the traditional list of alcoholism, drug addiction, gambling, and overeating (itself newly defined as an addiction, as opposed to the sinful trait of gluttony) (Anonymous, 1980; Greene & Jones, 1974) have been added addictions to a variety of "normal" drugs, including prescription tranquilizers (Cummings, 1979), nicotine, caffeine (Gilbert, 1976; Russ et al., 1988), and even sugar

---

[1] The relationship between leisure and addiction does not seem to be simple. Addictions certainly are not confined to leisured societies. Addictions to exceptionally rewarding activities – smoking, drinking, taking opiates – sometimes have occurred even in societies toiling on the edge of physical subsistence; but where daily activity is coerced by physical needs, there seems to be less susceptibility to addiction. This may be due simply to the monetary costs of most addictions: Historically (Braudel, 1973, pp. 86–92), when most people spent more than half their income on food, even beer was so wasteful of the grain from which it was made (Burnett, 1969) that they were obliged to find ways to control their appetite for it (Thompson, 1939/1973, pp. 64–75); societies too surprised by the introduction of a new addiction to develop controls have been ruined in their entirety, as witness the effects of alcohol on many tribes of American Indians.

In contrast to the apparent positive relationship between leisure and addiction in societies, among individuals resistance to addiction is a skill that probably is somewhat correlated with the skill of gaining leisure, and addictions tend to sap both skill and leisure. Thus, we regularly see the poor more strongly addicted than the rich, at least to those activities for which both have the means, such as overeating – the poor are several times as likely to be obese as the well-to-do (Stunkard et al., 1972). The influence of such factors as education and occupational level is especially well illustrated by their strong positive relationship to cessation rates for a newly recognized addiction: smoking (Kabat & Wynder, 1987), as well as success in treatment for alcoholism (Wiens & Menustik, 1983).

(Dufty, 1975; Falk, 1977), chocolate (Michell, Mebane, & Billings, 1989; Schuman, Gitlin, & Fairbanks, 1987), and water (which, in large quantities, intoxicates by diluting the electrolytes of the blood) (Langgard & Smith, 1962; Smith & Clark, 1980). In addition, there can be addictions to romantic relationships (Peele & Brodsky, 1975, pp. 141–169) and emotional dependence (Halpern, 1982), as well as promiscuous sexual encounters (Carnes, 1983; Ellis & Sagrin, 1964; I. Miller, 1969; Willis, 1967), masturbation (Latendresse, 1968), and a number of deviant sexual practices (Allen, 1969; Annon & Robinson, 1980; Carnes, 1983). The list continues: addictions to television and video games (Kubey & Csikszentmihalyi, 1990), to haste (Friedman & Rosenman, 1974), work (Kramer, 1977; Overbeck, 1976), and exercise (Kagan, 1987), to shoplifting and other kinds of thrill-seeking, to some kinds of self-inducible epileptic seizures (Faught et al., 1986), to physical self-mutilation (Asch, 1971; Bach-y-Rita, 1974; Pao, 1969) and aggression toward others (Bjorkqvist, Ekman, & Lagerspeth, 1982; Wilson, 1983), to spending money (Glatt & Cook, 1987; Krueger, 1988), to religiosity and fasting, to many maladaptive personality traits such as overcompetitiveness (Friedman & Rosenman, 1974), procrastination (Lachenicht, 1989; Lay, 1987), and obsessional jealousy (Schoenfeld, 1979), and even to some symptoms that usually have not been counted as behaviors, such as anxiety, depression, and "obsessional compulsions" (Hodgson & Miller, 1982). Adding the "compulsions to repeat" that psychoanalysts have described in various patients would make the list virtually endless.[2]

To some extent this growth reflects increased recognition of an addictive pattern in behaviors that have long been common, and to some extent it reflects a shift of public attention as the purely technical problems that have affected human welfare have been solved – addictions often are described as the "greatest preventable cause" of one or another kind of morbidity, as if they were somehow more easily preventable than other causes. Whatever the reason for the increased public consciousness of addictions, it confronts behavioral scientists with our chronic inability to fit them into any of our many theories of motivation. They are goal-directed behaviors and thus

---

[2] I am excluding the activities that have been called "positive addictions," such as an attachment to classical music that grows with practice (Becker & Murphy, 1988); these do not entail the experience of disowning one's own wishes, and hence they pose no problem for conventional motivational theory.

should respond to the many techniques that modern society uses to marshal motivation, but they do not. The persistence of this defiance after generations of study seems to demand a radical reexamination of our beliefs about motivation.

People have always had a tendency to defeat their own behavior. Since ancient times authors have complained of it, laughed at it, written tragedies about it. Addiction is a familiar phenomenon, but we understand it intuitively, through literature or through examples in our own lives. Science has never been of much help. A few psychologists, and philosophers before them, have claimed that such "incontinence" is avoidable and have offered to teach us how to avoid it. But from the viewpoint that usually is regarded as rational, the problem of addiction cannot even be explained, much less solved.

Why should there be choices that one does not feel that one wants to make, but nevertheless makes repeatedly? It is imaginable that an activity can feel so good that it overrides all other incentives, but how does one get to be "of two minds" about it, both wanting it and not wanting it, so that one may simultaneously buy it and buy an antidote for it? No accepted behavioral science accounts for that situation, and philosophers have had to engage in logical gymnastics to reconcile it with the idea of a single clearheaded actor (Davidson, 1980, pp. 21–42; 1983) (also see section 2.2).

A phenomenon that seems to accompany addictions is less paradoxical, although still unexplained: Jaded appetites for habitual pleasures are not inconsistent with a rationally ordered set of preferences, but conventional motivational theory does not say why the jading should occur. We can at least picture a simple defect that might create demands for more adventurous sexual techniques, more exotic fiction, and even more exciting meals – something like an exhausted tube in an old-fashioned radio whose waning power causes the listener to turn the volume knob higher and higher. We see a possible analogue in physiological habituation to a repeated stimulus (Solomon, 1980), although the failure of rest to restore the old appetites in all but the simplest cases suggests that such habituation is not literally involved in the creation of this kind of fatigue. After physical withdrawal from heroin, the addict's appetite for it is fresh again, but outmoded fashions remain uninteresting. Some kind of learning must have carried the process beyond just stimulus exhaustion.

Some authors suggest that something more deliberate – specifically perverse rather than just fatigued – governs the jading of modern appetites (Hendin, 1975; Linder, 1970; Maslow, 1970; Scitovsky, 1976). They suggest that people are not the passive victims of stimulus overload, but are the perpetrators of self-defeating consumption patterns. Many prosaic examples are widely complained of, if poorly documented, in our lore: the short attention span of the average modern reader, viewer, or diner (Corwin, 1983); the loudness and beat required of popular music if it is to capture attention; the level of violence required of an adventure film (Plagens et al., 1991); the impatience that leads more and more people to sacrifice family ties over childishly small frustrations (Hendin, 1975). This behavior is magnified in the patients whom psychotherapists see. Compared with those of Freud's day, modern patients more often complain of an unexplained loss of satisfaction, despite success – they get jobs and discard them, win friends and despise them, capture hearts but do not feel warmed by them (Giovachinni, 1975).

The decay of satisfaction seems to get worse the more subtle the source. People experience this as disillusion with their higher purposes, which usually have something to do with their relationships with other people. Many authors perceive social affiliation to be weakening in modern times. Alan Bloom's recent argument (1987) that a thorough renunciation of social commitments has occurred in the United States is only the latest of a progression of warnings that human relationships in developed society are becoming superficial (Bellah et al., 1985, pp. 275–296; Lasch, 1979; Marin, 1975; Packard, 1972; Riesman, Denney, & Glazer, 1950); the related concept of alienation is reviewed by Schacht (1971). To some, this development portends doom; psychoanalyst Marie Coleman Nelson (1984) has wondered that "as the twentieth century draws to a close, how shall we understand the burgeoning of evil?" The aloof bystander who lets tragedies run their course has become a cliché. Stanley Milgram's analog experiments (1974) inducing willing betrayals of social obligations offer, if not proof, at least agreement. The bare facts are that divorce has increased, intact families have decreased, and, in the United States at least, violence is at a new high (Holinger, 1979). The rate for the most alienated behavior, suicide, varies inversely with social integration (Gibbs & Martin, 1964); suicide among the young and others who would seem to have reason to be hopeful has increased markedly over the past two decades. More than 1% of deaths in the United States are now suicides (Holinger, 1979; Rosenberg et al., 1987).

The problem is complicated by our ignorance about what engenders our highest purposes to begin with. Addictions and their attendant behaviors might be said to be irrational in that they do not maximize what we think of ourselves as valuing most highly. However, it would be more accurate to say that we do not understand our higher values in any scientific sense and must reserve judgment about whether or not any given behavior toward them is irrational. Our theory of what rewards us has become increasingly systematized by economics and psychology, but that can describe few of our actual satisfactions.

1.2 Behavioral science has not dealt with our most significant decisions

Admittedly it is difficult to keep track of what people want – not starving people or those in pain, perhaps, for their motives are dominated by a single obvious discomfort. But biological need does not threaten most people in modern society, nor has it often been a sustained threat to the class of people who write books about motives. People usually are driven by incentives they choose for themselves (Csikszentmihalyi, 1977). Why do some people keep climbing Mount Everest, or running for office, or removing every speck of dust from their floors? How do they weigh the motives for these activities against a ticket to hear a comedian, or a new spring outfit in the latest fashion, or a great love?

Since ancient times, one school of thought has held that people can appraise the value of goods by simple experience, that incentive derives from the limited availability of such goods, and that motivational conflict results merely from failure to think choices through. This school essentially takes the desires that motivate climbing, cleaning, and loving as givens, assigns them values on the basis of their relative unavailability, and likens the task of choosing among them to shopping on a budget. That was the Epicurean approach, systematized in the modern era by Jeremy Bentham, who developed a hedonic "calculus" with which to analyze the budget. Its descendant is the widely accepted utility theory[3] that assumes that consistent preference requires only free comparison among the possible choices (Page, 1968).

---

[3] The difference between modern "utilitarian" and "hedonistic" schools lies in their

This approach has had many adherents in recent years. For instance, Skinner (1948b) extrapolated from his experimental research to an operant utopia where rational understanding of the contingencies of reinforcement permitted its maximization (see also Simon, 1955). Earlier, Samuelson (1937) had solidified economists' tentative assumptions that people and corporations, when allowed to choose freely, behave so as to optimize their objective prospects. Becker (1976) postulated a virtual price for each activity, in effect updating the hedonic calculus to modern economic standards. At about the same time, Atkinson and Birch (1970) were developing another hedonic calculus from purely psychological roots. From the cognitive therapist to the *Playboy Philosopher* there are many who believe that the only reason people cannot enjoy their wealth is a failure to use elementary utilitarian reasoning. But that approach still leaves unclear what determines higher motives – those that do not aim at the consumption of some physiologically active good. Furthermore, the growing catalog of self-defeating behaviors makes it evident that the relationships of motives do not compose a simple hierarchy and that a proper representation of human preferences requires more than the computation of relative values.

1.2.1 Utilitarian concepts of higher motives are primitive

Economists have almost unanimously avoided the problems of subtle reward and of self-defeating behavior (see chapter 2). They assume behavior to be utilitarian and, furthermore, have restricted their attention to those relatively concrete goods that can be easily priced. Conventional utility theory arose from the study of tangible commodities in limited supply – goods that, though they were not always necessities, could nevertheless motivate people powerfully if those goods were in short supply. Yet these are not the goods that command our energies, except in rather circumscribed situations. Under conditions of leisure, most of the value that commodities have for people is bestowed by the people themselves, depending on arbitrary processes that occur in

definitions of the goals of behavior, not in their tenets of how those goals are evaluated (Baron, 1988; Brandt, 1967). This definition will be unimportant for our discussion. I shall always use both terms in their psychological or economic, rather than ethical, sense.

their own heads, rather than on the properties of the commodities (Hardin, 1984). If the processes that bestow value are in limited supply, science has not identified the nature of the limits.

Granted that there are choices accurately described by current economic theory, most human decision making is beyond its laws. As seen in everyday experience or reported by normal subjects, only relatively small numbers of choices involve making or spending money. Most choices have to do with how much of an unpleasant emotion one is willing to risk enduring in the hope of reaching pleasant emotions – the unpleasant ones being embarrassment, tedium, doubt, confusion, apprehension, resentment, and so forth, and the pleasant ones being fellowship, comfort, amusement, pride, relief, inspiration, and other vaguely defined feelings that are nevertheless well known in the day's particular context.[4]

It is true that people make money much of the time, but with the possible exception of piecework payment schedules, the incentives bearing on their minute-to-minute choices are not monetary. They spend much of the workday in what Leibenstein (1976) called X-inefficiency, the adjustment of emotional well-being, with only tangential reference to productivity (Levinson, 1975). People also spend money – they wear out shoes, and their rents run continuously – but they are mostly concerned with buying the resources needed to take part in social or gamelike activities, rather than commodities that can yield significant rewards in their own right. They buy situations that help them feel masterful, or lovable, or admirable, or, through fiction, situations in which they can feel vicarious triumph, or even heartbreak or terror (Twitchell, 1985).

It has been argued that the limitation of economic theory for addressing the choices closest to the human heart may be simply that quantitative data on choice-making are not available for these areas of behavior. In the spirit of solving this problem, Gary Becker and a few other economists have recently expanded the economic data base by describing regularities in nonmonetary transactions like marriage (Becker, 1976), extramarital affairs (Fair, 1978), and criminal deter-

---

[4] Large time-diary studies reflect similar nonmonetary priorities in terms of the time spent on various activities (Robinson, Converse, & Szalai, 1972) and the contributions of those activities to reported well-being (Campbell, Converse, & Rodgers, 1976, p. 76).

rence (Becker, 1976), as well as addiction itself (Becker & Murphy, 1988). However, the problem is more serious than simply a lack of data.

A substantial number of people have always mistrusted hedonic reasoning. The Stoics said it was a sham (Zeller, 1870). The great religions often have declared that hedonism is misleading and sometimes have given elaborate explanations, such as the original sin of Adam, why this should be so. As secular philosophy and then psychology developed, some of the foremost thinkers in those fields opposed the strictly economic approach to value. However, the subtle goods they have proposed from time to time, such as existential authenticity and self-actualization, defy precise characterization. Such goods often have seemed to be irrational, or at least to be members of a different motivational system than that which is based on market economics. The true utilitarian does not have such doubts, of course, and asks why a person's behavior toward any good – self-actualization, transcendence, the salvation of the soul – cannot be handled with an approach like Becker's.

Indeed, some psychologists have made efforts over the years to explain how nonconcrete rewards might be related to concrete ones. But although concrete rewards have been studied thoroughly, no one has succeeded in expanding this nucleus of knowledge to include the subtle rewards. The psychological study of motivation has paralleled, rather than complemented, the economic study.

Studies of the concrete rewards that are effective because of physiological needs have produced a wealth of quantitative detail about how the reward[5] mechanism depends on previous deprivation, rate of delivery, the presence or absence of other sources of reward, and so forth. However, this information may not apply to the vast area of behavior motivated by the emotional processes that are occasioned by other people's social responses, or by tasks or games that are rewarding in their own right. Clearly it would be desirable if these

---

[5] "Reinforcer" was once supposed to be a value-free term and thus more appropriate than "reward," but it implies a specific hypothesis about the process of making choices – that choice depends on the relative strength of connections (absent or weak until "reinforced") from a cue to alternative responses – that does not now seem to be true (Brown & Herrnstein, 1975, pp. 115–162; Estes, 1969a). I shall revert to using the "reward" of common speech for both the internal process that confers value upon behaviors and the external occasion for this process.

subtle rewards could be understood in the same framework as concrete rewards, but psychology has had difficulty bridging the gap. It has not been able to study emotional processes in a controlled fashion, and its hypotheses about what parameters constrain the emotions have been improbable or incomplete:

An early approach was to make classical conditioning ("learning by association") the bridging mechanism. For instance, the rewarding value of an intangible reward like fame might be attributed to an infantile association between getting attention and getting food, thus in effect backing the soft currency of an activity reward with the hard currency of a visceral reward (Kempf, 1920, p. 76; Miller & Dollard, 1941; Sears, Maccoby, & Levin, 1957). However, observation has not been able to trace such tortuous paths of association from activity rewards back to actual visceral rewards. Furthermore, there is no reason to expect that the conditioned rewards should remain powerful once a person has discovered direct ways of getting the original visceral reward. The person who is not hungry should cease to value the conditioned food stimulus: attention.

Later, psychologists argued that there were elementary drives for the gamelike rewards (Fowler, 1967; Hunt, 1963). The problem with their exploration, curiosity, and mastery drives, and with the related concept of maintaining an optimal level of arousal (Hebb, 1955), is that the stimulus properties of the situation needed to satisfy the drive are difficult to specify. In general, stimuli of moderate complexity are preferred to stimuli of very high or very low complexity (Berlyne, 1971; Chevrier & Delorme, 1980; Simonton, 1990, pp. 117–119), but the phenomenon has not been robust, and the question of what limits satisfaction from this kind of activity has not been answered. Coombs and Avrunin (1977) pronounced the attempt to predict higher motives from this kind of elementary drive a failure.

Gamelike activities sometimes are explained as adaptive processes that train the player to get concrete rewards (Sutton-Smith, 1971). Although this explanation may well be valid, it is not useful at the motivational level: Adaptiveness selects for organisms, not behaviors, and must have its effect on behavior by causing the selection of particular differential reward contingencies within organisms. It is just such contingencies that the previously cited theorists have been trying to specify.

Discouraged in the attempt to account for subtle motives with simple principles, recent psychological writers have either bypassed motivation (e.g., by assuming that "goal hierarchies" or "agendas of living" are given) (Lazarus, 1989, p. 101) or turned to the same kind of shopping-list concept of reward that economists use: "That which a person will pay money for is a good." For instance, David Premack (1959) has pointed out that activities that a person will indulge in frequently when free to do so can be used as rewards for activities he ordinarily performs less frequently – in effect, "that which a person seeks is a reward." There is still argument as to the proper form of this principle (Timberlake, 1980), but in no form does it promise to discover the properties of gamelike rewards. Rather, its implication is that the reward process transpires just as much within a "black box" as does economic man's valuation of goods. Psychology as a quantitative science has merely arrived at utility theory.

1.2.2 Anomalies contradict current utility theory

Not only are subtle rewards terra incognita for utilitarian analysis – as this approach has become more microscopic and has examined individual behaviors more closely, it has yielded examples of apparent irrationality that contradict even the subjects' own beliefs about utility. Furthermore, this irrationality cannot be attributed to subjects' incomplete information about their options. Examples often are found in their deliberate, well-examined choices (creating a category of decisions for which Russell and Thaler, 1985, have suggested the name "quasi-rational") and include even purely monetary transactions. The first monetary anomaly to become widely known was the difference in a subject's valuations of two gambling propositions depending on whether he was asked to place cash values on them or choose between them (Grether & Plott, 1979; Lichtenstein & Slovic, 1971; Tversky & Thaler, 1990).[6] Subsequently, people have been found to report that they would accept different interest rates depending on whether those rates were in the form of extra money for

---

[6] I do not count the highly nonlinear interaction of probability and value that was first recognized by Bernoulli (1738/1954) and that, although frequently described as the "Allais paradox," only demonstrates the nonidentity of objective amount and subjective value, not a paradoxical concept (Schoemaker, 1982).

delaying pay that was due immediately versus a charge for immediately getting pay that was not due until later, whether the interest was on delayed money due them versus delayed money they would have to pay (Benzion, Rapoport, & Yagil, 1989), and even when the rates apply to identical transactions whether subjects reported their preferences in terms of an amount of money or in terms of a length of time they would wait (Loewenstein, 1988). People are more influenced by sunk costs than by the equivalent opportunity costs. They will accept greater risks to avoid losses than to obtain equivalent gains, and in experimental gambling situations they frequently do not maximize expected returns (Thaler, 1981; Toland & O'Neill, 1983; Tversky & Kahneman, 1981). For that matter, gambling in real life reduces one's expected income, yet gambling is a popular activity. The unrealistic economic activity with perhaps the greatest cost is compulsive shopping – knowingly spending money, often borrowed, at a rate that courts bankruptcy (Glatt & Cook, 1987; Krueger, 1988). There are sufficient examples of economic choices that do not maximize expected wealth for Richard Thaler to devote a regular column to them in the *Journal of Economic Perspectives*, beginning in 1987.

Some of these irrational choices constitute addictions – the person reports himself to be trapped in a choice pattern that he wants to abandon but somehow cannot. The distortion of even business choices, such as the sunk-cost fallacy in investing (the belief that past investment per se makes the option invested in more desirable), should be called an addiction if the choice-maker is aware of it but cannot overcome it.

Economics has also taken some theoretical interest in the much larger domain of nonmonetary addictions, but has been unable to handle the "two minds" problem that is the heart of the addict's paradox. Although some of his behavior can be described in conventional economic terms, for instance, as the combination of an inelastic demand curve for the addictive good with an increasing price for that good (Stigler & Becker, 1977), or as a high time constant for discounting future goods (Becker & Murphy, 1988), his fear of his own behavior and his consequent attempts to limit his own freedom cannot.

Conventional utilitarian logic does not fully describe human motivation. Granted that this logic is internally consistent, that it fully describes many people's *norms* for their motivation, and that it roughly describes much of their actual motivation, nevertheless its picture of motivation differs in detail from what is observed, even when the incentives people face are concrete and quantifiable. People often fail to maximize any conceivable shopping list of goods, but rather behave in ways that look internally contradictory. Furthermore, even where people do seek goods in a consistent fashion, utilitarian psychology does not specify the factors that make non-concrete goods scarce and/or necessary for the chosen reward process.

1.3 Utility theory fails to account for several major areas of behavior

Four phenomena that are unaccountable by existing utility theory have kept it from being of much use as a model of real life choice-making. I shall discuss these under the headings of ambivalence, participation in pain, dependence of rewards on taste, and the need for emotional objects. They constitute at the theoretical level what addiction and its relatives are at the observational level: warps in the linear economic model upon which modern society counts to put its values in perspective.

1.3.1 Ambivalence

When a choice-maker fails to reach a stable decision between two familiar alternatives, he is called ambivalent. Theories of choice have not often dealt with ambivalence, perhaps because cases of simple vacillation are unremarkable. When a person changes his mind because he has learned something new about unfamiliar alternatives, he poses no problem for utility theory. This is not ambivalence.

If the person has trouble choosing between two alternatives because he simply values them about the same, some observers might call him ambivalent, but only in the trivial sense of being unable to determine which is more valuable. This situation, too, is easily understood, but does not account for prolonged indecision. Buridan's fabled ass notwithstanding, no creature has ever been known to starve to death because it found itself equidistant between two piles of food: There is a cost to vacillation itself. Whenever an organism inclines slightly toward one of two competing alternatives, that cost becomes attached to wavering back again. Considering this, we would expect the chance of becoming paralyzed between two equal goals to be about the same as that of a pencil happening to balance on its point.

When such a situation appears to happen, as when a person clings to each of two incompatible alternatives, clinicians do not accept his close valuations of them as an explanation – too many such conflicts continue unresolved even after a major incentive is added to or removed from one of the alternatives. A person who agonizes at length whether or not he should violate a principle to get five thousand dollars probably will agonize just as long when he stands to get ten thousand.

A hungry rat that is shocked on approaching a food cup will pace around the cup at a safe distance, neither obtaining the food nor giving it up, but there is no evidence that he is ambivalent. He consistently prefers not to be shocked, even if the consequence is not eating, but he seems to prefer the activity of staying near the food, perhaps searching for a way to obtain it without shock, to the other behaviors that are then available to him. At least, it would not be possible to demonstrate true ambivalence in this situation. For all we know, the rat has reached a stable preference. As with close choices, deferral of a choice while exploring whether or not there is a way to obtain both alternatives is not an example of our problem.

These behaviors are easily understood as attempts to maximize reward. Ambivalence, on the other hand, is a puzzle. It is manifested by preference that changes, or that the subject expects to change, despite his familiarity with the alternatives. This is a phenomenon with which neither experimental psychology nor economics has dealt until recently. The incompatible preferences may even seem to be simultaneous, but somehow are not weighed against each other. In that situation, the person seems to perceive the outcome about which he is ambivalent as both a gain and a loss simultaneously, or in regular succession. For instance, a person may in the same hour check into an alcoholism treatment program and buy a bottle to take with him, without having discovered anything new about the consequences of these behaviors and without wavering in his decision to do either one. Consider this from economist James March (1978), citing Catullus' *Carmina* 85:

Our deepest preferences tend often to be paired. We find the same outcome both attractive and repulsive, not in the sense that the two sentiments cancel each other and we remain indifferent, but precisely that we simultaneously want and do not want an outcome, experience it as both pleasure and pain, love and hate it.

Such a conflictual valuation of a given outcome – in this case drinking alcohol – utterly defeats the Premack strategy of functional definition. It exemplifies the problem of addiction.

Examples of this kind abound. Many activities appear to be controlled by thoroughly familiar, mutually exclusive incentives that are never effectively weighed against each other: A student bites his nails or pulls his hair while wishing he did not; people smoke while "trying" to stop, gamble and repent, overeat and diet – with full knowledge of their own contrary wishes. Many passions can be added to the list of unwanted behaviors; although the name implies something that happens to a person, as opposed to something one actively does ("actions"), people have always recognized a temptation to entertain them and hence a choice. Thus, a typical counselor at the turn of the century, Aaron Crane (1905, p. 78), warned against seduction by a long list of "disruptive" feelings that a person might entertain even when he somehow did not want to: "anger, hate, greed, lust, jealousy, and all malevolent thoughts, also grief, regret and disappointment, fear, doubt, uncertainty, responsibility, anxiety, worry, and despair; condemnation, self-consciousness, self-abasement, shame and remorse."

Careful interviews of psychiatric patients often reveal their participation in their symptoms: A phobic patient gives in to an urge to panic, then regrets it, but can be taught to resist this urge by practice (Clum, 1989). A compulsive patient struggles with a repetitive urge to perform a ritualized but nevertheless voluntary behavior. He does not welcome the behavior, but still it is his behavior. How are we to understand his motivation for it?

This is a primordial problem. It is apparent by the age of five years, when children choose what they simultaneously report to be the less wise alternative of two rewards (Nisan & Koriat, 1977). It was apparent to the ancients. Aristotle's *Eudemian Ethics* turns it over and over, without making sense of it. His commentator, Anthony Kenny, summarizes a sample of this labor, regarding whether or not "voluntariness [can] be identified with being in accordance with appetite," that is, whether or not what a person wills is what he likes best:

> The incontinent man acts in accordance with appetite, so if we accept the identification he acts voluntarily. But he is acting against

what he knows to be best, and no one wills to do this; so he is acting against his will, and therefore involuntarily. [Kenny, 1979, p. 14].

However,

what conflicts with appetite is painful, what is painful is involuntary, so what is in accord with appetite is voluntary. [Kenny, 1979, p. 14]

After much equivocation, Aristotle left the paradox unsolved, and it has remained so through the ages.

I shall argue that this problem is central to the others and shall discuss it in chapters 2 and 3, in addition to returning to it throughout the rest of this book. Its consequences for motivational conflict, as described by clinical authors, are discussed in chapters 5 and 6, and in Ainslie (1986b).

1.3.2 Participation in aversion

Some of the preceding examples go beyond the subjective balance of feelings that would be called ambivalent in ordinary speech. They are wholly negative. Negative motives are the most problematic ones for existing theories of motivation. These are processes that not only produce little or no reward in their own right but also interfere with rewarding processes that are otherwise available. What makes a person participate in such processes as "self-abasement, shame, and remorse," or in the experience of pain itself?

The problem is not that some processes are poorly rewarded. If reward is to control an organism's behavior, it has to be distributed unevenly depending on his[7] various behaviors. There is no problem at all in conceiving that some situations greatly excite a neurophysiological reward mechanism and other situations do not. The problem is that some apparently unrewarding activities are still chosen over alternatives that are apparently more rewarding.

Archetypical of these activities is the experience of physical pain. Pain traditionally has been seen as an inevitable response to those innately determined stimuli that can unleash it, but the pain process is not in fact an obligatory response to "painful" stimuli. The aversive

---

[7] Because "organism" refers to both humans and lower animals, I believe that "his" is the correct pronoun. Recent proposals notwithstanding, it need not specify the male gender.

impact of pain requires motivated behavior on the person's part – at least attention to the stimuli,[8] perhaps a "motivational-affective" response to them (Fordyce, 1978). Thus, reaction to painful stimuli requires an explanation in motivational terms (Ainslie, 1987b). If it depends upon motivation, what creates the universally acknowledged urge to emit it?

Furthermore, it is not necessary to keep attention away from painful stimuli in order to avoid their reward-inhibiting effect. Under many circumstances – the heat of sports competition, battle, hypnosis, and various lesser forms of patterned activity such as those that are taught with natural childbirth – subjects say that they can identify and locate painful stimuli without making an emotional response to them, that is, without experiencing aversion (Beecher, 1959, pp. 157–190; Melzack, Weisz, & Sprague, 1963; Sternbach, 1968, pp. 140–141). Motivational aversion seems to depend not simply on the awareness of painful stimuli but on intervening processes that a person can actively control. If people are actually able to "gate out" pain, why do they not do it regularly? To put the problem another way, how does nature induce people to take an interest in their pains?

Admittedly, pain does not feel like a behavior to most people. Likewise, some readers might not want to count fear as a behavior, despite its responsiveness to behavior therapies. Traditionally, fear has been viewed as an obligatory response to anticipated pain. But there are many other aversive emotional processes, such as disgust, annoyance, embarrassment, and regret, that lack a releasing stimulus and thus a motivational explanation, if we must believe that aversion is stimulus-driven.

For instance, a person may arbitrarily set up standards for when he will call himself a success – attaining a skill, achieving entry to a profession, passing in a social circle – and yet feel unable to escape feelings of regret, guilt, or embarrassment if he does not meet his chosen standard. A person may interpret a dripping sound as a leaking faucet, and this interpretation may make him unable to go to sleep or concentrate; but if he finds that the sound comes from rainwater dripping from

---

[8] Motivated selective attention has not been studied specifically with painful stimuli, but is well known in general (Kahneman, 1973; Moray, 1969; Shiffrin & Schneider, 1977).

eaves, the same auditory stimulus may no longer be aversive. Such aversions are not biologically mandated, but depend on some personal bookkeeping system; yet they often have the same ability to compete for attention as "physical" pains. It is the basis for such a competition that is unsatisfactory in conventional motivational theory.

In sum, no existing psychological theory tells what motivates an organism to accept avoidable losses of reward. Without such an explanation, a major area of choice remains without so much as a possible hypothesis for it. This problem will be presented at length in sections 4.1.1 and 4.1.2, where its parallel with the problem of addiction will become apparent.

1.3.3 Dependence of rewards on taste

Conventional economics and psychological theory depict satisfaction as constrained by scarce resources – rewards or "goods" – that act like keys in a lock to turn on the reward process. Such a model has seemed necessary not only to account for the frequent association of satisfaction with specific rewards but also to explain why satisfaction itself seems to be a commodity of limited availability. But access to goods is both insufficient and unnecessary for the operation of the reward process. I shall present these problems, respectively, in this and the following section.

Goods themselves often lose their capacity to satisfy. Of course, examples of satiation or stimulus fatigue pose no difficulty for a turnkey hypothesis – It is easy to conceive of neural limitations to satisfaction that are not learned processes. The theoretical problem arises when an organism's appetite is fresh and a good seems to fit the physiological lock, but the organism is not rewarded by it. He is said not to have a "taste " for it, or even to have "lost his taste" for it, but this is description, not an explanation. Classical conditioning, itself a dubious explanation (see section 2.3.2), sometimes looks like a factor, but more often than not there is no credible conditioning stimulus. Since the loss of taste often persists longer than simple fatigue, sometimes permanently, some kind of learning is obviously involved; but why should an organism learn to be uninfluenced by available reward?

The action of nonconcrete rewards like art and play is so vaguely conceived that their dependence on taste represents no clear contradiction of accepted theory. However, it is hard to explain how rewards that are thought of as physiological reflexes can be modified or nullified by cognitive processes. There are many familiar examples: the food that the person has valued may lose its value because of habitual consumption or perhaps because of information that has no bearing on its physical effects, such as the fact that it contains horse or snake meat, or that a cockroach walked across it. Similarly, repeated exposure to the same mate tends to reduce sexual arousal, even in lower animals, with level of sexual deprivation held constant (Dewsbury, 1981).

Entire drive modalities that are thought to generate robust rewards, such as food, sex, and the opportunity for aggression following frustration, can cease to be the basis of rewards for psychological reasons. In cases of anorexia nervosa, a physically healthy person may voluntarily starve to death – food remains interesting, but no longer supports the behavior of obtaining and consuming it. In cases of sexual frigidity, the chance for sexual activity may become disgusting, and many people develop a similar disgust for anger. Distaste for a drive may come to be regarded as normal among whole cultures or subcultures, as when well-bred Victorian women were expected not to experience sexual pleasure, or when Jainists renounce anger (Stearns, 1986).

These cases are extreme, but changes in the rewarding power of all manner of goods are common occurrences. The events that will give rise to excitement, humor, anger, and sexual arousal change over the course of an individual person's life, and from decade to decade across a whole society. The problem of fashion has been described in economic terms (Stigler & Becker, 1977), but the psychological process that mediates between reward stimuli and the internal reward process in fashion and other changes in taste has not been characterized. If a good has the physical power to reward, how do mere thoughts get in its way? Even granted that an organism must learn some attitude or skill to make some goods rewarding, why should the organism later lose the ability he has learned to derive reward from that good?

Clarification of this process might allow us to study the jading of appetite that seems to be part of the addictive process. But to ask the question of current psychology simply exposes a gap in our basic knowledge. We shall return to it in chapter 7.

1.3.4 Need for emotional objects

With the exception of the taste factor just mentioned, concrete rewards seem to be roughly compatible with a turnkey model. The gamelike rewards that command the most effort in modern societies are quite another matter. People's active roles in setting their own rewards raise the converse question to that of how concrete rewards can lose their power. Insofar as people can set up the conditions under which they will be rewarded, why do they arrange for difficult conditions? Why, indeed, do people depend on any external objects when such objects are not physically obligatory?

In the modern world it does not take much effort for most people to avoid hunger, cold, and danger. But people show little tendency to rest when such motives are satisfied. Often they incur hunger, cold, or danger when they do not have to, in order to achieve some less concrete goal. Before we can examine the puzzles of higher motivation, we need to know something about its constraints. How are people moved to set themselves arbitrary goals? How does such a motive acquire binding power?

As was already noted, some properties of gamelike or "process" rewards are known. Higher organisms like to explore; they like to solve puzzles; they like stimuli that are moderately complex and those that lead to moderate arousal. In addition, humans follow some specific aesthetic rules (Empson, 1930). There is a well-known market for experiences that engender certain emotions; books and cinema sell laughter, excitement, romance, and even fear and sadness.

Yet the basis for these intangible rewards is poorly understood. If an activity is motivated, it must be in competition with other motivated activities. In effect, exploring or playing must bid against eating or avoiding pain to attract a person's participation. These potential activities are all in the same market.

The conventional view of the concrete rewards, such as food or the cessation of pain, is that they are based on a contingency outside of a person's control; food or noxious stimuli are said to be specific keys to perceptual locks, and the person is rewarded insofar as he inserts or removes these keys. If games are to share his attention with these concrete motives, such a view must also hold them to be limited by some circumstance that is outside of his immediate control. Otherwise the person's interest in the intangible activity might be unbounded, and he could free himself from the control of hunger or pain rewards by substituting limitless amounts of play. Thus, the authors who have dealt with process rewards have tried to formulate keys for them – necessary stimuli that release a finite amount of reward and that thus determine whether eating or playing or exploring will win the bidding.

However, turnkey stimuli for playlike activities have thus far eluded discovery. It seems unlikely that they exist. The emotions that are experienced as rewarding in play can be generated at will, or on the basis of very minimal stimulation. To do this in himself is an essential skill for the actor (Archer, 1888), but to "work oneself into" one emotional state or another is within anybody's repertoire. Some researchers have taken the trouble to demonstrate this ability under controlled conditions (Koriat et al., 1972; Lazarus, 1975a,b), but it is familiar enough:

Printed pages are sufficient stimuli for long sequences of intense emotions that clearly preexisted in the repertoire of the reader. Whether a person is reading or merely imagining, most of the images are his own memories and presumably are subject to voluntary recall; where there is a story, its bare words only organize these images. Conventional hedonic theory suggests no reason why a story should move us more if it is read or heard in a work of fiction rather than created by our own daydreaming, or why it should have even more effect if we believe the story to be true rather than made up. Assuming that it is irrelevant to our own prospects, this effect cannot be attributed to its information value. What are we doing when we "allow" ourselves to believe a story?

Hypnotic suggestion can produce similar involvement. Hypnotic images are fantasies generated within the person himself, with only minimal guidance from the hypnotist. In self-hypnosis, a person seems to be able to coin his own process rewards, and yet he usually does not become carried away by this activity (Kroger, 1963, p. 85). Even the occasional "fantasy-prone personality," who seems to have been born with an exceptional ability to create vivid fantasies, is not thereby lured away from the usual activities of life (Wilson & Barber, 1983).

This seeming abstemiousness is made even more puzzling by the fact that it sometimes fails to occur. Some schizoid and obsessional patients do become absorbed in fantasy to the extent that it interferes with other sources of reward, a process described clinically by Robert Lindner (1955), and well portrayed fictionally in *The Universal Baseball Association* (Coover, 1968) and "The Secret Life of Walter Mitty" (Thurber, 1942). They do not seem to have tapped great wells of joy by doing so, but they are sufficiently rewarded to maintain their investment in fantasy against the lure of "reality." Why not great wells? Why any trickle at all? And what are the rules that govern the competition between fantasied rewards and other kinds? Psychology does not tell us.

If we want to understand higher purposes in the context of other motives, and to evaluate the possibility that they are deteriorating in modern society, then we need to know how subtle rewards function in the same market as concrete rewards. This question will assume increasing importance from chapter 7 onward.

These four phenomena violate conventional utility theory, either obviously, as in the case of ambivalence, or by implication, given people's demonstrable abilities to modify aversiveness, tastes, and general emotional processes. They are not obscure phenomena, but processes that mediate most, if not all, of our motivation. Before scientists can deal with the pathologies of leisure, we shall have to reexamine utility theory and reconcile it with these phenomena.

Such a reconciliation does not necessarily depend on the findings of controlled research, but it must be consistent with such findings. Data for a powerfully predictive theory of human choice do not exist, but recent basic research on motivation does suggest revisions of the conventional, scarcity-based turnkey theory. I shall argue that utility theory can be rebuilt to be internally consistent and not to conflict with known fact. Even that would be a first.

2. In search of the two minds

The first clear illustration of self-contradictory behavior was Ulysses' problem of how to sail past the Sirens (Ainslie, 1975; Elster, 1979; Strotz, 1956). His conflicting motives were neatly separated in time: Beforehand he preferred to sail past these temptresses, but he expected to change his preference when he heard them. Acting on his earlier preference, he physically forestalled his later one. Since Homer's time, hundreds of authors in theology, philosophy, economics, sociology, and psychology have proposed models of ambivalent behavior. Fortunately, there are not many imaginable mechanisms for a person's regular pursuit of contradictory goals: We may believe that his conflict is really with another person; that his conflict is between two or more autonomous centers of decision making within himself; that it is between different principles of decision making that operate in tandem; that there is no real conflict but only misinformation; or that there is a conflict between differently delayed goals. Each mechanism has reappeared over the centuries, couched in new terminology and occasionally embellished with a new insight.

For an observer whose norm of decision making is the utilitarian free market, the question any such mechanism must answer is why choices that would maximize reward do not always win out over less rewarding alternatives. Until recently, all approaches have attempted to answer it by proposing added-on mechanisms, such as exceptions to the free market or multiple markets, or else they have assumed that failures to maximize come from simple errors in information processing. I shall argue that such proposals are neither adequate nor necessary. The traditional utilitarian model clearly has a problem with motivational conflict, as described in the preceding chapter, but the solution will not come from subdividing it or limiting its scope.

Rather, it will come from reexamination of the elementary nature of the model.

2.1 Conflict with other people does not imply ambivalence

Simplest but least adequate is the idea that ambivalence is due to conflict between the ambivalent person and others – that he is torn between his self-interest and the interests of his family or his society. This hypothesis usually is adopted when there is a conspicuous pleasurable component in the ambivalence, so that an observer can believe that the main motive for restraint comes from other people. For instance, often an alcoholic is depicted as pursuing selfish gratification, and as experiencing conflict only insofar as he has "internalized" the values or needs of others.

Admittedly the transactions between an alcoholic and his family often take this form – the alcoholic clutching his bottle while the family reproves him for the harm he is doing them. However, this model does not take into account the striking failure of alcohol to serve even the drinker's own interest. Even a few minutes after alcoholics begin drinking they report feeling more dysphoric than before (Cameron, Spence, & Drewery, 1978; Cappell, 1975).

Furthermore, there are, as Fingarette (1979) has pointed out, many cases of ambivalence in which no one else's interest is even seemingly at stake – for instance, concerning whether or not one will stay up too late, or bite one's nails. Here a person-versus-society model obviously is not applicable.

Even where there is significant conflict between the person and those around him, some hypothesis is needed to explain how he takes others' interests to heart in a way that makes him ambivalent. Few believe that murder, or even running stop signs, are largely restrained by the punishments threatened for those acts (Wilson & Herrnstein, 1985). But if that is not the case, then the conflict must be internal.

Psychological literature treats the "internalization" of social norms as a tenuous process, almost the result of a trick on the person in whom it occurs, in that he must be persuaded to give up what seems to be his own best interest. It is expected to fail unless the person receives careful training early in childhood. The most widespread conception of this training makes it little more than classical conditioning, the principle that "a burned child fears fire":

For a strict behaviorist like Eysenck, conscience is literally a conditioned reflex (1977, pp. 95–119); but at the ostensibly opposite pole of opinion, Freud's idea that conscience is motivated by fear of the father's anger in the Oedipal conflict differs from Eysenck's mainly in the extent to which the child attributes anger to the father or otherwise anticipates a conditioning stimulus that may not actually occur (Freud, 1930/1956o, pp. 123–133; 1933/1956p, pp. 61–65). Theories of positive incentives for internalization have been even more limited. As we have seen, the early behaviorists believed that the parents' attitudes became associated with the delivery of food or other kinds of comfort, and thus became valued. The later behaviorists have generally avoided theorizing about the point, but Skinner (1948b) implied in his novel *Walden Two* that gratification delay and other socialized behaviors are learned as operants (goal-directed behaviors) to get rewards from adults, and that these responses somehow generalize to situations where adults do not control reward.

Operant learning and conditioning often are proposed as mechanisms for ambivalence in their own right; we shall deal with these possibilities later. But as mechanisms for internalizing the wishes of others, they have an overwhelming flaw: In both processes, subjects come to discriminate between configurations of stimuli that will lead to punishment or reward or conditioning events, and those that will not. The person who has learned to escape social punishment or obtain reward should soon be able to recognize situations in which those options will arise, and withhold punished or nonrewarded behaviors only in those situations. If the punishment or reward is conditioned, it should extinguish when the conditioning stimuli stop occurring. Learning such realistic discriminations is not what is usually meant by internalization and will not lead to ambivalence.[1]

---

[1] The reader with a knowledge of experimental psychology may object that I have

Recently, sociobiologists have proposed that altruism is built into our genes and thus is perhaps not so tenuous as has been supposed (Dawkins, 1976, pp. 95–116). Altruism is certainly apt to have been selected for, like other social traits, but the genes that subtend it still must express themselves through a specific motivational mechanism, and it is just such a mechanism that has so far been lacking.

Even if we had a clear explanation of how a person takes others' interests to heart, a fundamental problem would remain: Why can he not weigh these interests against his other motives to reach a stable, unambivalent decision? The observation that people sometimes behave benevolently toward strangers without hope of recompense (Frank, 1988) has been validated experimentally (Caporael et al., 1989), but nothing in the extensive published commentary on the latter article suggests that unselfish behavior is *unhedonic*, that is, an exception to the utilitarian principle that all choices maximize expected satisfaction. According to such a principle, however, the choice whether to get drunk or please one's family should be no different in kind from the choice whether to drink Scotch or bourbon, a simple matter of expressing a preference. For the same reason, the "social trap" in which pressure from other people is said to push one into an unwanted behavior like smoking (Cross & Guyer, 1980) would not be an example of ambivalence.

There is something intuitively appealing about the analogy between interpersonal conflict and ambivalence, but the analogy alone is not an adequate hypothesis. Likewise, interpersonal conflict is a common finding in situations in which a person is ambivalent, but it does not explain his ambivalence.

---

ruled out conditioned fear too quickly. Under some circumstances, a substantial minority of people do not lose their "conditioned" fear reaction to certain stimuli that do not in fact predict danger (Eysenck, 1967; McNally & Steketee, 1985). However, the persistence and even growth of such fears seem to be determined by the subjects' particular proneness to fear, either in general or of innately "prepared" objects like snakes (Ohman, Dimberg, & Ost, 1985; Seligman, 1971), and that would be an undependable mechanism of internalization. Indeed, attempts to engineer socially useful phobias, such as conditioned aversion to cigarettes or alcohol, have failed (Lichtenstein & Danaher, 1976; Wilson, 1978). There is also reason to doubt that classical conditioning is governed by a process distinct from operant learning; this will be discussed later in this chapter.

2.2 Multiple centers of choice must compete on a common basis

Another venerable explanation for ambivalence is that there may be more than one center of choice within an individual. The oldest version of this theory is spirit possession. When someone acted against his own reported wishes, the ancient Greeks attributed that to the intervention of a god, whereas the Judeo-Christian tradition postulated possession by a demon or partial external control by a witch. The demon or witch could be happy while the possessed person was unhappy, and hence there did not need to be a resolution of the given motivational conflict.

Although modern society rejects these theories as literal mechanisms, the idea of separately motivated homunculi within the individual persists in less colorful form. For instance, Freud once speculated that the ego and the unconscious force he later called the id might be separately motivated, so that there could be "unpleasure for one system and simultaneously satisfaction for the other" (1920/1956k, p. 20). Elsewhere he likened the two to a married couple, saying that the relationship of a person and his unconscious wishes "can only be compared to an amalgamation of two separate people who are linked by some strong element in common" (1916–1917/1956i, p. 216). That was one of four identifiable mechanisms for ambivalence that he proposed at one time or another. We shall examine them shortly.

Modern evidence for distinct motivational centers in the brain (Olds & Fobes, 1981; Phillips, 1984) or separate "personalities" in right and left hemispheres (Dunaif-Hattis, 1984, pp. 6–36; Springer & Deutsch, 1981) might seem to support the possibility of multiple autonomous decision centers. The most abstract version of the multiple-center theory views the separate locations of reward as alternative consumption plans with no specific neurological or psychological substrates. For instance, Thaler and Shefrin (1981) described the competition of two apparently independent consumption patterns, such as a "doer" and a "planner," that opt for consuming and for deferring consumption, respectively. (They have since found this duality unnecessary (Shefrin & Thaler, 1988).) This formal solution to the problem of inconsistent behavior lets one plan be realized while another is being frustrated, without reconciliation to an overall plan. It echoes the Freudian topography that permits simultaneous id pleasure and ego unpleasure, and thus represents a multiple-center model.

Philosophers are also prone to try to solve the problem of weakness of the will (often called by Aristotle's term, *akrasia*) by proposing the existence of two selves, one of which can deceive the other. In the most coherent of these proposals, Donald Davidson argues that a person cannot behave contrary to his best reasoned judgment unless there can be "a mental cause that is not a reason" (1983, p. 298). In his view, "blind forces" in the mind do not adequately explain ambivalence (p. 299); however, "the breakdown of reason-relations" can cause partitioning of the mind into "two or more semi-autonomous structures" (pp. 303–304) that influence each other by some force other than reason. "Indeed, if we are going to explain irrationality at all, it seems we must assume that the mind can be partitioned into quasi-independent structures" (p. 300). David Pears, who proposes a similar partition, ascribes its origin to motivation that has escaped the person's "main system" of reasoning: "The sub-system is built around the nucleus of the wish for the irrational belief and it is organized like a person" (Pears, 1984, p. 87). This is close to Freud's picture of the origin of the unconscious, to which we shall come shortly; but because it does not invoke a different principle of motivation, but rather a separate, parallel motivated entity, it belongs here with the multiple-center theories (Davidson, 1983; Pears, 1984). Some philosophers have questioned the "curious metaphor of this divided personality" that can give orders to itself (Hare, 1963, p. 81), but only recently have any begun to develop other explanations (Mele, 1987).

Multiple-center models are easy to fit to inconsistent data. Just as the ancient Greeks had a god for every motive, so we can have a choice center. But this strategy does not meet our need for an explanation. For that we must look to Mt. Olympus to see how all these gods get along.

Perhaps Mt. Olympus is a car with tandem controls, tugged in different directions by differently motivated drivers. But even if these drivers were entirely autonomous, the tandem steering mechanisms would weigh their strengths to determine a single vector for the car. A close contest could produce indecision, but not ambivalence as it was described in section 1.3.1. Alternatively, Mt. Olympus may be an apartment house with a single telephone. Separate centers or personalities would react in autonomous ways to the events that happened to the person as a whole, but could express themselves only insofar as they got a turn on the phone. Clinical examples of multiple-personality disorder look like walking illustrations of this model (Putnam, 1989): Separate personalities are evident at different times, and must "go" somewhere while waiting their turns. But the question that a theory of ambivalence must answer is, How are the turns decided upon?

The lack of such a deciding principle is the fatal flaw of multiple-center theories of ambivalence. It is perhaps best illustrated by the most extreme version, which says that there is no general mechanism for decision making. Some schools of psychology and philosophy now entertain what could be called motivational nihilism – a belief that not all motives are comparable to all other motives, or even that motivation as an economic concept is a fancy of the Benthamite observer (Allison, 1981); regarding psychology, see Schwartz (1986), and for philosophy, Taylor (1982). That is, an organism may have particular hierarchies of preferences, but they have been partitioned from one another, perhaps by the happenstance of evolution, perhaps by learning, into unbridgeable niches, and they operate without reference to one another.

For instance, Schwartz says that "some sets of commodities are simply incomparable or incommensurable" (1986, p. 154), such as fifty dollars' worth of recreation versus fifty dollars contributed to charity. Underlying this assertion is the valid observation that choice is often arbitrary, dependent not on the innate feel of the objects chosen but on personal bookkeeping categories that are influenced by such factors as "habit" and "cultural norms" (1986, p. 155). However, he says that these factors are "noneconomic," that is, that the behavior of categorizing is itself unmotivated or is motivated by incomparable incentives. His point in describing the limitations of utilitarian theory is not to reexamine its properties but to call off the search for any general mechanism of choice, that is, to rebut "the unqualified claim that behavior is controlled by reinforcement" (1986, p. 225).

But if behaviors are not selected according to a single standard of choosability, the standard summarized by the term "reward" (or "reinforcement"),[2] how are they selected? The organism's means for expression are limited. A single channel of attention, if not a single set of muscles, is needed for the variety of behaviors that physically can be substituted for one another. Assuming that the selection of these behaviors is determinate, there must be a means of comparing them along some common dimension. Furthermore, most, if not all, behaviors can be substituted for most others. Otherwise we would continually encounter behaviors that an organism *could not* learn to emit following another behavior. Instead, what we find is that even "inborn" behavior sequences can be rearranged arbitrarily if the reward is sufficient and timely (Ainslie & Engel, 1974; Crawford & Masterson, 1982; Modaresi, 1989; Whipple & Fantino, 1980).

The down-east comedy team "Bert & I" told a joke about a farmer who was asked directions to Millinocket. After puzzling about the matter for some time, he told his questioner, "You can't get there from here." The farmer meant that it was difficult to get there, or difficult to understand how to get there, and perhaps not worth the trouble; but he said, "You can't get there." Motivational nihilists make just such an outrageous leap, from examples of apparent arbitrariness in choice to a theory of incommensurable choices. Although the alternatives of amusement and charity are widely disparate, to say that a person cannot weigh them so as to form a preference for one over the other is absurd. Among motivated behaviors, as among places on the map, one has to be able to get from anywhere to anywhere.

The argument is not much different if the competing entities are not behaviors but whole organs of behavior, that is, the separate centers of motivation that we have been evaluating. Of course, if motivational centers had the attributes of entire personalities, they

---

[2] A persistent need for such a term keeps generating new candidates, e.g., Freud's "libido," the economists' "utility," and Martin Hollis's quasi-facetious "micro-watts of inner glow" (1983).

could behave strategically toward each other, each predicting the other's preferences and acting at moments of relative strength to forestall the other's probable plans. However, it is most unlikely that entire personalities are duplicated, even functionally, in the brain; and insofar as separate motivational centers must share common resources for memory, perception, deduction, and so forth, they must somehow weigh in against each other to compete for these resources. Even entire internal personalities would have to compete on some common ground for the limited means of external expression. I shall soon argue that there are functional parts of an individual that do in fact behave strategically toward each other, but that they always do so on the basis of commensurable goals (see section 3.8).

In sum, there may be different motives or even anatomically separate motivational centers in the brain, but such motives or centers must compete and be chosen on the basis of a common dimension. In the language of cognitive psychology, behavior must be isotropic. The choice mechanism cannot be modular in the sense that perceptual mechanisms are sometimes held to be modular, that is, blind to part of the person's knowledge or motivation (Fodor, 1985). There must be a marketplace where the person's preference is decided. This marketplace need not be egalitarian – nature may give some alternatives a head start – but it must be comprehensive for all behaviors that can be substituted for each other.

It is the failure of this marketplace to produce a stable decision that we describe as ambivalence. Even if two or more discrete centers participate in this marketplace, we still must explain why the person's favor is not always auctioned off, as it were, to the highest bidder. The competition of all behaviors for a limited channel of expression requires that reward in one center have equivalents in the others; they must be like dollars and pounds, fully exchangeable and therefore fully commensurable.

2.3 Separate principles of decision making must also compete

The most important modern theories of ambivalence have postulated two separate principles of decision making, one of which is insensitive to reward or responds to reward in a different way than the other. In all these theories, one principle is rational and maximizes expected reward, whereas the other follows some "lower" principle. The second driver in the tandem car is a gremlin, not motivated the way the human driver is, perhaps not motivated at all.

2.3.1 Motivated lower principles

The classical Greeks first described a lower selective principle that was motivated but could not take long-term outcomes into account. The products of this principle were passions or appetites, animallike processes that could be tamed but not civilized. Plato divided the soul into three parts: reason and the two passions of anger and sensual desire (Kenny, 1979, p. 25). Aristotle expanded that theory by describing how the passions interact with reason: They will override reason unless reason sets up "continent habits" to reduce the strength of the passions. However, even a continent person's reason can be overcome by the "preternatural" operation of a passion (Kenny, 1979, p. 47). This basic outline of motivational conflict became generally accepted.

St. Paul put it in terms of sin versus the law. He and subsequent Christian theologians wavered ambiguously between a theory based on these two principles of decision making and a theory of two autonomous centers – a lower center serving the Devil or devils, and a higher center instructed by the "presence" or "grace" of God:

> I do not even acknowledge my own actions as mine, for what I do is not what I want to do, but what I detest. But if what I do is against my will, it means that I agree with the law and hold it to be admirable. But as things are, it is no longer I who perform the action, but sin that lodges in me . . . the good which I want to do, I fail to do; but what I do is the wrong which is against my will; and if what I do is against my will, clearly it is no longer I who am the agent, but sin that has its lodging in me. I discover this principle, then: that when I want to do the right, only the wrong is within my reach. In my inmost self I delight in the law of God, but perceive that there is in my bodily members a different law, fighting against the law that my reason approves and making me a prisoner under

the law that is in my members, the law of sin. [Romans 7, quoted by Hare, 1963, pp. 78–79]

Galen perpetuated a belief that apparently was ancient even in his time: He supported the "men of old" who spoke of "grief, wrath, anger, lust, fear and all the passions as diseases of the soul." Anger could be tamed like a horse, but the "concupiscible power" (sensual desire) was even more unruly, like a wild boar or goat that had to be controlled by starvation:

The chastisement of the concupiscible power consists in not furnishing it with the enjoyment of the things it desires. If it does not attain to this enjoyment, it becomes small and weak. The result is that the concupiscible power does not follow reason because it is obedient but because it is weak. [Galen, 1963, p. 47]

This model, too, the Romans sometimes combined with the idea of a second autonomous will that had gotten inside the self, as Ovid depicts in Medea's struggle against a growing love for Jason:

Meanwhile, Aeetes, daughter's heart took fire;
Her struggling Reason could not quell Desire.
"This madness how can I resist?", she cried;
"No use to fight; some God is on its side . . . "
[*Metamorphoses*, vii, 20, quoted by Hare, 1963, p. 78]

As the Renaissance questioned the knowledge received from the ancients, the distinction between passion and reason changed from that between two kinds of motives to that between motives and something that rode on top of motives, partaking of them yet somehow steering them. Some passions had come to be regarded as good; passions were now arrayed on a continuum of desirability (Hirschman, 1977, pp. 9–66). At this point the words "affect," "passion," and "emotion" referred to all motives, not just the lower, animal kind. Writing in the seventeenth century, Jean François Senault presaged unitary motivational concepts like utility and reward: "There is but one passion. . . . Hope and fear, sorrow and joy are the motions or properties of love" (1649, p. 27).

Spinoza still saw passions in opposition to a more ethereal "delight in blessedness," but pointed out for the first time that higher motives had to be weighed along the same dimension as passions in the process of choice: "No affect can be restrained by the true knowledge of good and evil insofar as it is true, but only insofar as it is considered as an affect" (Hirschman, 1977, p. 23). Knowledge had to generate motivation if it was to influence choice: "An affect cannot be restrained nor moved unless by an opposing stronger affect" (p. 23). Reason was then no longer an opponent of the passions, but a broker of them: "Reason . . . is nothing but the act of choosing those passions which we must follow for the sake of our happiness" (d'Holbach, quoted by Hirschman, 1977, p. 27). That concept is still proposed from time to time; in one of Piaget's rare references to motivation, he says that properly coordinated emotions "emerge as regulations whose final form of equilibrium is none other than the will" (Piaget, 1964/1967, p. 58).

But that view of motivation no longer explained ambivalence. If passions were not a lower principle of choice-making, but only the form in which the person experienced motivation, why did they not come into a balance representing the person's overall preference?

Even more of a problem was the idea that a passion might be in conflict with itself: "'Tis no great advantage to overcome *Avarice*, since she exerciseth her *fury* against her *self*, and deprives her *self* of that wealth which she hath deprived others of" (Senault, 1649, p. C1; italics in original). Senault's book purported to show how there was no passion "so despicable, but it may be changed into a *glorious Vertue*" by purifying it of the effects of "corrupt nature" (1649, p. C2). Hume developed this idea in more utilitarian language:

There is no passion, therefore, capable of controlling the interested affection [avarice], but the very affection itself, by an alteration in its direction. Now this alteration must necessarily take place upon the least reflection; since 'tis evident, that the passion is much better satisfy'd by its restraint, than by its liberty, and that in preserving society, we make much greater advances in the acquiring of possessions, than in the solitary and forlorn condition. [quoted by Hirschman, 1977, p. 25]

Again, in that era the separation of multiple-center and multiple-principle models was not complete. Contemporary allegory often implied that the passions were autonomous motivational centers, but that notion clearly was not applicable to the restraint of a passion by itself.

Freud reestablished the concept of a lower principle. What had been called "passion" he termed the id, "it," something outside of the "I" or ego. The id was the source of a person's motivational energy, much of it entirely acceptable to the ego. The "non-conflictual id" was passion purely as motivation (Freud, 1923/1956l, pp. 24–27). But the "conflictual" part was unacceptable, perhaps because it was intrinsically aversive, perhaps because it conflicted with the ego's values – Freud described both cases.

So far, a free market in motives was still operating. However, rather than simply leaving the inferior alternative unchosen, the person in Freud's model was apt to bar it from the market. In doing so, the person unwittingly created a lower principle of motivation, in effect a black market, in which his larger goals did not participate and which thus generated ungoverned passion as the ancients conceived it. Freud called this passion "impulse," or, more often, "the impulses," not implying suddenness but rather a motive force that was inferior and somehow external to the self.

We might ask what should motivate the person to make such a fateful move, not once but repeatedly, when maintaining his choices free would have served him so much better. Freud's explanation was not entirely clear, couched as it was in the hypothetical neurological constructs of his era. In his original concept of defense, incoming stimuli flowed reflexively into both consciousness (omega system) and motor activity unless blocked by opposing energy in the form of "side-cathexis" from the ego (Freud, 1895/1956a, pp. 295–307). The same "side-cathexis" could block flows into both outlets. That blockade did not eliminate the incoming stimulation, but diverted it into memory, which, like an electrical capacitor, fed it back into the original pathway when the blockade stopped. When the input was of a kind that would lead to extreme unpleasure, particularly threats to the person's values, he would try to maintain the blockade, creating a reservoir of energy that would intermittently pass the blockade to stimulate motor actions until it was painfully discharged through the other outlet, consciousness (Freud, 1895/1956a, pp. 305–321; McCarley & Hobson, 1977; Pribram & Gill, 1976).

Chronologically that was the second of Freud's four mechanisms

(1895/1956a); it seems to have been the one he had most in mind when elaborating his subsequent metapsychology. His capacitor model survived the many changes he made in his motivational concepts and remains a tacit part of modern ego psychology. In motivational terms, the mechanism seems to be driven by the wish to defer pain, implying that people give future pains less weight than present ones. Such a discounting hypothesis about the basic source of ambivalence is distinct from the two-principle hypothesis and will be discussed later. However, Freud assumed that it was natural and ordinary that future events were discounted and that threats to one's values were innately painful. The part of the mechanism that he claimed as his discovery was the repression of stimuli, the genesis of the repository of lower motives that he called the unconscious.

Stripped of its neuroanatomical images, Freud's second model of impulse creation can be characterized in this way: The defense guarding consciousness caused the accumulation of unsatisfied motives ("energy"), leading to increasingly intense urges to respond. Only this excessive accumulation of motivation could generate pathological impulses, which were the only forces that did not equilibrate with other motives (Freud, 1913/1956e, pp. 23–30; 1915/1956g, p. 147; 1920/1956k, p. 20). If it were not for this blockage of motivation and consequent transformation into impulses, a person would simply be motivated to maximize his pleasure; impulses would not occur. Thus, Freud's second theory of ambivalence apparently depended on the relationship of a higher principle and a lower principle of motivation. The higher was goal-directed and rational, but could not take some of the person's motives into account because they had become unconscious. The lower principle was also goal-directed, but it operated only on the basis of those motives that had been repressed by the higher principle.

Freud's therapy for ambivalence was founded on that model. Unlike his philosophical predecessors, he suggested more than a search for constructive passions that could battle the destructive ones. He said that it was possible for a person to stop repressing the relevant motives, thereby coming to see his goals in their true proportions (1923/1956l, p. 50n; 1916–1917/1956i, pp. 435–447). That strategy was described most clearly by a later psychoanalyst, Franz Alexander (1963, p. 440): "During treatment unconscious (repressed) material becomes conscious. This increases the action radius of the conscious ego; the ego becomes cognizant of unconscious impulses and thus is able to coordinate (integrate) the latter with the rest of conscious content."

Freud's hypotheses are notoriously difficult to test, but his assertion about the origin of a second principle of motivation seems both unnecessary and contradictory to available observations. Repression and a body of unconscious material demonstrably exist in everyone, but this is not evidence that repression is the fundamental cause of impulsiveness. On the contrary, repression often seems to be an impulsive act in its own right, in that it accepts a greater pain in the future in return for avoiding a smaller pain in the present. At other times it represents an attempt to control impulses (see section 5.3.2). For both reasons, repression frequently is found in the vicinity of impulses, and thus it was a natural object of Freud's suspicion; but he did not have to conclude that the repression caused the impulses.

Freud's concept of repression boils down to selective inattention. Although it is a weapon in the war of motive against motive, no finding from the several current lines of research on selective inattention suggests that it could be the cause of the war, as reviewed by Shevrin and Dickman (1980). What we know of repression itself entails no exception to the utilitarian model in which the greater motive always prevails over lesser ones.

Furthermore, even casual inspection of clinical data raises doubts that repression is the process that keeps one motive from being directly weighed against its competitors. Therapists from both psychoanalytic and other schools often describe decreases in patients' self-defeating behaviors unaccompanied by increases in the consciousness of their motives (Kohut, 1977, pp. 133–139; Thoresen & Mahoney, 1974; Yalom et al., 1967). Conversely, patients often acquire a vast knowledge of how their motives originate, without a decrease in self-defeating behavior, a finding that has led psychoanalysts to distinguish intellectual or "dictionary" insight from the kind that leads to resolution of the patient's ambivalence (Hatcher, 1973).

Often both alternatives of a choice are conscious and seem undistorted by defense mechanisms, yet the person remains unable to reach a stable preference. For instance, an addicted person who wants to break his dependence on a substance also wants not to, and consciously expresses both conflicting wishes. Where both sides are conscious, the role of unconsciousness in creating or curing ambivalence can at most be indirect. Furthermore, people who will become addicted to a substance do not necessarily use repression or other defense mechanisms in an unusual way: Examination of the defenses used by young adults cannot predict who will become alcoholic, for instance (Kammeier, Hoffman, & Toper, 1973; Vaillant, 1980); and the notorious difficulty of giving up a cigarette habit, even when the person is strongly motivated to do so, apparently is not related to psychopathology. Freud found his self-analysis useless against his own habit of smoking cigars, despite the fact that he was concerned about the effect of cigars on his health, and even after he learned that he had mouth cancer (Schur, 1972). There are some cases, at least, where ambivalence does not depend on repression.

Some authors ignore Freud's attempt to relate higher and lower principles, and continue to examine the traditional idea of passions. They have generally regarded passions as traps. For instance, Young (1972, pp. 20–30) described emotions as disruptions of rational behavior. Sartre (1948, p. 77) called them "degradations of consciousness," assertions of control over experiences that would be richer if left to take us where they might. Toda suggests that emotions are the basis of a separate ("compositional") kind of rationality that is lower only in that it conflicts with the analytical rationality newly evolved with "our large brain with its accompanying capacity for elaborate information processing" (1980, p. 142). Rapaport (1973, p. 179) avoids Davidson's two-center model (see section 2.2) of *akrasia* by ascribing lapses from one's own reasoned choices to "temptation," which can motivate the "spinelessness," deliberate ignorance, inattention, self-deception, or negligence for which philosophers have been trying to account. However, these authors have not suggested why people who know the consequences of their passions or temptations cannot integrate them with their other motives.

2.3.2 Unmotivated lower principles

The lower principles discussed so far have been goal-directed. They have sought gratification, sometimes of a different kind than the higher principles (e.g., joys of the flesh versus the spirit); but increasingly in modern times they have been seen as seeking the same gratifications as the higher principles, albeit in a less efficient way. Distinct from these hypotheses is the notion that a lower principle that is not goal-directed distorts the person's motivation, so that some appetites spring up in temporary opposition to the rest of his wishes. The implication is that a person's motives will not be in conflict until something triggers this blind mechanism.

For instance, it has been suggested that alcohol produces a sudden physical, almost reflexive, tendency to drink in some people. This hypothesis is based on the widespread reports by alcoholics that they remain in good "control" until they drink alcohol, and then they experience a sudden, involuntary "loss of control" of their drinking. In one study, 971 of 1,023 alcoholic subjects reported such a phenomenon (Evenson et al., 1973). Obviously, the behavior of drinking alcohol is not literally a reflex, and the reported loss of control is a change of motivation. If it is triggered by events outside the person's control and does not in turn cause a lasting change in his usual motives, it might produce the Jekyll-and-Hyde alternation that some alcoholics indeed experience. However, in experimental studies where either a strongly flavored punch or alcohol disguised in that punch was given in blind fashion to volunteer alcoholic subjects, some of whom believed they were getting alcohol and some of whom did not, the belief, not the actual presence of alcohol, was found to be the factor that determined an increased craving for drink (Engel & Williams, 1972; Maisto, Lauerman, & Adesso, 1977). Loss of control after drinking even small amounts of alcohol remains a striking observation, but the explanation for it cannot be the physical effects of alcohol.

Of course, many changes of motive have obvious physical causes. People go from being full to being hungry, for instance. That in itself suggests no reason for motivational conflict. But if the change were sudden – if chocolate ice cream triggered an appetite for itself the way alcohol was supposed to in the foregoing example, or if there were any other directly acting aperitifs or aphrodisiacs – it might be argued that such a change would cause a tendency for the person to undermine his own goals. However, we would not expect this to happen once a person was familiar with how and when a particular change occurred. Organisms learn to anticipate changes in appetite and take them into account like any other motive. People routinely buy food when they are not hungry, and satiated rats will run a maze for food if they have been receiving hunger-inducing brain stimulation on reaching the food (Mendelson & Chorover, 1965). If the organism does not learn to serve an expected motive, or even struggles against it – for instance, if a person, when full, locks his refrigerator so that he cannot eat when hungry – then some additional explanation is required.

Physical reflexes are not often proposed to explain ambivalence. Much more common are "blind forces" in the mind, the possibility that Davidson (1983, p. 298) rejected in favor of his partitioned mind (see section 2.2). Of these, the most popular have been those said to arise from classical conditioning.

Conditioning theories have been proposed since the time of the associationist philosophers. The commonsense version is that a person can be induced to change his wants by a stimulus that previously had been present at a time of emotional arousal. Pavlov's ability to override his subject's goal-directed behaviors by conditioning procedures apparently confirmed that here, indeed, was a lower principle of motivation, one that could pre-empt a subject's rational motives without being affected by them in turn.

Clinical hypotheses soon followed. J. B. Watson showed that a child's fear could be transferred to an arbitrarily chosen stimulus by pairing that stimulus with a loud noise, and a fear thus implanted was difficult to extinguish (Cohen, 1979, pp. 142–144). Some early writers in the behaviorist school described maladaptive behavior itself as being conditioned – so that there might be, for example, conditioned alcohol-drinking responses or even conditioned "verbal recrimination" (Watson, 1924). Interestingly, this awkward theory was similar to Freud's earliest explanation of ambivalence: that compulsively repeated behaviors represent an exact replay of behaviors that happened to occur during special "hypnoid" states of consciousness (Breuer & Freud, 1895/1956).

Neither theory went far in its original form, although Freud occasionally invoked repetition compulsion when he despaired of specifying a motive for a behavior: "Enough is left unexplained to justify the hypothesis of a compulsion to repeat – something that seems more primitive, more elementary, more instinctual than the pleasure principle which it overrides" (1920/1956k, p. 23). Similarly, references to "conditioned" motor behaviors still are encountered occasionally (Smith, 1982). However, after goal-directed ("operant") learning was clearly differentiated from classical conditioning in the 1930s, O. H. Mowrer (1947) proposed the conditioning theory of pathogenesis in its modern form. According to this "two-factor" theory, visceral states, particularly emotions, become maladaptively conditioned by chance pairings with environmental stimuli, and the person then performs ordinary goal-directed behavior to seek or avoid the stimuli that have come to produce these visceral states. For instance, a person might form a sexual fetish because the object was present during intercourse, or even imagined during masturbation. This theory was applied to psychopathology generally in Dollard and Miller's influential book *Personality and Psychotherapy* (1950), which provided an attractive explanation of how the defensive processes described by psychoanalysis might be providing relief from aversive conditioned emotions.

There are several problems with classical conditioning as a mechanism for ambivalence. The simplest is the argument made earlier against the unconditioned-reflex model of such motives as craving for alcohol: Mere demonstration of a cause for a motive in no way suggests that the motive cannot be weighed against the person's other motives. For classical conditioning to explain ambivalence, the conditioned motives would have to be somehow unpredictable or unimaginable even after much experience with them; otherwise the conditioned stimulus could not lead to the sudden change of motivation that the theory requires. In effect, the classical conditioning explanation relies on compartment formation: A person cannot imagine how good alcohol tastes until he encounters stimuli to which the taste or effects of alcohol have been conditioned, and a person cannot recall the extent of his fear of dogs until he encounters a dog.

Compartment formation does sometimes occur, the extreme case being multiple personalities. However, there are no laboratory findings on conditioning that suggest why conditioned motives should be partitioned from others. On the contrary, conditioning occurs to all stimuli that predict the occurrence of the relevant visceral state; any such predictive information is apt to induce a conditioned response

(Egger & Miller, 1962). Thus, the visceral state comes to be fully anticipated; no conditioned response should induce a sudden change of preference once it has become familiar. Given his total experience with alcohol or dogs, a person would be expected to make an overall evaluation whether or not seeking or avoiding them would be worthwhile, and not keep changing his mind.

A more fundamental problem is whether or not classical conditioning exists as a distinct principle of motivation. This question is relatively recent. Indeed, conditioning has always seemed more basic than operant learning, perhaps because a mechanism of causality is apparent. That stimulus A precedes stimulus B and wears a path to it seems a more robust hypothesis than the teleology of operant learning – that seeking stimulus B is reinforced in the presence of stimulus A. Perhaps this is one reason for the intuitive appeal of conditioning as a lower principle of motivation. Yet teleological behavior is observed in all higher organisms; it is unnecessary to know its underlying mechanism. Certainly we have no reason to believe that it is less fundamental than, or reduces to, classical conditioning, a point first made by Tolman (1932) more than 50 years ago.

It is classical conditioning that rests on shaky ground. Recent research has called into question its existence as a principle of motivation distinct from the goal-directed, "operant" kind (Ainslie & Engel, 1974; Atnip, 1977; Hearst, 1975, pp. 181–223; Herrnstein, 1969). The reader who does not want to explore this problem may skip to the last four paragraphs of this section.

1. Most visceral processes can be controlled by differential reward when it is promptly presented. The extensive data of biofeedback research refute the old belief that there are two kinds of behaviors, one responsive to operant reward and the other to unconditioned stimuli. Not only is operant reward effective generally, but stimuli that can induce classically conditioned responses seem always to be the kind that can also be operant rewards or punishments (Hull, 1943; N. Miller, 1969). In fact, when a stimulus can elicit a physical response but is neither rewarding nor punishing, as in the case of light that produces pupillary dilation, pairing it with a neutral stimulus does not lead to conditioning (Gerall & Obrist, 1962; Gerall, Sampson, & Gertrude, 1957). The fact that the same set of stimuli serve as both

operant and classical reinforcers makes it believable, but does not prove, that in classical conditioning procedures the reinforcing process is operant reward.

2. More convincing is the ability of operant reward to reverse a classically conditioned response. For instance, monkeys warned of unavoidable shock become "conditioned" to increase their heart rates in the presence of the warning stimulus. If the same subjects are trained in a biofeedback procedure to avoid shock by lowering their heart rates, and are then placed in a situation where both conditioning and operant contingencies are in force simultaneously (some shock unavoidable, additional shock avoidable by lowering the heart rate), they will lower rather than raise their heart rates in response to the warning stimulus (Ainslie & Engel, 1974).

In light of operant rewards' power to modify conditioned responses, N. J. Mackintosh concluded that "not only is any difference between classical and instrumental conditioning a graded rather than an abrupt one, but it is also largely a consequence of the differences in the operations involved in the two kinds of experiment" (1974, p. 139). He maintained even this distinction only because some rewards seem to elicit unrewarded behaviors, that is, responses that persist even when the response prevents the reward: In one procedure, food was delivered periodically to untrained pigeons in the presence of a lighted key. In that situation, pigeons would spontaneously peck the key, a phenomenon called "autoshaping" because it is easy subsequently to train ("shape") pigeons to peck the key to get food. However, pigeons would keep pecking at a low rate even if that behavior produced no extra food, and even if it reduced the rate of food delivery – the latter situation is called "negative autoshaping" (Williams & Williams, 1969). In such a situation, pecking clearly was sustained by something other than its reward by food, even though the pecking will eventually stop if food is never delivered.

Mackintosh (1974) calls it "implausible" that the unseen, unprogrammed sustaining force should be some kind of operant reward, such as the fun of pecking keys when food is around. However, such unseen, intrinsic reward is familiar in analogous human situations. For instance, a child spanked for crying will have the urge to cry more; he can resist this urge if the threat is great enough, just as the pigeon reduces his pecking rate somewhat during negative autoshaping (Schwartz & Williams, 1972), but otherwise he will be behaving in contradiction to his ostensible incentives. The point need not be resolved here. Suffice it to say that whatever force there is beyond reward is weighed against reward – the unseen urge to cry or peck is weighed against the visible consequences according to some common dimension of choosability, and therefore this urge must be said to possess a reward equivalence. As long as the organism's behavior is decided in a single marketplace, where any motivational force can be weighed against any other, the question whether or not other differences exist between classical and operant reinforcers will not matter.

3. Finally, conditioned responses differ from responses produced by the original biological stimulus in ways ranging from small details to complete reversal of the direction of the response (Siegal, 1983). Thus, "conditioned" responses are not transferred whole from the unconditioned to the conditioned stimulus, but are learned afresh, presumably on the basis of the differential reward for them in the conditioning situation. That is, the increase in heart rate that originally followed the warning stimulus in the monkey experiment described earlier may have prepared the subject in some way to meet the shock, or may have been rewarding in its own right, in the same way that crying when spanked must be regarded as rewarding in its own right; whatever the explanation, when a change in contingencies made a decrease in heart rate even more rewarding than an increase, the decrease supplanted the increase. Summarizing modern conditioning research, Rescorla has said that

> Pavlovian conditioning is not the shifting of a response from one stimulus to another. Instead, conditioning involves the learning of relations among events.... [1988, p. 158]

In other words, the acquisition of information may be somewhat independent of operant reward, but the production of behavior does not seem to be.[3]

In a clinical situation like substance abuse, too, operant reward probably is responsible for supposedly conditioned appetites. Substance abusers often are said to have developed conditioned emo-

---

[3] This distinction was well clarified years ago by Estes (1969a).

tional responses to the trappings of ingesting their substances – bars and shot glasses, or needle parks and "works," for instance – such that the sight of these stimuli will overwhelm all other motives and cause a loss of control even after years of abstinence. But the feature of these stimuli that leads to craving seems not to be the extent of their association with the substance, but rather the degree to which they predict its ingestion. Drug and alcohol abusers on experimental wards develop cravings if and only if the substance is scheduled to be available on that particular day, with environmental stimuli held constant (Meyer, 1981). Similarly, smokers who never smoke at certain times do not develop cravings at those times, even though their surroundings stay the same (Schachter, Silverstein, & Perlick, 1977). Craving seems best understood not as a response driven by a stimulus through association, but as a goal-directed preparatory response that is emitted when it is likely to be rewarded by consumption of the craved substance. There has even been a report that deprived narcotic addicts stop developing physiological symptoms of withdrawal when these are punished by shock (Wolpe, Groves, & Fisher, 1980), suggesting that these symptoms, too, are behaviors that can be controlled by differential reward.

Classical conditioning emerges as one means of shaping operant behavior. It is seen where reflexive behaviors also happen to be operants that are rewarded when the stimuli for these reflexes are present. Such operants can then be transferred to whatever other stimuli predict reward for them. Thus, in the autoshaping situation, for instance, a pigeon's innate tendency to peck a disk when it is being fed facilitates its learning to peck the disk *in order to get food.* Although the rewarding event sometimes is obscure (e.g., whatever incentive maintains the pecking in negative autoshaping), this obscurity certainly is not evidence that some process distinct from operant reward is occurring (Baer, 1981).

But if classical conditioning is just a special case of goal-directed learning, it cannot explain ambivalent motivation. On the contrary, when "conditioned responses" are experienced as unwelcome, their occurrence must be explained in turn. The problem, it should be emphasized, is not whether or not classical conditioning can be performed as a procedure, or whether or not this procedure can produce behaviors that the subject reports to be involuntary. Rather, the problem is whether or not the reinforcers that govern conditioned behavior have properties distinct from those of operant rewards. In particular, are conditioned reinforcers blocked from having the same interaction with operant rewards that operant rewards have with one another, the kind that should produce an overall preference for one of the rewarded behaviors over its competitors? In short, are conditioned behaviors exempt from some of the rules of the motivational marketplace? The evidence suggests that they are not, and thus that classical conditioning does not represent a separate motivational principle.

Recently it has been suggested that "automatic cognitive processes" or "automatized action schemata" can supersede a person's voluntary controls, leading to self-defeating behaviors like drug abuse (Tiffany, 1990). It is unclear whether or not these "tightly integrated associative connections . . . that always become active in response to a particular input configuration" (p. 152) are supposed to have been learned through a motivated process, but their functional properties, and hence shortcomings, seem to be the same as for the repetition compulsions and conditioned behaviors described earlier in this section.

None of the lower principles of choice discussed earlier constitutes the sought-after explanation for ambivalence. Each driver of the tandem automobile must tug at his wheel with a force measurable in dynes; and even if one wheel has a mechanical advantage over the other, the final force exerted on the turning arm to the front wheels will be composed of two simple quantities that will weigh against each other. It is possible, of course, to postulate cutoff mechanisms, whereby one driver could pre-empt the other under specified circumstances. Thus, appearances might suggest that repressed anger or conditioned fear disconnects other motives from the decision-making mechanism. But although strong emotions sometimes are experienced as unopposable, true independence from the person's internal marketplace would imply the kind of rigid stereotypy seen, for instance, in temporal-lobe seizures. This is not the case with emotions; even the strongest passion can be diverted by sufficient incentive or sufficient craft.

From earliest times, lower principles of choice have seemed to describe people's impressions of self-defeating behavior. But where theorists have proposed specific details about these principles, these have not accounted for how such behavior can persist in competition with adaptive behavior, and in many cases have been contradicted by careful observation. It is evident that a viable theory of ambivalence must stay within the rules of operant reward.

2.4 Misinformation cannot cause ambivalence

Some modern authors say that self-defeating behavior can be explained entirely as a person's erroneous perception of his situation. This approach dates back to Socrates' belief that no one knowingly does evil, but it was little advocated as an alternative to diabolical or lower-principle theories until modern times. Its first advocates were philosophers of the eighteenth and nineteenth centuries, both romantics and rationalists, who believed that ignorance, not an innate tendency to impulsiveness, was the true enemy of a person's best interests (Mill, 1871; Rousseau, 1959). That belief was common among the utopians who founded "rational" communities, some of whom expressly repudiated the doctrine of "original sin" by which intrinsic impulsiveness had been understood (Carden, 1969, pp. 11–15). The belief in human perfectibility through proper teaching has remained popular and in recent times has inspired a search for models of self-defeating behaviors based on either deceptive operant learning (Skinner, 1948b) or faulty logic.

2.4.1 Superstition

An experimental model of goal-directed learning was described by Thorndike (1905) at the turn of the century. Not until the 1940s did investigators describe systematic errors that developed with this kind of learning, errors that were not corrected by more extensive practice. Animals' tendencies to develop seemingly random bits of behavior and keep them even after the animals became otherwise efficient at getting their rewards were likened to human superstitions and, by extension, to clinically maladaptive behaviors (Gambrill, 1977, p. 34; Skinner, 1948b). If there is some fundamental tendency for goal-directed behavior to move off course and stay off course, the argument ran, then such a process could be a source of self-defeating behavior.

Therapists of the behavioral school have not tried to explain self-defeating behaviors to the extent that the psychoanalysts have, but in formulating their therapies they have had to make assumptions about why such behaviors persist. Those who have not invoked classical conditioning usually have implied that misguided operant learning is responsible for their clients' ambivalence. The superstitious operant behavior of animals once seemed to offer a model for such learning.

A closer examination of maladaptive laboratory "superstition," however, has shown that it is not caused by random pairings of behavior and reward, but by an innate preparedness to respond to particular features of the test situation (Staddon & Simmelhag, 1971). For instance, the pigeons' pecking of lighted keys in the negative-autoshaping procedure described in the preceding section might have been called superstitious. The most likely explanation is that there have been rewards intrinsic to the performance of such responses that cannot be detected except by their ability to counteract more readily observable rewards. Failure to observe these rewards directly means that more complicated explanations cannot be ruled out, but it certainly does not mean that such explanations are required. In any case, experimental superstition is not an example of ambivalence.

2.4.2 Hidden costs

Unlike schedule-induced "superstition," deceptive reward schedules probably are important in maladaptive behaviors; such schedules induce organisms to make choices that they would not make knowingly. In a taxonomy of "social traps" that lure people into making decisions they later regret, Cross and Guyer (1980) described "sliding reinforcers," rewards supporting a behavior that reduces the rewards for both itself and its alternatives on subsequent occasions (Platt, 1973). They described the example of a farmer who uses DDT: He is rewarded by larger crops in the short run, but he both selects for resistant strains of insects and kills some of the natural insectivores that represent his alternative strategy, thus trapping himself with poorer options than those with which he began. This phenomenon is readily replicated in the laboratory with both animal and human subjects. Herrnstein and Prelec (1988) have described several "distributed-choice" experiments in which a subject repeatedly chooses the larger of two rewards even though that choice regularly subtracts a large amount from both alternatives in all subsequent choices. Those authors suggest that such experiments provide a model for the "primrose path" taken by substance addicts. However, although the delayed costs seem remarkably difficult to detect in such experiments, human subjects often can detect them and, when they do, avoid them, although not with perfect regularity (Herrnstein et al., 1988). Such deception is apt to be an important factor in the bad long-range decisions that people sometimes make, but it cannot be a basis for motivational conflict; where a subject knowingly chooses inferior rewards in the primrose-path situation, some further explanation is necessary.

2.4.3 Misinterpretation

In the same vein, Paul Wachtel has suggested a revision of psychoanalytic theory that would hold misinformation to be the pathogen of some self-defeating behaviors. His view of motivational conflict is complex, but it can be summarized as recognizing cases in which symptoms are learned and maintained by a deceptive learning situation, thereby freeing therapeutic strategy from the implications of the repression hypothesis. For instance, a person who believes that others find him overly familiar, when they actually find him too aloof, may respond to their negative hints with greater aloofness. In such situations the patient seems innocently to misinterpret his failures as meaning that he is not performing enough of what is in fact the failure-producing behavior, and so he tries even harder at the wrong thing (Wachtel, 1977, pp. 41–75). Baumeister and Scher have reviewed a number of similar "counterproductive strategies" that are "mediated by misjudging either one's capacity to carry out the intended response or the contingencies associated with the response" (1988, p. 12). However, they have offered only ad hoc explanations for why such misjudgment persists in the face of contrary evidence. It is not clear why a patient should defend such an innocent error against the therapist's attempts to point it out. Simple misapprehension is not ambivalence and should respond to straightforward teaching.

2.4.4 Nonspecific errors of learning

Often behavior therapists refer to no particular model of pathogenesis. They seem to assume that some unspecified kind of overly narrow, albeit goal-directed, learning has led to maladaptive "habits" in their clients (Eysenck, 1964). However, they do not speculate about the reason for the pathological narrowing.

2.4.5 Errors in logic

Philosophy has been divided as to whether or not behavior is fundamentally a product of judgment (Davidson, 1980, pp. 21–42), that is, whether or not "the fit that confers rationality on actions and the fit that confers truth on sentences" (Pears, 1984, p. 181) are identical. If so, then "actions always go through the narrow gate of reason" (Pears, 1984, p. 195), and decisions will depend ultimately on logic rather than on force of motivation. Indeed, actions might never be examined as to their consequences at all, much less their consequences in terms of satisfaction to the actor – even in modern times philosophers have belittled this examination as "consequentialism" (Williams, 1973). Of course, even foraging and operant-reward theories can be translated into the process of making judgments, but the implication of such a change is that preference, once adequately deliberated upon, must be stable in the absence of new information and must be consistent with one's other preferences. Self-defeating behavior is then seen as a failure of realism, because "the agent's outright value-judgment and his action . . . form a representational couple aimed at the truth, like the conjunction of two beliefs" (Pears, 1984, p. 180); it should be said that Pears opposes the viewpoint he thus characterizes. Such a judgment-centered approach, in which motive is reduced to being one of a number of facts that the decision maker evaluates, provides the basis for a burgeoning school of psychotherapy:

Cognitive therapy explains "irrationality" ("any thought, emotion, or behavior that leads to self-defeating or self-destructive consequences," Ellis, 1976) as a defect in the subject's problem-solving skills (Beck & Emery, 1985; Ellis & Grieger, 1977). Cognitive therapists take negative cognitions about the self to be the pathogenic agents of their clients' self-defeating behaviors, but they do not explain why their clients should have selectively formed such cognitions. Some supposed pathogens imply misinformation, such as "dysfunctional meaning structures [that] develop as a result of deleterious interactions between man and his environment" (Perris, 1988, p. 12), or a "distorted or rigid . . . self-concept [determined by] relationships with significant others (i.e., parents)" (Dobson & Block, 1988, p. 27). However, the greater emphasis is on a misuse of logic, occurring unaccountably in otherwise intelligent people. Educated clients who commit "logical errors," such as overgeneralization, selective abstraction, or black-and-white thinking, to the detriment of their self-judgments, while otherwise retaining razor-sharp critical faculties, cannot simply be naive about logic. Even if they were, simple education should be enough to correct the error, just as with simple misinterpretations; but the cognitive therapists, like many before them, have observed that it is not sufficient: "When bright and generally competent people give up many of their irrationalities, they frequently tend to adopt other inanities or to go to opposite irrational extremes" (Ellis & Grieger, 1977, p. 17); see also Beck and Emery (1985, pp. 260–261). Self-destructive irrationality is another addition to the list of phenomena that do not explain, but remain to be explained.

2.4.6 Logical errors under pressure

Sjoberg (1980) has suggested that rational self-control requires sustained effort, and it fails under circumstances that increase that effort, such as emotional turmoil or the presence of a tempting object (Sjoberg & Johnson, 1978). His observations on self-control are astute, but the consequence of introducing effort as a factor in rationality is to convert the explanation from a cognitive to a utilitarian approach: that following one's own chosen path sometimes ceases to be worth the effort. Similarly, Cross and Guyer have described a social trap called the "Midas effect" (Why did King Midas forget that he would have to touch his food?), observing that "highly attractive reinforcers have the effect of inhibiting even ordinary reflections upon the consequences of one's behavior" (1980, p. 22). As was noted in section 1.3.2, selective attention is indeed a motivated behavior (see sections

4.2.1 and 5.3.2), but this fact does not explain how "highly attractive reinforcers" can sabotage the consistent operation of differential reward itself.

2.5 Most models incidentally imply that delayed events are devalued

Many of the authors discussed earlier have implied, or mentioned in passing, that intolerance of delay is an important property of their mechanisms of motivational conflict. However, they seem to have felt that it was not by itself a sufficient explanation for ambivalence. This rejection of an intuitively appealing and parsimonious mechanism is puzzling.

For instance, Freud did not need the repression-based lower principle of motivation to account for ambivalence. Implicit in his second hypothesis, in the *Project for a Scientific Psychology* (1895/1956a), is the assumption that people innately discount the importance of delayed events relative to imminent events: In that model, a person's blockade of painful stimuli does not eliminate the stimuli, but only stores them in a rumenlike reservoir for a later, obligatory passage through consciousness. This side-cathexis, or repression, is just a device to delay pain.

Freud made that assumption explicit in his third hypothesis (1911/1956d), where he proposed devaluation of the future per se as a cause of motivational conflict. According to the pleasure principle, a person seeks the course of "least resistance" rather than that of "greatest advantage" (1911/1956d, p. 223). This principle is sometimes restrained by the reality principle, which is not a separate decision-making mechanism, but a refinement of the pleasure principle, making the pair of principles function like Hume's passion that opposes itself: "Actually the substitution of the reality principle for the pleasure principle implies no deposing of the pleasure principle, but only a safeguarding of it. A momentary pleasure, uncertain in its results, is given up, but only in order to gain along the new path an assured pleasure at a later time" (Freud, 1911/1956d, p. 223).

Admittedly this passage does not make clear whether the original pleasure is given up because of its momentary quality or its uncertain results – oddly so, because the pleasure principle presumably operated in many situations where the outcome contingencies were thoroughly familiar to the actor. However, later psychoanalysts have consistently attributed discounting of the future to the pleasure principle and its descendant concepts. For instance, Rapaport describes the primary process, a concept closely akin to the pleasure principle, in this way: "The core of this change from the primary to the secondary process appears to be a change in the character of delay. The delay to begin with was due to external circumstances (i.e., the unavailability of immediate reward) and is turned into an ability to delay, into an internal control" (1950, p. 164).

However, pleasure and reality were still "principles" of motivation, and in Freud's fourth and final hypothesis he used ideas from his second hypothesis to elaborate on their distinctness, rather than follow his simpler idea that motivational conflict was a function of intolerance for delay. The pleasure principle and primary process became the id, a repository of repressed wishes that obeys a separate principle of motivation or even represents an autonomous motivational center distinct from the ego (1920/1956k, 1923/1956l). Nevertheless, just as repression itself implied a devaluation of future events, the id became the organ that could not defer gratification: "In contrast to the id, which refers to peremptory aspects of behavior, the ego refers to aspects of behavior which are delayable, bring about delay, or are themselves products of delays" (Rapaport, 1959); see also Klein (1954) and Blachly (1970).

Thus, in analytic theory the discounting of delayed events is what ultimately leads to ego-alien behavior. It is not clear why repression is needed as an intervening mechanism. The observed association of repression and unresolved motivational conflict need not lead to the conclusion that the former causes the latter. Most psychoanalytic findings are just as consistent with the hypothesis that discounting delayed events leads to ambivalence, which in turn motivates repression.

In fact, a single ingredient seems necessary to all the two-principle models: a person's current unresponsiveness to the motivational force of contingencies that will bear on his future behavior, even when he is intellectually aware of these contingencies. The person who represses his anger does not allow for it in planning his decisions and thus is surprised by its effects; the person who has been conditioned to crave alcohol in a given situation likewise does not weigh the conditioned craving in the absence of its conditioned stimuli, so he seems to change his evaluation of the alcohol suddenly when he encounters its conditioned stimuli. This apparent defect in the anticipation process has been described repeatedly in terms of one pair of factors or another, but it can be explained without resorting to a two-principle theory, as we shall see.

Similarly, cognitive theories for why people behave in ways they will later regret often involve a failure to picture delayed consequences adequately (Mischel & Staub, 1965), or even a disbelief that current behavior really affects later outcomes (Bialer, 1961; Strickland, 1972; Walls & Smith, 1970). The concept that the future appears less distinct as delay increases may be functionally the same as a simple devaluation of delayed events or an aversiveness attached to waiting; the latter formulation came from Mischel at about the same time as the failure-of-visualization hypothesis just mentioned (Mischel & Staub, 1965). Recently, Baumeister and Scher have attributed all self-defeating behaviors not caused by misestimation of their consequences to "judgment errors, especially favoring short-term benefits that are associated with long-term costs" (1988, p. 8). Also related are some of the "irrational beliefs" that people are said to form, such as the belief that they "can't stand" a particular complaint – the implication being that time will prove them wrong if they can only wait (Ellis & Grieger, 1977, pp. 8–11). Such authors are now dealing not so much with ignorance of future outcomes as with discounting their value. This was made explicit on one of the rare occasions when cognitive writers asked why "compelling schemata [rationales for action] that a patient will often 'know' are erroneous are hard to change. . . . People often find ways to adjust to and extract *short-term benefits* from fundamentally biased schemata that restrict or burden their *long-term capacity* to deal with the challenge of life" (Freeman & Leaf, 1989, p. 409; italics added).

Thus, cognitive hypotheses, like psychoanalytic and conditioning hypotheses, often imply a devaluation of delayed events relative to imminent events. Given the frequency with which this devaluation is mentioned in models of ambivalence, it might be wise to reach for Ockham's razor and see if the sought-after mechanism might be the elementary discounting function of delayed rewards per se.

3. Temporary-preference theory

3.1 Temporal distortion is a simple mechanism for ambivalence

The simplest explanation for why organisms fail to maximize their expected rewards would be that they discount the value of future rewards. Clearly we should not accept such an explanation without evidence that such discounting actually occurs. To be able to go a long step further and explain organisms' self-defeating behaviors by their discounting of future rewards we shall need evidence about the specific form of this discounting. The shape of the discount curve must generate the familiar manifestations of ambivalence, including (a) regular changes of preference in the absence of new information about outcome, (b) disproportionate motivational effect exerted by events with little intrinsic value (e.g., the events reviewed in chapter 2 as hypothetical triggers for reflexes, conditioned stimuli for appetites, and symbolic expressions of repressed issues), (c) motivational conflicts, that is, observations that "part" of the self regularly undermines some other part, however these parts might be defined, and (d) impulses, compulsions, and other subjectively involuntary conduct. The importance of a discounting phenomenon would be corroborated if it could also explain the other motivational paradoxes noted in chapter 1, even though they are not obviously based on ambivalence.

3.2 There is an innate tendency to devalue future events

Theorists of human irrationality have stopped short of saying that the human tendency to devalue future goods is fundamental. We have seen that they often mention relative unresponsiveness to future contingencies as part of the problem, but they portray it as exceptional and ascribe it to some more basic cause – repression, conditioning, illogical thinking, and so forth. This is natural enough. We are used to thinking of ourselves as consistent, and often we are right. People do not radically devalue the future for most purposes, but guard their interests over the years and save their money. Banks can attract ample deposits by offering single-digit interest rates. Even Freud, though he recognized many threats to the "reality principle," assumed that it was an intrinsically normal mode of functioning that did not need the explanation that impulsiveness did.

It is just as supportable, however, to say that living mostly for the present moment is our natural mode of functioning, and that consistent behavior is sometimes acquired, to a greater or lesser extent, as a skill. Some philosophers have even suggested that we should not acquire such a skill – that we would be happier if we abandoned our complex ways of banking on the future and lived for the present instant (Camus, 1955; Solomon, 1975), as Spengler (1926, p. 132) imagined "classical" man to have done. This message is even more conspicuous in modern fiction. A norm of consistency over time does not imply that such consistency is elementary; indeed, those who criticize the norm must believe that it is not.

Both a general tendency to discount future events and a valuable but elusive trait countervailing that tendency have long been recognized, as witness the maxims "Genius is nothing but a great aptitude for patience" and "Everything comes if a man will only wait" (Bartlett, 1955, pp. 334, 512). John Stuart Mill spoke of the conflict as commonplace:

> Many who are capable of the higher pleasures, occasionally, under the influence of temptation, postpone them to the lower. But this is quite compatible with a full appreciation of the intrinsic superiority of the higher. Men often, from infirmity of character, make their election for the nearer good, though they know it to be the less valuable; and this no less when the choice is between two bodily pleasures than when it is between bodily and mental. They pursue sensual indulgences to the injury of health, though perfectly aware that health is the greater good. [1871, p. 19]

The Victorian economist Jevons described the conflict similarly:

> To secure a maximum of benefit in life, all future events, all future pleasures or pains, should act upon us with the same force as if they were present, allowance being made for their uncertainty. The factor expressing the effect of remoteness should, in short, always be unity, so that time should have no influence. But no human mind is constituted in this perfect way: a future feeling is always less influential than a present one. [1871/1911, pp. 72–73]

In this century, another economist, Pigou, perceived the same split between rationality and human nature:

> People distribute their resources between the present, the near future and the remote future on the basis of a wholly irrational preference. When they have a choice between two satisfactions, they will not necessarily choose the larger of the two, but will often devote themselves to producing or obtaining a small one now in preference to a much larger one some years hence. [1920, p. 25]

When around 1900 E. L. Thorndike created the first systematic animal analogs of human choice situations, he found that "increasing the interval between the response and the satisfaction or discomfort . . . diminishes the rate of learning" (quoted by Benjamin & Perloff, 1983). Studies by an army of subsequent investigators have found that even short delays cause profound drops in reward effectiveness, even when subjects are signaled immediately that the reward is sure to come, as reviewed by Kimble (1961), Renner (1964), and Ainslie (1975). Preference for smaller, earlier rewards over larger, later ones persists over many days of continuous exposure to the choice, even when this reward is the subjects' sole source of food (Logue et al., 1988). However, it would not be difficult to believe that delay of reward is one area in which animal models can be misleading.

Empirical research on people's devaluations of future rewards had not been done until recently; perhaps the question seemed adequately answered by economic statistics on how the delay of a good decreases its value in the free market. Certainly there is a great deal of information on such discount rates and on their complements, the interest rates that must be paid to attract investment. However, when the notion that market discount rates reflect spontaneous preferences is tested systematically, it does not hold true, even in the realm of consumer economics. For instance, a study of actual air-conditioner purchases showed that in accepting higher operating costs in return for lower purchase prices, consumers devalued the future at annual rates as high as 89% (Hausman, 1979). Similar studies have sometimes found rates in the hundreds of percentage points (Gately, 1980; Ruderman, Levine, & McMahon, 1986).

It might be argued that in situations of consumer choice, people are forced away from their true preferences by various economic realities. In the air-conditioner study, it was the poorest subjects who chose the highest discount rates, perhaps because they could not pay the purchase prices for the more efficient units. However, in five studies in which people were asked how they would trade off the amount and the delay of extra income that was entirely hypothetical, the subjects' answers did not move closer to the ordinary interest rate; in fact, they moved somewhat in the other direction. In one study, subjects with at least moderate financial means were asked how large a bonus they would demand immediately in return for forgoing a bonus of $100 that would have been due in one year. Their reported discount rates ranged from 36% to 122% (Kurz, Spiegelman, & West, 1973). In another study, college students were asked how much money they would accept for delay of a payment due them by periods of 0.5 to 4 years, and how much they would pay to delay payments they owed for the same periods. Even though finance was their field of study, the mean annual discount rate for groups of these students was as high as 60% (Benzion et al., 1989). In a third study, 515 Israelis were asked whether they would rather have £1,000 immediately or an amount ranging from £1,100 to £2,000 in 1 year. Adults with a wide variety of backgrounds, ages, and educational levels gave remarkably uniform answers, reflecting mean annual interest rates clustered between 100% and 120% (Maital & Maital, 1977). Finally, graduate students and staff at an English university were asked how long they would wait for £10 rather than receive £5 immediately. Their answers reflected a mean annual discount rate of 5,000% (Lea, 1977).

I have studied the same phenomenon and have found still steeper discount rates (Ainslie & Haendel, 1983). For instance, employees and patients in a substance-abuse treatment unit were asked to imagine that they had won a certified check for $1,000 that could be cashed after 1 week, but that they had the option of getting a $2,000 certified check that could be cashed only after a greater delay. They were then asked to name the delay at which they would be indifferent between the $2,000 check and the $1,000 (1-week) check. They were told to assume that the checks were entirely sound, that they could be sure of getting the money at the stated time. The geometric mean time that patients would wait for the $2,000 was 31 days; the employees' answers were not significantly longer, at 43 days. These groups were reporting that they would have to get annual interest rates on the order of 30,000% to 300,000% to make it worth leaving their prize money invested.

It might be objected that the study involved hypothetical money and that the subjects were more careless with it than they would have been with real money. To some extent that probably was true, although there is no reason to suppose the subjects were not frankly reporting what they felt. If they had wanted to impress the interviewer with how good their judgment was, they should have reported less discounting than they spontaneously chose, not more. In fact, given a situation in which the patients could "invest" real money earned as subjects (from $2 to $10) for 3 days and collect 25% more, a third of them always chose not to do so, and another third sometimes chose not to do so. These patients were rejecting an annual interest rate of about 1 billion percent, even though they generally had little spending money and their earnings were significant to them (Ainslie & Haendel, 1983).

Such a finding should not lead us to believe that these subjects never put money in the bank at 6%, or even that they do so to a lesser extent than most people. Rather, it suggests that they are not *always* motivated to do so. They sometimes show another tendency, less well reflected in economic statistics, to devalue their future wealth. I shall argue in chapter 7 that there is a rationale predicting the circumstances under which people will do this (see section 7.1).

3.3 Discount curves must cross to produce ambivalence

For some theorists the simple discounting of delayed events explains all behaviors that are apparently imprudent or irrational. Logue

(1988) suggests that organisms change their preferences over time because of a "time window," that is, a limited awareness of the future. Similarly, those of Cross and Guyer's "social traps" that are not forms of ignorance or external social forces (see section 2.4.2) are simple "time-delay traps" (1980). Economists Becker and Murphy (1988) assert that all addiction is rational in that it must maximize a person's expected utility whenever he chooses it. They express the current utility of an alternative as the integral, from the present moment through the person's expectable life span, of $e^{\sigma d}$ times the momentary utility of that alternative at each delay, where σ is "a constant rate of time preference," and d is delay (their formula 3) [see section 8.1, equation (8.1)]. Their equations for computing these momentary utilities are complex, but the term that permits a highly destructive addiction is σ, which determines the steepness of the person's rate of exponentially discounting delayed events. In effect, theirs is another time-window hypothesis. The trouble with such hypotheses is not that a time window is nonexistent – a "time horizon" has been noted even in the plans of economically sophisticated people (Friedman, 1963; Landsberger, 1971) – but that these theories cannot deal with the common case in which an organism knows he will change his choice in the future and is still at pains to prevent this (Ainslie, 1988).

The hypothesis that the "true" or innate discount rate for future events is extremely steep accounts for disregard of the future, but by itself it does not explain ambivalence between "higher" and "lower" behaviors. A high discounting rate per se should simply enfranchise Freud's pleasure principle. A person might intellectually appreciate that his preferences are costly in overall reward, but, recalling Spinoza's rule that this kind of knowledge is idle unless it can be "considered as an affect" (see section 2.3.1), it is still not clear how such knowledge alone can weigh against the person's shortsighted motives. A high discount rate would mean, by definition, that the person did not care about this cost. Such carelessness might threaten the individual's survival as an organism, and an observer might wonder how this trait was ever selected for in evolution; but it cannot generate motivational conflict.

For a discount function to produce motivational conflict between alternatives, it must generate curves that lie so close together as to prevent one from dominating the other, or else the curves must cross one another as time elapses. The former situation must indeed arise from time to time, but in any important choice the value of reaching a resolution should add weight to an alternative that will get even a slight, temporary edge, as was said in chapter 1 concerning the fable of Buridan's ass (see section 1.3.1). However arbitrarily, the organism will tend to make a choice.

The latter situation, discount curves that cross as a function of time alone, does not arise from the conventional form of discounting: the exponential function. Exponential curves decline by a constant proportion of the remaining balance per unit of time elapsed. Unless different events are discounted at different rates, this kind of curve will never predict vacillations in their relative values.

Of course, there is no reason that different kinds of events, such as drinking alcohol and eating, could not be discounted at different rates. Thus, if a person valued drinking alcohol more than eating, when both were imminently available, but discounted alcohol more steeply than food, we would expect him to prefer alcohol only temporarily, when it was available in the near future. This example seems true to life as far as it goes. It could be that rewards that are commonly the subjects of impulses – addictive substances, "thrills," and escape from pain, for instance – are discounted in the familiar exponential curves, but more steeply than other rewards. However, many impulses seek the same rewards that are at stake in the long run, but on a schedule that delivers smaller amounts of them at shorter delays. Thus, a person may temporarily prefer immediate but transitory social approval, sexual gratification, or relief from pain at the expense of greater long-term occurrences of the very same events. A person may be avaricious or not, but exponential curves give no reason why shortsighted avarice should conflict with farsighted avarice, or why a reality principle is necessary to control the choices that would be made by the pleasure principle, in order to "safeguard" it.

Figure 3.1 shows two alternative amounts of a given good available at different times. Exponential curves drawn to show the discounted values of these alternatives at all times before they are due may decline sharply, but they remain proportional to one another. The only discount functions that can create conflicts between immediate consumption and delayed consumption of the same good differ from conventional discount functions not only in steepness but also in basic shape.

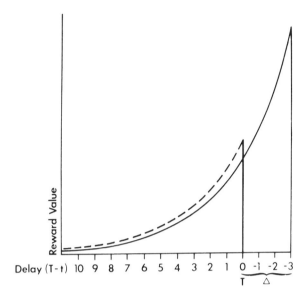

Figure 3.1. Exponential curves for the values of a reward available at time T and an alternative that is objectively twice as great but is available three units of time later, as a function of decreasing delay ($D = T - t$) before they become available.

3.4 Herrnstein's matching law describes discounting with a hyperbola

To produce temporary preferences between rewards of the same type as functions of time, the discount curve for this kind of reward must be more concave than an exponential curve (Figure 3.2). That is, it must decline steeply over small delays, but level out into a long tail that is higher at long delays than is the tail of an exponential curve. In fact, recent behavioral research has discerned an apparently universal discount function that has just such a form.

A brief description of the behavioral approach to studying choice will be necessary for understanding this research. The values of rewards are most commonly measured by studying choices on concurrent variable-interval (VI) schedules, which give subjects a continuous opportunity to opt for reward by selecting either of two behaviors, on two reward schedules that are in operation simultaneously. For instance, a subject might face two keys to press, each of which is

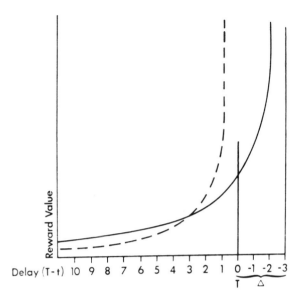

Figure 3.2. Hyperbolic curves for the effectiveness of the same alternative rewards as in Figure 3.1, drawn according to the original matching law, equation (3.1).

scheduled to deliver a reward independently of his presses on the other. On each key, a reward is delivered at the subject's first response after the elapse of an unpredictable time that is specified by that key's schedule. VI schedules are good models for common life situations in which repeated choices of a single option yield diminishing returns relative to its alternatives. In such varied activities as eating the same food repeatedly, seeing one person to the exclusion of others, and reusing the same strategy in a competitive game, the relative values of the unchosen alternatives build up by some increasing function of time. Likewise, in a concurrent VI schedule, a recent reward for one option reduces the likelihood that reward is scheduled for the next choice of it, and repeated eschewal of an option makes it increasingly likely that choosing it will be rewarded; thus, the schedule cannot be "solved" by an exclusive preference, and a subject's behavior stays flexible. The reward may be either a good that is rewarding in its own right or the opportunity to work on still another schedule that will produce such a good. In the latter case, the successive schedules are referred to as links in a chain of schedules.

Three decades ago Richard Herrnstein (1961) described a simple principle predicting subjects' relative preferences for the alternatives in concurrent VI schedules. The relative rate of work on one schedule was proportional to the relative rate of reward from that schedule:

$$B/B' = R/R'$$

where the B's are rates of behaviors, and the R's are rates of reward. Analogous experiments soon showed that relative choice also responded proportionately to relative amount of reward (Neuringer, 1967). More important, when the second links in concurrent-chain schedules contained only a delay followed by delivery of the reward, relative choice was proportional to this delay (Chung & Herrnstein, 1967). The matching equation then became

$$\frac{B}{B'} = \frac{R}{R'} \cdot \frac{A}{A'} \cdot \frac{D'}{D} \tag{3.1}$$

where the A's and D's are the amounts and delays of the rewards (Killeen, 1972). This formula was parsimonious in the extreme, containing no empirical constants. It described preference as simply proportional to reward rate and amount, and inversely proportional to delay. Shortly afterward, I pointed out its relevance to the problem of ambivalence, because the simple proportions it contains become hyperbolic curves when graphed (Ainslie, 1974); hyperbolae have the bowing required to cross as a function of time, thus predicting temporary preferences in many cases. However, this equation could not be directly applied to the case of a single choice between two amounts of a good available at different delays.

The problem with equation (3.1) for this purpose is that rate usually is not independent of delay. Because subjects usually respond several times in the hope of getting a given reward before that reward is actually delivered, rewards delivered at a lower rate on a simple VI schedule also have a greater average delay from the time of the responses (Ainslie, 1974). For instance, if I am key-pressing on a VI schedule for puffs on a cigarette and my pressing is rewarded after an average (but unpredictable) interval of 30 sec, then pressing at an even rate throughout the interval will lead to a mean delay of 15 sec between press and puff; if I am rewarded only half as often, I shall experience not only half the rate of puffs but also double the mean delay, 30 sec, from press to puff. It will not be clear whether my reduced rate of pressing is mainly due to the longer delays or to the reduced rate of reward.

Separation of rate and delay was achieved without abandoning the VI method by Shull, Spear, and Bryson (1981). They periodically gave pigeons the choice of staying on a VI schedule that delivered food every 2 min, on the average, versus taking periods of time out from that schedule, during each of which there was a single delivery of food. They parametrically varied both the total length of that period and the delay from when the subject chose it to when the single food delivery occurred. Period length affected the rate of food delivery for the time-out option (periods of more than 2 min representing a decreased rate from the VI option, and those of less than 2 min an increased rate), but the delay of food delivery from the moment of choosing the time-out did not. The authors observed that the main factor affecting choice of time-out periods was not the length of the periods but the delay of the reward within the periods. This finding suggests that the delay consequence of reward rate is more important than the frequency consequence.[1]

Thus, preferability seems to be inversely proportional specifically to delay, and to rate mainly insofar as the rate affects delay:

$$\frac{B}{B'} = \frac{A}{A'} \cdot \frac{D'}{D}$$

If we take a good's value to be its ability to compete with alternative goods in such a comparison, the expression for this attribute is even simpler:

$$V = A/D \tag{3.2}$$

where V is the value of a given reward, A is its amount, and D is its delay. The curves drawn from the rewards are hyperbolic and indeed predict that in some choice situations preference will temporarily change as a function of time alone. That is the case shown in Figure 3.2.

Consider two alternative rewards, one of which, A, will be available

---

[1] This effect was not obtained because the period lengths were so great as to be beyond the pigeons' comprehension: For a given delay, the subjects also responded to the lengths of the periods, showing that they could detect differences in times when these periods were as long as 8 min.

at time T, and a greater one, A', will be available at time $T + \Delta$ (Figure 3.2). Equation (3.1) says that subjects will prefer them equally when

$$\frac{B}{B'} = \frac{V}{V'} = \frac{A}{A'} \cdot \frac{(T + \Delta) - t}{T - t} = 1$$

where t is the time the choice is made, and the "rates" of reward drop out because they are equal (a single occurrence in each case). Solving for t,

$$t_{\text{indifference}} = \frac{A(T + \Delta) - A'T}{A - A'} \tag{3.3}$$

If A' were twice as great as A, and Δ were 3 units of time, as in Figure 3.2, then $t_{\text{indifference}} = T - 3$; the delay at which the subject will be indifferent, $T - t_{\text{indifference}}$, is 3. At all choice points before $T - 3$ units, the alternative rewards should be preferred in the order of their amounts, which is to say that later, larger alternative rewards should be preferred. (For instance, at $t = T - 5$ units, the later reward should be preferred by $\frac{2}{8}$ to $\frac{1}{5}$, or 1.25.) However, at all choice points after $T - 3$ units, the smaller alternative should be preferred over the larger one (e.g., at $t = T - 2$ units, by $\frac{1}{2}$ to $\frac{2}{5}$, or 1.25).

It has been reported that the matching law accounts for more of the variance in concurrent VI schedule behavior than any previous model, and that this is true for human subjects as well as a variety of animals (Buskist & Miller, 1981; deVilliers, 1977; DeVilliers & Herrnstein, 1976; Stevenson, 1986). Furthermore, it is a law not only of response rates but also of preference, because it holds true when the B's are merely the subject's allocations of time between the schedules – expressed, for instance, by standing on one side or the other of the experimental chamber (Baum & Rachlin, 1969).

3.4.1 Fine-tuning the matching law

The original matching law has been remarkably robust, but as it has been tested in an increasingly broad variety of situations, mostly with concurrent VI schedules, it has failed to account for variations in individual subjects' sensitivities to delay, as well as for some subtler deviations from simple matching. Furthermore, most authors now believe that overall matching is not a fundamental process, but the result of a simpler mechanism, and some have suggested that it is a temporary phenomenon that disappears as learning reaches equilibrium. Because of the central place that the matching law will occupy in the theory of ambivalence presented here, I shall use the rest of this section to discuss these problems. However, the discussion will serve mainly to justify selection of a recently proposed variant of the matching law [equation (3.7), plotted in Figure 3.3] as our working assumption in subsequent examples about how delayed events are devalued. The reader who is not interested in the arguments that have been made about the exact form of this devaluation should merely note this equation and figure and proceed to section 3.5.

In its original form, the matching law has not accounted for individual differences observed in the tendency to discount delayed rewards. This problem has led to several proposals to add a parameter to the discount equation describing individual sensitivity to delay. For instance:

$$V = B = \frac{kRA}{RA + r_e + (T - t)I} \tag{3.4}$$

where k is the asymptotic rate of behavior B, R, and A are the rate and amount of reward for B, r_e is the total reward for *not* emitting B, $T - t$ is delay, and I is the organism's sensitivity to delay (Herrnstein, 1981). This formula was flexible but was never explored empirically.

An early problem was that its additive denominator did not account for apparent deviations from simple matching with respect to delay that have been found with concurrent VI procedures. For instance, alternative rewards delayed by the same amount from the moment of choice should be preferred in the same proportion whatever that delay is, but it has been reported that with relative amounts and delays held constant, preference for the larger reward changes as the absolute length of delay increases. Navarick and Fantino (1976) reported that this change was upward, but Logue and Chavarro (1987) said that it was downward. Furthermore, both used concurrent VI schedules, which means that literal delay was not calculated. Another reported discrepancy is that in many concurrent VI experiments, subjects choose the less productive alternative slightly more than the original matching law predicts, a finding called undermatching (Myers & Myers, 1977; Wearden & Burgess, 1982).

To permit fine adjustment for these discrepancies, several authors have adopted the power function suggested by Baum (1974, 1979):

$$\frac{B}{B'} = c \cdot \left(\frac{A}{A'}\right)^{sA} \cdot \left(\frac{T' - t}{T - t}\right)^{sD}$$

where c is a parameter expressing side bias, sA is a parameter expressing sensitivity to amount, and sD is a parameter expressing sensitivity to delay (Green & Snyderman, 1980; Hunter & Davison, 1982; Logue, 1983; Myers & Myers, 1977).[2] Raising the delay and amount factors to powers permits the equation to account for both undermatching and individual differences in sensitivity to delay (Logue et al., 1984; Wearden, 1980). There are also mathematical reasons why the function predicting the ratio of choice on the basis of another ratio, such as amount or delay, must be a power function (Allen, 1981; Prelec, 1984); however, if the exponents are close to 1.0, they will have little effect. With Baum's approach, the value of one alternative is

$$V = \frac{c \cdot A^{sA}}{(T - t)^{sD}} \tag{3.5}$$

Data recently reported by Mazur (1987) suggest that these exponents may be unnecessary after all, that is, that they may not differ from 1.0 in any significant way. The need for adjusting them was suggested by concurrent VI schedules, which is not the best method of measuring the fine properties of delay. This is true for much the same reason that they confound the effects of rate and delay: Usually the

---

[2] Rachlin has presented evidence that the probability of occurrence is evaluated by a similar function, so that value is a decreasing hyperbolic function of both delay and improbability (Rachlin, Logue, Gibbon, & Frankel, 1986). However, there are few situations in which probability systematically increases in the way that delay decreases with the passage of time; this value function is unlikely to be an important source of motivational conflict, although it may sometimes prevent an individual from maximizing his prospects. For clarity, this book discusses conflicts over rewards that are both familiar and certain to occur, even though many life situations are also complicated by the need to estimate probability.

subject makes several responses to obtain each reward, and the reward occurs after its ostensible delay from only the last of these responses. In pigeons, the animal most studied, an innate tendency to peck in bursts also adds "noise" to the data obtained with VI schedules (Wearden, 1983). VI schedules have been popular because they easily keep subjects from becoming fixed in their preferences, that is, unresponsive to changes in schedule. However, with somewhat more effort there are ways to keep choice flexible in discrete choice trials, so that literal delays can be employed. In such designs, subjects must make single choices between alternative rewards at fixed delays – for instance, between a small amount of food at 2 sec delay and a large amount at a greater delay – with nonchoice trials interspersed to prevent rigidity of choice. The delay of the large alternative is varied until a value is found that produces stable indifference. With this titration or "adjusting" procedure, Mazur reports that undermatching does not occur and that the best equation is a fairly slight modification of equation (3.2):

$$V = \frac{A}{1 + K(T - t)} \tag{3.6}$$

where V is the value of a given reward, A is its amount, K is an empirical constant representing the individual subject's sensitivity to delay, and $T - t$ is the delay of reward. Figure 3.3 plots value according to this function.

A specific time dimension is needed for this equation because of the "1"; in the research reported it was seconds. Mazur added 1 to the denominator to fit his data, but it also has the fortunate effect of giving a finite value to a good that is not delayed at all, rather than sending its value to infinity as equation (3.2) does.[3] In human subjects, the value that needs to be added to the denominator is also 1 when the delays they face are on the order of a few seconds (Rodriguez & Logue, 1988), but the available data do not say whether that is the amount that should be added to the denominator in other situations (e.g., as a fixed limitation on the immediacy with which a reward can have its effect) or whether that amount should be larger when delays

---

[3] A detailed mathematical description of the consequences of hyperbolic discounting, as described here and in chapter 5, has been presented by Prelec (1989).

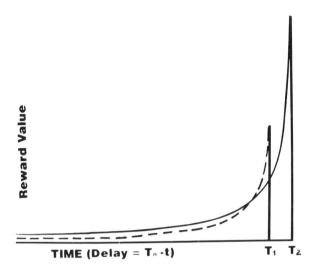

Figure 3.3. Hyperbolic curves for the effectiveness of the same alternative rewards as in Figures 3.1 and 3.2, drawn according to Mazur's correction of the matching law for discrete trials, equation (3.7).

are orders of magnitude longer (e.g., when the organism is facing delays of weeks). However, because a reward that is meaningful at delays of weeks or longer usually cannot be consumed in time periods on the order of seconds (Prelec, 1989), the minimum offset from immediacy of its point of action can be assumed to be significantly larger than 1 sec. The general form of Mazur's equation probably should be

$$V = \frac{A}{Z + \Gamma (T - t)} \tag{3.7}$$

where the additive constant Z replaces the 1 in equation (3.6) to determine value at zero delay, and Γ is used instead of K to name the constant that determines the delay gradient.

In the absence of data on the behavior of Z in other situations, predictions of preferences as functions of specific times will not be possible. When I use equation (3.7) to supply hypothetical values for occasional illustrations, I shall choose time units so that delays will be small numbers and shall set $Z = 1.0$, realizing that this will yield

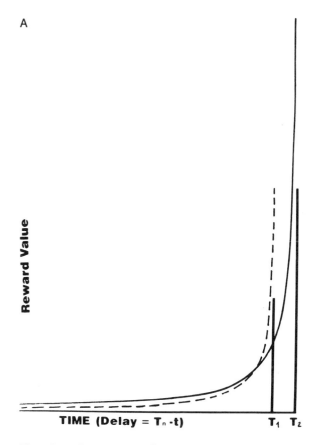

Figure 3.4. Effects of varying Z in the matching-law equation (3.7). A: Z = 0.5; B: Z = 1.0; C: Z = 2.0.

only the roughest estimate of the value of a near-immediate reward. One second was a large fraction of the delay in Mazur's experiments. Values of Z that are smaller fractions of the delays under study will yield a taller spike of value at short delays, as Figure 3.4 shows; increasing this fraction will blunt the spike. All but very high Z's will yield the same qualitative predictions: A reward's value will be proportional to the size of the reward at long delays and will rise to much greater, but not infinite, heights as delay approaches zero. The same is true for all possible sensitivities to delay (Γ), which, again following Mazur, will be taken as 1.0 Figure 3.5.

To account for the converse of impulsiveness, why discount rates

B

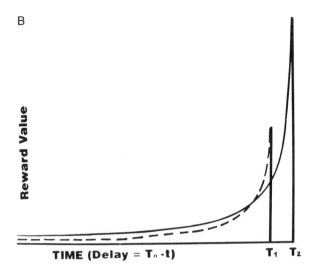

C

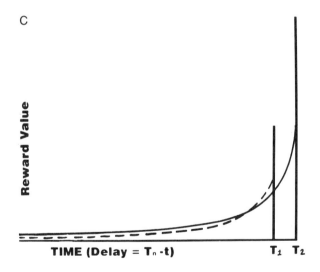

at very *long* delays (decades) seem much *less* than bank rates, economist Charles Harvey has proposed a similar formula in which $\Gamma = 1.0$ and Z is multiplied by the amount in the numerator as well as being added to the delay in the denominator (unpublished ms., U. of Houston). This change would make Z easily measurable as the delay at which an event's nondelayed value was halved, which Harvey

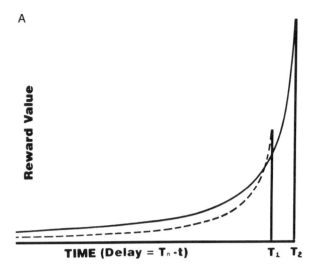

Figure 3.5. Effects of varying Γ in the matching-law equation (3.7). A: $\Gamma = 0.5$; B: $\Gamma = 1.0$; C: Γ 2.0.

calls the "temporal midvalue," but so far there are no systematic data on the point. At $Z = 1$, the value I shall be assuming in subsequent illustrations, Harvey's formula is the same as equation 3.7.

Some authors have suggested the possibility of further refinements of the matching law. Rodriguez and Logue (1988) replicated Mazur's work, but found that raising $T - t$ in equation (3.7) to a power (another free parameter) improved its fit to their data. However, because they found that this parameter was greater or less than 1.0 depending on how the size of the food reward was measured, it is evident that calculating its value strains the resolving power of this observation method. Equation (3.7) allows the matching law to fit individual differences in behavior about as well as current data permit.

Matching (or near-matching) choice behavior probably results from an underlying mechanism that is not designed to produce matching per se. It is unlikely that organisms compute the actual ratios of rewards they are getting from various sources (Staddon & Hinson, 1983), rather than using a more elementary estimating device. Several mechanisms have been suggested that do not assume the organism to be doing more than simple data processing of his recent reward experience. The differences among them are in their hypotheses about

B

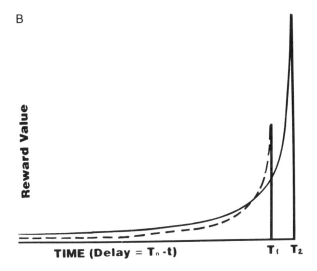

C

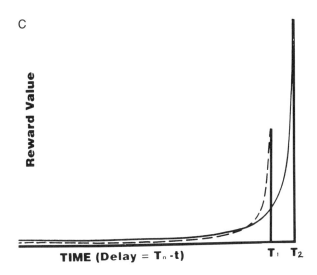

what elementary units an organism uses to keep track of his rewards. All assume that something is maximized or minimized, but they differ as to what. Suggested mechanisms include maximizing the momentary probability of reward per response ("momentary maximizing") (Silberberg et al., 1978), maximizing the rate of reward per "interchangeover time" between alternatives ("molecular maximizing")

(Silberberg & Ziriax, 1982), minimizing expected time to the next reward (Fantino & Abarca, 1985), and maximizing the current rate of reward per response ("meliorating") (Vaughan, 1981; Vaughan & Herrnstein, 1987).

However, it is also possible that there is a direct process of valuation in which an organism discounts an expected good according to its expected delay and maximizes the value of his choices only after this discounting has taken place. That is, the discount curve, equation (3.7), may describe an elementary process rather than the end result of other processes. In that case, what the organism maximizes will be the "momentary discounted value" of expected consequences.

3.5 Temporary preference can be observed directly

We need not examine the increasingly technical arguments for choosing among the possible mechanisms of valuation that have been proposed. The crucial aspect of any of them as an explanation for impulsiveness is the degree of concavity in the discount curve it implies – whether rewards delayed by different times lose value in proportional curves like exponential curves (Figure 3.1) or in more concave curves that can cross, creating a conflict between present and future motives (Figures 3.2 and 3.3). Conventional concepts of motivation have assumed that the discount curve is exponential, probably *because* a more concave function produces intertemporal conflict and hence apparent irrationality:

Maximization of aggregate reward over time, discounted only in a shallow exponential curve, is still the basic valuation process in the eyes of most economists, even those dealing with individual irrationality (Stigler & Becker, 1977). In fact, justification for any intrinsic discounting of future events (a "positive time preference") was still seen as necessary as late as the 1980s (see Olson & Bailey, 1981). Even those economists who have dealt with cases such as addiction, in which a person seeks to discount his future massively, regard his discount function as exponential (Becker & Murphy, 1988). Only recently have some economists begun to accept R. H. Strotz's suggestion (1956) that choice naturally changes over time and begun to catalog behaviors that are paradoxical from the viewpoint of overall utility maximization (Thaler, 1980; Winston, 1980); see also Thaler's

"Anomalies" series in the *Journal of Economic Perspectives* beginning in 1987.

Philosophers rarely address the issue of discounting per se. When they do, they generally count as irrational any devaluation beyond that which reflects risk or an objective decline in the value of the good over time, as in Parfit's "self-interest theory" (1984).

The ecological counterpart of economics, foraging theory, has assumed a choice principle that maximizes aggregate net energy gain to have been a necessary outcome of evolution (Krebs, 1978; Maynard Smith, 1978) and has not examined the discounting process until recently. When investigators have done so, they have found that animals will regularly choose poorer, imminently available prey over better but delayed alternatives to the detriment of overall foraging efficiency (Lea, 1979; Snyderman, 1983).

In behavioral psychology itself, theories that assume consistent maximization of reward, or "molar maximization," are still advocated (Kagel, Battalio, & Green, 1983; Rachlin, 1983; Rachlin et al., 1976, 1981; Staddon & Motheral, 1978). However, behaviorists have been able to use the very property that makes molar maximization intuitively attractive to test it decisively: As we have seen, molar maximization implies an exponential discount curve and thus stable choice over time once an organism is familiar with the contingencies of reward (Figure 3.1). Conversely, the highly bowed curve generated by matching predicts that there will be some pairs of alternative rewards such that a larger but later reward will be preferred when the choice is seen from a distance, but the smaller, earlier reward will be preferred as it becomes imminent (Figure 3.3). Rather than wait for the shape of the discount curve to be quantified precisely, some researchers have bypassed this issue, rendering moot the question of how well data obtained on concurrent VI schedules apply to discrete choice situations. Temporary change of preference is an empirical phenomenon in its own right and has been accessible to study.

The experimental paradigm to elicit temporary change of preference follows equation (3.7): A reward is made available at time T, and a larger alternative reward at time $T + \Delta$. The subject is offered the choice at some earlier time t. With Δ held constant, the delay $T - t$ at which the choice is made is varied parametrically. A switch of choice from the larger but later reward to the smaller, earlier reward as t approaches T represents a temporary change of preference.

A number of experiments have shown preference for the smaller, earlier reward when the delay $T - t$ is short, and preference for the larger but later reward when this delay is long. Such a switch has been produced in animals choosing between two amounts of food at different delays (Ainslie & Herrnstein, 1981; Boehme, Blakely, & Poling, 1986; Green et al., 1981; Navarick & Fantino, 1976; Rachlin & Green, 1972), in retarded adolescents also choosing between amounts of food (Ragotzy, Blakely, & Poling, 1988), in undergraduates choosing between longer and shorter periods of access to a video game (Millar & Navarick, 1984) or relief from noxious noise (Navarick, 1982; Solnick et al., 1980), in women deciding whether or not to have anesthesia for childbirth (Christensen-Szalanski, 1984), in substance-abuse patients choosing between different amounts of real money (Ainslie & Haendel, 1983), and even in the conscious self-reports of various human subjects choosing between hypothetical amounts of money (Ainslie & Haendel, 1983; Stevenson, 1986; Thaler, 1981).[4] For instance, most people say they would rather have a prize of a $100 certified check available immediately rather than a $200 certified check that could not be cashed for 2 years; the same people would not prefer a $100 certified check that could be cashed in 6 years to a $200 certified check that could be cashed in 8 years, even though that is the same choice seen at 6 years' greater delay ($T - t$). They generally do not notice that these choices differ only in the time at which they are made, and they cannot give an economically consistent explanation for their reported discrepancy of choice when this is pointed out to them.

These experiments are evidence that a discount curve more deeply bowed than an exponential curve governs the subjects' choices in the situations tested. Such findings do not establish a precise shape and do not rule out a curve that is deeply concave but not hyperboloid, such as that suggested by Logan (1965). However, the differences

---

[4] Stevenson's amounts and delays do not permit direct observation of preference reversal, but it can be inferred by extrapolation from her Figure 13. For instance, her undergraduates report preferring $160 in 3 months over $320 in 1 year, but the value that would be plotted for $160 at 2 years and 3 months is below that reported for $320 in 3 years – the same choice seen at 2 years' greater distance. Thaler's data do not show change of preference itself, but discount rates that fall with delay.

among deeply bowed curves are not important for the model of motivational conflict proposed here. It is temporary preference per se
that explains persistent ambivalence (i.e., the recurrence of impulses
despite adequate familiarity with the situation).

Aside from the theoretical expectation that the matching law's
hyperbolic curve would be maladaptive as the basic mechanism of
choice, the main arguments against it have come from certain experimental findings: Human subjects often come to maximize aggregate reward, especially when they know the nature of the reward
schedule or have some sophistication in economics (Mawhinney,
1982), and even lower animals sometimes move in the direction of
maximization of reward after long experience. It has been proposed
that the acknowledged examples of matching be relegated to the
status of special cases, either as derivable from maximization theory
(Rachlin et al., 1976; Staddon & Motheral, 1978) or as one end of
an evolutionary spectrum of sensitivity to "post-reinforcer delay,"
with maximization at the other end (Logue, 1988).

The ability of adult humans to maximize income is not a surprise.
People are known to be capable of great feats of gratification deferral.
An organism who can spare next year's seed by rationing his food
over long periods of scarcity, and is known for resisting torture, is
unlikely to be coerced by immediate reward in a laboratory experiment. However, the question is not whether or not a person's choice
pattern is limited to matching, but whether or not matching is the
underlying mechanism of choice. If it is, it should remain detectable
as a factor in decision making even after the person has largely
achieved consistency over time. How he can achieve consistency
within the constraints of the matching law will then be an important
topic, somewhat overlapping the existing area of ego psychology; it
will be taken up in chapter 5.

To observe human matching directly, we have to observe situations
in which the subject is not challenged to exercise self-control and in
which the delays studied end in primary rewards or punishments, not
tokens or warnings that these will come in the relatively distant future.
Matching would not be expected in a procedure like that reported
by Logue et al. (1986), in which undergraduates chose between schedules of accumulating points that would later be converted to cash:
Keeping cumulative scores challenges a subject to maximize these

scores as a game in its own right, that is, as a rational task that "should" override current feelings of comfort or discomfort; and differences in such feelings are minimized by rewarding with tokens exchangeable for money, which is in turn only a token exchangeable for still more delayed rewards. In the experiments just described, in which human subjects showed temporary preference, there was nothing inducing them to play a maximizing game, and the rewards were either primary experiences or money delayed by periods much longer than the time it would take to buy such experiences.

The human subjects in the latter experiments undoubtedly had shown better self-control at other times in their lives. However, in the experimental situations, they expressed a spontaneous preference for impulsive alternatives. I shall argue later that a one-time windfall, such as a prize or earnings for serving as an experimental subject, is exactly the situation in which people tend not to apply their self-control (see section 7.1). Here it is enough to note that some experimental procedures reveal a persistent tendency for people to form temporary preferences; these subjects have apparently not outgrown the matching law, but rather have acquired impulse-avoiding skills which they apply only selectively.

As for the experiments showing an apparent shift toward maximizing in animals, some pigeons have learned to be slightly less impulsive than they were at first, after long experience in an amount-versus-delay choice situation; but their gratification-delaying behavior is easily disrupted (Ainslie, 1989; Logue & Mazur, 1981) and never arrives at a pattern consistent with noncrossing discount curves (Todorov et al., 1983).

The universal reports that temporary preference is observed when it is looked for in animals, together with human subjects' similar behavior when expressing spontaneous preference, strongly suggest that deeply bowed discount functions and consequent temporary preferences for imminent rewards are fundamental properties of motivation.

3.6 Hyperbolic discounting seems counterintuitive

The wisdom of the ages has held that future events should not be discounted. On just that basis the medieval Christian church made it a sin to lend money at interest. Ever since then there has been a stubborn belief that it is irrational to discount for delay beyond an allowance for uncertainty, a belief expressed even by economists until quite recently. For instance, Jevons said that "all future events... should act upon us with the same force as if they were present...." (1871/1911). Even more recently, while acknowledging the prevalence of discounting, Pigou called it abnormal:

> Generally speaking, everybody prefers present pleasures or satisfactions of given magnitude to future pleasures or satisfactions of equal magnitude, even when the latter are perfectly certain to occur. But this preference for present pleasures does not – the idea is self-contradictory – imply that a present pleasure of given magnitude is any greater than a future pleasure of the same magnitude. It implies only that our telescopic faculty is defective. [1920, pp. 24–25]

Many writers in psychology have also disregarded delay. For instance, the literature of the "need for achievement" (Raynor, 1969) did not recognize an effect of delay per se on the value of a goal until recently (Gjesme, 1983).

A more pragmatic school has existed all along, composed of the people who pay and receive interest, that is, those who perceive a realistic cost for waiting itself. However, even they usually see this as a relatively small rate, one that is constant for a given length of delay regardless of when that delay occurs (i.e., exponential). When payers and receivers of interest bargain in a free market, they are said to set a price of about 3% per year beyond expected inflation and a factor representing the uncertainty of repayment.[5] Three percent is not a sharp rate for discounting delayed events, and any "rate" in the usual sense of the word remains the same for a given unit of time regardless of when that time is. The orthodox belief is that the value in constant dollars of a guaranteed delivery will be 3% less if it is not available for a year than if it is available now, and 3% less if it is available in 11 years than if it is available in 10 years. This is

---

[5] This assertion seems to be widespread in the oral lore of economists, but it is rarely documented in print; examples include Ashton (1948, pp. 9–10) and Kiplinger (1986).

not a great change from the square corners of a world without discounting.

We have just seen modern theories in both economics and psychology that allow for steep discounting, but even they have mostly stuck to the conventional exponential discount curve that leaves temporary preference unexplained. Yet hyperbolic functions are commonplace in the perception of quantities that do not involve delay. According to a principle known since the nineteenth century, the Weber–Fechner law, a change in a physical stimulus is perceived not proportionately to the absolute amount of change but as a ratio of the change to the prior stimulus intensity (Boring, 1950, pp. 280ff.). For the perception of value specifically, recognition that it is based on a ratio dates back to Daniel Bernoulli: "Any increase in wealth, no matter how insignificant, will always result in an increase in utility which is inversely proportionate to the quantity of goods already possessed" (1738/1954, p. 25). Accordingly, Gibbon (1977) has suggested that the ratios described by the matching law simply represent the Weber–Fechner law as applied to the perception of delay. As applied to discounting, this law predicts that a delay from tomorrow to the day after tomorrow should be spontaneously perceived as 30 times as great as the delay from next month to next month plus a day.

But something seems wrong with this analysis. If we have reason to do so, we can correct for our human distortion of brightness, or loudness, or the dimension to which we analogize time, length (Benjamin, 1966; Kummel, 1966). The photographer can train his eye to estimate true light levels at least roughly, and it soon becomes second nature to a child that the telephone pole down the street is as tall as the one nearby. Where an educated eye does not suffice, we easily believe the data of the light meter or tape measure. It requires little effort to abstract a "real" object from our changing sensory impressions (Piaget, 1937/1954). That is, we adjust our sensory impressions to agree with our best information, and we do so without the feeling that we are wrestling with some inner resistance.

Our norms call for the same adjustment when we are evaluating goods at various delays, but despite data from clock and calendar, such adjustment seems to occur irregularly, sometimes not at all. It typically takes some kind of effort, like "willpower," to evaluate a present good as less desirable than a greater one in the future. This is where the analogy of delay to length breaks down. A person may move through time toward a goal just as he moves through space toward a building. The matching-law formula describing his spontaneous valuation of a goal, equation (3.7), is close to the formula for the retinal height of the building: $Y = 1/X$, where Y is the magnitude in question, and X is the distance to the building or goal; equation (3.2) is actually identical. The building does not seem to get larger as it gets closer, but the goal often seems to get more valuable. Insofar as a person fails to make the analogous correction, poorer goals that are close can loom larger than better, distant goals.

This is the heart of the temporary-preference hypothesis: The original evaluation of delayed goods takes place in the same way as the perception of other magnitudes, but a person cannot learn to correct it as well, just as Pigou said. A larger image on the retina does not of itself pull him one way or another and thus does not resist transformation by abstraction; "satisfaction," on the other hand, is the fundamental selective force of choice, and however a person perceives or categorizes it with his "telescopic faculty," he is still acted upon by its direct influence. That is, there is a raw process of reward that constitutes the active determinant of value. Although it can be perceived abstractly, it does not occur differently because of this abstraction – just as gestalt length illusions are not modified by insight, value, as it determines choice, seems to be one of the perceptions not "penetrated" by cognition (Fodor, 1985). Of course, a person's expectations of his goals can be manipulated by intellectual processes (see section 5.3.4), but his valuation of these expectations is strictly constrained by this application of the Weber–Fechner law. Abstraction occurs downstream, as it were, from where motivation occurs.

The inconstant valuation of events that results from this property of motivation causes preferences to change between a given pair of alternatives as time elapses. In ordinary speech, the process of establishing a stable preference, when acknowledged as an activity in its own right, is called "making" a decision. The term implies that this process is indeed not as automatic as is the correction for retinal size, for it requires deliberate action from time to time. Still, once we have "made" a decision in a particular direction, we expect it to continue in that direction over time unless acted upon by new events, almost as if it obeyed Newton's first law of motion. To not make decisions, that is, to undergo vacillation, is called weak, impulsive, or otherwise pathological, an extraordinary situation that needs explanation.

Some writers have suggested that a person's natural valuation of goods is not constant over time (Parfit, 1984). The psychologist Janis (1968) did extensive work on the way in which certain decisions, like giving up smoking, require "commitment," although he assumed that the contrary forces, even "[repeated failure to] tolerate the withdrawal symptoms," came from new information rather than from a shifting valuation of familiar facts. The economist Strotz (1956) took it for granted that people's preferences change from time to time and that their economic planning for themselves will have to take that property into account. Hollis (1983) has identified intrinsic change of preference at the root of such diverse problems as why young people do not plan for old age and why the "judgment of Paris" favored Aphrodite rather than a goddess who promised better long-range rewards. By way of confirmation, the matching law says that this is the elementary situation, the way decisions evolve in the absence of some additional factor. The matching law says that decisions will not behave like objects with Newtonian momentum. Rather, they will obey Aristotle's older idea of motion, tending to decelerate or change course unless something continuously pulls them.

Because people sometimes stick to their original decisions and sometimes do not, it might seem arbitrary to say that sticking to them, rather than abandoning them, is what requires special explanation. But that could have been said also of Newton's first law of motion: The objects of everyday experience tend to come to rest; why not see this behavior as the norm?

The answer is obvious. When Aristotelian philosophers looked for propellants rather than retardants, they actually found none and had to account for momentum with ad hoc constructs that lacked predictive power, such as streams of air doubling back from the front of a thrown stone to push it from behind (Andrade, 1954, pp. 8–9). When we have looked for factors that change preferences rather than maintain them, we seem to have been equally misled; existing theories of "irrational" or ambivalent behavior are a hodgepodge. Given experimental evidence that preference intrinsically tends to change as a function of time, it makes sense to look for what factors produce constancy, and the circumstances under which they do so.

Deeply bowed discount functions tell us that a shift in preference in the absence of new incentives is not an exceptional event that attacks some naturally linear perspective on value through the intervention of extra centers of motivation, reflexes, lower principles of decision making, or gods. Rather, they predict that preference tends to be dominated by skewed momentary perspectives. Other things being equal, it will shift as our perspectives shift, even if we have experienced these same shifts until they are thoroughly familiar. They say, in effect, that what Eve did in the Garden of Eden was not to eat the fruit of knowledge but to swing on the universal discount curve from delayed rewards, bending it permanently from a shape that had always generated simple preferences to a shape that generates persistent motivational conflicts.

3.7 Matching may be more adaptive than maximizing

Of course, the actual mechanism that must have bowed the curves was the natural selection of organisms. The reason evolution would have done such a thing is not immediately obvious. Would not hyperboloid curves lead organisms into maladaptive behaviors? And even granted that conspicuous examples of maladaptive behaviors in human individuals have survived the selective process, lower animals in their native habitats are widely believed to maximize their expected incomes over time (Krebs, 1978). Can this observation be consistent with a fundamentally hyperboloid curve?

It might seem that natural selection should favor not only exponential discount curves, but very shallow ones at that, the kind Jevons called rational. This might be true and still not have been a sufficient factor to overcome vertebrates' apparently basic tooling for Weber–Fechner perception patterns. It is unlikely that modern humans will grow wheels, adaptive as that might be (Simon, 1983). However, hyperboloid curves might actually be the most adaptive ones possible. As I have argued previously (Ainslie & Herrnstein, 1981), the biological value of a low discount rate is limited by its requiring the organism to detect which one of all the events occurring over a preceding period of hours or days led to a particular reinforcer. As the discounting rate falls, the informational load increases. Without substantial discounting, a reinforcer would act with nearly full force not only on the behaviors that immediately preceded it, but also on those that had been emitted in past hours or days. The task of factoring out which behaviors had actually led to reward could exceed the information processing capacity of a species.

Because even human information processing (e.g., estimation of probability) is subject to gross biases in everyday situations (Kahneman, Slovic, & Tversky, 1982), there may be no species whatever for which this is not the case.

According to this reasoning, the most adaptive slope for an organism's discount curve will depend on the rate at which his environment changes. The same discount curve that is optimally steep for an organism's intelligence in a poorly predictable environment will make him unnecessarily shortsighted in a more predictable one. The simplest adjustment for changes in the information-processing demands of the environment would be to make the discount curve deeply concave. Curves such as those in Figure 3.3 are high at short delays, and fall off rapidly. In a poorly predictable environment, they will motivate choices of those alternatives most closely associated with reward, which is apt to be the most adaptive behavior under the circumstances. However, unlike exponential functions, these curves flatten out at long delays, at heights that are roughly proportional to the sizes of their rewards – as long as the delay before both rewards is somewhat greater than the lag between them. In an environment predictable enough to make choice at a distance meaningful, these curves will motivate organisms to choose "objectively" when no alternative is imminent, whereas exponential curves will fail to correct at any distance a perspective distortion that occurs close up. With deeply concave curves, the first judgment an organism makes when approaching familiar alternatives at a distance will tend to maximize expected reward.

In effect, a deeply concave discount curve imposes an information-processing bias. It gives more weight to immediate prospects and to those long-delayed prospects that arise regularly enough to be recognized despite their distance; it reduces consideration of prospects in the middle. Thus, if a foraging organism arrives at a point *A* for the first time and chooses between a small berry patch just to the east and a large berry patch some distance to the west, the matching law may be maximizing his probable income by moving him to the small patch. Once he is familiar with the area, that may no longer be true; but then he can learn to approach the large berry patch without getting too close to the small one, that is, without going through point *A*. This will not be because he is self-aware in any sense, but only because the rewards he has experienced when coming by a more direct route from point *B* have been greater when he has not gone through point *A* and been attracted by the smaller patch. The matching law may maximize overall income for organisms that live in both familiar and unfamiliar environments, even though it imposes a motive not to maximize in some situations.

Such a biphasic learning pattern can be discerned in child development. When Yates and Mischel (1979) offered children a preferred food if they could wait for it, and a nonpreferred food if they gave up too soon, they found that 4-year-olds preferred to watch the actual foods while they were waiting, even though that tended to make them so eager that they would regularly give up waiting for the preferred food. Children who were only 1–2 years older apparently had learned to be wary of that phenomenon, and they chose not to be able to see the foods while waiting.

Again quoting from my earlier article with Herrnstein,

> two discontinuous time zones are defined by the operation of highly concave, continuous discount functions on an organism's preference. The persistence of learning in both time zones undoubtedly leads to the enduring patterns of motivational conflict that have been described elsewhere (Ainslie, 1975). Even counting the cost of this conflict, a combination of rapid learning favoring the earlier reinforcer and countervailing slow learning favoring the later reinforcer probably reaps a greater proportion of the available reinforcement than the learning that could be based on an exponential or other noncrossing curve. [Ainslie & Herrnstein, 1981]

In sum, a curve that has both a steep zone and a shallow zone may provide organisms with the flexibility needed to make the most adaptive choices in a mixture of familiar and unfamiliar environments.

The apparent consequences of this situation for human choice are momentous, and their discussion will require the rest of this book. For most organisms, farsighted behaviors, such as staying inactive in the dark, hoarding food for winter, and begetting progeny, do not depend on planning, but on shortsighted obedience to drives, the timing of which has been shaped by evolution and is beyond the organism's ability to tamper with. As long as they sleep and hoard and mate when the relevant urge arises, they will behave more or less adaptively in the environment in which those urges evolved. People, however, dissect their urges. We learn to divorce sleep from darkness, to cultivate appetites for hoarding what we do not need, to mate without reproducing, indeed to obtain many of the rewards of mating vicariously, through fiction or fantasy, and in general to cultivate motives that overwhelm our spontaneous ones. We have also changed our environments radically from those in which we evolved. We have increasingly taken our long-range plans into our own hands, and thus we are increasingly threatened by the operation of our deeply concave discount functions. As we overcome the historical limitations imposed by poverty and primitive technology, the scope of the decisions governed directly by these discount functions becomes broader.

3.8 The parties to intrapsychic conflicts resemble political interests

The conflicts created by highly bowed discount curves are unresolvable, because each alternative is dominant at a different time. Figure 3.3 could describe a number of the conflicts discussed in chapter 1. At most points along the time axis, a person will prefer a "rational" behavior – eating prudently, saving, being moral, avoiding bad habits – but when an opportunity to lapse is imminent, he will change to an equally sincere preference for its alternative. Objectively, the rewards for rationality are greater, but the highly bowed discount curve should make these rewards ineffective from some perspectives.

People often report just such frank reversals of preferences, but usually only in some areas of their lives, the "problem" areas where they experience their wills as weak. These reversals seem to be the exception, whereas by the matching law we would expect them to be the rule. In fact, most people save at least some of their money, and many alcoholics stop drinking. It is easy to see how a deeply concave discount function like the matching law can account for impulses; the question remains how it accounts for controls.

The matching law does not describe a person's inevitable behavior – only the behavior to which a particular set of rewards will move him if additional motives do not override them. People do not endlessly choose a larger, later reward at a distance and then choose a small alternative when it is imminent. In situations where they always choose the smaller reward, they soon realize that the larger one is not within their grasp for practical purposes, even though it is they themselves who keep it out of reach. In that case, any motivation to go through the idle behavior of "choosing" the larger reward will die away, because the behavior will not be rewarded.

However, behaviors that include ways of forestalling the change of preference, or at least the change of behavior, will result in delivery of the larger, later reward. Such behaviors will be valued according to the original curve from the larger reward. If this reward has not been discounted too much at the time that these precommitting behaviors are available, they will be adopted. If, however, the person thinks of a behavior that can evade this precommitment at a time when the curve from the smaller reward is uppermost, he will adopt this behavior in turn. The value of the precommitting behaviors will then decline, because they will no longer guarantee the reward on which they are based. Thus, the effect created by successively dominant rewards is not simple turn-taking, but a struggle for survival by the set of behaviors that tend to produce one reward against those that tend to produce its alternative. As we shall see, the turnings of this struggle can generate the whole range of seemingly paradoxical behaviors that are seen in motivational conflicts.

The incentives that give rise to these conflicting motives may equally well be called rewards (the common term), reinforcers (favored by behaviorists), or goods (favored by economists). These terms may also be applied to relief from aversive events (punishments). The actual parties to the struggle are best described as "interests."

In political economy, an interest is an identified motive that acts on a group of people, or would act on them if they were thoroughly familiar with the situation (as "they have an interest in outcome X"). At the same time, it refers to the group that is defined by this motivation (as "the votes of the X interest"). Within the individual, both the particular motive that gives rise to a set of behaviors and the set of behaviors themselves can be called interests.[6]

Regularly recurring rewards create internal interests in the same way that economic opportunities create businesses to exploit them. Whether or not the converse occurs – that is, whether or not there are behavioral systems that hunt for rewards that can sustain them, just as members of the British Parliament can hunt for electorates that will elect them – is a separate question. The process I have described is simply an example of selection by reward, as that process is conventionally understood.

Interests are separated when the goods on which they are based are mutually incompatible. Interests that could be based on compatible goods cannot be practically distinguished from each other, and there would be no point in trying to do so. Interests may coalesce or divide over time, because they need not have an institutional life of their own. If I want to drink coffee, which keeps me awake, but I also need sleep for an early appointment tomorrow, I have competing interests based on the rewards of coffee and sleep. If my appointment is changed so that I can sleep late tomorrow, they cease to support discrete interests. Thus, the term is one of convenience and implies nothing profound.

Furthermore, the concept of internal interests is convenient simply because contradictory goals that are preferred at different times are not weighed against each other to produce a single, unambivalent purpose, but rather tend to produce conflicting sets of processes that persist as long as they sometimes obtain their respective goals. Examples of this alternation of power may be trivial. Take, for instance, a person who stays up too late at night, and at the time that he is

---

[6] Speaking of relationships among people, interests have historically been opposed to passions, irrational processes that subvert some individuals' rational goal-seeking (as in "the conservatives' passion moved them away from their true interests"; Hirschman, 1977, pp. 31–42). Within the individual, passions may be interests in their own right, viable strategies to exploit a source of reward. That they might interfere with the person's overall income of reward (his "best interests") is no more contradictory than that a political/economic interest interferes with the overall welfare of a nation.

staying up he is not particularly concerned about what he will feel in the morning when he has to get up. His interest in staying up could be said to win out over his interest in feeling good in the morning. When his alarm rings in the morning, he regrets having stayed up so late and perhaps plans how to avoid staying up so late the following night – the balance of power between these interests has shifted. Now we also see an interest in going back to sleep, which may win out over the interest to get up and go to school or work; if the sleep interest prevails, he will regret it in turn later on, when the work interest regains its dominance. This alternation may be discerned on many successive nights and mornings, even though at each of these times his motives will be different in some respects from his motives at each other time. Despite such differences, the pattern boils down to the conflict between a short-range interest involving immediate gratification (staying up a little bit later, or staying in bed a little bit longer) and a long-range interest that requires adherence to some plan, such as getting enough sleep, or making it to class or work. The application of the matching law to the decision about staying up or not is diagrammed in Figure 3.6.

Where conflicts cannot be resolved into shorter- and longer-range components, there is not much point in analyzing the interests involved. For instance, having overslept, a person may debate whether or not to have breakfast, knowing that if he does not he will feel vaguely dysphoric as he does his work, but if he does, he will make himself late for work. There is no obvious short-term interest here unless his major interest in eating breakfast is that he is very hungry right at the moment. Otherwise he is weighing two relatively delayed consequences against each other. There is no reason to expect that he will not simply decide which seems the lesser evil, and choose it without later wanting to change his choice.

Thus, the case that is important for the problem of ambivalence entails a short-range interest based on the upward spikes of the discount curve when a smaller reward is imminent and a long-range interest based on the "objective" valuations described by the tail of the curve from a more delayed alternative reward. The long-range interest is based on heavily discounted motivation, but has the advantage of foresight – it can take steps in advance to forestall the temporary change of preference toward the poorer alternative, like

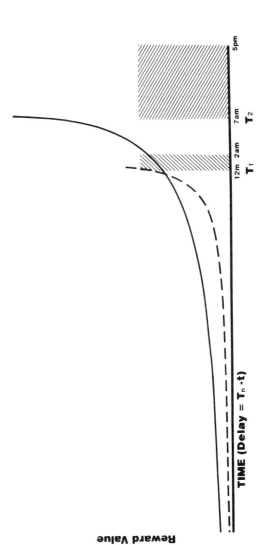

Figure 3.6. Hyperbolic curves for the value of staying up late (from midnight to 2 a.m.) and the value of feeling rested at work the next day (taking the period during which fighting sleep would be unpleasant as 7 a.m. to 5 p.m.); the person expects that the differential value at a given delay for each hour of staying up versus going to bed will be the same as for each hour of feeling rested versus fighting sleep. This illustration assumes that the values for a series of hours are additive.

Ulysses tying himself to the mast.[7] The short-range interest is powerfully motivated by the proximity of its reward and can be expected to prevail if it has not been forestalled.

Interests must be based strictly on increases in aggregate expectable discounted rewards. A person has no interest in modifying his future motives except when such modification will increase his present discounted expectation of reward. An interest based on getting chocolate ice cream for dessert does not increase the expectable reward by forestalling an interest based on getting lemon meringue pie, even if the two rewards are alternative to one another. Neither interest includes a motive to interfere with the person's free choice between them. But an interest based on not gaining weight may increase the overall discounted reward by leading him to adopt precommitting devices against the dessert interests.

The point of temporary-preference theory is that many incompatible interests will not reach a stable resolution in which one of them will simply win, because they take turns being preferred. Any behavior in this situation must allow for the fact that the interest upon which it is based may not be dominant long enough for one to actually obtain the goal. In this respect, interests within a person operate under the same constraint as parties in a legislature. Mutually incompatible programs tend to define opposing parties, which in mature democracies alternate in power. A party putting forward a long-term program must plan for the fate of that program during the time that the opposing party is in power. Indeed, the power of a minority party does not come from the weight of its current votes – a loss by one vote is a loss. Rather, such power as it has comes from the likelihood of its becoming the majority party at some time in the future. This power cannot be measured as easily as current voting strength, but it is more meaningful. Similarly, if a person is ever to see his current long-range plans realized, he must, in his current frame of mind, take into account the tendency of currently unpreferred goals to become preferred at a later time.

The reader may object to the idea of internal interests. They may seem to be a set of little homunculi within the person, like the ego

---

[7] This comparison was first suggested by Strotz (1956) and has been explored in detail by Elster (1979).

and id, or angels and devils. Such pairs of personifications of higher and lower motives have reemerged so often (see section 6.4) that they probably refer in some way to actual observation,[8] but they have been defined only vaguely and have tended to deteriorate into allegory. However, the problem with homunculi has not been their personlike qualities, but the lack of a principle that could relate them to the whole person, on the one hand, and to the known elements of motivation, on the other.

In temporary-preference theory, a person's motivation in general is divided into interests by the operation of the matching law. These interests are limited in their duration of dominance, but not necessarily in their access to any of the functions that compose the "self" in any of its definitions. Again, like parties vying to rule a country, internal interests gain access to most of a person's resources when they prevail. The person who wants to stay up later at night and the person who wants to rest in the morning are indeed entire personalities, in the sense that they have the person's whole psychic apparatus at their disposal; and yet they are clearly in conflict with one another. When an intelligent person is acting in his long-range interest not to smoke, he may use that intelligence to devise better stratagems to precommit his future behavior; but when he acts in his short-range interest to have a cigarette, he can marshal that same intelligence to evade these devices.

Of course, an interest based only on immediate rewards will not have all the options for using this intelligence that a longer-range interest will have. Furthermore, each interest does not necessarily have access to all of the person's current resources. As we shall see later, one interest may, to some extent, learn to deprive another of information. Thus, an infrequently dominant interest may be able to keep its activities secret from the "government" of the usually dominant interests; it may then form not a political-party-like interest but a Mafia-like interest (see section 5.3.2). Everyone has known gifted people whose gifts were harnessed to the cause of self-destruction.

---

[8] Most vivid is Henry Murray's declaration that "a personality is a full Congress of orators and pressure-groups, of children, demagogues, communists, isolationists, war-mongers, mugwumps, grafters, log-rollers, lobbyists, Caesars and Christs, Machiavels and Judases, Tories and Promethean revolutionists" (quoted by Beck, 1976, p. 24).

3.9 Summary

Many of the theories of ambivalence reviewed in chapter 2 seem to have been attempts to explain why people sharply discount future goals, as if that could not be an elementary property of motivation that required no additional explanation. There is good evidence that all organisms have an innate tendency to discount delayed rewards roughly in proportion to that delay, and that process creates temporary preferences for poorer, earlier goals over objectively better goals that are more delayed. Insofar as an organism learns to predict these temporary preferences, the rewards upon which each is based will motivate him to develop mechanisms for disarming the opposing preferences. He is then apt to spend a good proportion of his attention "getting along with" himself, the way a legislature gets along with itself – through the interaction of interests.

4. The interaction of interests: The effects of short-range interests

4.1 The duration of a temporary preference determines its nature

Interests are apt to have characteristic periods of dominance, a length of time when an interest's discount curve rises above those of competitors. These periods will depend on the kinds of rewards the interests have arisen to exploit and on the intrinsic limitations of their particular modes of exploitation. These periods, in turn, will have major effects on what behaviors particular interests typically favor. The duration of dominance will affect not only how they defeat and are defeated by other interests but also the affective quality of their motivation and whether or not behaviors based on them will feel voluntary.

For example, conflictual sexual behaviors are temporarily preferred for various durations: The most obviously ambivalent are dysphoric sexual rituals like exhibitionism, which are strongly preferred for the period in which they are executed (usually a matter of minutes to hours), but are disowned at other times. Other preferences are longer lasting: Driven, rather hollow behaviors, such as the "Casanova complex" (Trachtenberg, 1988), may be dominant for months or years at a time in someone who nevertheless believes that the trait is harmful and sometimes tries to cure himself of it. Conversely, some preferences are brief, such as the surrender to a premature urge for ejaculation, which the man is motivated to avoid even a second before he gives in to it. Other processes, such as performance fears, are experienced as lacking a preferred period altogether; yet they must compete with other emotions for dominance, which suggests, as I shall argue shortly, some form of preferability.

Differences in affective quality and perceived voluntariness serve

Table 4.1. *Zones of temporary preference duration*

Descriptor	Distinguishing feature	Duration of cycle	Time until recognized as a problem	Examples
Optimal	Never aversive	No cycle	Never	Conflict-free satisfactions; "to love and to work"
Sellouts	Ambiguous feeling of aversion	Months to years	Decades	Constrictions of personality; anorexia nervosa, "false" goals
Addictions	Clear periods of pleasure and aversion	Hours to days	Years	Substance abuse; rage attacks, exhibitionism
Itches	Ambiguous pleasureable phase, but conscious participation	Seconds	Seconds to minutes	Physical itches, obsessions, tics, mannerisms, hypochondria
Pains	Never pleasurable, no sense of participation	Fractions of second	Fractions of second	Physical pain, panic

to define five rough zones of preference duration, four of which are temporary (Table 4.1). The fifth zone contains activities for which one never regularly changes his preference, making it perhaps the equivalent of Heinz Hartmann's "conflict-free ego sphere" (1958). Its member choices, like those of the conflict-free ego sphere, are not necessarily of exalted importance, but may range from the momentous to the trivial. Their defining characteristic is that preference for them is consistent, absent new information about them.

4.1.1 Addictions

The behaviors that best seem to fit the description "temporarily preferred" are often called addictions. They have a clear phase of conscious though temporary preference, followed by an equally clear period of regret. Many of these activities involve the consumption of drugs that produce physiological habituation as they are consumed and aversive withdrawal states when consumption is discontinued, but that is not characteristic of thrill-seeking behaviors like gambling compulsively, courting fights, running risks with the law, the ritualized sexual offenses (e.g., exhibitionism, voyeurism), or kleptomania. Some addictions do not involve a thrill, but rather shortsighted relief from chronic dysphoria. For some people, that is the value of drugs, especially the opiates; it is also the basis for social withdrawal in schizophrenic, schizoid, and simply shy people (Baumeister & Scher, 1988), for self-laceration in some borderline characters (Asch, 1971; Bach-y-Rita, 1974; Pao, 1969), and for the avoidance of stimulation in patients with chronic pain (Philips & Jahanshahi, 1985). Many addictive activities are seen as ordinary habits, bad habits perhaps, but not badges of psychopathology. The "type-A" person who tries to reform finds himself overwhelmingly tempted to drive his car competitively, step on others' sentences, and otherwise indulge his impatience (Friedman & Rosenman, 1974). People may find themselves unable to give up a habitual stance in relationships – obsequious, clownish, bullying, and so forth, or, more subtly, the "games" in Eric Berne's perceptive taxonomy (1964) – and there are many eating and sexual habits that people say they want to give up. Many characterologic "addictions" were listed in section 1.1. The weakness for late hours, discussed in section 3.8, exemplifies a temporary preference in the addiction range that involves neither a physical stimulus nor apparent psychopathology.

It is in the addictive behaviors that the influence of proximity on the temporary preferences is especially evident: For instance, an alcoholic may plan not to drink, succeed if he keeps sufficiently distant from the opportunities, become overwhelmingly tempted when faced with an imminent chance to drink, but later wholeheartedly regret this lapse. Accordingly, the most elementary addiction is procrastination – simply postponing the relatively unrewarding parts of an activity (Lachenicht, 1989).

4.1.2 Sellouts

Many behaviors are indulged for years at a time, despite the individual's sense that they impair richer, longer-term activities. Complaints based on this kind of conflict are the most difficult to understand because they arise in the context of an apparently healthy life-style: A person is successful at his job, but undergoes a crisis because he is not getting the satisfaction he expected; another is successful in romance, but finds himself losing interest in his partners; and so on. Often these conflicts are seen in philosophical or religious terms rather than clinical terms. For instance, the seven deadly sins described in medieval times (lust, wrath, avarice, pride, envy, sloth, and gluttony) include activities that can be highly stable and may never be renounced or even questioned, but that tend to become "empty" in the long run. These are major strategies for reward-seeking, and they often become stabilized as character traits – the Don Juan, the Narcissus, the embittered loser, the miser, and so forth. More complex but equally confining patterns are described among Eric Berne's "scripts" (Berne, 1972; Steiner, 1974). Such strategies tend to be more narrow or more concrete than other possible activities, but only some of their habitués come to identify them as unsatisfactory; others do not simply prefer these strategies temporarily, but follow them, however erroneously, as their best guesses about how to obtain long-range satisfaction.

Individuals may or may not ultimately reject these patterns of behavior. The process of rejection is apt to involve long periods of reform, alternating with surrender to the trait in question, during which the trait's character as a long but temporary preference is apparent. However, sometimes rejection comes decisively in a sudden "conversion," with no further changes of preference. And often a person expects to regret a given trait years before he ever rejects it, making this category somewhat atypical of the temporary preferences. There is no widely accepted generic term for these slowly changing preferences that have a clear-cut attractive phase and an ambiguous or variably experienced aversive phase, but they are sometimes called "sellouts," and I shall adopt that term. I do not mean it to include any behavior that an observer might deem a sellout but that the subject himself does not expect to regret – for instance, the substitution of monetary gain for art as one's goal in writing a novel.

4.1.3 Itches

Some temporary preferences are briefer than the addictions. Unlike the sellout – which a person has at one time taken to heart and which may seem to be part of his "self" – preferences that are briefer than addictions are apt to seem external to the individual. A person is able to report participating in or "going along with" such activities, but describes his motive not as pleasure but as a response to an urge. The prototype of such activities is an itch, which the person wants to be rid of and which will abate if ignored, but which he usually maintains because of brief preference for the sensation of scratching. Many pathological forms of thought and behavior seem to follow this pattern, including hypochondria, persistent self-consciousness, obsessional doubts or worries, intrusive thoughts, compulsive rituals, and the brief outbursts of social offensiveness called Tourette's syndrome, all of which are perceived by their sufferers as undesirable and all of which get worse with repetition, but which nevertheless seem to be difficult to give up. Even schizophrenic hallucinations (Anderson & Alpert, 1974) and the seizures of photosensitive epilepsy (Faught et al., 1986; Jeavons & Harding, 1975) may represent briefly preferred activities: A patient sometimes will report trying to bring them on, and they occur less frequently when a behavior therapy program offers incentives to avoid them. In everyday life, mannerisms of speech and behavior such as teeth-grinding, lip-smacking, nail-biting, hair-pulling, psychogenic coughing, the use of "um," fidgeting, and so forth, are all patterns that produce some relief or satisfaction but that the person generally wants to be rid of (Azrin, Nunn, & Frantz-Renshaw, 1982; Gay et al., 1987). Mere self-consciousness about the steps involved in what is usually an automatic behavior can distract a person from that behavior, thus producing an itchlike pattern (Baumeister & Scher, 1988).

Unlike the case for literal itches, most of these activities lack a physiologically stereotyped need state. The signal that they are available to be indulged in cannot be dismissed as an innate releasing stimulus for some kind of reflex.

4.1.4 Pains

As periods of preference get shorter, the motivation to participate in one of these activities is increasingly experienced as ego-alien. This relationship suggests that there is a fourth zone of temporary preference on the brief end of the scale that has the basic properties of pain: aversiveness combined with a great tendency to attract some kind of involvement, an involvement that is related to but apparently not identical with paying attention to the painful stimulus. Like many of the implications of highly bowed discount curves, this concept of pain is counterintuitive and needs justification. I shall use much of this chapter to argue that the highly bowed discount curves that create temporary preferences can indeed provide a solution to the problem of aversion (viz., how genuinely aversive events can nevertheless attract the organism's involvement), the second of the four paradoxes of behavior presented in section 1.3.2.

4.2 Pain is an intense, very brief, rapidly recurring reward that undermines other rewards

Aversive events – variously called pains, punishments, annoyers, or unpleasant stimuli – superficially appear to be the simple opposites of rewards, and they were conceived in that way by philosophers of behavior until the current century. It was held that rewards simply deepened the pathways that led to them, whereas aversive events obliterated those pathways.

In formulating the precursor of the law of effect, Thorndike (1905) adopted that convention at first, theorizing that satisfiers strengthened learned connections, and annoyers weakened them. Later he acknowledged an asymmetry in these processes, in that punishment turned out not to efface learning. He formulated the following solution, which anticipated Mowrer's two-factor mechanism by 12 years:

> The idea of making [the] response or the impulse to make it then tends to arouse a memory of the punishment and fear, repulsion, or shame. This is relieved by making no response to the situation . . . or by making a response that seems opposite to the original responses. [Thorndike, 1935, p. 80]

This passage implies that punishment induces learning, and not just by selecting for nonpunished responses – details of the sequence leading to punishment are affirmatively remembered as "fear, repulsion, or shame." That is, punishment has to reinforce at least some kind of learning, in the most fundamental sense that it causes attention to, and later rehearsal of, the aversive experience. The problem that Thorndike's latter theory raises is that if punishment strengthens learned connections leading to it, how does it come to be avoided?

4.2.1 Two-factor theory

O. H. Mowrer's solution (1947) appealed to a difference between two principles of learning that had just been distinguished from each other: classical conditioning and operant learning. The connections of classical conditioning appeared to be strengthened by both rewards and punishments, whereas the connections of operant learning were strengthened only by rewards. Mowrer hypothesized that organisms learned to emit aversive emotional responses through classical conditioning, and then avoided the objects that gave rise to those responses by using operant learning, thus seeming to solve the problem of aversion. However, closer examination reveals three major flaws in that proposed solution:

1. The existence of classical conditioning as a mechanism for maintaining behavior has been called into doubt, as was discussed in section 2.3.2. Briefly put, there is evidence that conditioning is a form of operant learning, rather than a separate principle for selecting behaviors. Even assuming that conditioning is a separate principle, the finding that some conditioned responses can be modified by operant reward implies that conditioning must at least be able to compete with operant reinforcement on the basis of some common dimension of choosability. If conditioned responses can be modified by operant incentives, the question reasserts itself: Why do organisms generate the unpleasant affects that supposedly motivate them to avoid an aversive stimulus?

2. Organisms avoid punishment just as efficiently when there is no conditioning stimulus as when there is (Herrnstein, 1969). In fact, rats will work to hasten the appearance of stimuli associated with shock if by doing so they can delay the actual shock (Hineline, 1977). Here Mowrer's two factors clearly are not operating. Indeed, measures of "conditioned" emotional reactions correlate poorly with measures of behavioral avoidance; this and related discrepancies have been reviewed by Hugdahl (1981) and Hineline (1981, p. 501).

3. It is not clear what obliges the organism to pay attention to the

unconditioned stimulus itself (Erdelyi, 1974; Smith, 1954). It may seem only common sense that pain is peremptory and must be attended to. It is easy enough to conceive of attention to pain as automatic, an arbitrary reflex in an otherwise free market of operants, but there is a great deal of evidence that pain does not have such absolute priority. The effects of painful stimuli seem to be readily modified by interpretation or even simple distraction:

(a) People who are engaged in highly involving tasks, such as competitive sports or combat, often fail to notice injuries that others would report to be extremely painful (Beecher, 1959, pp. 157–190).

(b) Lesser pains can be overcome by the performance of ordinary structured activities, and they notoriously become worse at bedtime, when ordinary activities cease (Zborowski, 1969, p. 147). The behaviors of subjects in "audio analgesia" experiments strongly suggest an active competition for attention between pain and the auditory stimuli (Melzack et al., 1963). Obstetricians and dentists often find that patterned activity or simply distracting stimuli will reduce reports of pain (Licklider, 1959).

(c) Evidence from hypnosis research (Hilgard & Hilgard, 1975; Spiegel & Spiegel, 1978), neurophysiology (Melzack & Casey, 1970; Wall, 1977), and neurosurgery (Mark, Erwin, & Yakovley, 1963) suggests that a motivational-affective, or aversive, aspect of pain can be separated from a sensory-discriminative, or informational, aspect, perhaps with the former representing a response to the latter (Sternbach, 1968). This response can be withheld totally under hypnotic suggestion (Hilgard & Hilgard, 1975). Hypnosis does not act through a detectable change in alertness, but probably by guiding the focus of the subject's attention (Galbraith, Cooper, & London, 1972). Hypnotic suppression of aversion to pain should certainly be regarded as an operant.

(d) Under some circumstances, organisms not only withhold their aversion responses to pain stimuli but also seem to use the stimuli to generate rewarding affective states. Nonhuman mammals will scratch, bite, and even chew themselves vigorously in certain stressful situations, and these behaviors are followed by reductions in their levels of excitement (Jones & Barraclough, 1978). Similarly, a majority of people who intentionally slash themselves with sharp objects report not only that the slash is not painful but also that it reduces their feelings of tension (Conn & Lion, 1983; Jones et al., 1979). Torture may even become an occasion for joy, as in cultures that ritualize it as a rite of passage (Wissler, 1921), and as in the supposed ecstasy of some martyrs.

(e) Influenced by peer modeling, people can experience physical pain to a stimulus that is otherwise not painful (Craig & Weiss, 1972). This finding suggests that motivational-affective pain is freely available in people's repertoires and does not require an innate releasing stimulus.

(f) All aversion does not depend on physical pain. Recall that Thorndike listed fear, repulsion, and shame as the affects that were avoided, the latter two presumably arising from stimuli other than physical injuries. To this list could be added guilt, self-consciousness, worry, and numerous other vaguely defined but definitely aversive subjective states. These have no qualitatively distinct stimulus that could be hypothesized to pre-empt attention. For instance, a person walking on a cliffside path with no railing finds it aversive to look down, and even notices that his gait becomes unsteady when he looks down, but he nevertheless has a strong tendency to do so. Such a tendency cannot be accounted for as a reflex, or even as a reaction to the expectation of physical pain. The example will work as well if the person is simply carrying a tray of priceless antique cups, and dwells on this perception even though it makes his hands shake; Baumeister (1984) gives a detailed description of "choking under pressure."

Thus, aversive stimuli must compete, sometimes unsuccessfully, for the organism's attention, and beyond that for his active generation of the emotions of aversion. Like the reinforcers of classical conditioning, these stimuli must have a common dimension with operant rewards along which this competition can take place. The subjective term that best captures the nature of this dimension is "urge." An urge clearly is a motive and can be resisted, but it expresses an instinctive, demanding quality that a term like "temptation" does not. There is an urge to attend to aversive stimuli, or, more precisely, to generate affective pain or other negative emotions in response to aversive stimuli; but it probably does not differ in kind from the urge to shiver when cold, scratch what itches, or drink alcohol when tense.

Because of these three problems, the hypothesis that aversive events are unconditioned stimuli for conditioned emotional reactions does not solve the problem of aversion: Conditioning as a principle for maintaining responses over and above the principle of operant reward has not been established. Even were it established, there is evidence that the motivational-affective pain response to a painful stimulus is not obligatory. Lastly, even if there were stimuli that were sufficient to cause aversion, why should not all people routinely suppress them or otherwise gate them out in the way some people have been observed to do under some circumstances?

4.2.2 One-factor theory: Pain as nonreward

Some authors have interpreted behavioral data as supporting a single principle of reward. In their view, classical conditioning of responses does not occur; all behaviors are operants. However, organisms' learning of new information may follow connectionistic principles that resemble classical conditioning, a possibility that does not seem to be contradicted by data as was the case for the conditioning of behaviors (Bindra, 1974; Estes, 1969a,b; Prokasy, 1965, pp. 208–225; Rescorla, 1988). This interpretation returns to a position held by Tolman (1932).

With such a separation of learning and performance, a new formulation of punishment as the symmetrical opposite of reward has seemed possible (Herrnstein, 1969). According to this formulation, perceptions that follow one another become connected without the need for reward; as for behaviors, those that are followed by reward are retained, whereas those followed by punishment cease to occur. This theory might solve the first two problems encountered by two-factor theory, although the connection of stimuli still should depend heavily on the operant direction of attention (Kahneman, 1973; Moray, 1969; Tulving, 1985). It does not solve the third, namely, why organisms do not regularly evade the motivational impact of aversive stimuli even though such evasion is in their repertoires. It has to assume that aversive events can exert direct control of the reward mechanism, that is, that organisms have no operant that changes their receptivity to these events. If this is true, then (1) motivational-affective pain cannot be an operant unless an additional source of reward is postulated, and (2) absent such additional reward, operant rewards cannot compete with pain stimuli for attention, because any reward would always win out over nonreward; and events that lack direct control of the reward mechanism cannot be aversive.

We have already seen evidence that contradicts both parts of conclusion (2), except insofar as they depend on conclusion (1). Operant theorists have recently discussed conclusion (1), the mediation of an extrinsic reward. Two extrinsic rewards have been postulated: (a) greater efficiency of reward-getting when an organism can avoid injuries and (b) social reward in the form of sympathy.

(a) The first theory says that organisms emit pain behavior because that is the adaptive thing to do. This argument confuses the forces governing natural selection with those bearing on the individual organism. Pain clearly helps organisms to survive. The question is how it does so using the laws of reward as we know them.

The conventional answer has been that painful stimuli warn the organism of impending losses of rewards (Bakan, 1968, pp. 67–70). They certainly seem to do so, and they require only the sensory-discriminative aspect of pain for this function. However, mere information that foretells future loss of reward is apt to be of too little significance for the organism to motivate behavior. As was discussed in chapter 3, delayed incentives are relatively impotent in competition with immediate incentives. Indeed, credible information about the eventual harmfulness of various habits (type-A behavior, smoking, lack of exercise) in the absence of current punishment for them has remarkably little impact on most people. If organisms were adequately motivated to avoid distant losses, the sensory-discriminative aspect of pain would be enough. Because they are not so motivated, the adaptiveness hypothesis must hold pain-avoidance behavior to be governed by the threat of motivational-affective pain in the near future.

But if motivational-affective pain is a threat, how are we also to understand it as an operant behavior? We have been drawn into a line of reasoning that says in effect that self-punishment in the presence of pain stimuli will maximize the long-term rate of reward by motivating the organism to avoid injurious circumstances. Missing in this reasoning is a motive for such self-punishment, that is, for the motivational-affective pain response. Certainly it cannot be the threat of delayed loss of reward; if that were an adequate motive for current behavior, a motivational-affective response would have been super-fluous to begin with. There seems to be no incentive for an organism who recognizes a painful stimulus as injurious to generate aversive emotions, instead of just avoiding the stimulus.

There is another problem with the theory that pain behavior is an operant to preserve future sources of reward. Under its terms, naive or sheltered organisms who have not yet learned the value of this behavior should not emit it. There is no evidence that organisms ignore pain at first and only gradually learn its significance. Likewise, if pain were such an operant, organisms should learn to withhold those responses to pain stimuli that do not predict loss of reward. The shocks administered in most animal experiments, for instance, are not cues that require a response to preserve future rewards, and they may even predict an increase in reward, as when they are paired with food in approach–avoidance paradigms (Holz & Azrin, 1961). However, subjects usually do not cease to respond to them. Similarly, many people who have been hurt in dentists' offices are not able to withhold their particular reactions to dental procedures, either before or during them, even though they recognize these reactions to be maladaptive. The person on the cliffside path may not be able to refrain from looking down, even though it interferes with adaptive behavior. On the contrary, emotional responses to cues associated with aversiveness have an extraordinary tendency to persist after numerous extinction trials, the phenomenon that Solomon and Wynne (1954) called "partial irreversibility," and even grow larger in the absence of new punished trials, the notorious Napalkov effect that exacerbates the clinical problem of phobias (Eysenck, 1967). People buy large quantities of medication for pain, a behavior that would make no sense if they were imposing the pain on themselves to begin with as a means of increasing their long-term rewards.

(b) The other extrinsic reward that has been suggested for pain behavior encompasses the social behaviors of other organisms. For instance, Rachlin (1985) discerns in Fordyce's clinical research on chronic pain (1978) a paradigm for the motivational-affective pain response. He calls this response "pain behavior" and notes that it can come under the control of social rewards, such as sympathy or escape from duties. He does not propose this process as a model for all pains – some he depicts as classically conditioned, a model we have already discussed. However, if we are to avoid resorting to classical conditioning as a mechanism, Rachlin's model requires us to see all expressions of pain as social demands. Thus, we do not need to ask if environmental shaping of pain behavior sometimes occurs, but whether or not it always occurs, that is, whether or not external rewards are adequate rewards for all motivational-affective pain responses.

Such a theory would require, among other things, that organisms reared in social isolation not show pain behavior and that people not show pain behavior when they believe they are alone. These are empirical hypotheses that should be tested by direct experimentation, but such evidence as exists does not seem to support them: Although animals reared in complete isolation do not avoid external painful stimuli effectively, they still respond to them with obvious distress, as if "to a bellyache" (Thompson & Melzack, 1956). Animals reared in lesser isolation, but still enough to produce extensive social disorientation, have not been reported to show aberrant reactions to painful stimuli (Harlow, 1973). Furthermore, solitary pain is a common experience, although people who disallow self-reports as data would need to observe subjects who believe that they are alone to be certain that solitary pain exists.[1] There have been reports, uncontrolled observations, that people from some cultures bear pain silently, and groan only when they believe they are alone (Zborowski, 1969). It is not clear why radical behaviorists balk at recognizing the very existence of solitary experiences (Ainslie, 1988; Alston, 1974).

There are even greater problems with this theory that pain behavior is mainly an operant to gain sympathy: If "real" pain does not occur, how does pain behavior get to be a basis for sympathy to begin with? Furthermore, however aversive pain might be in itself, social compensation for it that would be enough to overcome this aversiveness would be the only known example of a culture spontaneously overcompensating people for their misfortunes. This discrepancy is especially striking when we consider that the apparent experience of

---

[1] Such observations could be obtained from an experiment analogous to Orne's behavioral differentiation between true hypnosis and subject compliance (Orne, Sheehan, & Evans, 1968).

pain is immediate, whereas the compensatory sympathy is delayed and hence presumably discounted.

The social shaping hypothesis was originally meant to account for the apparent participation of some patients in the generation of their pains and the effectiveness of certain social responses in halting that participation (Fordyce, 1978). Social shaping undoubtedly occurs, but the social responses that shape pain behavior would not be available if pain were not intrinsically aversive. For this reason and the others just discussed, it cannot be a sole explanation for pain behavior. The social shaping of pain behavior can be only a secondary process that relies on the fact that the aversive property of pain itself is well known.

We have to conclude that aversiveness is not simply a diminution of reward, because such diminution cannot adequately motivate the affective pain response or "pain behavior." Nor can any extrinsic source of differential reward account for most examples of pain behavior. It should be obvious that the same difficulties attach to an inverted one-factor theory like Freud's, that is, one that makes aversiveness the driving force and reward merely the absence of aversiveness (1920/1956k, p. 22). So far, no psychological theory has told us why "paradoxically, pain is both psychologically determined and phenomenally ego-alien" (Bakan, 1968, p. 73).

4.2.3 An alternative one-factor theory: Pain as a reward–nonreward sequence

Explaining responses that are emitted by an organism despite nonrewarding consequences clearly is a difficult task. Nevertheless, it can be accomplished using established operant principles. Although the matching law deprives us of long-term maximization as a mechanism for attending to pain, it provides us another one: It predicts that a pattern of intense but brief reward, followed by a longer inhibition of reward, will be temporarily preferred during the time when it is imminently available.

Recall our problem: An aversive stimulus cannot be simply rewarding, or it would not deter motor behavior; it cannot be simply nonrewarding, or it would fail to support attention and the motivational-affective pain response. However, hyperbolic discount curves drawn according to the matching law from delayed rewards do not describe a single hedonic level, but a level that shifts regularly from low to high reward as delay decreases. Consider such a curve from a certain kind of event: a brief spike of reward that undermines the effectiveness of other rewards for a relatively long time after it occurs. This curve will describe temporary preference for the event over background rewards during the period when it is imminently available, but nonpreference at all other times. This succession of preference and nonpreference, repeated rapidly enough, will produce the motivational pattern characteristic of pain (Figure 4.1)

That is, pain may consist of a spike of reward that is dominant long enough to reward a motivational-affective or attention-directing response, but not long enough to reward motor behaviors. The response made when this spike is imminently available both consumes this reward and commits the organism to a subsequent period of nonreward, thus supplying the "self-punishment" that has heretofore seemed inadequately motivated. For the whole pattern to appear as pain, the period of the obligatory fall in reward will have to be long enough so that the aggregate, discounted value of this alternative will be less than that of the background reward at all times except just before the initial spike of reward is available. In effect, such a stimulus seems to reward attention but punish behavior.

The behaviorally oriented reader might find it useful to imagine pain as a schedule of rewards that becomes available simultaneously with the existing schedules in a given situation; the organism can choose freely among these schedules. Aversiveness is a schedule that makes available an immediate, brief, intense reward for the first response after a refractory period of fixed duration following the previous occurrence of this reward. Each occurrence of the reward is followed by a period in which reward is unavailable in most or all modalities. That is, aversiveness is a fixed-interval (FI) schedule of immediate, brief reward in the first link of a chain, followed by a fixed time out from reward on all schedules in the second link. If the capacity for the aversive process to produce spikes of reward regenerates rapidly, that is, if the FI is on the order of fractions of a second, the aversive process as a whole can reward some intrapsychic behaviors, such as attention, but will punish processes with longer latencies, such as motor behavior. Furthermore, if responses occur more rapidly than the relevant flicker-fusion frequency, the organism

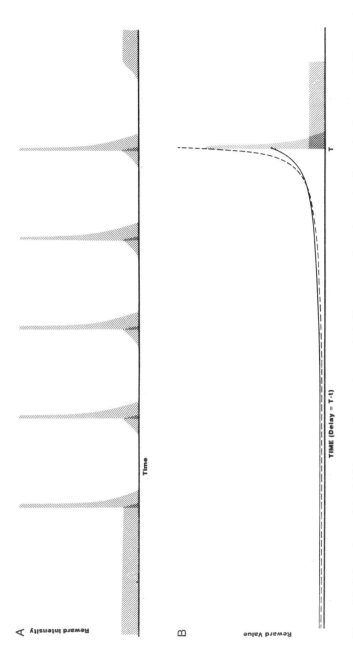

Figure 4.1. Spikes of reward that inhibit an ongoing, steady reward. A: Time course of actual reward as five such spikes occur. B: Discounted values of a single spike versus the steady reward that is alternative to it. To produce the experience of pain, the times involved are hypothesized to be fractions of a second.

will not be able to identify its separate phases, but only a blend of attraction and aversion. Given our current state of knowledge, it would not be profitable to speculate about the events that make this schedule available or the processes in the central nervous system that subtend the operant response.

To test this model directly, it would be necessary either to dissect out the distinct rewarding and reward-inhibiting components in known aversive stimuli or to create aversive stimuli from known rewarding components. The former probably is beyond the current ability of physiological psychology. The latter seems to have been done, although on a slower time scale than the one I have proposed for pain: When pigeons are given an increasingly lean fixed-ratio (FR) schedule of food reward, they come to actively prefer time out from the schedule to the schedule itself (Appel, 1963; Azrin, 1961; Zimmerman & Ferster, 1964). That is, the mere chance to perform an operant behavior has become aversive, even though subjects perform this behavior when it is possible, or perhaps *because* subjects perform this behavior when it is possible. In the same way, it can be argued, organisms are briefly motivated to perform the operant that generates motivational-affective pain, but most of the time they prefer a schedule that does not offer such an opportunity.

This argument does not lead to the conclusion that pain is "really pleasure," nor will it shed light on the puzzling finding of motor behaviors that seem to be maintained by punishment (Dweyer & Renner, 1971). It does not require that the rewarding component of aversive events be conscious, nor the attention to the events deliberate. However, some awareness of an alluring aspect to aversive events does seem to be discernible in our culture.

The idea of the fatal temptation to pay attention to something forbidden is common both in mythology and everyday experience: Orpheus lost Eurydice because he could not resist looking at her; Pandora unleashed all the world's troubles because of curiosity (Bulfinch, 1948, pp. 201–204, 12–15); and Lot's wife was turned into a pillar of salt because she could not help looking at the destruction of Sodom (Genesis 19:12–29). Similarly, our cliffside walker has a difficult time not looking down, and drivers who cannot avoid noticing the proximity of death at highway speeds may become unable to drive. E. B. Titchener, listing those stimuli that people "cannot help" paying attention to, included "newspaper accounts of fires and murders [which] have a morbid fascination for us" (1910). Unpleasant rumination about traumatic events that occurred in the past is widespread, being reported by 71% of elderly subjects in one study (Tait & Silver, 1989).

The hypothesis that unpleasant stimuli lure us rather than push themselves upon us should not be difficult to accept. Similarly, there are many familiar behaviors that we find unpleasant and can withhold, but only with the greatest effort: biting a canker sore, rehearsing a bygone humiliation, or reacting with arousal when we hear a dripping faucet while trying to go to sleep. Indeed, the combination of attention-drawing and behavior deterrence that is characteristic of physical pain is shared by a number of other aversive processes. These hinge on behaviors as brief as a person's mere notice. Phobias compose the most important category, the participatory nature of which is shown by their responsiveness to behavior therapies that give patients practice in resisting the urge to panic, as reviewed by Clum (1989). Tinnitus (ringing in the ears) seems to be another example of a perception that can be reduced by training in structuring attention (Ince et al., 1984). There are many other "feelings" that are experienced as "happening to" a person but that can be cultivated or, conversely, starved out by some kind of practice. If a person experiences them as happening without his participation and regrets them from their first appearance, they should be regarded as temporary preferences in the pain range of duration.

To some readers, the most unacceptable aspect of this one-factor model of pain may be that it blurs the line between "respectable" symptoms like pain or fear and "disreputable" behaviors like sexual crimes or excessive drinking. If the urge of some people to drink excessively is of the same kind as most people's urge to emit pain responses to certain stimuli – both incentives that can be resisted, but only with extreme difficulty – then an awkward question arises: To be consistent, must not society either forgive all drinking or blame all victims of pain? Certainly it is most practical, in both social and personal situations, to invoke self-control against the addictions, but give up on pains, lest the sufferer's capacity for self-control be overstrained. This could be the optimal attitude despite cases of addiction that do not respond to self-control and cases of pain that do. This issue will become clearer in the next chapter when we have examined the nature of self-control and the usefulness of distinct boundaries between feasible and unfeasible objects of control. Here it is enough to say that such boundaries will have to be somewhat arbitrary, for pains and addictions seem to exist on a continuum, with an even more ambiguous case, itches, right between them (see section 9.5.1).

4.3 Interests interact according to their durations

Deeply bowed discount functions suggest that there should be a radical change in our traditional binary perception of motivation. Apparently, the sharpest division of incentives is not between pleasures and pains but between those rewards that are temporarily preferred and those that are preferred without conflict. Simple nonreward probably is neutral rather than aversive, a barren contingency that is avoided routinely and without much notice as a by-product of the quest for reward. Aversive stimuli are at one end of the continuum of temporarily preferred incentives; they are not experienced as having a rewarding component because their duration of reward is so short. We must infer the rewarding aspect of aversive stimuli from their ability to reward pain behavior. There has been little opportunity to view it directly – only, arguably, in the poor schedules of reward that have led subjects to prefer time-out periods rather than the schedules. However, no previous hypothesis concerning aversion is consistent with both attention-drawing and behavior deterrence, although these are well-known properties of pains.

The other temporarily preferred activities tend to be subjects of conscious ambivalence, which is felt differently depending largely on the duration of the preference. The classification of temporary preferences for given kinds of activities according to the rough experiential benchmarks described in Table 4.1 often will change from one situation to the next. For instance, the feelings called "pain" and "fear" usually are aversive throughout their durations. However, when a person seeks pain to prove his virtue or bravery, or as an adjuvant to sexual pleasure, he may prefer it temporarily in the addiction or sellout range (as in masochism), or he may prefer it unambivalently. Similarly, a person may wholeheartedly cultivate an appetite for frightening movies, but when a child repeatedly seeks to watch them and suffers nightmares after each one, he is preferring them in the addiction range; if he experiences an unpleasant urge to rehearse scenes from them during the day, such activity (as opposed to the activity of going to these movies per se) would be called an itch. The same person may be subject to related fears, though he never feels like he is bringing them on; these are pains in the sense described earlier.

Some feelings have no characteristic zone of preference, but play different roles depending on their use by the individual and the particular occasions that evoke them. Anger, for instance, may be felt unambivalently or may be cultivated in the sellout range as self-righteous hatred, perhaps as one of the many cult hatreds (Ku Klux Klan, anarchism, etc.) in a person who "knows better." Those with explosive personalities who lose their tempers and feel remorse over a cycle of hours to days can be said to be addicted to anger, whereas for an obsessional patient angry thoughts may be an itch, and for some schizophrenic or terribly inhibited patients anger may be a pain that breaks through their consistent attempts to avoid it.

Preference duration for a given activity may change with experience. The anger in the foregoing example may start out unconflictual in a person's youth and gradually grow into an addiction. Probably most addictions and sellouts first appear to be blessings that individuals embrace wholeheartedly – alcohol is a tiresomely frequent example – and only gradually come to be seen as specious rewards.

To further complicate classification, a given reward-getting process may have separable components that are preferred over different time courses. When an organism prepares for a behavior by generating an appetite, that appetite probably should be considered a behavior in its own right, an argument that I shall defer until section 7.3.1. What needs to be noted here is that many of the short-range preferences associated with addictions are for the appetites that precede the addictive behaviors themselves. Thus, an exhibitionist is apt to prefer that sexual behavior for periods of time in the addiction range (a few hours at a time), but also prefer generating fantasies about it in the itch range (seconds to minutes before suppressing them). An alcoholic not only prefers drinking in the addiction range but also is apt to entertain cravings for alcohol in the itch range and also emit motivational-affective withdrawal symptoms in the pain range. A vegetarian who classifies the eating of meat as an addictive behavior may or may not suffer cravings for meat in the itch range. Where preference for a behavior is not temporary, the appetite for it is not apt to be subject to ambivalence either.

4.3.1 "Higher" interests

There are many activities that are preferred consistently over time, that is, that are never regularly avoided or regretted. These may be trivial, routine tasks: a manner of walking, a particular job, combing one's hair. However, they also include the subtle "higher purposes" of life that tend to be spoken of rather mystically, evoking concepts such as harmony with God or nature, self-actualization (Maslow, 1968), or ego autonomy (Loevinger, 1976). The differences are in the time frames of their payoffs – how long it is before an activity yields rewards. There are unconflictual activities that can pay off either seconds or decades after their inception, although activities that produce intense rewards after short delays have such ability to compete with other behaviors that they are very apt to be preferred only temporarily, indeed to be major nuisances. Rich but slow-paying interests transcend shorter-term interests only tenuously and always remain vulnerable to a vast array of nearsighted alternatives.

Thus, the model suggested here differs from the many other hierarchies of maturity or ego function that have been proposed, as reviewed by Loevinger (1976), in that those hierarchies are nonconflictual; they depict a person as simply advancing upward as he learns more about life, abandoning leaner activities as he discovers richer ones. The interests described here also form a hierarchy (Table 4.1), but the lower activities remain temptations that threaten higher ones, and what is learned as a person matures is a range of operant behaviors that can potentially join any of these interests in its competition with any other. The other models predict that a person who has learned self-actualization should give up nail-biting and overeating. In the model proposed here, the highest or richest activities stay in competitive equilibrium with bad habits, forestalling them when a person both knows how to pre-empt and is so motivated, succumbing to them when the person knows how to evade such prior forestalling and is so motivated.

In this model, too, many itches and pains that usually are counted as involuntary are brought into the hierarchy. In a model in which people are supposed to outgrow lower behaviors, reaction to a painful stimulus with pain behavior will be evidence of immaturity; but in a model that includes robust temporary preferences there is no such implication.

4.3.2 The constitution of short-range interests

The competition of interests, then, is what creates the "whole" person. When two interests interact, I have postulated that their goals are timed differently – otherwise one would simply be preferred, or they would not be truly separate interests. Thus, there can be only one longest-term interest, one set of goals never avoided or regretted, and each of its member goals either must be compatible with all the others or must be rankable against them in a way that stays unchanged in the absence of new information. However, there can be a number of shorter-term interests, even many with the same term if their goals are available at different times.

For instance, a person may be interested both in rich, mutual friendships and in developing great skill at his job, so that both are included in his longest-term interest. Both are rewarding mainly over a period of many years, so there will not be a time when one is significantly more immediate than the other. When he must devote attention to one or the other – going to night school versus visiting his friends, for instance – he can weigh the alternatives and make a decision that is not apt to change simply as a function of time. There will be no time that this person, acting under the incentive of one of these goals, will be motivated to forestall the other goal, for such motivation could find a much simpler expression: He could simply change goals. Insofar as he is familiar with the outcomes of his choices, his longest-term goals should form a unitary, coherent set. Of course, these are also the goals that are the most difficult to know at first hand or evaluate from available evidence; a person may have great difficulty in setting them, but because of limited information, not because of conflict among them.

On the other hand, there can be many interests that achieve dominance only through the proximity of their goals. These interests do not constitute a single, larger short-range interest, or even a single interest in one range of durations. The person who wants to stay up too late in order to obtain immediate excitement does not at that moment want to oversleep the next morning, or even stay up too late the following night. He wants to stay up just this once, and he may arrange to get himself up, despite next morning's short-term interest, by putting his alarm clock across the room so that he will have to get up to turn it off. Likewise, he may resolve that he will go to bed early the next night.

At the current moment he may have other desires that he can expect to regret having indulged in when morning comes. He may want to stay up and drink, gamble, and so forth. These desires compose a single, multifaceted interest, but only for this night. He does not want to go on staying up late (or gambling, etc.) for years, only for the immediate future – "For tonight we'll merry be; tomorrow we'll be sober."

Tomorrow he may in fact want to be merry again, but again just that once. This is a defining property of short-term interests. They cannot ally with other short-term interests, even identical ones, that will be dominant after their current term is over. Looking purely at expected reward, behaviors to get the poorer reward that is available now *and forestall* all subsequent choices of the poorer reward will be more productive than behaviors to get the poorer reward every time this choice comes up. Only the immediate poorer reward is overvalued. Its interest does best to dissociate itself from the prospect of later, poorer rewards.

If, in the future, a short-range interest seems to be allying with similar interests, then they probably are all parts of a longer-range interest. The person's interest in staying up late tonight is a short-range interest only insofar as there was a time beforehand when he would have preferred to avoid doing so and there will be a time afterward when he will think he should not have done so; the length of the range is the distance between those two times. The person's short-range interest is in the addiction range, for instance, only if the period when he prefers indulgence to nonindulgence is on the order of hours to days. If he controls his drinking or gambling so as not to get in actual trouble, he may embrace his pattern of indulgence for months or years at a time. If he still has periods when he rejects this indulgence because of subtler costs – the superficiality of his personal relationships, say, or diversion of his energy from other goals – he may go through years alternately involved and uninvolved in gambling and drinking (or money-making schemes or self-destructive romantic relationships, etc.); however, because of their durations of being preferred, these are not addictions but rather the weaknesses of character I have called sellouts.

We can, in turn, call this a sellout only if, while he is indulging in the activity, he is not planning to spend the rest of his life that way. If he does not know that his preference is temporary, we have to say that his problem is imperfect information, not ambivalence. The person engaged in a sellout has a sense that he will regret his activity in later years. He may expect to give it up, even to atone for it – but not this year. Afterward he plans to repair his relationship with his family and avoid the seduction that he has fallen for this time. As with the addictions, his sellout-range interest may merge with other interests in the same range, but the prospect of later, similar sellouts reduces, rather than increases, its current preferability. Like an addiction, it is most apt to succeed if the person expects it to do so "just for now."

This situation is even more evident for itches and pains. Even while the person succumbs to the urge, he is looking for a way not to do so next time – for a "cure" of the itch or pain. In sum, it is always in the person's short-term as well as long-term interest not to seek future repetitions of the choice he temporarily prefers.

4.3.3 Impulses as a chain of predation

While attacking a longer-range interest, a short-range interest must also guard against attacks by interests of still shorter range. Figure 4.2 shows that hyperbolic curves permit such a complexity; the middle reward, if incompatible with both others, threatens the later, larger one and is threatened by the smaller, earlier one. This possibility makes sense of Elster's paradoxical predicament:

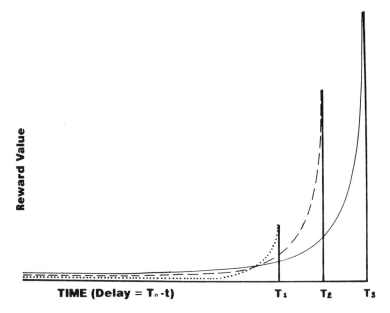

Figure 4.2. Discounted values for three alternative rewards with amounts in the ratio 20:70:100. Each reward becomes dominant successively.

I wish that I didn't wish that I didn't wish to eat cream cake. I wish to eat cream cake because I like it. I wish that I didn't like it, because, as a moderately vain person, I think it is more important to remain slim. But I wish I was less vain. [1989a, p. 37n]

His long-range wish is not to be vain, which defines vanity as a temporary preference in the sellout range. His vanity is in turn threatened by an appetite for cream cake, a temporary preference in the addiction range. Note that, given only what the example tells us, we would not call the appetite for cream cake a temporary preference if the vanity were not present.

In theory, there could be any number of different activities, each with slightly more immediate goals than the next and incompatible with it, that would form something like a chain of predation within the person's repertoire of choices. However, it is difficult to think of examples with more conflicting elements than there are in Table 4.1, that is, about five. An example with just that many elements might be a person with bulimia nervosa. This person's longest-range interest is to eat normally, that is, so that he will be pleased when looking both forward and backward over periods of years. However, he derives shorter-range satisfaction from mortifying his appetite to the extent that no evidence of fat remains on his body – a preoccupying asceticism (called anorexia nervosa if pursued consistently) that interferes with richer satisfactions and that he knows he will ultimately regret. This person does not pursue it consistently, but episodically binges on food and then tries to undo the damage by inducing vomiting. His preferences for binging last a matter of an hour or so and thus are in the addiction range. Now suppose that he has read of injuries caused by self-induced vomiting, and he develops a hypochondriacal preoccupation with having damaged his throat. When he is binging, he repeatedly feels compelled to examine his swallowing sensations for evidence of damage, an urge in the itch range that interferes with the reward of eating. Finally, if he confronts clear evidence of injury, he may surrender to a panic that undermines even his ability to worry; this is experienced as happening without his participation and thus falls in the pain range.

The temporary preferences in the preceding example all carry diagnostic labels, but everyday concerns can fall into similar hierarchies. For instance, a person may believe that he will get the most satisfaction in the long run by consistent generosity to others. However, such generosity conflicts with behaviors he has long cultivated to maximize his saving and investment. Whenever he tries to relax his hoarding tendencies, he is opposed by some concrete, well-learned money-saving activity that is a reliable source of fairly long range satisfaction and that tends to prevail over his more subtle project for character reformation. However, his hoarding is itself undermined by fantasies of getting rich quickly, which can be intensified by a night of gambling to the point that this activity becomes irresistible even though he regularly loses money when he gambles. Gambling, in turn, often is spoiled for him by nagging worries about being cheated. He gets urges to check up on the dice or cards, and if he gives in to those urges they become so preoccupying that he cannot get satisfaction from playing the game. Lastly, on a particular night when he is gambling, he gets a toothache that throbs so annoyingly that he cannot focus his attention even on his worries about being cheated.

In each of these competitions between a longer- and a shorter-range goal, there are chance factors that could tip the balance in favor of the long-term interest. Increases in the expected value of the longer-term goal (including its probability and believability) will advance the interest based upon it: Thus, a persuasive minister or philosopher may make it easier to avoid hoarding; a robust money-making project may make gambling less attractive; the excitement of gambling may make the person forget his worries about being cheated; and the excitement of either gambling or investigating his worry may make it possible for him to ignore his toothache. As in any chain of predation, each participant has its resources.

5. The interaction of interests

The existence of political parties in a legislature dictates that negotiation will be its principal day-to-day activity. Just so, the existence of durable interests within an individual predicts that intertemporal conflict and its resolution will have first call on his energies. His longer-range interests will have difficulty in maintaining their existence unless they devote close attention to forestalling the temporary dominance of his short-range interests. However, the problem of temporary preference usually has been conceived in different terms. There has not been much empirical research on how an organism learns to precommit his subsequent behavior.

5.1 A direct increase in an organism's valuation of the future is unlikely

People and even animals often are observed to increase their preferences for larger, later rewards when those are repeatedly alternative to smaller, earlier rewards. In people, this development is so familiar as to have become the norm of healthy conduct. Human subjects doing operant tasks for money often learn to maximize on concurrent schedules (King & Logue, 1987; Logue et al. 1986; Mawhinney, 1982); children choosing between larger-later and smaller-earlier experimental rewards tend to shift toward the larger over trials (Nisan & Koriat, 1984; Schweitzer & Sulzer-Azaroff, 1988); and in real life many people invest prudently and consume abstemiously. Animal examples are more remarkable, particularly where no physical precommitting mechanism is available: A substantial minority of pigeons choosing between smaller-earlier and larger-later food rewards will increase their tendency to wait for larger-later alternatives (Ainslie,

1989; Mazur & Logue, 1978), and most pigeons run on concurrent VI schedules over many sessions will slightly reduce their sensitivity to delay, appearing to change their sD exponent [equation (3.5)] downward by about 0.1 or 0.2 (Todorov et al., 1983). Thus, even animals seem to move toward maximizing their overall incomes in many cases (Logue & Mazur, 1981).

As we saw in section 3.5, such examples have been cited as evidence that matching or "local maximizing" is an aberration, or at most an unstable stage on the road to global maximizing (Rachlin et al., 1981). Of course, the simplest suggestion for why people or pigeons reduce their impulsiveness would be that they have learned to discount the future less sharply (Logue, 1988). If the discount function is taken to be a description of subjects' actual behaviors, that suggestion must be accepted, because those behaviors have in fact shifted toward delay of gratification. However, the important question here is whether such a change is direct or is mediated by other processes. If it is direct, we cannot easily ask how organisms make it; it will function as a given. However, if it is mediated, the process of mediation becomes crucial for our inquiry into self-defeating behavior.

A direct-change hypothesis faces one monumental difficulty: If organisms can directly change the steepness of their discount functions, they will always be motivated to discount the future as little as possible, because the current effectiveness of a given delayed reward is greatest when there is least discounting. Given a choice, they should always choose to make delayed rewards be worth as much as possible. A process that is learned must depend upon reward. If the discounting that governs an organism's reward process is itself shaped by reward, then there is the potential for an awkward positive-feedback system in the mechanism – to learn to discount the future less would be to learn to coin reward. Any hypothesis that organisms such as those in the experiments described earlier can directly learn changes in their discount rates must deal with the question of why such learning had not already been shaped maximally by ordinary experience. If an organism can learn to make waiting less aversive, even by such mundane means as making distant rewards seem closer or, as Logue suggests (1988), by making time seem to go faster, such learning should be intrinsically rewarded not just by a shaping experiment but by all experience with all rewards the organism has encountered since birth. Why should he have waited until an amount-versus-delay experiment to learn it?[1]

The foregoing problem is a theoretical one, but there have also been suggestive observations that bear on the question of direct changes in discounting. For instance, if animals can learn to change whatever the basic mechanism is that controls the discounting phenomenon, such a change ought to generalize to new situations, making them less impulsive across the board. This does not happen. Furthermore, the impulsiveness of which psychiatric patients commonly complain does not resolve through a lessening in the aversiveness of delay of gratification. Rather, patients with addictions and other impulse disorders report intense, continuing urges to backslide even after years of continence, urges controlled by processes vaguely reported to involve foresight and effort of will. Although an observer without access to the self-reports of recovering addicts might see their behavior as compatible with a direct change in discount rate, careful observation can still rule this out: Minor disturbances in a person's regimen can produce episodes of renewed impulsiveness (Polivy & Herman, 1985, p. 195), and such episodes increase the likelihood of further episodes. Once an organism had learned the trick of making remote rewards act as if they were imminent, its great motivational value should prevent him from forgetting it again. For these reasons we should be chary of concluding that organisms learn to modify their fundamental rate of discounting delayed events.

5.2 Consistent choice requires precommitment

If the intrinsic discount function remains constant, exponential curves offer no mechanism for learning delay of gratification. Even where their steepness has created sharp overvaluation of an earlier reward relative to a later one, these curves predict that the rewards will be valued in the same proportion at a distance as up close. Hyperbolic

[1] In reply to a similar statement of this point as commentary on her article (Ainslie, 1988), Logue said that in real life "there are some situations in which impulsiveness is the better alternative" (1988, p. 699). This clearly is a use of "impulsive" to mean just shortsighted, rather than self-defeating (see section 5.2). Granted that sometimes it could be better, in the sense of *more adaptive*, for organisms to have a high fixed discount rate (see chapter 3), it would never be *rewarding* to an organism who could directly change his rate to do so in any direction but downward.

curves, on the other hand, predict the same original overvaluation of imminent reward, but also suggest that an organism can compensate for that by indirect means in order to attain long-range goals. The most obvious method is for him to precommit his motivation or behavior before his preference changes toward an inferior good.

Precommitting devices involving both modification of future motives and physical limitations on future behavior have been described in several literatures, usually under the title of "impulse control." This term is sometimes used too broadly for our purposes. By "impulses," people sometimes mean behaviors that are merely spontaneous, that is, motivated by a whim. Sometimes (Barratt & Patton, 1983) people use the term for the quasi-delinquent behaviors, symptoms of "dyscontrol" that used to be called "choleric" (Schalling, Erdman, & Asberg, 1983), behaviors that might or might not be preferred only temporarily. However, much of the literature is applicable to organisms' attempts to forestall their own temporarily powerful motives.

Mechanisms by which short-term interests escape the effects of precommitment have also been described. Naturally, when one's long-term interest learns to forestall the expectable victories of short-term interests, it is setting the stage in turn for the growth of those short-term interests that have learned to undermine these measures. This contrary process that attacks precommitments has received almost no attention, with the exception of some of the things Freud said about defense mechanisms.

5.2.1 Some authors have described simple precommitments

Skinner (1953, pp. 230–241) listed nine ways that an individual can control his impulses. However, he did not portray the problems of impulse control as a private conflict, but rather a clash between the individual's wishes and those of society. He said that the incentive to adopt self-controlling devices comes from social pressure. He did not mention the changes of preferences implied by the need to constrain future behavior. Kanfer and Phillips (1970) came closer to recognizing these changes of preferences when they pointed out that Skinner's devices act by "interruption of an [impulsive] behavioral sequence at an early stage."

An economist, Strotz, was the first modern author to specifically postulate an expectable change of preference:

> An individual is imagined to choose a plan of consumption for a future period of time so as to maximize the utility of the plan as evaluated at the present moment. ... If he is free to reconsider his plan at later dates, will he abide by it or disobey it – *even though his original expectations of future desires and means of consumption are verified*? Our present answer is that the optimal plan of the present moment is generally one which will not be obeyed, or that the individual's future behavior will be inconsistent with his optimal plan. If this inconsistency is not recognized, our subject will typically be a "spendthrift." ... If the inconsistency is recognized, the rational individual will do one of two things. He may "precommit" his future behavior by precluding future options so that it will conform to his present desire as to what it should be. Or, alternatively, he may modify his chosen plan to take account of future disobedience, realizing that the possibility of disobedience imposes a further constraint ... on the set of plans which are attainable. [Strotz, 1956, p. 166]

These two responses are not actually alternatives. Strotz is saying that the rational individual should make no plans that are unlikely to be realized and should enlarge the category of realizable plans by precommitment. His precommitting devices include irrevocable contracts, compulsory savings plans, telling friends to "Kick me if I don't ... ," and so on.

A sociologist, Becker, apparently came independently to a similar device. He spoke of a commitment as a making of "side bets," irreversibly arranging to forfeit something valuable, especially social standing, if the given decision were not maintained:

> Decisions not supported by such side bets will lack staying power, crumpling in the face of opposition or fading away to be replaced by other essentially meaningless decisions until a commitment based on side bets stabilizes behavior. [Becker, 1960, p. 38]

March suggested that the interplay of commitment and its evasion can become complex:

We treat our preferences strategically. . . . In effect we consider the choice of preferences as part of an infinite game with ourselves in which we attempt to deal with our propensities for acting badly by anticipating them and outsmarting ourselves. [March, 1978, p. 597]

5.2.2 Freud's defense mechanisms confound precommitment and its evasion

Freud's concept of defenses against impulses had much in common with that of precommitting skills, but his hypothesis that defenses also cause impulses has led to ambiguity in psychoanalytic thinking, as discussed in section 2.3.1. Recall that in his underlying concept of defense, repression diverted painful stimuli away from both awareness and motor responsiveness into the unconscious, which, like an electrical capacitor, fed them back into the original pathway when the blockade stopped. Thus, he depicted the avoidance of conscious perceptions as taking place on the same occasion as the avoidance of immediate behavior. This concept of consciousness and behavior as alternative outlets has led to the confounding of two distinct motives for ego defense: (1) the avoidance of unpleasant perceptions per se, for instance, pain, or information that the person is unsuccessful or deficient (White & Gilliland, 1975, pp. 83–85), and (2) the avoidance of impulses, that is, avoidance of those reward-seeking behaviors that could lead to disproportionately unpleasant perceptions in the future (Fenichel, 1945, pp. 129–167; A. Freud, 1966, pp. 30–32, 54–62; S. Freud, 1926/1956n, p. 164).

The avoidance of impulses is a process distinct from the avoidance of unpleasant perceptions, but the two forms of avoidance have shared the same name. If a person cultivates a benign, magnanimous nature in order to avoid beating up his little brother, he is said to be defending himself against his impulses. If he cultivates this attitude in order to resemble Christ and thus avoid perceiving himself as powerless, this is also called a defense mechanism, even though its purpose is not impulse control.

The psychoanalytic literature usually does not distinguish between defense mechanisms whose target is an unpleasant perception and those whose target is an impulsive behavior. Where this distinction is made, it is held to be unimportant:

One and the same ego can have at its disposal only a limited number of possible means of defense. At particular periods in life and according to its own specific structure, the individual ego selects now one defense method, now another . . . and these it can employ both in its conflict with the instincts [i.e., against impulses] and [in] its defense against the liberation of affects [by unpleasant perceptions]. [A. Freud, 1966, p. 32]

There are two reasons why this distinction has been largely ignored:

1. Because apprehension about an impending impulse and its consequences can be considered an unpleasant perception, the impulse-avoiding function of the defense mechanisms is sometimes described as a special case of avoiding unpleasant perceptions (Hendrick, 1958, p. 97). Such a synthesis obscures the fact that these motives can be contradictory: A person may change his perception of a situation just to serve his impulses, and thus put this defense mechanism into direct opposition to his impulse controls.

2. Even when this potential contradiction is recognized, psycho-analysis sees its components as parts of an integral sequence of action and reaction. Defenses against impulses are thought to be necessitated by the defenses guarding consciousness. If it were not for the defensive blockage and consequent accumulation of impulsive energy, a person would simply be motivated to maximize his pleasure, and impulses would cease to occur. Because of this view that ties all defenses to the pathogenesis of impulses, psychoanalysis has traditionally taught that every kind of defensive process should be eliminated where possible.

In practice, modern analytically oriented therapists often acknowledge the usefulness of defense mechanisms, which they see as either the last chance to forestall impulses that cannot be diverted through insight or a necessary veil over harsh facts that the patient is not otherwise equipped to handle. However, they have stopped short of trying to teach actual defensive skills to patients. Behavior therapists have not been so reticent. Many behavioral approaches implicitly recognize motivational states within a person that cannot equilibrate with the current self, and thus must be influenced by the same concrete means one might use on another person; this literature has been reviewed elsewhere (Ainslie, 1986b).

5.3 There are four ways to precommit future behaviors

Impulse-controlling devices have been suggested spontaneously by our culture, hypothetically by motivational theorists, warily by psychoanalytic practitioners, and enthusiastically by behavior therapists. Much of what little systematic research has been done has been organized according to the psychoanalytic list of defense mechanisms, elaborated most fully by Sjoback (1973), and thus has necessarily confounded impulse control with self-deception. These studies have shown that individuals' self-reports about their personality traits do cluster into patterns like those described by analytic writers – obsessional, hysterical, or "oral/paranoid," according to one line of inquiry (Lazare, Klerman, & Armor, 1966, 1968), principalization, reversal, turning against self, turning against object, or projection, according to another (Gleser & Ihilevich, 1969). This research has not explored the specific roles of these traits in impulse control, much less how those roles might be performed.

By contrast, clinical reports and other descriptions of self-control give a rich selection of self-control methods. Critical examination of these descriptions shows that all of them rely on one or more of four basic tactics for influencing future motivational states to accommodate the current state: extrapsychic mechanisms, control of attention, preparation of emotion, and personal rules. It is important to note that these tactics work both ways: There are also circumstances in which each can serve a shorter-range interest against a longer-range interest.

5.3.1 Extrapsychic mechanisms

Devices of the extrapsychic kind involve arranging for either physical or social action upon a person's future motivational state. These have been recommended since ancient times, not only in the literary example of Ulysses and the Sirens but also in the physician Galen's advice to the person trying to control his passions: This person should find someone who will "disclose his every action which is wrong... none of us can succeed unless he has someone to point out his every error" (1963, p. 44). Many such devices are ingrained in the culture of a community. For instance, the economist Alfred Marshall observed early in this century that small vendors survive in poor neighborhoods despite their high prices because large stocks of a good "tempt to extravagance." For instance, those "who cannot keep away from any alcohol they may have in the house . . . pay the retailer a very high wage for taking charge of their stock of it, and serving it out to them a little at a time" (1921, p. 814).

Extrapsychic controls are widely proposed in manuals on behavior therapy (Stuart & Davis, 1972, pp. 61–98; Thoresen & Mahoney, 1974). A person who is trying to avoid overeating, for instance, has variously been advised to take a drug that will suppress his appetite, to keep fattening foods out of the house (perhaps by the expedient of going shopping only when he has just eaten), or even to have his jaws wired together. If he can enlist the cooperation of a friend, he might ask the friend to put pressure on him when he seems about to overeat, he might deposit money with the friend that is to be given away whenever he overeats, or he might simply make a public statement of his intention to lose weight, so that he will look foolish if he does not. Psychodynamic therapists have described how a person may "act up" in order to attract the attention of someone in authority, someone who will then guard him and prevent the occurrence of more serious impulsive behavior. This maneuver has been called "asking for controls."

In situations in which a temporary preference arises regularly, even pigeons sometimes will learn a precommitting operant and will perform it regularly once it is learned. In the basic experiment, pigeons were periodically offered a choice between a small, immediate food reward and a larger food reward a few seconds later (Ainslie, 1974). All subjects made their choices in favor of the immediate reward on virtually all trials. If several seconds before the choice was due to come up again they were allowed to make a response that rendered the smaller reward unavailable, some of the birds came regularly to choose that precommitment. The birds did not make that response in control conditions where it had no effect, where it was *required* to make the earlier reward available, or where it was made possible only a very short time before the choice was due to be offered. Pigeons learn a precommitting operant even more readily when it is programmed on a separate key (Hayes et al., 1981). Similarly, rats will learn to press a bar that commits them to accept a smaller, earlier electric shock and thus avoid a larger, later shock; their likelihood of making that commitment is proportional to the delay before the earlier shock is due (Deluty et al., 1983). Thus, at least one kind of device to forestall temporary changes of preference can be learned in the absence of "higher" mental functions, entirely on the basis of the differential effect of the better outcome before the poorer outcome becomes dominant.

It is obvious that the potential committing power of extrapsychic devices is variable, and they also depend on what the environment makes available. When their clinical effectiveness has been studied, they have been shown to be most effective against temporary preferences in the addiction range, particularly in the form of social support groups dealing with alcoholism (Alford, 1980), opiate abuse (Nurco & Makofsky, 1981), gambling (Scodel, 1964), and the social withdrawal of schizophrenics (Low, 1976). Contracts enforced by fines have been found to be effective against smoking, but, as we would expect, only for as long as the contract stays in force (Paxton, 1981). Drugs to reduce unwanted urges are used against targets in the itch and pain ranges, as well as addictions, but in the absence of additional therapies they have produced disappointing results when deployed against alcoholism (Azrin et al., 1982; Fuller & Roth, 1979), overeating (Munro, 1979), pain behavior (Fordyce & Steger, 1979), and phobic avoidance (Marks, 1976).

People who report that this kind of device makes sense for "someone like" them are slightly more apt to be male than female and to show "oral" rather than "obsessional" personality traits (Ainslie, 1987a). However, it is apparent that everyone makes use of extrapsychic constraints where they are convenient and that societies make it easier for their members to control some kinds of impulses than others by selectively supplying such constraints in the form of social pressure. Social sanctions usually have made it easier for Western, middle-class individuals to avoid opiates than to avoid alcohol or cigarettes, for instance, and easier for Jainists to avoid rage than for Westerners to do so.

Extrapsychic devices are the most readily discoverable devices.

They form a concrete platform upon which other devices can be built, but they also may get in the way of other devices, as we shall see.

5.3.2 Control of attention

Repression, which Freud at one time held to be the cornerstone of all defensive processes (1914/1956f, p. 16), is said to operate by keeping one's attention away from thoughts that might lead to impulses:

> A repressed instinctual impulse can be activated (newly cathected) from two directions: from within, through reinforcement from its internal sources of excitation, and from without, through the perception of an object that it desires. The hysterical anticathexis is mainly directed outwards, against dangerous perceptions. It takes the form of a special kind of vigilance which, by means of restrictions of the ego, causes situations to be avoided that would entail such perceptions, or if they do occur, manages to withdraw the subject's attention from them. [Freud, 1926/1956n, p. 158]

Repression can be seen in terms of simple information processing. When deciding whether or not to pursue a given activity, a person does not call up all his knowledge of it at once, but begins with a label by which he has categorized that knowledge (Shiffrin & Schneider, 1977; the aspect he is likely to remember first is its emotional meaning (Zajonc, 1980). He is apt to evaluate his options for further information processing according to the likely payoffs for those options, perhaps arrayed in what has been called a "sentry matrix" (Bruner, Goodnow, & Austin, 1956, p. 75). If he has categorized his knowledge of the activity according to its impulsiveness, and the capsule he recalls first tells him that the activity is indeed impulsive, he will know that further review will risk revealing it to be imminently available; thus, he may be motivated to stop the review at that point.

Such avoidance of further information represents the act of repression. Of course, if he estimates the risk of discovering its availability to be high already, that very estimate may change his preference in favor of further review, and the repression will have failed. Furthermore, if the capsule contains information that further review is apt to be unpleasant – using what Williams et al. (1988, p. 171) call "affective salience" – he may decide in his *short-range* interest not to pursue it further. He will then be using repression for its other defensive purpose: maintaining short-range comfort. Whatever its purpose, if the person were able to report his decision to avoid further information, that would be called "suppression," rather than "repression," a distinction that is not important for this discussion.

Freud believed that all repression was pathological and particularly apt to lead to "hysterical" symptoms (Breuer & Freud, 1895/1956). Normal subjects who say that attention-diverting tactics make sense as impulse controls are indeed more likely to be female, but no more likely than other subjects to report "hysterical" personality traits (Ainslie, 1987a).

Before Freud's time, forgetting about one's impulses was not only a spontaneous behavior but also the recommendation of professional advice-givers. For instance, the writer of a book called *Right and Wrong Thinking and Their Results* advised the reader to "avoid discordant thoughts," by distraction if possible, and, if necessary, by "the rule at Donnybrook Fair: 'whenever you see a head, hit it.' The least is not too small to be terminated if it is wrong" (Crane, 1905, p. 115). This would seem to be an attempt to describe sheer suppression. Behavioral writers even today advocate "stimulus control" as a useful way of avoiding impulses (Goldiamond, 1965; Kanfer, 1975, pp. 309–355). It is common lore that "if you speak of the Devil, he'll appear." I have had patients describe being able to "fight off" panic attacks, dissociative episodes, and even epileptic seizures by vigorously directing their minds away from the feeling that those things were about to occur.

Denial, the misinterpretation of what one notices, may also serve this purpose by distorting information about environmental opportunities for impulses. Often it is advocated in the form of hypnosis, particularly against preferences of brief duration, such as pain (Hilgard & Hilgard, 1975) and panic, although its effectiveness against panic has been limited (Schenck, 1954; Wolberg, 1948). However, psychoanalytic writers recognize denial mostly as serving to avoid painful perceptions, rather than as a precommitting device. For instance, White and Gilliland cite as examples of denial a mother denying the recent accidental death of her child, a scientist denying a failure to get a professorship, a widow denying the death of her husband, and a child denying culpability (1975, pp. 78–80). Recently, cognitive psychology seems to have rediscovered the pain-avoiding kind of denial as "cognitive deconstruction" (Baumeister, 1990, p. 92).

The disadvantage of attention control as a defense against impulses is that it may hinder the gathering of useful information, possibly leading to serious gaps in a person's orientation to reality. To impair one's own information gathering can be awkward. J. M. Russell pointed out in an introspective example that even the need for suppression may need to be suppressed:

> I suspect that I may be getting seasick so I follow someone's advice to "keep your eyes on the horizon." ... The effort to look at the horizon will fail if it amounts to a token made in a spirit of desperation. ... I must look at it in the way one would for reasons other than those of getting over nausea ... not with the despair of "I must look at the horizon or else I shall be sick!" To become well I must pretend I am well. [1978, pp. 27–28]

It complicates our classification slightly that some extrapsychic devices operate by controlling attention, the archetype being the wax with which Ulysses stopped his ears to avoid hearing the Sirens. Real-life examples would include a gambler's cancellation of his subscription to a betting sheet, or an acrophobic pulling down the blind on his airplane window or high-rise window. Because they have the comparative stability and also the limited availability of other extrapsychic mechanisms, these overlapping devices will be classified with those mechanisms rather than with attention control.

5.3.3 Preparation of emotion

Freud initially included in his concept of repression the disconnection of thoughts from feelings (1895/1956a, p. 58), a distinct process he later named "isolation of affect": A person pays attention to experiences that would be expected to cause emotionality, but reports feeling no emotion (1926/1956n, pp. 120–122, 163–164). This may be understood as an example of precommitment if we notice the effect that an emotion has on subsequent motivation. It is commonly recognized that basic emotions such as anger, sexual arousal, and fear are, up to a point, vicious circles. After the emotion has gotten under way, there is a lower threshold for further emotional activity of the same kind, until some satiation point has been reached (Skinner, 1953, pp. 235–236, 239–240). If a person expects an emotion to make an otherwise unpreferred reward temporarily dominant, he may commit himself not to choose the reward through early inhibition of that emotion.

A concrete example of this strategy is the advice that used to be given to teenagers in dating manuals on how to avoid sexual intercourse by avoiding foreplay. Avoidance of the emotion usually produced by foreplay would be expected to have the same result. Although there has been little research on voluntary control of the emotional processes, Lazarus (1975a,b) has described credible examples from everyday life. He and his associates have demonstrated experimentally how human subjects can learn to voluntarily "distance" themselves from a stressful film, as confirmed by reductions in their galvanic skin responses (Koriat et al., 1972). The recent discovery that people can learn extensive voluntary control of vegetative functions, such as blood pressure, organ perfusion, and brain waves (Kimmel, 1974; Schwartz, 1975), tends to confirm the practicality of voluntarily controlling emotions. Perhaps the most persuasive example is the well-known ability of actors to "put themselves into" their performances, to "make themselves feel it" (Russell, 1978, p. 35); see also Archer (1888).

Early inhibition of emotions appears to be a powerful means of precommitment, although this device costs whatever reward is dependent on that emotion for its consumption. For instance, a person who controls his sexual temptations by early avoidance of sexual affects might run the risk of losing his capacity for sexual enjoyment.

A person can also decrease the attractiveness of a particular activity by cultivating a contradictory emotion. For instance, when entering a situation that he expects to provoke unwanted tender feelings, he might forestall those feelings by summoning his rage at the earliest opportunity. Conversely, if he is worried about rage, he might cultivate tender feelings. Examples of this device have been discussed under the name of "reversal of affect" (A. Freud, 1966, pp. 29–40; S. Freud, 1915/1956g, pp. 126–127). This device has also been proposed by behavior therapists, as we shall see presently.

Reversal seems to represent a special case of general strategy: finding activities that will reduce one's appetite for, or increase one's appetite for the alternative to, a particular reward. This general strategy has been called "reaction formation" (A. Freud, 1966, pp. 37–38; S. Freud, 1926/1956n, pp. 157–158). Again, Russell (1978) points out that this strategy need not be unconscious, but may be pursued deliberately by means of "affect-constitutive statements." He identifies private and public verbalizations that are uttered to manipulate mood because of a self-confirming property, although just as often to serve a short-range interest as to combat one ("Oh, God! I am going to be seasick!" versus "I am feeling better already").

Hirschman (1977) has recently pointed out that descriptions of this strategy antedate Freud by nearly three centuries, having originated with Bacon and Spinoza. Bacon, for instance, commended those who described how to "set affection against affection and to master one by another: even as we use to hunt beast with beast. . . . For as in the government of states it is sometimes necessary to bridle one faction with another, so it is in the government within" (quoted by Hirschman, 1977, p. 22). In the eighteenth century, this tactic was sometimes held out as the only practical precommitting device: "Nothing can oppose or retard the impulse of passion but a contrary impulse" – David Hume (quoted by Hirschman, 1977, pp. 24–25).

Where a long-range interest cannot forestall a shorter-range interest simply by cultivating a nonimpulsive alternative, it may nevertheless be able to prevail by finding a still more briefly preferred activity that is incompatible with the target activity. That is, a long-range interest may ally itself, in effect, with a short-range interest to forestall a midrange interest. Recall from chapter 4 that an interest that can temporarily dominate a longer-range interest may also be temporarily dominated by a shorter-range interest (section 4.3.3). This is perhaps illustrated by the ancient myth of Atalanta, the swiftest runner alive, who could be married only if she were beaten in a footrace. The myth does not tell us whether or not she really wanted to be married, but assuming that she did, her interest in winning races undermined what presumably was her longer-range interest in marriage. It was one of her suitors, Hippomenes, who thought of distracting her from the race, that is, of appealing to an interest of still shorter range, by throwing golden apples near her as she ran. The myth would serve our purpose better if the apples had been made of something objectively less valuable than gold, but if Atalanta had dispassionately preferred the gold to winning the race, Hippomenes could simply have bribed her. Furthermore, the truth of the myth does not depend on having her suitor, or any outside party, to supply the distraction; if she had despaired of waiting for someone clever enough to deal with her midrange interest in winning races, she could have cultivated some other kind of distractibility to set herself up to lose. The point is that Atalanta was not one who could simply rank her preferences in order, but rather experienced a sequential competition among them, and finally was able to realize her long-range interest by appealing to the competitor of its competitor.

Examples from ordinary life are common enough. For instance, a person may have a long-range interest in asserting himself in a relationship in which he is being bullied, but may always shrink from doing so when the opportunity arises. This interest might need to find a short-term interest, such as getting drunk, an indulgence he might not ordinarily allow himself, in order to "get his courage up." Without the help of the long-range interest, a midrange interest in avoiding embarrassment might forestall the urge to get drunk. This midrange interest might, in turn, undermine his long-range interest in rising above his usual role in order to stop the bullying. Such relationships are quantified in Figure 5.1.

Consider again our hypothetical person from chapter 4 who wants to be generous, a project undermined by miserly character traits that are in turn undermined by urges to gamble. His longest-range interest may defeat the miserly, sellout-range interest by allying with his addictive interest in gambling. His motive to gamble when it is "for a good cause" (e.g., at a church lottery or casino night for the arts) may be enough to secure his money for that cause even though he would not otherwise be adequately motivated either to give the money away or to gamble. This is because his long-range interest is backing the short-range urge to gamble, not trying to defeat it. Similarly, his miserly interest may try to forestall urges to gamble by cultivating his fears of being cheated.

The obsessional patient seems to be making a similar encircling alliance when he defeats urges for sexual intimacy by pairing them with vivid, disgusting ideas – ideas that he would normally avoid, but that, if he does not avoid them, briefly have enough attraction to parasitize the longer-range romantic plans he wants to sabotage. Such cultivation of itch-range activities to combat addictions has been recommended by some behavior therapists, who call them "coverants" (Cautela & Bennett, 1981; Homme, 1965). For instance, a person trying to give up smoking would be advised to imagine that the cigarette smoke is automobile exhaust or some other disgusting substance. Making smoking the occasion for this kind of emotionally provocative fantasy may spoil the pleasure of smoking somewhat without interfering with longer-range interests.

The behavior therapy technique that ostensibly conditions pain or disgust to addiction-range activities like drinking, smoking, and unwanted homosexual arousal probably works by a similar mechanism. Even though patients often stop the unwanted activities, actual conditioned responses have not been documented, and patients report still having the appetites that were to have been destroyed by counterconditioning (Clairborn, Lewis, & Humble, 1972; Hunt & Matarazzo, 1973; Lichtenstein & Danaher, 1976; Wilson, 1978). Because delivering an aversive stimulus before a person's response works as well as delivering it afterward (McConaghy & Barr, 1973), and having a person imagine aversive stimuli works as well as actually delivering them (McConaghy, Armstrong, & Blasczyski, 1981), it is likely that this kind of treatment works not by conditioning but by suggesting vivid, itch-range thoughts that the patient can use to undermine his addictive pleasure.

The disadvantage of the emotion-control tactic seems to be that the activities that forestall a particular temporary preference may not happen to be otherwise productive in the long run, and they may thrive to the point that they represent nuisances in their own right. Obsessional thoughts seem to be examples of this, but iatrogenic examples from coverant therapies have not been reported. There is also the potential that short-range interests will look for long-range interests to protect them. When the cream-cake eater described in section 4.3.3 (Elster, 1989a) says "I wish I was less vain," he becomes suspicious of that lofty goal: "But do I think that only when I wish to eat cake?" In any case, the need to maintain a close balance of emotions might greatly reduce the person's reward-getting efficiency.

Some extrapsychic devices operate by controlling emotions. For

A

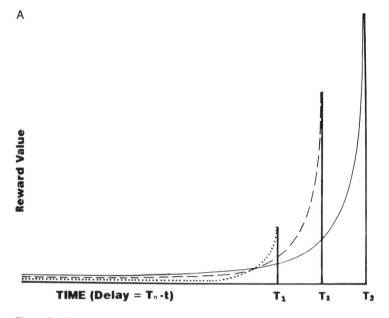

Figure 5.1. Discounted values for three alternative rewards, such as "getting drunk," "sober but bullied," and "overcoming a bully." A: Amounts of 20:70:100, so that, with this timing, the first is temporarily preferred to the second; these values will cause the first to be chosen in its own right, whether or not it helps the third. B: Amounts of 8:70:100, so that, with this timing, the second always dominates the first, which will never be chosen in its own right. C: Amounts of 8:70:100, with the first seen as compatible with the third and thus summed with it; with these values, the first will be chosen only when this compatibility exists.

instance, naloxone spoils the appetite for opiates, and alcohol facilitates anger, as in the case just described. As with the physical controls on attention, their properties are determined more by their extrapsychic mechanisms than by their psychological effects, and thus they should be classed with the extrapsychic devices.

The distinction between controls on attention and on emotion is sometimes more difficult to make. Information processing is part of any mental activity; the cultivation or inhibition of an emotion is apt to be experienced as "getting one's mind" on or off that emotion. Whether the person's intent is to restrict the processing of information or to prepare an emotional climate may sometimes be just a matter of emphasis. For instance, it is difficult to separate the two processes in the observations of Mischel and associates:

B

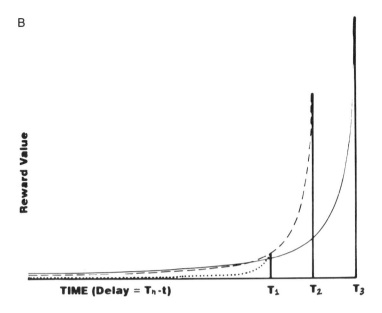

TIME (Delay = T$_h$-t)   T$_1$ T$_2$ T$_3$

C

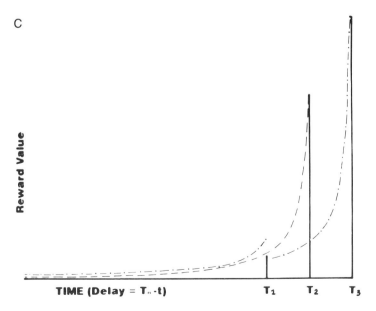

TIME (Delay = T$_n$-t)   T$_1$ T$_2$ T$_3$

Around the age of 5 years children can understand a problem in gratification delay, but they cannot yet solve it internally with any regularity (Mischel & Mischel, 1983). That situation has been exploited in several experiments. Mischel and Ebbeson (1970) gave children their choice of an unpreferred food (often marshmallows) immediately or a preferred food if they could wait 15 min without eating. The children devised "self-distraction techniques" to take their attention off the food. These usually succeeded if the food was not present. A similar study by Mischel, Ebbeson, and Zeiss (1972) found that children could refrain from eating for longer periods if given things to play with or think about. It could be argued that the successful techniques were examples of attention control, ways for the subjects to "forget" or mentally block the information that a tempting food was imminently available. However, subjects waited *longer* when they could look at pictures of the reward they were waiting for than if shown irrelevant pictures (Mischel & Moore, 1980). Further research by the same group showed that the crucial ingredient in delaying consumption was for the children to think about the reward in nonconsummatory ("cool") ways or to think about the task of delaying itself, so as not to stimulate their appetites (Mischel & Mischel, 1983; Mischel & Moore, 1980). Interviews showed that the older children were sophisticated about this strategy; some had even hit upon the kind of "coverant" described earlier: "Think about gum stuck all over [the marshmallow rewards]" (Mischel, 1981), or "I won't eat the marshmallows 'cause they're all moldy and spoiled" (Mischel & Mischel, 1983). Thus, successful delayers in those experiments seem to have been modulating their affect more than blocking information about the imminent availability of the food rewards. However, it may be difficult in practice to determine what mixture of these two endeavors a subject is using.

5.3.4 Personal rules

Only a few of the many defense mechanisms that have been described in the psychoanalytic literature seem to be simple precommitting devices: asking for controls, repression, denial, isolation of affect, reversal of affect, and reaction formation. Furthermore, simple precommitment does not seem to account for the kind of impulse control we call willpower, which allows a person to resist impulses while he is both attracted by them and able to pursue them. Such a power is well known in common experience, but it has never been precisely characterized by behavioral science.

Galen, for instance, who was quoted earlier on the value of getting other people to help control one's passions, also proposed an internal technique: A person should consider, for each daily task, whether it is better to be the slave of passion or to go by reason. That is, he should classify every behavior into one of two accounts: passionate or reasonable (Galen, 1963, p. 44). Galen implied that a decrease in the passionate behaviors would follow as a matter of course, but gave few clues as to what he thought the mechanism would be. He did say that it was more difficult for people who were out of practice: "A man who has for a long time habitually fallen into error finds it difficult to remove the defilement of the passions from his soul." Galen also implied that a little backsliding would be disproportionately damaging: "He must not relax his vigilance for a single hour" (1963, p. 45).

This short list of properties had not changed much by the time of the Victorian psychologists, who were the last group to subject the will to serious analysis. Sully did say a little more about the formation of mental accounts:

> When the child begins to view each individual action in its bearing on some portion of his lasting welfare, his actions become united and consolidated into what we call conduct. Impulse as isolated prompting for this or that particular enjoyment becomes transformed into comprehensive aim and rational motive. Or to express the change otherwise, action becomes pervaded and regulated by principle. The child consciously or unconsciously begins to refer to a general precept or maxim of action, as "maintain health," "seek knowledge," "be good," and so forth. Particular actions are thus united under a common rule, they are viewed as members of a class of actions subserving one comprehensive end. In this way the will attains a measure of unity. [Sully, 1884, p. 631]

He reaffirmed Galen's point about the cumulative effects of choices: "Every repetition of this kind of action . . . tends to fix conduct in this particular direction" (1884, p. 663).[2] His contemporary, Bain, noted again the disproportionate damage done by backsliding: "It is necessary, above all things, never to lose a battle. Every gain on the wrong side undoes the effect of many conquests on the right" (Bain, 1886, p. 440).

The gist of those descriptions was that a person defined a category of similar choices, such that each would have an effect on those still to come. The motive to shore up subsequent choices in the category might be substantially greater than the motive to control an individual impulse for its own sake. The great virtue of willpower was that it left perception and emotion undistorted. As William James said, "both alternatives are steadily held in view, and in the very act of murdering the vanquished possibility the chooser realizes how much in that instant he is making himself lose" (1890, p. 534). Unfortunately, in casting about for a mechanism for willpower, James (1890, pp. 562–565) also suggested that it *was* a matter of keeping the vanquished alternative out of view, thus retreating to the simple idea of attention control (Ainslie, 1975, pp. 483–484), which is the mechanism still advocated by those cognitive psychologists who speak of will (Fiske, 1989).

Freud indirectly said even more about willpower, although he characterized it as something frequently pathological, or at least suboptimal, the loosely bounded realm of the "compulsive defenses." Discussion of his complicated contribution to the concept of will is best deferred until we have explored the motivational basis of such a force (section 6.1).

5.4 Hyperbolic discount functions predict personal rules

It is possible to deduce a mechanism for willpower from the existence of deeply concave discount curves, like those in Figures 3.2 and 3.3, if we assume only that curves from multiple rewards combine in an additive fashion. In brief, choosing rewards in aggregates rather than individually gives later, larger rewards a major advantage over smaller,

---

[2] Likewise, Emerson said, "as the Sandwich Islander believes that the strength and valor of the enemy he kills passes into himself, so we gain the strength of the temptation we resist" (quoted by Stevenson, 1967, p. 1980).

earlier ones; and the perception of one's current choice as a precedent predicting a whole series of choices leads to just such aggregations.

Little research has been done on the summation of a series of rewards separated by intervals of time. Some kind of summation clearly occurs, even in pigeons, although one article has reported that by the fourth reward from the moment of choice no effect is apparent in that species (Shull et al., 1981). Mazur (1986) has recently shown that the value to pigeons of up to three rewards delayed by up to 30 sec is the exact sum of their individual values discounted for delay, thus confirming a report by McDiarmid and Rilling (1965):

$$V = \sum \frac{A_i}{Z + \Gamma(T - t_i)} \tag{5.1}$$

where V is the value of a series of rewards, A_i is the amount of the ith reward, $T - t_i$ is its delay, Z is the intercept adjustment, and Γ is the subject's sensitivity to delay ($Z = \Gamma = 1.0$ in Mazur's report; see section 3.4.1). The precision of this finding suggests that the same effect could be found for still later rewards if the method of measuring were sensitive enough. Because equation (5.1) is just an extension of equation (3.6), it also describes the simplest assumption about the summation of rewards. For these reasons it will be adopted here.

If an organism must make a series of choices between rewards of amount A_i, and later, larger rewards of amount A'_i (i.e., all $A'_i > A_i$, and all $T'_i > T_i$), each choice will be described simply by equation (3.7) and Figure 3.3 – unless the choices are linked. If, for instance, the whole series of choices must be made all in the same direction and all at once, then the choice will be governed by the summed values of the rewards on each side. The crucial time at which preference between the two whole series of rewards changes will be represented by the t at which the value V' of the series of larger rewards equals the value V of the series of smaller ones, called $t_{\text{indifference}}$:

$$\frac{V}{V'} = \frac{\Sigma A_i/[Z + \Gamma(T_i - t_{\text{indifference}})]}{\Sigma A'_i/[Z + \Gamma(T'_i - t_{\text{indifference}})]} = 1 \tag{5.2}$$

If the choice is made before $t_{\text{indifference}}$, it will favor the series of larger, later rewards, and if it is made after $t_{\text{indifference}}$, it will favor the series of smaller, earlier rewards.

This would be a trivial application of equation (3.7) to the case of multiple rewards except for an important phenomenon: $t_{\text{indifference}}$ between the series of larger (primed) rewards and the series of smaller (nonprimed) rewards will move closer to the moment when the first smaller reward is available as the series is made longer. This means that the period $T_1 - t_{\text{indifference}}$ will become shorter and may disappear; that is, the period of temporary preference for the smaller reward will be reduced or eliminated.

To illustrate this effect (with Z and Γ equal to 1): In the choice between a reward A at time T and a reward twice as great, A', available at $T + 3$ units of time, $t_{\text{indifference}}$ will equal 2. That is, preference between these alternatives will change 2 units of time before each earlier member of a pair is due (Figure 5.2A):

$$\frac{1}{1 + T - (T - 2)} = \frac{2}{1 + (T + 3) - (T - 2)}$$

Curves from two pairs of alternatives will cross 1.3 units of time before the earliest reward is due:

$$\frac{1}{T - (T - 1.3)} + \frac{1}{(T + 6) - (T - 1.3)}$$
$$\cong \frac{2}{(T + 3) - (T - 1.3)} + \frac{2}{(T + 9) - (T - 1.3)}$$

(Figure 5.2B), and summed curves from six pairs of alternatives will cross 0.6 unit of time before the earliest reward is due (Figure 5.2C). By the time there are 20 choices in the series, the summed discount curves from the two series of rewards no longer cross at all; the series of larger rewards is preferred at all times, even when the first of the smaller rewards is available immediately (Figure 5.2D).

The results of simple addition of recurring, discounted values are tabulated in Appendix II: Ten iterations of a unit reward separated by a unit time multiply its value by anywhere from 2.92 to almost 10 times, depending on how delayed the first reward in the series is; an additional 90 repetitions add only about twice again its undiscounted value, but without much sensitivity to when the initial reward occurs; and an additional 900 repetitions add its undiscounted value only twice again. Thus, as increasingly delayed rewards are added, their value becomes both smaller and more stable. Calculation of values by the original matching law [i.e., simple inverse proportionality to delay, equation (3.2)] yields a similar pattern, except that the already huge relative value of rewards delayed less than 3 units or so becomes even larger.[3]

In most life situations, rewards are not concentrated at a single point, and larger rewards often differ from smaller ones in being more prolonged rather than more intense. However, if we continue to assume that reward value is the sum (or integral) of the values of a series of reward segments, the value of a prolonged reward will be simply the aggregate of all of its discounted segments. Furthermore, equation (5.1) can be used to equate the value of a relatively steady, continuous reward to the value of a reward of the same magnitude occurring all at one particular moment, a transformation that generally will make illustration easier (Appendix III contains a table of such transformations). However, note that insofar as the moment of choice is close to the beginning of a continuous reward, the moment of effective reward moves earlier, from nearly halfway through the reward to only about a fifth of the way through (Figure 5.3).

Bearing this shift in mind, we can obtain the effective delay values from Appendix III for use in Appendix II to estimate the effect of repeating prolonged rewards. It should be the same as that of repeating brief rewards at the relevant times. Of course, where Z differs importantly from 1, the relative contributions of imminent rewards will change accordingly; but the pattern of aggregation, which is the aspect important to our discussion, will keep the same form.

Appendix II makes it clear that the practical effect of choosing a whole series of rewards at once will be to increase the individual's tendency to choose the larger rewards. He can approach much closer to the smaller, earlier rewards, and therefore be more flexible in his behavior, without forming temporary preferences for them. This predicted phenomenon obviously might be relevant to the problem of human impulse control.

But how does a person arrange to choose a whole series of rewards at once? In fact, he does not have to commit himself physically. The

---

[3] To obtain original matching-law values from Appendix II, read from the table *one line above* any given initial delay; values at delay = 0 will be infinite.

A

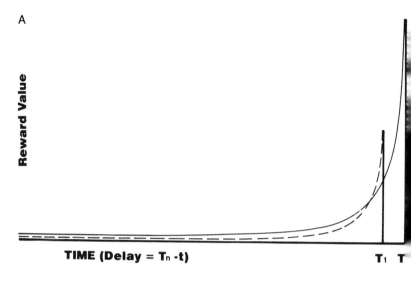

B

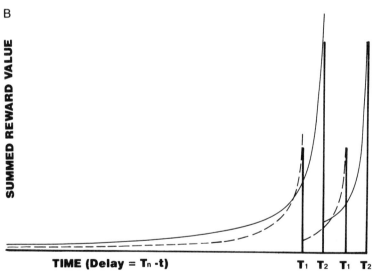

Figure 5.2. Summation of the values of expected rewards: hyperbolic curves drawn according to equation (5.1): a single pair of alternative rewards (A) and series of 2 (B), 6 (C), and 20 (D) pairs. Before 20 pairs, the temporary dominance of the series of smaller rewards is almost eliminated.

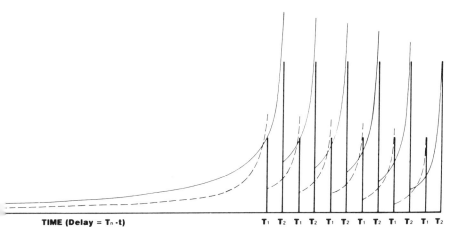

TIME (Delay = T_n -t) T_1 T_2 T_1 T_2 T_1 T_2 T_1 T_2 T_1 T_2 T_1 T_2

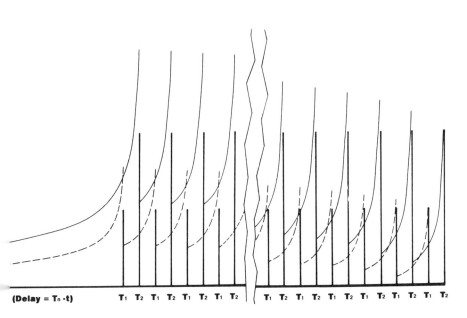

(Delay = T_n -t) T_1 T_2 T_1 T_2 T_1 T_2 T_1 T_2 T_1 T_2 T_1 T_2 T_1 T_2 T_1 T_2 T_1 T_2 T_1 T_2

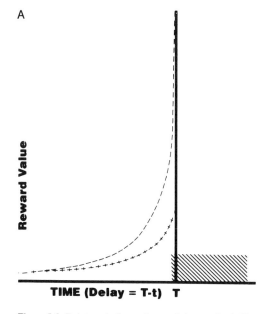

TIME (Delay = T-t) T

Figure 5.3. Point equivalents of extended rewards: A: If an extended reward is represented by a bar of equivalent amount at its beginning, the value of the bar (dashes) is drawn much higher than the summed value of the extended reward (pluses) in the period just before it is due. B: If the bar is drawn at the midpoint of the extended reward, the fit is better, but slightly undervalues the reward just before it is due. C: Appendix III gives a point at which the discount curve from a bar coincides with the summed curve of the extended reward.

values of the alternative series of rewards cannot depend on whether or not he will actually get them, an event that has not yet occurred. Rather, they depend on his expectation of getting them. Assuming that he is familiar with the expectable physical outcomes of his possible choices, the main element of uncertainty will be what he himself will actually choose. In situations where temporary preferences are likely, he is apt to be genuinely ignorant of what his own future choices will be. His best information is his knowledge of his past behavior under similar circumstances, with the most recent examples probably being the most informative. Furthermore, if he has chosen the poorer reward often enough that he knows that self-control will be an issue, but not so often as to give up hope that he may choose the richer rewards, his current choice is likely to be what will swing his expec-

B

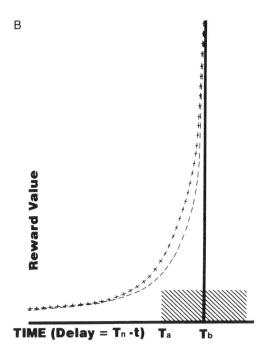

Reward Value

TIME (Delay = T_n -t) T_a T_b

C

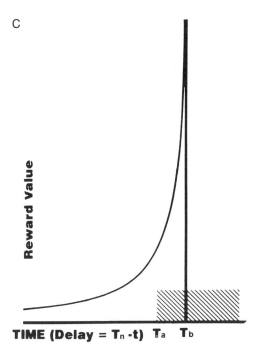

Reward Value

TIME (Delay = T_n -t) T_a T_b

tation of future rewards one way or the other: If he makes an impulsive choice he will have little reason to believe he will not go on doing so, and if he controls his impulse he will have evidence that he may go on doing so.

Consider, for example, the predicament of a person on a weight-reducing diet who has been offered a piece of candy. He knows that the calories in one piece of candy will not make any noticeable difference in his weight, and yet he is apt to feel that he should not eat the candy. What would it cost him? Common experience tells us: his expectation of sticking to the diet. He will face many chances to eat forbidden foods, and if he sees himself eating this one, it will not seem likely to him that he will refuse the others. If he succumbs to the temptation to eat the candy, it will cost him not only its small caloric burden but also the expectation of getting whatever benefits he had hoped for from his diet. And yet the very knowledge that he is in this predicament may make him refuse the candy where he would otherwise accept it. His behavior will then be controlled by equation (5.1) rather than equation (3.7).

According to this logic, amplification of impulse control can be expected to occur to some extent whenever a person perceives a series of confrontations with impulses as similar to each other. He will not necessarily notice the process itself, or develop any way of describing it. He might develop an extensive practical understanding of it by trial and error, but have only tangential theories about how it works – for instance, by identifying a "higher level of action," such as staying thin, as opposed to simply avoiding candy (Vallacher & Wegner, 1985), or by taking an oath that invokes supernatural help for the kind of choices it covers (Ainslie, 1975). However, insofar as he has become aware of this phenomenon, he will be able to induce it where it has not occurred spontaneously, by arbitrarily defining a category of gratification-delaying behaviors that will thereafter prevail or not as a set (Ainslie, 1975).[4]

---

[4] In fact, a person's awareness that his current choice will tend to serve as a precedent for future choices will further enhance this self-perpetuating property. That is, someone who makes a choice while aware that it will set a precedent will subsequently interpret that choice as not just additional evidence about his future choice propensities, but as a *test case*, for in making such a choice he is aware of saying, in effect, "let me decide such cases this way ever after," and a choice made in light of that awareness will be stronger evidence about his future behavior than a choice that is merely spontaneous.

By such a perception the person stakes his expectation of getting the whole series of larger rewards on a single choice, and the relative values V and V' of the two alternatives will be determined by equation (5.2). Some psychologists might see the stake in terms of secondary reward (Longstreth, 1971; Wyckoff, 1959): If the person has reason to predict that he will get the series of larger rewards, he will derive a secondary reward from that prediction. If that prediction changes, he will lose this secondary reward, and gain only the secondary reward induced by the series of smaller alternatives. But the theory of precedents just described does not depend on the existence of a secondary reward or any other specific mediating mechanism between expected reward and current motivation. Only the highly concave shape of the effective discount curve is needed.

This means of precommitment is an example of side betting, because it works by putting additional reward at stake in each individual choice. Schelling (1960, pp. 21–80) and Becker (1960) have described side betting as a way people sometimes commit themselves to a course of action by arranging to forfeit things of value – money, reputation, freedom – if they do not make a particular choice in a specified direction. For instance, a person who wishes to commit himself not to tell lies may do so by cultivating a reputation as a truthful person, which would be lost if he were caught lying. In Schelling's and Becker's examples, however, the side bets are held by other people, who exact the penalty if the person does not behave as he said he would. A public side bet like that is a case of an extrapsychic precommitting device. In the interdependent series of behaviors described earlier, no one need hold the bet; if the bettor perceives himself not to have waited for a large reward, he will automatically pay the forfeit, and at once, by losing his expectation that he will wait for similar rewards in the future. The dieter who has, in effect, bet himself that he will not eat candy pays for any lapse by a decrease in his own expectations.

Thus, a person can bind his behavior by a private side bet that does not depend on the cooperation of any other person. It has the same properties as the promise one entrepreneur makes another, where the value to each of their sustained cooperation is greater than what is at stake in the situation at hand, a promise that has been called a "self-enforcing contract" (Klein & Leffler, 1981; Macaulay, 1963). In effect, a private side bet is a self-enforcing contract with the person's own future motivational states.

Private side bets have the properties that the Victorian writers cited earlier ascribed to force of character or willpower: They arise when a person sees "each individual action in its bearing on some portion of his lasting welfare." They gain strength as repetition makes consistent self-control more believable, but insofar as the value of each choice as a precedent exceeds its intrinsic importance, "every gain on the wrong side undoes the effect of many conquests on the right." Attention control is not required, and may actually do damage, because to evaluate precedents it is necessary that "both alternatives are held steadily in view." Finally, because the increased motivation for self-control comes from no tangible process, but only a shift of mental bookkeeping, it seems somewhat magical, "some new force distinct from the impulses primarily engaged. In making an effort the will seems to throw in its strength on the weaker side . . . to neutralize the momentary preponderance of certain agreeable sensations" (Sully, 1884, p. 669).

Nowadays we are less in awe of the will and its force – some authors have even thought the concept unnecessary, as when Gilbert Ryle called it "the ghost in the machine" (1949, p. 15). Clinicians of all schools seem to go out of their way to avoid invoking it. However, modern concepts are no clearer. For instance, behavior therapists regularly observe that when patients systematically record either impulsive behaviors or avoidances of those behaviors, the occurrences of such behaviors decrease, a practice called self-monitoring (Broden, Hall, & Mitts, 1971; Fremouw & Brown, 1980). Where they propose a mechanism it is either the mysterious "intrinsically reinforcing properties of self-control" (O'Banion, Armstrong, & Ellis, 1980) or a reward that the person somehow gives himself, as in Kanfer and Karoly's "beta control" (1972), an equally mysterious process without the concept of constraint by personal rules (see section 6.2.2). The phenomenon of clear-eyed, wholly mental impulse avoidance described casually by terms such as "resolutions" and "willpower," and often intended by the generic term "self-control," has not been explained by any other mechanism.

Personal rules are the most flexible and accessible precommitting device. They are not without grave side effects, however, as will become apparent. As a deliberate tactic they are endorsed by male subjects more than females, and endorsed by all subjects more than the preceding three tactics (Ainslie, 1987a). Not surprisingly, approval of the use of personal rules is correlated positively with self-reported obsessional traits; it is correlated negatively with self-reported "oral" traits and with endorsement of extrapsychic self-control devices.

5.5 Personal rules solve a bargaining problem

The temporary-preference phenomenon creates a relationship among an individual's successive motivational states that can be described as limited warfare (Schelling, 1960, pp. 53–80): Successive motivational states will have some interests in common, but others that are peculiar to one state. The interests in common are identical with the person's long-range interest. The peculiar interests are short-range interests in whatever rewards happen to be imminently available. At any given time, the alcoholic wants to drink less in the aggregate – he does not want to be an alcoholic – but he may currently want to drink a great deal. That is, his long-range interest, common to all his successive motivational states, is to be generally sober; that interest is challenged, and often overwhelmed, by a succession of short-range interests in getting drunk just once.

Each person has, in Winston's phrase (1980), a "stock of human capital" – in sobriety, health, goodwill, reputation, and many other goods besides money itself. He is called upon daily to decide whether or not to cash in some of it for immediate consumption. Each day he has much the same interest in preserving his capital for the future, but he is also drawn to consumption plans that would consume a disproportionate share of it in the present. His successive motivational states may either cooperate with one another in their mutual long-range interest or abandon that interest for the sake of each one's short-range interest. A person's long-range interest is apt to prevail if and only if he believes that he can generally preserve that interest from one time to the next, that is, if at each decision he expects future motivational states to cooperate with his long-range plan. An effective personal rule is one that specifies a common interest in such a way that the person never prefers to abandon it.

The regular occurrences of temporary preferences and the consequent limited warfare between successive motivational states lend themselves to analysis in terms of the same concepts that have been used to understand interpersonal or international conflicts. As March put it,

> the problem of intertemporal comparisons . . . is technically indistinguishable from the problem of interpersonal comparison of utilities. When we compare the changing preferences of a single person over time to make [trade-offs] across time, we are in the identical position as when we attempt to make comparisons across different individuals at a point in time. The fact that the problems are identical has the advantage of immediately bringing to bear on the problems of intertemporal comparisons the apparatus developed to deal with interpersonal comparisons. [1978, p. 600]

For instance, the making of personal rules can be seen as a learnable skill,[5] similar to the skills required of a lawyer or a negotiator. Indeed, recently described principles of interpersonal negotiation closely fit the interaction of impulses and impulse controls (Schelling, 1960, pp. 21–80; Shefrin & Thaler, 1978; Taylor, 1975). As has just been described, the most important aspect of the relationship among those processes is the fact that they must operate together over a long and repetitive lifetime, so that current decisions may be more important as precedents for future decisions than as events in their own right. The need of the long-range interest to draw a line against impulses is like the interest of the negotiator who must face an opponent not just once but repeatedly, a position Schelling defines well:

> To persuade the other that one cannot afford to concede, one says in effect, "If I conceded to you here, you would revise your estimate on me in our other negotiations; to protect my reputation with you I must stand firm." [1960, p. 30]

This logic does not change if it is the self, not the other, who must be convinced. By similar logic, players in experimental bargaining games, such as the prisoner's dilemma, are motivated to choose the cooperative solution if that choice will be seen as a precedent for

---

[5] This point has been controversial even in modern times: "What sort of a notion is that of 'improving at operating one's will'? It sounds like 'improving at throwing one's voice . . . ' " (O'Shaughnessy, 1956).

Table 5.1. *Outcomes for country A*

If country A chooses	If country B chooses	
	Gas	No gas
Gas	2	10
No gas	0	5

future games, but often choose the noncooperative solution if it will not (Taylor, 1975, ch. 3 and 5; Telser, 1980). Theories of bargaining and games may let us make explicit much of the logic of impulse control, which, like bargaining itself, has long been left to intuition.

To put the analogy another way, the relationship among successive motivational states is similar to that of larger entities, such as countries at war, that may preserve some common interests (fair treatment of prisoners, avoidance of poison-gas warfare) only if each expects the other to cooperate in those areas. The paradigm for this relationship is the prisoner's dilemma. Table 5.1 shows the values to country A of using poison gas in a given battle if country B does or does not use gas. If this will be the only battle, it seems to be in country A's interest to use gas, for A is better off using gas both if B uses it and if B does not. If a similar payoff also faces B, both will probably use gas and get a lower payoff than if both did not. However, if there should be several battles, each country will have some reason not to use gas, as an offer to the other to cooperate on this aspect of the war and get a series of "5" payoffs instead of "2" payoffs. Because following suit is both the most obvious strategy and the most successful one in the prisoner's dilemma (Axelrod, 1984), it is reasonable for each side to expect the other to follow it, knowing only that the other's payoffs are in a prisoner's-dilemma pattern (i.e., "both defect" being worth substantially less than "both cooperate").

Notice that in the game with repeated moves, the two players do not have to make their decisions simultaneously for the prisoner's dilemma to arise. Each country will base its decision about using gas on the other's known moves, and the occurrence of a simultaneous, as-yet-unknown move will not affect the rationale for choice. Thus, the choices made by a legislature that is dominated alternately by conflicting interests are also apt to follow a true prisoner's-dilemma pattern: One party may want to build arms and the other to disarm, but neither wants to waste money. When each is in power it must choose between cooperation – a middle level of armament – and defections, and a series of such choices would mean alternately building and scrapping expensive weapon systems.

But this is the pattern of payoffs faced by successive motivational states within the individual. An example in which the payoffs occur regularly and at discrete times was mentioned in section 3.8. Say that a person at midnight faces the choice of staying up for about 2 hours more and having fun before he finally gives in to fatigue, but feeling tired at work the next day, versus giving up his present fun and expecting to feel rested at work. He values the imminent fun at 60 units per hour (for simplicity, a gradual decrease with fatigue will not be computed, and the whole value will be computed from the midpoint of the hour) and expects to lose comfort at 60 units per hour from when he gets up at seven the next morning until he leaves work at 5 p.m. At midnight the value of staying up will be

$$V_{up} = \Sigma_{i=0.5\to1.5}60/(1 + i) = 64$$

and the differential value of feeling rested at work will be

$$V_{bed} = \Sigma_{i=7.5\to16.5}60/(1 + i) = 49$$

Given only this one choice, he will stay up and suffer the next day. (This is the choice illustrated in chapter 3 by Figure 3.6.)

However, if he must face this choice nightly, he may perceive his current choice as a precedent for future nights as well. Assuming that he believes that he will go to bed on time on subsequent nights if he does so tonight, and not otherwise, the values of his alternatives are

$$V_{up} = [\Sigma_{i=0.5\to1.5}60/(1 + i)] + [\Sigma_{i=24.5\to25.5}60/(1 + i)] + [\Sigma_{i=48.5\to49.5}60/(1 + i)] + \cdots + [\Sigma_{i=216.5\to217.5}60/(1 + i)] = 78$$

for staying up on the next 10 nights, versus

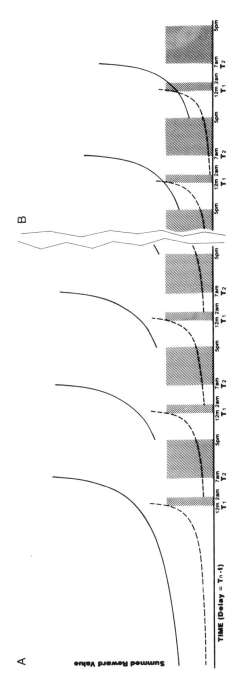

Figure 5.4. Summed curves from a series of 10 choices like that depicted in Figure 3.6: Early in the series the summed value of staying up (dashes) never rises above that of going to bed (solid curve).

$$V_{\text{bed}} = [\Sigma_{i=7.5 \to 16.5} 60/(1 + i)] + [\Sigma_{i=31.5 \to 40.5} 60/(1 + i)] + \ldots +$$
$$[\Sigma_{i=223.5 \to 232.5} 60/(1 + i)] = 105$$

for going to bed early on the next 10 nights (Figure 5.4). He will go to bed *if* he expects that he will also be motivated to follow suit on the subsequent nights.[6]

Considering separately the present values of the alternatives in his first choice (64 versus 49) and the present values of two subsequent series of nine choices all in one direction (14 for always staying up vs. 56 for always going to bed), his incentives form a prisoner's-dilemma matrix (Table 5.2). From his present point of view, going to bed on time both today and in the future is worth 105, and staying up both today and in the future is worth 78. However, if he can stay up today and still expect to go to bed on time in the future, that is worth 120. Conversely, if he goes to bed today but fails to go to bed in the future, that is worth only 63. The latter two outcomes respectively represent (a) his success in finding a loophole that will except the present case from the string of precedents and (b) his false hope that his current cooperation will give him sufficient incentive to follow suit in subsequent choices. The nature of the matrix does not change if we consider a series of 99 future choices (worth 25 for staying up versus 110 for going to bed, almost the 1 : 5 ratio of the "objective" rewards).

Thus, his best move at present will depend on how he forecasts his

---

[6] Computations for this example assume that Z = 1 hour, and Γ = 1.0, and that the entire reward for each hour is concentrated at the midpoint of that hour. According to Appendix III, the reward for an hour starting immediately acts as if it occurred at 0.39 hour, not 0.5, and the reward for the second hour at 1.42 hours, not 1.50; only at delays of many hours does the virtual action point reach the midpoint of the hour. However, the difference is not enough to affect the outcome of this example, and it is noticeable at all only in the first period of staying up, which at midnight will be worth 68 rather than 64. The precise calculations would be much more difficult for the reader to repeat and would imply more precision than is intended. The effect of using different values of Z underscores our lack of precise knowledge about the discounting of nearly immediate rewards: If Z is set at 0.1 hour instead of 1 hour, the value at midnight of staying up jumps to 180, even if the 2-hour period is divided into 6-min segments for analysis. If it is 1 min, staying up is worth 260, 90 of which is contributed by the first 0.1-hour segment. The very fact that impulses like staying up too late are not unopposable argues that Z must be substantially larger than 1 sec in situations involving longer periods of time than Mazur's pigeon experiments (1987).

In calculating the present value of being rested tomorrow or on subsequent days, or staying up tomorrow night or subsequent nights, neither the point during the reward at which it is taken as occurring nor the value of Z makes any noticeable difference.

Table 5.2. *Present value of present and future choices*

Present	Future	
	Stay up	Go to bed
Stay up	$64 + 14 = 78$	$64 + 56 = 120$
Go to bed	$49 + 14 = 63$	$49 + 56 = 105$

future perceptions. He must ask two questions: (1) In the future, will he see this choice as having been a precedent for his bedtimes? (2) If so, will the aggregate expected value of going to bed on time usually be enough to motivate this behavior? If he stays up tonight and sees it as a precedent, he should expect to go on staying up. If he goes to bed now and sees it as a precedent, that will increase his likelihood of doing so in the future, but if that likelihood is still low, he will have wasted the effort. If he stays up or goes to bed, but sees it as an exceptional case, he will not have changed his prior expectations.

A person's situation facing a succession of his own future choices is just like that of the country deciding about poison gas or the legislature deciding about armaments. Unlike the single game, which is changed completely if one player knows the other's move, a repeated prisoner's dilemma makes players predict each other's future moves on the basis of known past moves. The incentives stay the same whether the players move simultaneously or take turns. Thus, a player on Monday predicts Tuesday's move, whereas Tuesday's player does not predict Monday's move, but rather Wednesday's, and those of the following days in turn. This is true whether the players on different days are two people, or a single person, or N people, as long as each plays repeatedly. Whether or not Monday's player is a different person from Tuesday's player, Monday's move will be the Tuesday player's best predictor of Wednesday's move and subsequent moves.

To summarize this hypothesis about force of will: The will is created by the perception of impulse-related choices as precedents for similar choices in the future. This perception generates the same pattern of incentives that operate in a repeated prisoner's-dilemma game. Personal rules are promises to cooperate with the individual's own subsequent motivational states in such a game. They are self-enforcing insofar as the expected value of cooperation exceeds that of defection at the times when the choices are made. This difference in value can also be regarded as the stake of a private side bet that the person "makes" to precommit his future behavior. It is this stake that gives the will its force.

5.6 The properties of a personal rule depend on the set of choices it covers

To be cost-effective, a personal rule must be drawn with three characteristics: (1) The series of rewards to be waited for must be long enough and valuable enough so that it will be preferred over each impulsive alternative. (2) Each member of the series and its impulsive alternatives must be readily identifiable, without ambiguity. (3) The features that exclude a choice from the series must either occur independently of the person's behavior or have such a high intrinsic cost that he will not be motivated to bring them about just for the sake of evading the rule.

These three requirements can be illustrated by the common problem of trying to lose weight:

1. To succeed, a person must expect enough cumulative reward from weighing less to motivate each of the many acts of abstinence that will be necessary. This amount will depend not only on the daily reward differential – the value of being thin on Tuesday versus eating ad lib on Tuesday – but also on the number of days for which the person expects this differential to remain in force. Someone who stays thin mainly because of a modeling job and plans to retire in the near future may suddenly find it impossible to eat sparingly. This person may even find it difficult to diet at the beginning of a vacation, because early rewards for dieting – the most influential of the series – will not be present. Similarly, it is easy to estimate the effect on Figure 5.4 of interposing a weekend before the person has to get up early.

2. The person must also have clear guidelines that identify which food choices are permissible: He might find it difficult not to see his eating a piece of candy as a violation of his plan to reduce, but what about eating a relatively large piece of steak? Or a medium-size piece

of steak? In the absence of clear boundaries between impulsive and adaptive eating behaviors, it will be difficult for him to know when he has violated his rule. Similarly, rules that require him not to have "large" helpings or to eat "only when hungry" are apt to be defeated by shifts in his threshold for detecting largeness or hunger, because this detection must be done during the period when the temptation to overeat is temporarily dominant. Mark Twain told of limiting himself to one cigar per day for the sake of his health. He shopped for bigger and bigger cigars, until finally "I was getting cigars *made* for me – on a yet larger pattern. . . . Within the month my cigar had grown to such proportions that I could have used it as a crutch" (Twain, 1899, p. 10). Doubtless it is the absence of a simple cue distinguishing adaptive eating from overeating that makes people turn to the cumbersome legalism of a formal diet. What a dieter gains from the trouble of classifying, counting, and sometimes weighing foods is a two-way division of his eating behaviors into the good and the bad.

3. Finally, it would be evident folly for a person to rule that he will eat only what he puts on his plate or only what he buys. W. C. Fields's temperance lecturer (n.d.) clearly was on a slippery slope when he permitted himself a swig of alcohol-based snakebite remedy, "which I always keep handy. Only, however, after first being bitten by a snake . . . which I also keep handy." However, it might be practical for a person to permit himself to eat all the caviar he buys or all the food he wants when he gives a party, if the cost of buying caviar or the effort of giving a party would deter him from doing these things too often.

5.6.1 Redefining personal rules: The role of bright lines

These three requirements – adequate size, adequate clarity, and criteria that do not depend on the person's own behavior – are all that should be necessary for the success of personal rules made in advance and maintained without modification. However, in a changing environment, a person is apt to find that he has committed himself to forgo an unexpectedly large amount of reward. Such a commitment will lead him either to break his rule or to forgo more reward than he had expected to in order to follow his commitment. He might be able to get more reward out of the situation if he could redefine his rule without undermining its effectiveness.

For instance, our dieter might find that he has committed himself to forgo a meal with great sentimental value (Thanksgiving dinner, say), or to offend a host by refusing food, or simply to avoid a kind of food that he likes more than he had thought. There are any number of ways he can make the necessary loopholes in his diet: calling it off on major holidays, or in company, or when the food would be wasted if he did not eat it, or just this once, and so on. It is almost always possible to formulate a principle that will grant an exception in the case at hand, but that very fact makes indiscriminate redefinitions fatal to a personal rule.

If the dieter is going to redefine his rule in such a way that he keeps his expectation of losing weight, the occasion he uses not only must be rare but also must stand out in some way from other possible occasions that are not rare enough. He must detect some feature that will separate his current, adequately rare excuse from other excuses that will be available too often. If for him Thanksgiving stands out against Sunday or against a cousin's birthday, if he can name only a few specific hosts who might be hurt if he refused large portions, or if an infrequently encountered dessert actually has a unique place in his heart, only then might he make an exception without losing the credibility of his rule.

The interest based on the smaller, earlier reward finds countless ways to say "just this once"; facile reclassification of behaviors that were originally forbidden is called rationalization (Hollitscher, 1939). The long-term interest must defend itself by arguing, "This, too, is a matter of principle." Ultimately the decision between the two will depend on the person's guess about whether or not a particular exception will in fact lower his expectation of generally adhering to his rule. He may even accept some probable lowering of that expectation so long as he is left with enough to deter most lapses – calculation of that quantity is an internal equivalent to estimating how many defections there can be in a multiperson prisoner's dilemma without making cooperation generally unprofitable (Schelling, 1978, pp. 217ff.).

The problem of defining exceptions is inherent in all real-life examples of repeated prisoner's dilemmas. The cooperation between the countries in the choice about poison gas is threatened by the possibility of choices that are marginal in their aptness to be seen as precedents, such as the use of gas against a third nation or the use of an explosive that happens to give off toxic fumes. A country might hope to engage in such marginal behaviors without being perceived as having betrayed its tacit agreement to cooperate. Because of that hope, there is substantially more risk that the country will engage in them and find that it has hoped falsely than that it will commit an unambiguous betrayal.

Thus, the tacit cooperation that limits warfare depends on the clear identifiability of defections. That, in turn, depends not only on the astuteness of the rules for cooperation but also on what could be called the topography of the choice situation – the physical features of the various alternatives that might be chosen. Schelling describes the problem succinctly:

> Two opposing forces are at the points marked X and Y [on the map (Figure 5.5)]. The commander of each force wishes to occupy as much of the area as he can, and [he] knows [that] the other does too. But each commander wishes to avoid an armed clash and knows [that] the other does too. Each must send forth his troops with orders to take up a designated line and to fight if opposed. Once the troops are dispatched, the outcome depends only on the lines that the two commanders have ordered their troops to occupy. If the lines overlap, the troops will be assumed to meet and fight to the disadvantage of both sides. If the troops take up positions that leave any appreciable space unoccupied between them, the situation will be assumed "unstable" and a clash inevitable. Only if the troops are ordered to occupy [abutting] lines or lines that leave virtually no unoccupied space between them will a clash be avoided. In that case, each side [rules over] the area it occupies, the advantage going to the side that has the most valuable area in terms of land and facilities. [Schelling, 1960, p. 62]

Schelling goes on to argue that the only good solution for each commander is to order his troops up to the river. The river is shallow and thus has no military value per se, but it is the only boundary that stands out from other possible boundaries, and each commander should assume that that is what the other is looking for.

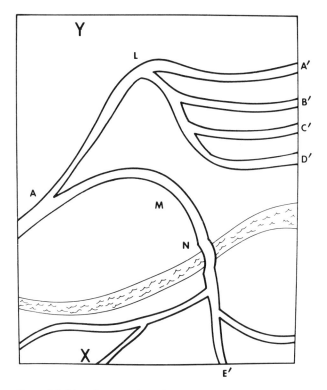

Figure 5.5. Map of contested terrain.

Troops in an army are in a limited-war relationship not only with the enemy but also with one another. They have a common interest in holding ground for their side, but each has an individual urge to flee. Even if they have no commander or other extrinsic source of discipline – even if they just belong to a hostile mob – they can be expected to wind up at the river by similar logic: Each fighter will obey his own individual desire for safety wherever such action will not cause a much greater retreat by the whole group. If he edges backward from a random spot on the map, his comrades will scarcely notice; in fact, they probably are edging backward themselves, for the same reason, and he would be increasingly exposed if he did not stay with them. At each step the small gain in safety seems worth the small loss of territory.

But suppose he is from the X side and is deep in Y territory. If someone calls out, "Fall back to road AA'," he must evaluate this public proposal as to its effect on the tacit bargaining among the soldiers. If the group does not stop at this line, where can it be expected to stop? Perhaps at the next road back, AB', which would not be a significant loss of territory. But then someone on the right flank might call out, "Fall back to road AC'," and because the individuals on the far right flank still can expect most of the line to hold, they will fall back. Having done so, might they not call for a retreat to D' as well, because it is still more forward than A? But that would leave the people in the center far forward, with an obvious road to retreat to (AN) that is about as far advanced as the right wing at D'. And once some of this mob has reached the river, why should not the right wing do so, too, especially because the river is no farther from D' than D' is from C'? Similarly, members between M and N do not have far to go to reach the river, but once the retreat starts from AN to the river, there is no point at which it can stop. Better to retreat to the river at the outset, each individual concludes; the right flank still will be more advanced than the left, but whatever line anybody calls out at that point, no one will be able to believe that the group will stop there if it has not stopped at the river. If any individual retreats from the river, he can expect to precipitate a rout, and that very expectation should keep him from retreating.

Happenstances of the layout of roads might enable the same leaderless band with the same motives to hold a position farther forward. If the roads LB' and LC' did not exist, for instance, the retreat from A' to D' might be too great for the right wing to accept, and thus the contingent near fork A would have a strong reason to occupy AL instead of AM. Similarly, if a road existed from M to D', or the segment MN did not exist, the band might avoid a retreat all the way to the river. Of course, if the band had a commander, the line between obedience and disobedience to an order might be more prominent than the lines on the map, assuming that he was skilled enough to avoid ambiguous orders. But even when there is a strong military command structure, the bargaining relationships among the troops constrains what a commander can get his troops to do: "Armies must be analyzed as collections of independent individuals who are, in some senses, as much at war with one another and their own leaders as they are with enemy forces" (Brennan & Tullock, 1982, p. 226). Indeed, those authors argue persuasively that a commander's main task is to foresee and manipulate the prisoner's-dilemma incentive structure that motivates his troops in battle.

The logic that confronts the individual mob member in predicting his comrades' moves is the same as that for someone at the present moment predicting his own future moves. It can even be illustrated by the same map. Movement in the direction of Y then depicts the choice that will increase overall reward, and movement toward X a yielding to short-range temptation. The fighters are the person himself at different times, as time moves from left to right. The person takes up positions successively, in view of where he has moved in the past and in anticipation of where he will move in the future. As in the preceding example, overvaluation of imminent reward will lead him to move at each successive moment farther in the X direction than he would have chosen in advance, unless he makes a rule for the situation. The roads and river on the map represent the facts outside of his control that can be used as criteria for his rule. At point A he might rule that he will hold the line AA', but if he can expect to change this rule at L to LB', he will have no reason to expect that he will not then change to LC' and LD' in turn. He may decide at A not to waste his effort, but rather consider specifying AN, followed by the "river." But if he is going to wind up at the river, he will have little motive not to retreat there to begin with. Conversely, he will have overwhelming reason never to move to the X side of the river; it will be his Rubicon.[7]

The availability of boundaries that cannot be moved just a little bit is crucially important to the long-term interest. Activities like smoking and drinking have such a line in an obvious place, that is, between any indulgence and no indulgence; but people who eat too much or spend too much money cannot completely give up those activities, and so must find some way to make a single diet, or budget, stand out from all the others to which they are tempted to retreat under pressure. Lawyers call such a unique boundary a "bright line."

---

[7] Freud made use of an embattled migratory horde of people to illustrate the nature of individual impulse control (1916–1917/1956i, pp. 339–341). His idea was more specific than the age-old religious allegory of doing battle against sin, but he did not recognize the limited warfare among group members.

The concept is familiar to people whose profession it is to negotiate between interests in the larger world. It expresses why countries blessed with unique boundaries, such as a mountain range or a river without large tributaries, have fewer wars than countries simply set out on a plain.

Whether people, or nations, in a limited-war situation must depend on a bright line to maintain cooperation or can use less prominent lines to gain more flexibility will depend on factors such as their history and skill in that situation and the amounts at stake. For instance, since World War II, war between the great powers may have been prevented by the widespread belief that even skilled policy-making would not be able to restrict it to conventional weapons.[8] Thus, their very history of failing to avert the escalation of wars, added to the new threat of nuclear destruction, may have deterred them from venturing beyond the bright line between some war and no war at all. Similarly, alcoholics find that they cannot engage in "controlled drinking" – following somewhat arbitrary rules to stop after two drinks, or three, or when they feel high, or when their spouses say they have had enough – and are advised by Alcoholics Anonymous to regard themselves as "helpless against alcohol."

To be helpless means that an alcoholic cannot use his willpower flexibly in this area, that is, cannot successfully choose one principle of drinking or another, but can only hope never to be lured across the bright line between some drinking and no drinking. Strictly speaking, these alcoholics are still using willpower, in that their choice is constrained by the logic of a repeated prisoner's dilemma among successive motivational states; but because that constraint is determined by a single bright line in their environment, rather than by their own activity in defining what their rules will be, they may indeed feel helpless (see chapter 7). People for whom drinking is not so rewarding, and those for whom willpower has not lost its credibility in the area of drinking, are able to follow the constraints of less prominent lines or even their spontaneous preferences without losing control.

Robert Frank has recently pointed out that a morality higher than

---

[8] "No government has ever been rational with conventional weapons. You expect them to be rational with nuclear weapons?" (Blessing, 1988).

the simple prudence that requires one not to risk getting caught may still be consistent with strict self-interest (1988, pp. 71–95). The logic is exactly that of Alcoholics Anonymous: Because of the tendency to overvalue immediate gratification of one's own particular vices, a person who tries to indulge them in a controlled way according to rules for prudence often will find loopholes that will lead him beyond prudence into behavior for which he will be caught and blamed. A person who draws a line further from his impulses – for instance, to be virtuous for the sake of virtue – has the same improved chance of suppressing his impulses as does the alcoholic who perceives himself to be helpless against alcohol. This may be the only person who succeeds well enough at being prudent to keep a reputation for virtue. Unless he sincerely renounces the relevant vice, the person may be like the "dry drunk" who is just waiting for a loophole.

This example incidentally reinforces Elster's astute observation (1981) that there may be states, such as contentment, spontaneity, dignity, and perhaps even sleep, that cannot be achieved by direct effort – see Kroger's "law of reverse effect" (1963); the direct approach to them tempts a person into those shortsighted behaviors, such as hedonism, silliness, pomposity, and "trying to sleep," that undermine the original goals.

Of course, the most effective belief in one's helplessness cannot be willed either, but must arise from unforced observation of the facts. To achieve it deliberately, a person can do no more than honestly ask if the term "helpless" applies to his will in a given kind of situation. However, where the answer is ambiguous or even apparently negative, he still may be able to force a belief that is more effective than nothing. Such a belief is called a tenet, "something held," an act of faith. Belief-holding behavior will be discussed further under the heading of testing reality in section 8.4; suffice it here to say that a rule to act as if helpless, regardless of spontaneous perceptions to the contrary, may succeed in suppressing lawyerly activity with the specified rules; but because this tenet is itself based on a rule, it is apt to be overcome by the same temptations that assault the rules it is trying to protect. If an alcoholic declares himself helpless against alcohol out of mere prudence (i.e., as a ploy of his will), this tenet is more apt to bend in the face of temptation than is a belief forged of experience – but it may still be worth a try.

5.6.2 Behavioral research on the perception of precedents

It is innately difficult to conduct controlled experiments on personal rules. The act of serving as an experimental subject is an exception par excellence to anyone's usual rules. That is, an experimental example of a choice (e.g., getting less money now versus more money later) is readily distinguishable from all other examples in a person's daily life; a subject should behave toward it as an isolated instance, not as a precedent. Indeed, that probably is why the subjects in section 3.5, who were asked to choose between different amounts of money at different delays seemed such spendthrifts. Of course, animals can be obliged to get most of their food over long periods in an experimental situation; but although there is no theoretical reason why pigeons cannot use their own current choices as predictive information about their future choices, they seem not to do so (Ainslie, 1989).

Subjects can report on their use of personal rules (Ainslie, 1987a, and unpublished data), as did the child (Mischel & Mischel, 1983) who described his gratification-delaying tactic as "I would say ... 'I shouldn't eat 'em ... so I won't eat 'em' "); however, their use of language in this area is idiosyncratic, especially when they are describing what happens when the will fails (Sjoberg, 1980; Sjoberg & Johnson, 1978). Sjoberg's lapsed smokers who said that logic failed them under the pressure of temptation were telling no more than Aristotle did about the effect of an incontinent person's passion on his beliefs (Bogen & Moravcsik, 1982). When asked about their wills, people theorize rather than observe, and the theories of modern subjects are not nearly as explicit as those of the great Victorian psychologists discussed in section 5.3.4.

However, even if actual personal rules are inaccessible, it may be possible to study the components of rule formation. There seem to be two antecedents of rule-governed behavior: the discounting of delayed reward that creates the temporary-preference situation, and the definition of categories of choice that determines the importance of possible behaviors as precedents. Research on discounting was discussed in sections 3.4 and 3.5. The study of categories of choice has just begun.

The cognitive process involved in judging internal precedents should be much the same as that for judging precedents in interpersonal bargaining. If human subjects are repeatedly offered alternative outcomes that simulate the motives predicted by matching-law discount curves, these alternatives should pose these players the same strategic problems that people face in intertemporal choices. It should make no difference whether the successive players are the successive motivational states of a given person or different people who move successively. Each player has a whole person's resources at his disposal, as does each successive motivational state within an individual. Although individuals doubtless can keep secrets from each other more effectively than can successive motivational states, this difference should not be crucial to the conduct of the game: As long as past behavior is the best predictor of future behavior, it will not much matter whether or not each choice-maker's intentions, stratagems, or other considerations are secret. Individuals also seem to differ from groups in being able to form intentions, but that is the very process to be studied – the intention as a solution to the problem of conflicting interests, which, I have hypothesized, follows the same logic as tacit agreement in an interpersonal limited-war situation.

In some experiments we are conducting, pairs of human subjects use computer terminals to play a prisoner's-dilemma game with an outcome matrix similar to the nightly bedtime problem described earlier, though with values of 100 and 80 for defection versus cooperation, instead of 64 and 49 (Ainslie, Lyke, & Freeman, in press). No attempt is made to use actual delays to generate the differential incentives. The objective is not to study the effect of delay, but the effects of differential incentives typical of those that delay is assumed to produce within the individual. The subjects choose between distributions of points that are all exchangeable for money at the end of a session. Each subject is given a scheduled but unpredictable number of turns at choosing between two distributions of points to be added to his score and his partner's score: On most turns, the choice is between 80 points for both ("cooperation") versus 100 points for the player himself and none for his partner ("defection"). At these baseline values, players usually cooperate, but defections are not uncommon. After five consecutive baseline cooperations, the self-only option for one subject on one turn is made higher, anywhere from 120 to 400 points (a "lure"). His partner is offered a lure subsequently, but only after five more cooperations. Subjects are allowed to communicate with each other only by their choices on their computer terminals.

In an experiment already completed, it was hypothesized that a player would interpret his partner's defection to a lure differently depending on whether the lure was high or low – that defection to a low lure would be seen as a sign of low willingness to cooperate, often leading the player to defect himself on his next (baseline) turn, whereas defection to an infrequent high lure would be more apt to be seen as an exception to the tacit agreement to cooperate and thus not a cause for retaliation. Lures were observed to produce defections on about half of the turns at which they were offered, and the subsequent move by the other player confirmed the stated hypothesis 71% of the time.[9] On the same point, observations of treated smokers trying to stay abstinent have shown that lapses that occur in situations that the patient encounters frequently will lead to his return to smoking at a much higher rate than will lapses that occur in unusual situations (Baer et al., 1989).

The somewhat primitive experiment shows the feasibility of studying human cognitions about personal rules and their loopholes by a repeated prisoner's-dilemma analogy. To summarize this analogy: Although there are many concrete differences between the cooperation of individuals who face a limited-war outcome matrix and the cooperation of one individual's successive motivational states as predicted by the matching law, the basic incentive structure for these situations is the same. In both cases, a given choice about cooperation will depend on the prediction made by a whole choice-maker regarding whether another whole choice-maker with only some interests in common is apt to act in the common interest or in his own particular interest. In both cases, this prediction will depend more on what evidence one choice-maker expects his choice to provide the other choice-maker than on other forms of communication between them, including even the "inside knowledge" a person might be thought to have regarding his future motivational states.

[9] The reason this percentage is not higher probably is because on any given turn, subjects were remarkably apt to ignore their partners' recent behavior, as if using a very long range average or even the "homemade prior probability" that subjects in other repeated games have been reported to add to their expectations of partners' behavior, with no experiential basis (Camerer & Weigelt, 1988).

5.7 Precommitting methods interact

Clinicians have reported that the various precommitting tactics are effective against different kinds of impulses, as reviewed elsewhere (Ainslie, 1986b, pp. 149–158). Extrapsychic devices depend on happenstances of invention, but have been most useful against addictions. Attention-controlling devices work against preferences of very short durations, namely, the itches and pains. Emotion control has been used mainly against addictions. Clinical experience with personal rules will be discussed in the next chapter; they cover all ranges of preference duration, but seem least effective against the shortest.

Adequate coping with temporary preferences in a complex world probably requires the use of all four kinds of tactics, although there is ample room to vary their mixture. A choice of tactics is complicated not only by their potential to serve both long- and short-range interests but also by their expectable tendency to interact. There is clinical lore, but little research, suggesting that some devices tend to occur together, whereas others tend to be alternatives to each other.

For instance, the use of external constraints where personal rules might have served may undermine the maintenance of personal rules. The force of a personal rule is proportional to the number of delayed rewards that are perceived to be part of the series at risk. Choices that are externally forced cannot form part of this series, because they will be made according to the external force without regard to how other, unforced choices are made. Because that is the case, a person's choice does not provide evidence about how he will respond in unforced choices and thus does not contribute to the personal credibility he can stake on personal rules. A manipulated child or other prisoner simply depends less on his will than does a free person, and for that reason his will has less force. Furthermore, a person who often places himself under external constraints is apt to find that he is sometimes forced by those constraints to disobey personal rules, which will injure the rules if he is not skillful at distinguishing the forced choices from the others. Thus, strong, externally regulated motives should reduce the strength of the will.

This prediction seems to be borne out by the fact that children who are largely restrained by parental pressure grow up to use fewer internal controls (Aronfreed, 1968, pp. 308–309; Freedman, 1965;

Lepper, 1981). In addition, an extensive literature has found an internal (versus external) perceived "locus of control" to be correlated with more autonomy (Rotter, 1982), and subjects' endorsement of extrapsychic self-control tactics is negatively correlated with their endorsement of personal rules (Ainslie, 1987a).

Extrapsychic constraints and attention control could well be found together. There is no reason to predict that they would undermine each other, and each one is apt to be limited in its applicability – extrapsychic constraint by the availability of appropriate external forces, and attention control by its interference with information gathering. Because extensive use of either one should undermine a person's personal rules, they might sometimes wind up supplementing each other. "Hysterical" traits (largely inconsistencies attributable to mental blocking) often have been attributed to people who experience unusual amounts of coercion, such as slaves, members of impoverished cultures, and women who have adopted a subordinate role (Smith-Rosenberg, 1972), but there is little evidence on the point.

Emotion control is unique among the precommitting devices in that it can work simply with any of the others. It is like the flywheel on an engine that creates momentum, thus reducing the need for other decision-preserving methods. Attention control probably is best facilitated specifically by anger, which clinical lore holds to be an aid to repression. Personal rules may both direct the preparation of emotion and conversely be spared strong opposition by the isolation of affect, which is often observed in people who rely extensively on rules.

The most important interaction of precommitting devices is between attention control and personal rules. These are widely thought of as alternatives, and an analysis of interview transcripts to detect subjects' habits of ego defense has in fact found a negative correlation between the use of compulsive and hysterical defenses (Vaillant, 1976). In self-reports of self-control tactics, however, that negative correlation does not appear (Ainslie, 1987a). Nevertheless, a self-control strategy based on ignoring information is apt to interfere with the maintenance of personal rules, because these rules depend on a person's receiving accurate information about whether or not they are being followed:

To some extent, attention control can conceal behavior that violates a rule, or conceal the applicability of the rule to that behavior. That is, a person may be aware that certain information is apt to make a rule relevant to his current choice before he has actually collected that information. On that basis he may avoid collecting the relevant information. Although such a course evades his rule, it does not violate it; it is as legitimate as the congressional practice of "stopping" the official clock when the members do not want to observe a previously imposed time limit on their deliberations. It permits the behavior to be performed without regard to the rule, rather than in violation of it. A person skilled in using attention control may examine an impulsive behavior fairly thoroughly, but still not ask the questions that would lead him to declare it either "deliberate" or a lapse. The easiest targets will be behaviors that can be completed in short periods of time and those that are already ambiguous as to whether or not they follow the rule.

Thus, the short-range interest accomplishes an evasion that makes the behavior unconscious, as Freud called it (see section 2.3.1), or "cognitively deconstructed," as it has recently been called (Baumeister, 1990). But the point is not for a person to be spared knowledge of the behavior per se, but rather not to have it tested by his rules. As is notorious with "unconscious" behaviors, a person may remain extensively aware of it, missing only its key implications for issues about which he is in conflict with himself. "Unofficial" describes the status of these behaviors better than "unconscious."

Acting in his long-range interest, the person can in turn formulate rules for information gathering that will combat this evasion by formulating rules for the attention-controlling decisions themselves (i.e., by prescribing what kinds of information must be sought). Where the person wants to commit himself not to let a certain thing escape his attention, he can make rules governing his attention-directing behavior that will at least necessitate more motivation to evade them. For instance, a person who evades his rule against biting his nails by doing it "unconsciously" may make a further rule to note whenever one of his hands is above shoulder level, or note whenever he is ruminating about his nails. Thus, attention control and personal rules limit each other.

However, the usual relationship between attention control and personal rules probably is symbiotic. Although attention control often is used by short-term interests to defeat long-term interests, especially by undermining personal rules, it is also needed to save personal rules from their most serious failing: an inability to discriminate important cases from unimportant ones. The cost of this inability is reduced efficiency at foraging: If a person sticks to a rigid schedule, he cannot take advantage of big opportunities offered by the environment if they also represent any kind of small lapse. He is apt to become "penny wise and pound foolish," a widespread trait that has heretofore lacked a behavioral explanation. Likewise, in a situation in which a person can always do a little more work, or be a little more careful, or show a little more concern, he will be the prisoner of a rule that requires completeness. His only remedy will be to hedge on his rules, and doing that without impairing them takes skill.

It is not in a person's long-range interest to examine all behaviors as precedents. Just as courts keep – or used to keep – their dockets manageable by the doctrine *de minibus non curat lex* ("the law does not care about trivia"), a person must tolerate some spontaneity in his decisions. Furthermore, to decide deliberately whether or not to evaluate choices as precedents would invoke the very encumbrance he is trying to avoid; he must simply not notice the possible legal implications of much of his behavior, while staying alert to signs that significant short-range interests have begun to take advantage of the consequent blind spots in a particular area. Nevertheless, a small lapse is still a lapse, a genuine precedent that can endanger a person's expectation of getting his long-range rewards as much as a large lapse does. Where great and small cases are not separated by a clear boundary – thoughts versus actions, for instance, or, less reliably, petty cash versus major expenses – then any rule enforced with perfect information will become intolerably picky, and a person's resources will be absorbed by preventing or repairing innumerable tiny lapses that nevertheless threaten the major rule because they set genuine precedents.

Small lapses do differ from major ones in that it is easier not to notice them, and this property seems to offer the only practical way out of the difficulty. A person who has ruled that he will never get angry without just cause can throw an angry glance or pull in front of another car a bit too quickly without having to recognize such behaviors as examples of anger, whereas he would have to recognize them as such if the anger lasted longer than a glance or the motive for the driving could not be seen as haste more than anger. Likewise, a person fighting his tendency toward social withdrawal can get away with "not seeing" an acquaintance in a crowd, whereas active flight from a clear invitation would surely damage the credibility of his resolution. In this way, attention control can keep a person's legal system from getting clogged with small cases.

Of course, greater use of the same device can weaken rules, and the person can respond in turn in his long-range interest by mandating exhaustive vigilance. The tedium of such vigilance might then invite more daring examples of repression, and so on. It is easy to see how the sequence of overly demanding rules and blind evasions might become a vicious circle, leading to the pattern often noticed in failing despotisms, "tyranny tempered by anarchy." The use of attention control to obscure the minute implications of rules can be expected to deviate frequently in both directions from optimality.

There is another problem to which personal rules may be vulnerable without the help of attention control. Equation (3.7) predicts that a reward available at a near-zero delay will be much more effective than at any other delay. Personal rules that are otherwise adequate may sometimes be unable to recruit enough additional reward to offset this effect during the short period just before a smaller, earlier reward is available. Attention-controlling mechanisms, which are especially effective in blocking out information over short periods of time, may be needed to bridge such periods of vulnerability.

Thus, we see an ironic situation. Although attention control often may block the information that personal rules need, they depend upon that very process to compensate for two of their weaknesses: They sometimes cannot marshal enough motivation to overcome a temptation that is actually immediate, and so they must bridge that moment with a diversion of attention; and, being categorical, they cannot curb their own wasteful application to trivial cases, and so they must count on those cases not coming to their attention. The microscopic interactions of attention control with personal rules must have major consequences, but at present there is little basis for speculation about them.

5.8 The selection of behaviors is different from the selection of organisms

As we come to the end of this chapter on competing interests, it is worth noting a parallel that has been proposed with the evolutionary competition of organisms. Some authors draw an analogy between the selection of organisms and the selection of behaviors within an organism (Gilbert, 1972; Skinner, 1981). Vaughan and Herrnstein (1987) have suggested that the two processes are formally identical. There are indeed many similarities between them, but also two major differences: Organisms (or their genotypes) are literally separate entities, and their selection is based on the complex happenstances of their environment, most of which are not in turn subject to natural selection; for instance, the cold wave that selects for cold-adapted organisms does not do so because that selective function improves the cold wave's own chance of survival. An organism's behaviors, on the other hand, are related by a common dependence on the activity of that organism's reward center (or interacting set of reward centers), which at least partially unites behaviors that are separated in time; that selective function has in turn been shaped by the natural selection of organisms to serve a coherent purpose, the survival of that organism and its progeny. For instance, seeking warmth during the cold is selected for by the organism's reward mechanism because that reward process has been adaptive. The evolution-shaped function by which the reward process discounts delayed events is apt to be different from the unselected mathematical function that simply describes the survival of the fittest over time.

Indeed, these functions are necessarily different if organisms discount the value of delayed rewards according to a hyperbolic curve. As long as an inborn trait's selective advantage remains the same relative to its competitors (i.e., as long as the consequences of success do not change that advantage), the trait will be selected according to the exponential function described by Lotka (1957, p. 123):

$$u_n = (1 - k)^n u_0 \qquad\qquad (5.3)$$

where u_n is the proportion of organisms with a given trait after n generations, k is the coefficient of selection, and u_0 is the starting proportion of these organisms. Selective pressure that stays the same over time will never shift from favoring one trait to favoring its alternative; thus, this situation cannot be a model for the conflict of successive preferences within the individual organism.

Of course, the differential reward for behaviors and the selective factor for organisms both actually change with the changing frequency of the behavior or organism – as either becomes commoner, its advantage tends to decrease, although there can be special cases in which it increases. For behaviors, such diminishing returns commonly come from satiation of reward, or, in competitive activities, from the organism's increased predictability; they may have any number of particular mathematical functions. For organisms, frequency-dependent selection commonly results from increased competition for resources as a population grows, but also, positively, from increased cooperation (e.g., against enemies). Frequency dependence, too, may take any number of forms.

Vaughan and Herrnstein (1987) give a representative example of frequency-dependent natural selection of traits in a species, to be compared with the selection of competing behaviors within an individual; they use Maynard Smith's example (1982) of two mutually exclusive inborn behavioral traits or "strategies" that can exist in a hypothetical species, governing behavior when another member of the species is confronted:

> The first strategy is termed hawk and is characterized by the individual always fighting until one of the combatants wins and the other loses; the loser is always injured. The second strategy is termed dove. If a dove meets a hawk it runs away; the hawk wins the contest but neither is hurt. If a dove meets a dove, both posture for a while. Both doves lose time, and one wins the contest and the other loses, but neither is injured. [Vaughan & Herrnstein, 1987, p. 199]

Assuming, plausibly, that "winning confers 50 fitness points on the winner and 0 on the loser; that an injury costs 100 points; and that time spent posturing costs 10 points," the average payoffs are as follows: for a dove meeting a dove, 15 points; for a dove meeting a hawk, 0; for a hawk meeting a dove, 50; for a hawk meeting a hawk, −25. The "fittest" population will then consist of all doves, but individual hawk mutants will be selected for until there is a significant probability that hawks will meet hawks; it can be shown that the average fitness payoff for confrontations among members of a stable mixture of hawks and doves is only 6.25, much less than the 15 for an all-dove population. [This reasoning is condensed from Vaughan and Herrnstein (1987).]

In this situation, hawks arise to prey upon doves at a cost to the overall fitness of the combined population, a process somewhat similar to the generation of shorter-range interests within an individual to prey upon longer-range interests at the expense of aggregate reward. Doves, like long-range behaviors, will be motivated to prevent hawks from being born if possible; hawks, like impulses, will *also* be motivated to prevent the birth of other hawks, but not the birth of the doves on which they prey. In the grip of compulsive spending, the spendthrift wants to waste money only this once; the thriftier he has been and expects to be in the future, the fatter the pickings for his impulse.

However, although the reward and natural selection processes are grossly similar, they are not identical. In terms of natural selection, the enmity of hawks toward other hawks is limited – those that suppress competition by their own species too severely will not be selected, for they would reduce the population of their own genes. An impulsive behavior, however, is not chosen according to the number of similar behaviors to which it leads, but according to expected reward. An impulse that would kill the possibility of similar impulses in the future (e.g., a binge that would lead to the alcoholic's commitment to a treatment program) might be all the more attractive for that reason.[10]

A proper intrapersonal analogy to the hawks and doves would be

---

[10] One of the excuses that William James's famous drunkard gives for a binge is that "it is a means of stimulating him to make a more powerful resolution in favor of abstinence than any he has hitherto made" (1890, p. 565).

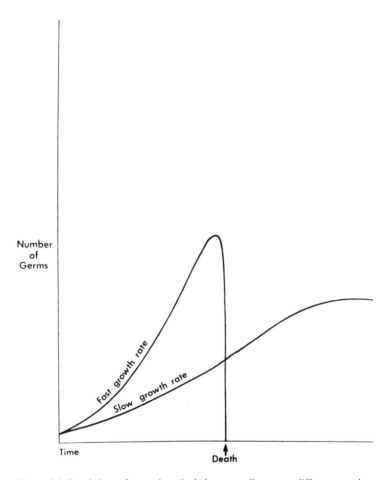

Figure 5.6. Populations of germs in a single host according to two different growth rates, the faster of which is lethal to the host.

a case that did not involve discounting, such as the "primrose path" dynamic described in section 2.4.3. If a person did not keep track of the effects of individual purchases on his disposable income, he might find that decisions to spend usually would be more rewarding than decisions to save, not noticing that his range of choices would be getting progressively poorer. The "hawk" spending choices would replace the "dove" saving choices, despite the resultant drop in his overall utility.

The difference in mechanisms can be seen most clearly if we look at evolutionary blind alleys, which look roughly like the temporary preferences induced by deeply bowed discount curves in the selection of behaviors. The frequency dependence of an organism's fitness does not necessarily create deeply bowed curves, or indeed any particular shape. However, there seem to be many cases in which the coefficient of selection [k in equation (5.3)], which determines the evolutionary analog of the discount rate, changes as such a function of time as to create a "discount curve" that is deeply bowed. For instance, the short-term success of a trait often endangers its long-term survival. A disease germ that multiplies so rapidly that it kills its host will leave fewer descendants than will a germ that can limit its growth so as to parasitize its host efficiently. Because the "value" of a trait is reflected in the number of organisms that carry it, the value of the growth-limiting trait can be diagrammed as crossing that of its alternative, just as the value of a larger, later outcome does in a behavioral choice: lower in the short run (i.e., for the next few generations), but higher many generations hence (Figure 5.6). Just as the repeated operation of such a reward pattern will lead an organism to adopt means of forestalling the smaller, earlier reward, so a species of germ will "learn" not to grow maximally, and an observer will see the disease grow tamer as decades pass; see the examples offered by Christie (1980, pp. 357ff., 935ff.). The apparent discount curve for the "value" of a certain virulence of a germ, in terms of the germ count to which that trait will lead after many generations, will not be hyperbolic or any other simple shape, but it will be bowed enough to make the germ species' "choice" of individual germs roughly coincide with impulsiveness and impulse control.

There are other interesting parallels between reward and natural selection. Of special relevance to intertemporal conflict is D. S. Wilson's hypothesis (1980) that organisms may increase their selective fitness if they compete in groups ("structured demes") rather than as individuals, as described by Vaughan and Herrnstein (1987). Such a change suggests the advantage gained by long-range interests when a person chooses behaviors in categories rather than as isolated instances. But again, the underlying mechanism has a different form: Groups of organisms obviously are not formed because one organism is seen as a precedent predicting others. The mathematics of the natural selection of organisms cannot be applied wholesale to the selection of behaviors by differential reward, at least where the discounting of delayed rewards is an important factor.

6. Freedom and compulsion

The explanation of behaviors that are experienced as involuntary was Freud's special concern. We have looked at his four theories of impulsiveness (see sections 2.3 and 2.5). Now that we have an alternative mechanism, or perhaps just a simplified mechanism, for temporary preferences, and have explored the consequent growth of particular interaction patterns among intrapersonal interests, it will be profitable to return to some of Freud's ideas about motivational conflict. We shall see that the internal bargaining activity described in chapter 5 should generate many, though not all, of the conflictual processes Freud described.

The reader with little interest in psychodynamics or the defense mechanisms can skip this next section and turn to section 6.2 without missing anything essential to the argument. There I shall develop an economic theory of the involuntary processes usually called compulsive, followed by a deterministic solution to an old philosophical puzzle: freedom of the will.

6.1 Freud's energy theory can be revised in motivational terms

The opposition of shorter- and longer-range interests in ambivalence creates the appearance of separate principles of mental functioning, as Freud described them: the pleasure and reality principles (1911/1956d, pp. 219–223), or their descendants, the id and the ego (1923/1956l, pp. 24–25). In choice situations that can be described by the diagram in Figure 3.3, functions based on the differential effectiveness of smaller, earlier rewards in the period after the curves have crossed will necessarily be functions that will seek instant gratification. There will be as many of these mental functions as there are situations that create temporarily preferred rewards. These functions will be transient and will have no necessary connection with each other, except that they will share a negative relationship to the long-run interests of the decision maker. They will be reward-seeking functions and hence will operate according to Freud's pleasure principle, and because they are closely followed by reward, they will be the functions a person will learn first.

However, as a person discovers delayed rewards that are more valuable, the mental functions that seek the poorer, earlier alternatives will become a nuisance to him. The functions based on the delayed rewards, which will be dominant before the curves of effectiveness cross, will be farsighted but must stay in control of behavior over the long run if they are to obtain the rewards that are their raison d'être. In particular, they must include devices to forestall the temporary attractiveness of the poorer alternatives. If they succeed in preventing changes of choice based on the poorer rewards, they can be said to be "safeguarding" the pleasure principle.

Freud meant "psychic energy" to be "motivation" (1916–1917/ 1956i, pp. 339–340; Rapaport, 1960, pp. 91ff.). However, when one mental agency (or "principle") had energy "at its disposal," that did not refer to the motivation on which it operated, but rather its ability to motivate another agency. Translated into picoeconomic theory, the energy of the ego functions will be the differential effectiveness (Rapaport, 1960, pp. 92–94) of the better, delayed rewards in the period before the poorer alternatives become temporarily preferred. Because these better rewards are not consumed in this period, Freud would have described their energy as "bound." On the basis of this energy, the ego functions must prevent the discharge of enormous but temporary concentrations of id energy that occur when a poorer reward is imminent, using the leverage afforded by foresight (i.e., by their being dominant at an earlier time). Freud described a similar relationship between id and ego when he compared the id to a horse controlled by a weaker but more farsighted horseman, the ego (1923/ 1956l, p. 25; 1926/1956n, p. 97).

Although Freud seems to have been talking about very much the same intrapersonal split that is induced by deeply bowed discount curves, he made three theoretical assumptions that seem unnecessary, and he also neglected the will as a phenomenon relevant to motivational conflict:

First, Freud believed that psychic energy was conserved in all transactions, that is, that it was neither created nor destroyed, but only moved from one object to another (Freud, 1938/1956q, p. 148; Rapaport, 1960, pp. 76–77). There seems to be no need to postulate this strict conservation of energy, understood either as motivation or the drive that gives rise to it. The reward process must necessarily operate with greater intensity at some times than at others if it is to establish differential motives. However, if one source of reward ceased to be productive, a person would be motivated to find other sources, and sources that previously had been unable to compete for his attention would become able to do so. A person's continuing susceptibility to reward is all that is needed to account for the substitution phenomena that Freud was trying to explain by the conservation of energy.

Second, Freud said that the demand of "reality" for gratification delay came from social authorities, particularly parents (1920/1956k, pp. 20–21; Rangell, 1968). But a highly concave time curve of reward effectiveness predicts that a person will be confronted by the need for gratification delay even in the absence of any social demands. His ability to get fast, costly rewards will be a threat to his more adaptive, long-range skills, and he will be motivated to adopt precommitting devices purely to suit himself. He may even want to guard against the rapid but wasteful consumption of the same reward he seeks in the long run (see section 7.3.2). Entirely personal motivation for the use of defense mechanisms was indeed suggested by Anna Freud as "instinctual anxiety" (A. Freud, 1966, pp. 58–61, 152–172); this proposal has been controversial (Fenichel, 1945, p. 140; Waelder, 1960, pp. 160–162), although it has recently been supported and amplified by Kohut (1977, pp. 93–111).

Third, Freud implied that the cost of using a defense mechanism is the energy spent in operating the mechanism itself and that this energy matches the energy of the target impulse. Specifically, he held that dangerous "cathexes" (roughly, "attractions"; see section 7.3.1) had to be restrained by opposite and equal anticathexes (1895/1956a, pp. 323–324; 1920/1956k, pp. 29–30; 1926/1956n, pp. 157–158). Psychodynamic writers often have referred to the ego's use of bound

energy to block the discharge of free energy and have spoken as if
the bound energy were itself the substance from which the blockade
is formed:

> In the course of development, hierarchically layered structures arise
> (defenses and controls) which act as "dikes." These not only delay
> or prevent discharge, but also diminish the drives' tendency toward
> immediate discharge. These structures are conceived of as built by
> "binding" drive energies to heighten the originally given drive-
> discharge thresholds. Their effect of diminishing the drives' ten-
> dency toward immediate discharge is conceptualized as "neutral-
> ization," special instances of which are referred to as
> delibidinization, deaggressivization, or sublimation. [Rapaport,
> 1960, p. 51]

Precommitment to forestall a temporary preference for a reward
could certainly be described as a binding of energy, in that it prevents
the consumption of the reward; and internal self-control probably
has some cost in effort, as reflected, for instance, in subjects' longer
estimates of the length of a given delay during internal versus external
control (Miller & Karniol, 1976). However, the differential in reward
effectiveness needed to set up a precommitment bears no fixed relationship to the future reward differential that is thereby rendered
ineffective, and it is generally apt to be much smaller because it acts
at a longer distance from the rewards. To further confound calculation, the cost of a precommitment also includes a variable amount
of harmless reward that also bears no necessary relationship to the
particular reward being avoided; the wider the berth a person must
give his impulse, the more sources of harmless reward he may incidentally have to give up. An alcoholic, say, who must stay away from
parties and all his drinking friends in order to stay off the bottle will
lose more sources of reward than will a person who can simply use
willpower. If Ulysses had not found an easy way to forestall the Sirens,
he would have had to use the much more costly device of not sailing
in that direction at all – although that still might have been less costly
than letting himself succumb to the Sirens.[1]

---

[1] Such defenses as displacement and sublimation are difficult to picture as the
deflection of energy by other energy. They lose none of their characteristics if they

Thus, as viewed by picoeconomics, the cost of avoiding a given impulse may vary from one device to another, and given one device, it may vary as both skill and environmental opportunities vary. The most costly defenses will be those that are the most restricting and inflexible.

Finally, Freud and his followers neglect the topic of will, which they usually note as a manifestation of resistance when they discuss it at all. Wheelis (1956), however, described the will as a frequently beneficial ego function. In his view, the will was the comparatively small amount of energy at the disposal of the ego ("attention cathexis and neutralized drive energy") that if "committed" at a crucial point could change the balance of power between drives. He noted two of the prerequisites for successful personal rules, adequate motivation and clear criteria:

> Will is usually ineffective when ego energy is pitted in a simply negative way against drive energy, as when an alcoholic wills to stop drinking or an adolescent to stop masturbating. Will is ineffective, also, when directed toward a goal which remains general in its formulation – as a will to be happy, to become a better person, or to overcome a neurosis. [Wheelis, 1956]

It would be difficult to say for sure why psychoanalysis has paid so little attention to the will. When Freud was young, it was widely extolled as the highest form of mental organization (Bain, 1859/1886). Perhaps it had become so much the norm of rationality that when he began to explore its shortcomings he took it as a given and saw no need to explain it. In any case, he and his followers have written a

---

are understood as redefinitions of personal rules that initially forbade a whole category of impulses, but afterward permitted an impulse under circumstances that reduced its harmfulness. For instance, a person's anger that was directed at family members and was too costly to be totally prevented later becomes permissible, but only when displaced to a scapegoat, or when sublimated into the effective performance of the person's duty as a policeman. The difference between a pattern that would be called displacement and a pattern that would be called sublimation is mainly one of rule-making skill: If a person finds fault with his neighbor to justify anger that was inspired by his brother, the change probably will not increase his long-range reward; but if he refines the criteria he uses to justify anger, his passion may serve his longest-range interests, and he may become much more effective at getting rewards. In addition to the skill factor, the topography of possible bright lines laid down by one's history or environment (cf. the roads in Figure 5.5) may make the task more difficult for one person than for another.

great deal about compulsion, which, I shall argue, is a natural side effect of personal rules. Likewise, the important defenses of projection and regression, which we have not discussed yet, and other processes that have received psychoanalytic names, such as "cathexis," "object-hunger," and the "superego," will be shown to arise from the modification of spontaneous motivation into will by means of personal rules.

6.1.1 Defense mechanisms vary in their usefulness as precommitments

A few recent analytic writers have said that some defense mechanisms are more benign than others, and some may even be associated with emotional health. Not surprisingly, the better mechanisms are said to be learned at a later age than the poorer (A. Freud, 1966, pp. 30–35; Gedo & Goldberg, 1973; Menninger, 1963, pp. 153–270; Vaillant, 1971). If we look at the functional classes of defense mechanisms proposed in chapter 5, we might indeed guess that some are learned earlier than others. Certainly, reliance on external constraint must come first, probably followed by the child's discovery that he can avert his attention from temptation. The children studied by Mischel's group were forming verbal concepts of this tactic around the age of 5 years (Mischel & Mischel, 1983); younger children not only failed to describe precommitment as a need but also, in their actual attempts to wait for the better but later of two foods, did not make choices that had precommitting effects. Conversely, "the self-control rule that does not seem to become available until some time between the third and sixth grades requires recognition of the value of abstract rather than arousing thoughts" (Mischel, Shoda, & Rodriguez, 1989, p. 937), that is, manipulation of affect.

The perception of one's own current behavior as a precedent predicting future choices in similar situations must be the subtlest possibility that one discovers. Mischel's children sometimes spoke of "oughts," and matters of principle often are discerned in the "anal" struggles of late infancy; but there is no evidence that young children notice the importance of precedents for personal rules or even know that the enforcers of external rules have some choice as to what those rules will be. The belief that rules come from some authority on high and must not be tampered with persists into late childhood (Piaget, 1932/1965) and on into adolescence (Perry, 1981). Children's knowledge of the necessary properties of personal rules, as opposed to their legal skills with external rules, has not been studied. Awareness of personal rule-making is apt to begin begin with a sense of being able to cooperate differentially with various externally given rules.

In the only hierarchy of adaptiveness that is backed by systematic research (Semrad, Grinspoon, & Feinberg, 1973; Vaillant, 1971), the strategies of defense described earlier seem to develop in parallel; most are present even at the least sophisticated level of self-control. Vaillant's table of defense mechanisms (1971) assigns 15 defensive strategies to four levels of adaptiveness, ranging from the least adaptive "narcissistic" level through "immature" and "neurotic" to "mature." He does not deal with external constraint, unless that is the purpose of "acting out" (an "immature" defense). But the attention-controlling defenses are represented on every level: suppression (mature), repression (neurotic), schizoid fantasy or denial through fantasy (immature), and psychotic denial (narcissistic).

Mature emotion control is represented by altruism ("benign and constructive reaction formation"). Reaction formation, the archetype of the emotion controlling defenses, is listed as neurotic in Vaillant's table, as are the reversal of affect and counterphobia that he groups with dissociation and the isolation of affect that he groups with intellectualization. Emotion control is represented at the immature level by passive–aggressive behavior, to the extent that such behavior results from the inhibition of overt rage, and at the narcissistic level by distortion, in which "unpleasant feelings are replaced with their opposites."

Insofar as Vaillant's "anticipation" represents a defense mechanism, it probably uses personal rules; he groups it among the mature defenses with "control through thinking" and "conscious control," typical of the inexplicit terms with which authors have described willpower. At the neurotic level, personal rules are approximated by intellectualization. If, as I shall argue presently, projection is a way of perceiving commitment by personal rules, then rule formation occurs at the immature (projection) and narcissistic (delusional projection) levels. Redefinitions of personal rules are present at two levels: as sublimation (mature) and displacement (neurotic).

It seems that there can be an efficient way to use all four tactics of defense, and none is inconsistent with a mature defensive style. Haan (1963) has reached a similar conclusion, stating that for each of 10 defense mechanisms there is a corresponding coping mechanism.

Vaillant (1976) has added that there is one defense mechanism, suppression, that is associated with signs of emotional maturity in normal adult males. This might be an example of an attention-controlling defense, because he defines it as "the conscious or semi-conscious decision to postpone paying attention to a conscious impulse or conflict." However, the illustrations he lists include "employing a stiff upper lip" and "deliberately postponing but not avoiding," which suggest willpower and thus personal rules. Therefore, we cannot be sure whether his "suppression" represents a single precommitting tactic or combines attention control and personal rules.

People generally endorse personal rules above other self-control tactics in hypothetical situations (Ainslie, 1987a), and this is true of such diverse groups as college students and prisoners. Personal rules seem to be both the most powerful and the most adaptable of the four precommitting tactics. The other tactics seem to function at the edges of the domain of rules, sometimes extending them, sometimes hedging against them, but never coalescing into an overall system. They lack the leverage to govern choice comprehensively as rules do.

6.2 Personal rules transform the nature of choice

Three consequences of rules are particularly important: Personal rules turn the sequential preference pattern described by simple hyperbolic discount curves into the kind of conflict people more often experience, where the prudent and impulsive incentives exert pressure simultaneously. Second, rules tend to change the evaluation of events from a weighing of amounts of reward to a prediction of risks, namely, the risk that an impulsive choice will set a precedent. Third, the magnification of small choices through their importance as precedents gives them a self-confirming property that often overshadows the influence of the incentives that are literally at stake. This positive-feedback effect can produce either a sense of being compelled by forces beyond a person's control or, near the balance point of the choice, the experience of free will.

6.2.1 Impulses exist simultaneously with their controls

In principle, personal rules make it possible for a person never to prefer small, early alternatives at the expense of the series of larger, later ones. He may be able to keep temptations close at hand without succumbing to them. However, although he may always prefer a series of larger, later rewards to the small, early reward at hand, he must even more strongly prefer to have both. The danger is no longer that of the poorer reward coming so close that he will suddenly choose it, but of his finding a credible distinction between that choice and the other members of the series that form the stake of his private side bet. Proximity is still a contributor to his temptation, of course, but the deciding factor is no longer whether or not a prior commitment is too weak, but whether or not a tentative loophole currently appears such that he thinks that he can get away with a transgression. He will not experience this situation as an exotic voyage past some Siren or other, but as a simultaneous struggle between two ways of conceiving a choice. His rules have enabled him to live in close proximity to his temptations, but while he is there the struggle will be continuous rather than episodic. Lapses will occur through loopholes, variously clever and inept, rather than through a global shift of preference in favor of the forbidden activity. A person is apt to express preference for the course of action required by his rule even as he is evading it, as Sjoberg (1983) found in his study of smoking lapses.[2]

6.2.2 Failures of will lead to "vice districts"

The perception of precedents transforms a diffuse array of choices into a single, highly charged dichotomy, which results in more con-

---

[2] Smokers who kept daily logs of their resolve against smoking while attempting abstinence reported no decrease in resolve on days when they lapsed. Sjoberg interpreted this finding as evidence against a change of preference when reward is imminently available, but his design did not provide a way to test the question: Cigarettes were *always* imminently available, and the self-report questions were framed to elicit effort of will, not strength of craving.

sistent behavior toward temptation. The major side effect of such perceptions is that when a lapse occurs, a person is apt to fear that he will lose his ability to control impulses. He might call this fear anxiety, guilt,[3] or foreboding, and unless he is conscious of his internal bargaining process in some way that makes sense to him, he will be apt to say that the fear is unaccountable, that he "knows" there is nothing to be afraid of. Another perception might be that his self-esteem or self-respect is in danger. What is actually in danger is his expectation of following the rule in question, and perhaps rules generally. The danger is proportional to the degree to which he has staked his expectation on that choice. Insofar as he has lost the expectation of following his rule, he is apt to redefine it so as to abandon part or all of it (Marlatt & Gordon, 1980), lest repeated failed attempts to follow it damage the credibility of his rule-following generally.

The smallest retreat would be to redefine his rule from "I will not do X" to "I will not do X without inflicting punishment Y," a rule that he would not have violated. Such a rule might be resilient against temptations of highly variable strength, because the strongest temptations will not ruin it, but will buy their way past it with the prescribed penance. The difficulty with this strategy lies in finding a punishment that will be sufficiently aversive but that the person still will not avoid when it becomes imminent. To do this, he might either set up a long-lasting punishment that never reaches great intensity (e.g., drudgery) or else yield to some impulse that usually commits him to being punished (fighting with family or authorities, say, or getting drunk), hoping that the punishment part of the sequence will deter further lapses more strongly than the opportunity for his new impulsive behavior will encourage them. Preserving personal rules by permitting lapses, followed by punishment, may account for some clinical examples of self-punitiveness (White & Gilliland, 1975, pp. 87–89), which are said to arise from a process of turning sadistic impulses against the self (Freud, 1915/1956g, p. 127), or from an "unconscious sense of guilt" or "need for punishment" (Freud, 1924/1956m, pp. 165–167). As Freud pointed out (1924/1956m, pp. 168–170), it

---

[3] The finding that guilt after a smoking lapse predicts eventual return to smoking (Baer, Kamarck, Lichtenstein, & Ransom, 1989) supports the hypothesis that guilt primarily reflects a decline in expectation of self-control, rather than being a force that strengthens self-control.

may be difficult in practice to tell whether a person is seeking deprivation as a penance or is simply being scrupulous about avoiding impulses.

Other redefinitions in the face of lapses usually will be rationalizations, which will have about the same practical effect as simply giving up on part of the rule. Although this retreat represents a victory for some short-range interest, it may nevertheless have been necessary in order to preserve something of the person's rule structure. By abandoning his most vulnerable rules, a person accepts some impulsive behavior in return for a greater likelihood of following narrower, perhaps more fundamental rules. Here is Freud's migratory horde retreating to hold a less exposed position, a move he called "regression" (1916–1917/1956i, pp. 340–341).

In regressing to a less ambitious rule, a person abandons an area of functioning to the sway of his short-term interest. For example, a person who normally resists thoughts of danger while driving, or self-conscious feelings while talking in public, or the urge for a cigarette while under social pressure, may have his will "broken" by conspicuous failure in one of these endeavors. Subsequently he will have less expectation of control to stake against his urges. However, he might preserve that expectation in some areas by distinguishing the area of loss from his urges generally. That is, if he can interpret his lapse not as a sign that "my will is weak" but that "I can't resist cigarettes," he can save his credibility against other impulses at the cost of virtually abandoning the task on which he was defeated. He is apt to experience a loss of control over these urges when he drives, or talks in public, or faces smoking peers. Such a situation will form a large, stable loophole, a circumscribed lacuna in his impulse controls that may even be experienced as an automatism or irresistible urge. He will "automatically" panic in traffic, freeze while speaking, or reach for a cigarette.

Given such a lacuna, it will be difficult for a person's long-term interest to retrieve its credibility, because the self-confirming property of personal rules works both ways. Once a person has identified a feature that has accompanied past failures, it will be used by the relevant short-range interest to argue that "once more won't make any difference," and by the long-range interest to avoid making losing investments. Such a labeling process has been described by "attribution theory" (Peterson & Seligman, 1984), but as a simple deductive error rather than a compromise between strong motives. Abandonment of a sector of choice-making to one's impulses creates a strongly motivated tendency to lapse that is unlikely to change through mere logic.

Again, the situation has an analog in social groups: Disreputable activities that have been too strongly motivated to outlaw completely become encapsulated in what used to be called "segregated vice districts," areas where by tacit or even explicit agreement the relevant laws are not enforced. The purpose, of course, is to preserve other, "good" neighborhoods from vice.

People's instincts apparently tell them to respond to lapses by enlarging the scope of their rules still further, resolving, for instance, to perform even stricter tasks of abstention or to reform their entire life-styles. In theory, such an addition to the long-range reward at stake could make up for a decreased probability of getting it, but such an act of desperation is rarely convincing. The best strategy to restore a broken rule seems to be to keep resolutions small, as in the Alcoholics Anonymous dictum of "one day at a time," so that a cumulation of actual choices in the right direction can gradually rebuild the kitty of the private side bet. Even so, the area will long be suspect and will be abandoned at the least sign of backsliding.

The periodic accumulation and loss of one circumscribed kitty is the basis of binging. For instance, if temporarily abstinent alcoholic subjects are led to believe that they have taken a drink of alcohol, they report a marked increase in craving, whether or not they have actually had any alcohol (Engel & Williams, 1972; Maisto et al., 1977). Loss of control after the first drink is universally reported at the beginning of binges (Evenson et al., 1973). Likewise, binge eating has been observed to result from a combination of dieting and the person's belief (whether accurate or not) that he has just consumed an over-large caloric load, an event that "triggers overeating by ruining the diet temporarily" (Polivy & Herman, 1985). A person who is suspicious of his self-control in such an area will repeatedly build up some credibility in the area, but hesitate to add his expectation of self-control in other areas to the stake, thus leaving the behavior in question prone to crises of confidence and consequent "losses of control." Without periodic recoveries of some self-control, an abandoned sector takes the form of a stable symptom.

By the time a patient encounters a psychotherapist, the patient will have reached the point that he has given up trying to use his will against his symptom. I have argued elsewhere that the common denominator of successful psychotherapies is that they define a real example of the conflictual situation and give the patient actual experience in resisting a previously rampant urge (Ainslie, 1986b). Techniques to dissuade a patient from using maladaptive defense mechanisms may make such practice easier, but the final result must be that the will regains its credibility. This difficult, subtle achievement could be the same thing as "remoralization," the process that Jerome Frank (1984) identified as the common factor allowing many diverse schools of psychotherapy to produce similar results.

6.2.3 The internal marketplace is no longer free

The second consequence of using rules is a shift in the person's concern from evaluating the magnitude of rewards at stake in a given choice to estimating the risk that he will subsequently perceive himself to have committed a lapse. That is, for individual decisions that are perceived as precedents for much larger categories of decisions, it matters less how profitable the immediate choice promises to be and matters more how likely the person himself is to see it as a violation of a rule. Of course, the ultimate determinant of choice is still the total discounted reward that is expected on each side. But the loss from disobeying a personal rule is difficult to estimate, just as it is difficult to know how the failure of a particular business will affect the stock market. In the wake of a loss, a person might conceive it as unique and not predictive of further lapses. Alternatively, he might see himself as having broken a narrow rule, say a diet, thus reducing his expectation of getting the benefits of that rule, but not boding ill for his behavior toward other rules. However, he might see the lapse predictive of lapses against similar rules, or even of lapses generally, and thereby suffer a much greater decrease in expected reward.

Perhaps he has been barely restraining a very important impulse, say to murder someone, and he suddenly sees himself violate a diet he has hitherto been obeying. He might reasonably interpret this event as indicating that "my impulses are getting stronger," or "I am going out of control." That decrease in his expectations would give him less incentive with which to control his murderous impulses. The consequence would be much greater than the loss of his expected reward from dieting. Furthermore, a person contemplating new loopholes will never be in a position to make confident predictions about consequences. He is apt to conclude that he is best off being cautious and to treat almost any lapse as a potential disaster, however small that lapse may be.

The interface between the process of weighing rewards and the process of estimating the danger from lapses is always an uneasy one. It resembles the interface between the regulated and free-market sectors of a country's economy. In commerce, goods that are priced by regulation distort the prices of related goods and tend to become unavailable, and their price will rebound once controls are removed (Mitchell, 1978, chs. 2 and 10). They generate a black market operated by interests willing to put a cash value on the risk of legal action against them. Analogously, an individual choosing between honor and expedience has always been known to face more than arithmetic difficulties: "The man of honor prices the doing of actions, whereas [economic man] prices only their consequences. It is not clear that 'prices' refers to the same metaphor in each case" (Hollis, 1983, p. 258).

It is not hard to decide which of two foods to eat or which of two friends to visit if these are only matters of taste. The most serious problem in such a case will arise when the person expects them to be about equally rewarding and has to decide arbitrarily. If, however, eating one food would violate a personal rule, or if he has resolved to see or not to see one of the friends, the situation is different. Now he is weighing simple reward against a duty, still an economic process, but one complicated by the need for self-prediction. He must estimate the likelihood that consuming the simple reward will make him lose the expectation of getting a series of larger, later rewards.

Thus, maintenance of categorical rules in the midst of the free motivational marketplace is apt to require skill. In deciding whether or not to obey his diet in a particular case, a person cannot just weigh the value of the proposed indulgence against the value of a series of abstentions. If that series is an example, in turn, of still larger self-control projects, such as "controlling physical desires" or "using will-power generally," he must figure in the estimated damage to the credibility of those projects. He must evaluate additional options, such as finding loopholes to permit consumption in the case at hand, or avoiding the perception of a lapse by not gathering or processing the necessary information – the equivalents, in intrapersonal negotiation, of a businessman hiring lawyers or keeping a false set of books, respectively. By such means the dieter may justify a contemplated excess, or direct his notice away from the properties of his food that are relevant to his diet. Insofar as these evasions have worked, it will be in his long-range interest to study the need for more rules to protect the original rules from just such evasion, redefining them to close loopholes or requiring more systematic testing of whether or not they are being followed.

Personal rules necessarily replace a simple marketplace with a contest between regulation and evasion, but the service they perform for a person's long-range interests often is worth the difficulty. Again, by analogy to commerce, it is rational for a businessman both to vote for a regulation and to try to evade it (Schelling, 1967), but the process is much more complex than simple trading.

Utilitarian theories heretofore have depicted choice-making organisms as analog computers, weighing the values of alternative rewards against each other and reaching a quantitative solution. However, because of the deeply bowed shape of the discount curve and the consequent need for personal rules, the more important tasks facing at least some organisms are digital tasks: People must construct sets of categorical requirements that will permit some kinds of weighings but not others.

Furthermore, a person must use a combination of these two somewhat incompatible modes of analyzing his options. A simple weighing of preferences will leave a person open to temporary changes of preference. On the other hand, a decision-making process that does not respond to weights, but only to categories, will have difficulty in distinguishing between trivial and vital incentives. Individual solutions to the awkward problem of mixing these modes may constitute a large component of people's character styles.

6.3 Prediction of one's future choices tends to be self-confirming

The third consequence of using personal rules is a sensation that some choices are free, and others unfree. The choices that are labeled free are not those dictated by any single motive, whether arising from the environment or from internal pressures like desires or passions. Apparently they must involve some subtlety of the self. Once a train of causality is seen to determine a choice reliably, that choice is called unfree. Thus, freedom has seemed to suffer from a paradox of definition, in that as soon as an author specifies the steps by which he imagines choice to proceed, he takes choice away from the self and thereby renders it unfree. For instance, the philosopher Hollis complains that conventional economic rationality reduces a person to a calculating machine: "Preference is automatically transmitted into outcome so as to solve the maximizing problem. The agent is simply a throughput" (1983, p. 250); see also Dennett (1984, pp. 74–81).

Explanations of the experience of free will that do not violate strict determinism have focused on the unpredictability of free choices. Because the most conspicuous feature of choices that one feels to be free is the sensation that one "might have" done something else (Broad, 1962; James, 1884/1967a), a situation that will render prediction imponderable may suffice to make choices in that situation seem free. Because simple maximizing tasks often can be solved by a formula that will make choice predictable, choices that are free in principle need to be buffered against such external solutions, as, for instance, by being self-referential in some way. Thus, Hollis points out that choices often lead not only to their expected consequences but also to changes in the person's valuation of those consequences; in choosing, the choice-maker is transformed, so that he is "always shaping his identity by his choices" (1983, p. 158). Choice is then no less determinate, but is much less predictable, than a simple choice among goods.

However, changes in tastes or values occur relatively slowly, a fact that would seem to allow for predictability in the short run. By contrast, the self-prediction that is basic to personal rules can shift with each new bit of evidence about one's disposition and thus seems a more likely source of the sensation of freedom: The perception of choices as precedents creates the kind of prisoner's-dilemma payoff matrix seen in Table 5.2. The relative values in such a table fall into one of two rough zones: balanced, so that small changes in the prospects for future cooperation will swing the decision between cooperation and defection, and unbalanced, so that changes in decisions appear to be unlikely. In the balanced zone, an assumption about the direction of the current choice will be a major factor in estimating future outcomes. But this estimate in turn affects the probability that the current choice will be in that direction. Thus, the decision process is recursive – not tautological, but continuously fed back like the output of a transistor to its own input. If a person's prediction about his propensity to make the choice in question is at all open, this feedback process may play a larger role in his decision than any given incentive, external or internal.

A dieter faces a tempting food, guesses that he will be able to resist it, applies the consequences of that guess to the expected outcome matrix as an increase in the likelihood that he will reap the benefits of his diet, and thus has more to bet against the temptation. Then he discovers a possible loophole and thereby incurs a decrease in his expectation of a successful diet because of the chance that he will try the loophole and not get away with it. This decrease may be so great as to make the expected values of lapsing versus continuing to diet about equal, until some other consideration tips his self-prediction one way or the other. Such a process is not subtle conceptually, but it eludes any calculation based only on the contingencies of reward, and it buffers the person's decision against coercion by these contingencies. It may thus generate the experience of exercising free will.

Furthermore, such an explanation allows us to characterize free choices better, rather than saying that they are too close to predict. After all, many behaviors are quite predictable in practice and still are experienced as free. What becomes crucial is the person's belief that a given choice depends on this self-prediction process, in whatever terms he has found to describe his experience of that process. If he believes that a preference is subject to change through such "reflection," he identifies it as free even though it never actually changes.

Because of the force of precedent, the most ordinary examples of decision making are apt to follow this transistorlike pattern. For instance, a person might try to save quarters because he is always needing them for parking meters, but he rules that he will never actually pay a fee to obtain them – certainly not by buying two quarters for a dollar. However, when leaving a tip at a lunch counter, he may find that the usual formula calls for $1.50. The consideration of wanting to save quarters may lead him to leave $2, even though his rule states that he is not to pay money for quarters. The point is that he is weighing neither the current value of half a dollar against the effort of replenishing two quarters in his change supply nor a series of half dollars against a series of such efforts. If he were, then, given figures for his feelings, he could simply calculate the values of the choices as he has defined them. But, on the contrary, he is weighing the effort of getting two quarters against the *risk* that he will see his subterfuge as a lapse *and* the risk that he will see breaking his rule about quarters as a breach of more important rules about the value of money as well. The issue of self-prediction has come to overshadow the ostensible incentives.

Perhaps he recalls a better waiter whom he did not tip extra, which will render a $2 tip in this case clearly suspect. If this consideration tilts the balance away from the larger tip, the risk of his subsequently perceiving a lapse will fall, and his expectation of getting the rewards attendant on following his rules will rise, thus solidifying the decision for the smaller tip. If he notices that this recollection fails to tilt the balance, he may conclude that his motive to leave a larger tip is stronger than he thought, which will increase the risk of a perceived lapse, decrease his confidence that he will win the stake he has bet on his following his rules, and thus move his incentives still further in the direction of the large tip. These effects will be fed back, in turn, to his decision-making process, always positively (i.e., in a direction that will multiply their original impact). Unless the shift is overwhelming, however, he may search for memories that will have a contrary impact, reasons to distinguish the present case from remembered precedents, distractions that may make him lose sight of what he has just recalled, principles that contradict the "don't buy quarters" rule (e.g., not to waste time applying rules to tiny transactions), and so forth. He will search in the service of both his motive not to spend quarters and his motive not to waste money, until one line of reasoning takes him decisively far from the balance point.

The recursive nature of the volition process bridges the distinction between diagnostic and causal acts, about which those involved in the psychology of rationality have lately had much to say, using the name "Newcomb's problem" (Campbell & Sowden, 1985; Elster, 1989b, pp. 186–214; Quattrone & Tversky, 1986). Diagnostic acts are symptoms of a condition, but do not cause it, such as the involuntary movements of a person with mercury poisoning; causal acts bring on the condition, such as exposing oneself to mercury. Acts governed by willpower evidently are both diagnostic and causal. Drinking too much is diagnostic of a condition, alcoholism out of control, but it causes further uncontrolled drinking when the subject, using it to diagnose himself as out of control, is discouraged from trying to will sobriety.

Early in this century Max Weber puzzled over how Calvinist theology could have increased its adherents' self-control when it preached predestination, that is, when it held people to be helpless as to whether or not they would be damned for their behaviors. His solution was, in effect, that the doctrine of predestination transformed a person's array of individual choices about whether or not to do good into a single, comprehensive private side bet, the stake of which was his whole expectation of being saved:

> [Good works] are the technical means, not of purchasing salvation, but of getting rid of the fear of damnation. . . . [The Calvinist] himself creates his own salvation, or, as would be more correct, the conviction of it. But this creation cannot, as in Catholicism, consist in a gradual accumulation of individual good works to one's credit, but rather in a systematic self-control which at every moment stands before the inexorable alternative, chosen or damned. [Weber, 1904/1958, p. 115]

Under such a belief system, doing good is sometimes held to be a superstitious behavior, in that it is purely diagnostic, so that emitting it for the sake of seeing oneself emit it is fooling oneself (Quattrone & Tversky, 1986). The several authors who have pointed this out have not considered an important possibility: Doing good for its diagnostic value may not invalidate that diagnostic value. That is, if one can do good for any reason, that may be valid evidence of being among the saved; such a situation would not contradict predestination, but only provide another mechanism through which destiny might act. The expectation of salvation might be self-confirming, and the ability to maintain such an expectation might be the defining trait of the saved. This is much the same thing as saying that a higher power will grant sobriety to some alcoholics and that one's acknowledgment of helplessness against alcohol is a sign that one may be among those who will receive that favor. Such a shift in a person's concept of causality is not casuistry. It marks the formation of a more thorough personal rule, one that apparently deters the hedging that weakens personal rules whenever they are recognized as such (see section 5.6.1).

The celebrated James–Lange theory of emotion also seems to have been based on the observation of recursive decision making: When a person is in doubt whether or not he will succumb to a negative emotion (or achieve a positive one), the appearance of a physical manifestation of the emotion will be evidence that the emotion is gaining ground, evidence that may, like the alcoholic's first drink, throw the decision beyond the zone of balance. "He anticipates certain feelings, and the anticipation precipitates their arrival" (James, 1890, vol. 2, p. 458). Darwin had said the same thing:

> The free expression by outward signs of an emotion intensifies it. On the other hand, the repression, as far as this is possible, of all outward signs softens our emotions. He who gives way to violent gestures will increase his rage; he who does not control the signs of fear will experience fear in greater degree. [1872/1979, p. 366]

That is, a person does not emit a simple behavior, either an emotion followed by physical signs or physical signs followed by an emotion, but rather makes a series of predictions of the apparent strength of an emotion vis-à-vis his controls – predictions that tend to be self-confirming.

Such analyses go beyond Albert Bandura's recent assertion that free will represents the operation of "self-generated influences" on behavior (1986, p. 39). If a person merely acts upon himself, he may be just as much a "throughput" as in Hollis's complaint. It is the interdependence of self-action and self-prediction that undermines the possibility of a single maximizing solution to a person's motivational puzzles. Of course, both self-prediction and self-action would in turn lack any rationale without the underlying problem of temporary preference.

Thus, the problem of free choice still can be solved within the marketplace, but the estimation of the risks, leveraged by the feedback process just described, introduces an element of self-prediction that moves the problem beyond any straightforward calculus. Furthermore, decisions will change, not just over a series of behaviors or moves in the prisoner's-dilemma game, but over a series of forecasts of the consequences of a single move. Here is an ample hiding place for the mystery of free will.

6.4 Compulsiveness is a side effect of personal rules

Conversely, unbalanced decision matrices are only driven further out of balance by the self-prediction process. If a person knows of no way of defining precedents and no manipulation of his attention that would change his expected line of choice, he is apt to feel unfree, despite, or rather because of, the fact that his behavior is strongly motivated.

Two kinds of coercive motivational forces have been described by philosophers and theologians since antiquity: a capricious, seemingly irrational force that is commonly called an impulse, and a relentless, highly consistent force that is often called a compulsion. For example, Aristotle described not only passions, which could overcome people suddenly, but also dispositions, forces that develop through consistent choices (habit) in one direction and subsequently impel further choices in that direction (Kenny, 1963, ch. 8). Similarly, Kant depicted an egolike part of the will, the *Wilkür*, that can let itself be led on one side by impulses and on the other by personal maxims for conduct (the content of the *Wille*) (Kant, 1960, pp. 15–49). He said that choice in either direction creates a disposition that impels further choice in that direction. The philosopher of religion, Paul Ricoeur, has said that freedom of will is encroached upon not only by sin but also by moral law, through the "juridization of action" by which "a scrupulous person encloses himself in an inextricable labyrinth of commandments" (Ricoeur, 1971, p. 11). It has long been recognized that a person can experience coercion in two distinct modes.

From the perspective of the matching law, the subjectively unfree choices of single imminent rewards known as impulses represent the ordinary state of nature. Compulsions, on the other hand, seem to result from overcommitment by personal rules:

A person with little skill at formulating rules or with unusually strong impulses is apt to compensate for those defects by increasing the number of behaviors that he classifies as covered by each private side bet, or by connecting each bet with some or all of his other bets. Either way of making his choices more interdependent will increase the differential reward for turning down each temptation, but at the expense of making his behavior more rigid: Increasing his tendency to classify his behaviors as impulsive or not will give his experience a dry, rational, lawyerly quality, because he will choose his actions less and less for their intrinsic value, and more according to whether or not they meet the terms of a bet. Increasing the interdependence of his bets will give every choice a cataclysmic, life-or-death quality, because he will incur an enormous decrease in expectations if he perceives himself to have violated any personal rule. This is entirely realistic: There is evidence that the damage to self-control following a lapse is proportional to the perceived generality of the rule[4] over both time and kinds of choices, at least for smokers (Curry, Marlatt, & Gordon, 1987). In consequence, the person will come to feel that he acts at great peril, and he will begin to examine each choice with such care as to render himself utterly indecisive.

Clinicians would label the behavior just described, bound to a restrictive set of rules to the point that it feels unfree, as compulsive. I shall also use "compulsive" in that way, realizing that the term sometimes has been applied to behaviors that I would call impulsive (as in "compulsive drinking"), a usage that seems especially common when their isolation in a vice district has made them seem uncontrollable.

According to psychoanalytic wisdom, the lawyerly, scrupulous person just described would be apt to exhibit the "compulsive defense mechanisms": undoing, reaction formation, isolation of affect, and

---

[4] Curry and many cognitively oriented researchers are reporting on subjects' "attributions" rather than personal rules specifically. However, "internal" attributions of causality in a current choice clearly are part of the process of predicting future choices; the extent to which these predictors interact will be proportional to how general they are seen to be over diverse categories ("global") and over time ("stable").

regression (A. Freud, 1966, p. 43; Sandler & Joffe, 1965). But his symptoms – the inordinate fear of impulses, overconcern with principle, rigid behavior guarded by the threat of guilt, and indecisiveness – are not explained by the presence of these defense mechanisms. It is difficult to imagine how undoing could ever be of any practical help in forestalling impulses, although it may well be inspired by a "defensive purpose" (Freud, 1926/1956n, pp. 119–120, 164). Going through the motions of avoiding or undoing an impulse that has already prevailed might be a favorite kind of self-punishment (see section 6.2.2) to make the impulse less likely in the future (White & Gilliland, 1975, pp. 65–68), but should not be more effective than any other mild self-punishment. It might be just an attempt to imagine that the impulsive behavior did not take place, which, insofar as it succeeded, would decrease the effectiveness of the relevant personal rule, like any other way of ignoring lapses.

Reaction formation, which operates by cultivating an emotional process that reduces the motivation for an impulse, would not be expected to lead to the compulsive person's timid, legalistic style. In fact, Freud did not say that reaction formation was specific to compulsive neurosis, but only that it took on a "universal," generalizing quality when used by a compulsive person (1926/1956n, pp. 157–158). Isolation of affect, another emotion-controlling device, would not in itself lead to a legalistic style. However, as was explained in chapter 5, a person who controls himself largely by personal rules should prefer it to attention control as a supplement to his defensive strategy. Regression, as I have just argued, is not an impulse-controlling device, but a response to failures of impulse control; it represents a retreat to more elementary personal rules from rules that have proved untenable.

Although undoing, reaction formation, isolation of affect, and regression often can be found together with compulsive characteristics, the use of personal rules must be a defensive operation in its own right, and central to the phenomenon of compulsion. We recognize this when we say that a relatively healthy patient has "good compulsive defenses." Certainly no one would be pleased to see a defensive style that was simply a combination of undoing, reaction formation, isolation of affect, and regression. The operation that gives compulsive defenses both their power and their symptomatic side effects seems to be the making of personal rules. This mechanism can account for compulsive symptoms in much greater detail than have previous explanations derived from learning theory, which have held that compulsions arise from excessive timidity (Carr, 1974) or excessive arousal.

6.4.1 Even compulsive people may be unable to report their rules

However, the reader may object to this explanation. Rules are conventionally understood to be conscious things – deliberate, reportable, "ego-syntonic." A problem with explaining compulsive phenomena in terms of personal rules is that people usually are only vaguely aware of judging their behaviors as precedents, if they are able to report such a process at all; and far from feeling like the architects of their compulsions, they feel imprisoned by them, moved by a force that is outside of the will and often contrary to it (Fenichel, 1945, p. 268; Shapiro, 1965, p. 33). It was such considerations that led Freud to explain compulsions and defenses generally in terms of repression and a realm of unconscious functioning created by repression.

I have described personal rules as solutions to intrapersonal bargaining problems. But can bargaining occur without awareness? Furthermore, if bargaining does occur without awareness, is it not then unconscious, the very theoretical construct I have just found unnecessary in Freud's account? If I am going to invoke repression, how have I improved on existing theory?

Interpersonal bargaining often occurs trivially, without awareness, that is, without the participants noticing that it is an example of bargaining: A newcomer to a community establishes a place in the pecking order while seeming to be just "socializing"; an official enforces a regulation more or less strictly depending on how "deserving" a citizen seems to be; a young couple establish their respective roles without mentioning them in words. Likewise, internal bargaining can be second nature; and, once completed, neither need be repeated often.

For instance, procrastination is not often described as an example of bargaining with oneself, but introspection will almost always discover elements of bargaining. In the simple example of getting up in the morning (for those who must make an effort to do so), a person may initially report only that it happens on time or that it does not, but when asked about the time of decision, often he can recall his thoughts, such as "I do not have to get out of bed this minute, I can rest for the time being without spoiling the possibility of eventually doing it." His reasoning may even have run like this: "I will enjoy my rest now and not examine the long-term consequences." Usually he will have noticed that not getting up on time is a bad sign and that failure to carry through a current resolve to get up undermines future resolve. Futhermore, on most days he will not try to estimate the effects of his choice even intuitively, but go by past estimates in the same way that people in a pecking order or a negotiated role come to assume that reopening past negotiations would not produce a new outcome. That is, few of his decisions will involve fresh conflict, even though they are determined by a history of conflict. His failure to examine the contingencies that determine his motives, and to reexamine his motives on most occasions, does not set this topic apart from most areas of psychological functioning.

However, the question remains whether or not his behavior is "unconscious" as Freud used the term. The category of reward-governed behavior is clearly larger than that of conscious behavior. Many of our skeletal-muscle movements are unreportable – mannerisms, postures, facial expressions that we learn about only when someone says we look angry, or tired, or anxious. Differential punishment may even shape behavior during sleep (Granda & Hammack, 1961). But Freud distinguished only two categories of mental processes of which a person is not aware: "preconscious" processes, which are not reportable simply because the person is not entertaining them at the moment, and "unconscious" processes, which the person resists noticing because to do so would be aversive. The former category is trivial as far as motivational conflict is concerned, and Freud did not enlarge upon it. The latter category lay at the heart of his theory of psychopathology.

Neither category seems to fit most people's experience of their personal rules. The operation of a person's will is not preconscious, because he cannot report how it operates even when his attention is directed toward that area. But we should not call it unconscious unless he resists noticing its operation. A third category is logically possible: processes that are not noticed because a person does not have the concepts that would let him appreciate their importance, although he is not motivated to avoid such notice.

Consider a person who resists the temptation to go off a diet but does not know why. He may even know that he can violate the diet under some circumstances (on his birthday, on Thanksgiving day, etc.) without doing the same damage as if he had violated it arbitrarily, but still not know why that is the case. This kind of unreportability is due to the fact that a person has not noticed certain aspects of his experience, just as a person may become a skilled bicycle rider without being able to explain how he does it. Such functional knowledge is not unconscious in Freud's sense of being resisted, but it is not preconscious either. It might be called unsymbolized.

Freud believed that a compulsive behavior was the resultant of an impulse and a moral prohibition, and his belief is consistent with the model of personal rule formation developed here (Freud, 1913/1956e, pp. 26–35). However, he believed that compulsions are experienced as involuntary because a person is motivated to keep his attention away from the motives that govern them, that is, to repress those motives. Many personal rules, perhaps most, are unreportable, but there is no reason that a person should have repressed them. They represent neither impulses that might be forestalled by attention control nor facets of the self that a person should want to deny.

It is true that a person might have reason to repress the fact that he can modify his rules. As we noted earlier, that could protect them in the same way the Alcoholics Anonymous dictum of "helplessness" against alcohol protects a rule that forbids any kind of drinking (see sections 5.6.1 and 6.3). Certainly children who are not yet skilled with *interpersonal* rules are loath to notice their changeability (Piaget, 1932/1965). But a person's inability to report even the existence of established rules probably is due to his having no sensible way to explain their function. Even though a person has developed a practical facility with personal rules through experience, our culture's belief that discounting the future occurs in shallow exponential curves, when it occurs at all, denies him a rationale for that knowledge. Thus, rules tend to remain unsymbolized.

6.4.2 How a rule becomes a compulsion

The degree to which a rule for behavior takes on a compulsive, externally imposed quality may partly depend on how actively a person sets up the private side bet that enforces it. Private side bets may be formed spontaneously whenever a person notices that his individual choices to resist or yield to minor temptations are members of a larger class. He begins to refer his recurring choices to crude, possibly unnamed, categories having to do with when he will give in to the urges for procrastination, lying, or wasting money, as well as the urges for such unwelcome but controllable emotions as panic, disgust, and anger. For instance, he may notice that if he does not get up as soon as his alarm rings, he begins to lose his ability to get up on time. After some experience with this problem, he may find that he "cannot" stay in bed once the alarm has rung.

Likewise, for a person who is susceptible to panic, fear is never far away. Where he can resist the urge, he must resist it, lest he take warning from the failure and abandon another area of functioning to his fear. He is unlikely to describe this requirement as a rule, but simply as using some kind of effort to fight the fear; those cues that, according to the foregoing analysis, lead him to abandon the effort by predicting its failure he will simply describe as objects of fear. Conversely, if some coincidental circumstance has been accompanied by a period of confidence, he may "superstitiously" begin seeking repetitions of that circumstance in order to ward off panic. But if the superstition is merely a guess about his likelihood of panic, its true nature will soon be revealed, and it will be abandoned. A durable superstition functions as a rule (e.g., "I will not panic when my spouse is beside me," or "when my horoscope is good," or "when I have performed the correct ritual"). The stake of such a rule is the person's expected freedom from panic in the area that is in doubt. He has gained power over an urge, but at the expense of being bound to his particular talisman – take it away, and what may once have been an open choice becomes helpless abandonment to the relevant vice district. In either case, the effect appears to be magical.

Many phenomena called supernatural probably are examples of an unrecognized private side-betting process, as I have argued elsewhere in the case of oaths (Ainslie, 1975, p. 483): An oath defines a category of behaviors – "things sworn to" – that a person thereafter performs or fails to perform as a set, with the goodwill or wrath of the sacred entity sworn upon explaining the consequent double-or-nothing quality of his motivation. As we have just seen, Max Weber ascribed the behavioral consequences of Calvinism to a similar mechanism. Without a concept of private side betting, people naturally postulate a supernatural version of ordinary public side bets, a perception that in no way diminishes the effectiveness of the bets.

A personal rule that has gravitated into being as in the example of counterphobia just described may seem to be more alien than one that a person sets up by a deliberate oath or resolution. However, most rules for most people arise through just such mindless practice, without seeming like alien forces. The compulsive quality of a rule may depend more on the extent to which the person is actually bound by it. If the impulses that necessitated the rule seem disastrous, if the person knows no other defenses that would be adequate to forestall these impulses, and if he does not see safe ways to redefine the rule to make it adapt to his changing needs, then he will be apt to say that he is compelled by a force outside his own will.

For instance, if he saw the act of stepping on a crack as symbolic of an urge to break his mother's back, and feared that his anger at his mother, once aroused, would be so compelling that any expression of it must be forbidden, he might become "unable" to step on cracks. He would be said to have developed a compulsion. The actual force of the compulsion would be the aggregate effect of the whole category of long-term rewards at stake, that is, everything he would fear losing if he hurt his mother. Even if, in the course of therapy, he were led to remember how he had originally come to classify stepping on cracks as an antimother gesture, he probably would continue to experience the compulsion unless he actually braved a revision of his rule against ever hurting his mother.

A person may or may not realize that he can voluntarily modify the force of his personal rules. When people are aware of this power, they sometimes try to nullify a rule by violating it. For instance, a person may deliberately break a perfect attendance record, or "discard" his virginity, simply so as not to have the incentives that have collected along those boundaries as forces in his future decision making. Arnold Bennett, a popular novelist and advice-giver early in this century, warned against the way arbitrary rules seem to grow and solidify in some people by a process he called "fussiness." His remedy was to break such rules systematically before they acquired a force greater than the person's other motives could counteract:

> [If the fusser has developed a rule never to wear black clothes,] let him proceed to the shopping quarter at once. Let him not order a suit-to-measure of black. Let him buy a ready made suit. Let him put it on in the store or shop, and let him have the other suit sent home. Let him then walk about the town in black.... He is saved! [Bennett, 1918, p. 80]

From a clinical viewpoint, Fenichel described how the voluntary avoidance of phobic objects can gradually acquire an obsessive or compulsive quality, that is, the sensation that "I am compelled to feel as if this or that were the case" (Fenichel, 1945, p. 552). What he and Bennett seem to have been pointing out is that a rule can grow larger than the other motives that bear on a particular behavior and that a person has some opportunity to encourage or thwart that growth.

It is such growth, then, modifiable as the growth of a tree or a sand bar is modifiable, but not deliberate in itself, that builds unopposable compulsions. Personal rules may arise without a person's active participation; they can make large categories of differential rewards hinge on decisions of little intrinsic importance, and they may be very difficult to modify once established. Their conflict with impulsive attempts to define loopholes, if carried to an extreme, can be expected to result in those things that characterize the compulsive personality: lawyerly overconcern with principle; timidity, from fear of setting or violating a precedent; and rigid behavior, guarded by the threat of guilt or foreboding. The experience of compulsion simply represents a person's accurate perception of a binding commitment.

6.4.3 Ordinary coercion by rules is experienced as conscience

Freud's elaboration of the two forces coercing choice is consistent with the picoeconomic model: He called them the id and the superego (Freud, 1923/1956l). He meant the id to be the source of all psychic energy, that is, the source of a person's capacity to be differentially rewarded (Freud, 1923/1956l, p. 30n). Only a portion of the id was said to be in conflict with the person's long-range goals. Similarly, in the behavioral model described here, not all imminent rewards will be temporarily preferred to later alternatives (Freud, 1923/1956l, p. 24, fig. 1; Waelder, 1960, p. 84). Depending on which frame of reference is used, impulses can be seen either as those behaviors that are temporarily preferred or as that part of the id that is in conflict with the ego. Imminent rewards that do not interfere with major delayed rewards combine with them to produce unambivalent motives, which, as was noted in section 4.1, probably are the bases of the "conflict-free" mental functions (Hartmann, 1958).

Freud depicted the superego as the function most people would call conscience (1930/1956o, p. 127), though without the usual implication that the person had to be conscious of its operations. Because he did not discuss the will as such, we cannot know how he thought they were related. The one psychoanalytic writer who has discussed willpower has assigned the superego a key role in its generation, giving as an example the case "when one says to one's self ... 'I'll stake my honor on it' " (Wheelis, 1956). Often people use the terms "conscience" and "superego" to imply more than simply willpower: The will is thought of as a tool that serves the current self, whereas both conscience and superego usually are described as partially outside this self, a "voice" or a second awareness – "conscientia" (Lehmann, 1973) – that measures a current choice against an inflexible standard. However, the essence of both willpower and the conscience/superego is to define choice as a matter of principle in order to counteract the promptings of impulse.

Freud said that the superego develops through internalization of the perceived demands of others, mainly parents. His mechanism was indirect – the child's fear of the parents' anger leads him to take their side against himself and thus direct his own anger inward – but still it was driven by the child's experience of their "unattackable authority" (1930/1956o, p. 129). Fear of authority is also the basis of behavioral and commonsense notions of socialization (see section 2.1) (Aronfreed, 1968, pp. 268–272; Eysenck, 1964, ch. 5; Fenichel, 1945, pp. 162–169; Freud, 1923/1956l, pp. 28–39; Freud, 1938/1956q, p. 145; Waelder, 1960, pp. 187–195).

But if that were the mechanism, the most punitive parents would be expected to produce the most conscientious children, whereas in fact they are likely to produce psychopaths. A child's adoption of parental rules is not proportional to the force with which they are laid down (Aronfreed, 1968, pp. 308–309; Freedman, 1965; Lepper, 1981). Furthermore, conscience does not operate to enforce only one's duty to other people (i.e., morality). As the philosopher Fingarette has pointed out, purely personal impulse control, such as sticking to a diet, is a matter of conscience: "We can have a conscience and feel guilty in matters entirely non-moral" (1979, p. 162).

Although the people around a child have some power to affect, through reward and punishment, which of his behaviors will be especially costly, hyperbolic discount curves predict that he will have an intrinsic problem of impulse control quite apart from the demands of his society (see section 6.1). Therefore, it is unnecessary to postulate that the major motivation for adopting personal rules comes from parents. Rather, it makes sense to say that a child inevitably forms a superego because of his general need for impulse control, and frequently the leadership of other people will furnish the terms for the necessary personal rules. For instance, obedience to his parents' demands may provide a child with a safe boundary against his impulses. The undertaking may require him to forgo a fair amount of harmless reward but still may be more responsive to his need than any rule he can construct using purely arbitrary criteria – especially when he is a novice at rule-making. A parent's role is ultimately as model, showing him both effective rules and skillful rule-making; but parental authority may also provide the motivation necessary for the child to practice some rules long enough to discover their usefulness.

A person can even use the memory of his parents' behavior as an effective criterion for a personal rule. For instance, if he has trouble controlling his temper and remembers the situations in which his parents got angry, he may let himself get angry only when he perceives himself in one of those situations. Such a detailed rule for his anger may serve some of his purposes better than more general rules he might construct from logical principles (having to do with whether or not another person was being deceitful or was endorsing reprehensible opinions or represented an immediate danger, etc.) and may replace or supplement such logical boundaries.

Using parents or other leaders as sources of criteria for personal rules could correspond to the defense mechanism called "identification," although this term might also refer to simple avoidance of the unpleasant perception of being inferior to a leader (Fenichel, 1945, pp. 268–269; A. Freud, 1966, pp. 109–121). When a person experiences such pressures toward impulsiveness that he has little feeling of being able to choose his rules, he may find himself compelled by a parental example he would otherwise like to reject. Insofar as personal rules that hinge on parental leadership become irreplaceable, in the sense that the person could not achieve acceptable impulse control without them, he will report that he is stuck with his parental precepts whether he wants them or not, and he can be said to have "introjected" them.

The parents with whom children most strongly identify are those who are most useful in teaching criteria for rules, but no child is completely able to avoid using material from his parents to form boundaries between his impulses and his own long-range interests. The parents who most interfere with good superego formation are those who make internal impulse control less necessary because of their willingness to manipulate their children's motives directly and those who leave their children to their own impulse-controlling devices too early. The former should cause children to rely relatively more on impulse-controlling devices other than personal rules; the latter should produce the harsh superego and resulting compulsive traits that are said to be associated with "precocious ego development" (Sandler & Joffe, 1965). Of course, children rarely are able to report the properties of their personal rules (see section 5.6.2). A child may attribute the force of his personal rules to his parents' demandingness and thus seem to himself and to others to be experiencing the conditioned fear that has been so often described.

6.4.4 Personal rules may serve midrange interests

Every author who has dealt with the two apparent forces impinging on the self has agreed that coercion by the "lower," or impulsive, principle should be minimized. However, the desirability of coercion by powerful personal rules has been in dispute. Before the nineteenth century there seems to have been general agreement that safety lay on the side of lawfulness. The Romans applauded the kind of iron will that allowed Mucius Scaevola to plunge his right hand into fire when his purposes called for it. Kant said that people should use their free will to embrace an inflexible moral law (Kant, 1960, pp. 15–49). Even in modern times, personal rules sometimes are valued uncritically. For instance, neither Piaget (1932/1965) nor Kohlberg (1963), the two authors who have most studied the development of moral judgment in children, described in their original theories a stage higher than one in which the individual has the ability to choose the principles by which he will be bound.[5]

However, modern man has been warned by a number of writers that his sense of will may decrease rather than increase if he binds himself too extensively to rules. Shortly after Kant and Hegel developed bookkeeping tools to test all particular behaviors for their conformity to universal, rational standards, Kierkegaard began to point out how that kind of rationality could erode the vitality of human experience, a view that grew into existentialism (May, 1958). Existential values such as authenticity and living in the present (Ellenberger, 1958) are clearly threatened by a perception that gives one's current choice more importance as a precedent than as something in itself; such a perception is close to what existential therapists, following Kierkegaard, call an "idealistic orientation," an improvement over the pursuit of transient pleasure, but still inauthentic because of rules' legalistic side effects (Kobasa & Maddi, 1983). Victorian novelists such as Hardy and Chekhov are said to have begun illustrating that "obedience to [moral] prescriptions may constitute moral weakness" (Evans, 1975). Theologians have long known of the dangers of "scrupulosity," the attempt to govern oneself minutely by rules (Davison, 1888, pp. 156–183; Ricoeur, 1971, p. 11). The psychologist Loevinger put conscientiousness ("the internalization of rules") high in her sequence of ego development, but below an "autonomous" stage characterized by "a toleration for ambiguity" (Loevinger, 1976, pp. 15–26). In effect, she warned her readers against settling even for principles as the final arbiters of choice.

---

[5] Kohlberg (1973) has actually proposed a seventh stage that reaches beyond morality to an Eriksonian "integrity," but its mechanism is somewhat mystical, and its relationship to personal rules is unclear.

Writers in the tradition of empirical utilitarianism have sometimes come to similar conclusions. Freud said that the goal of therapy was not only to expand the functioning of the ego at the expense of the id but also to "make it more independent of the superego" (Hatcher, 1973). William James said that "the highest ethical life . . . consists at all times in the breaking of rules which have grown too narrow for the actual case" (James, 1890, p. 209). Martin Hollis's recent criticism of "economic man" raised the same concern:

> A Rational Economic Man . . . must be able to reflect on whether the upshot of his calculations is truly the rational course of action. This is to raise a query about the base of the calculation. . . . A person may find himself locked into his preferences against his real interests. [1983, p. 260]

The message is that personal rules can become prisons.

It is unlikely that such self-imposed prisons serve a person's longest-range interest. He must, of course, expect his rule to serve a longer-range interest against a shorter-range interest; it is only this property that gives a rule its self-enforcing power. However, a rule can serve a midrange interest against both shorter- and longer-range interests. The motivations for activities that are preferred in the sellout range may combine to form rules, as depicted in Figure 6.1. Such a situation is especially apt to arise when a rule that formerly served a person's longest-range interests becomes gradually more rigid and less productive (see section 9.3), leading to the penny-wise, pound-foolish choice pattern noted earlier. The retreat from difficult rules that is sometimes called regression (discussed in section 6.2.2) may occur not only from a strict rule to a more permissive one but also from a subtle rule to one that is more concrete. When a person is at his best, he may maintain a rule to eat, or spend money, or behave sexually according to a criterion of whether or not he thinks he will feel good about the choice in retrospect, but otherwise he may have to choose concrete rules like diets, budgets, or social prescriptions, rules that serve his longest-range interest poorly but that are at least able to forestall addiction-range preferences. Similarly, a person serving his longest-range interest may be able to base his choices on empathy with other people generally, but he may regress to a position of empathizing only with those who are conventionally moral, or even only with those who are of his nation, religion, or family. He may even abandon empathy and serve only duty.

Rules may serve sellout-range interests from their inception. Referring again to the example in section 4.3.3, a person may believe that his greatest long-range reward will come from being generous, but find that relatively distant incentive overwhelmed by long-standing rules for thrift. He might try to make a rule requiring generosity, of course. However, that might be defeated not only by the greater discounting of its more delayed rewards (in the same way that a rule can be inadequate to defeat an impulse) but also by the greater ambiguity of the concept; it is more difficult to be sure that a person has been ungenerous than that he has exceeded a budget. This ambiguity may allow his midrange interests to prevail by rationalizing or overlooking behaviors that at a distance he himself would call miserly. Thus, the rules for thrift may prove more robust than those for generosity.

Rules maintaining sellouts may be especially difficult to overcome where they have been toughened by struggles with still briefer preferences like gambling or addictive shopping or getting drunk; the moral rigidity of reformed alcoholics is notorious. Don Juans are said to be fearful of sexual passivity, and the frigid of sexual spontaneity. Miserliness is apt to represent a mastery of financial impulsiveness, perfectionism of carelessness, workaholism of procrastination. A person who inhibits his aggressiveness too rigidly becomes a "weenie" (Chance, 1989). Anorexia nervosa seems to represent a preoccupation with maximizing perceived self-control with respect to food. Less evident but still probably pathogenic are the forestalling of one's spontaneous empathy toward others, seen in posttraumatic stress and other disorders, and the achievement of insensitivity to emotions generally, which characterizes the syndrome of alexithymia described by Peter Sifneos (Nemiah, 1977). An examination of why personal rules come to serve interests in the sellout range with some frequency will have to wait until we have discussed more of their properties (see sections 9.3 and 9.4).

The defining feature of those temporary preferences that are maintained by personal rules is an absence of the sharp urge that marks individual impulses. They are dispassionate, and what pleasures are attached to them are those of the collector, not the lover.

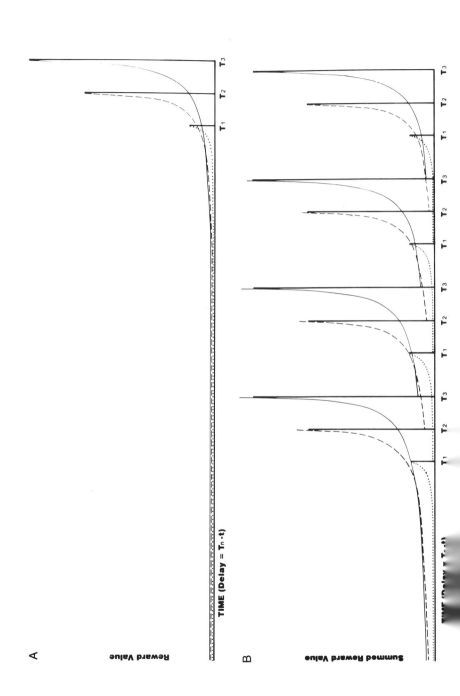

A

Reward Value

TIME (Delay = T_n-t)

B

Summed Reward Value

TIME (Delay = T_n-t)

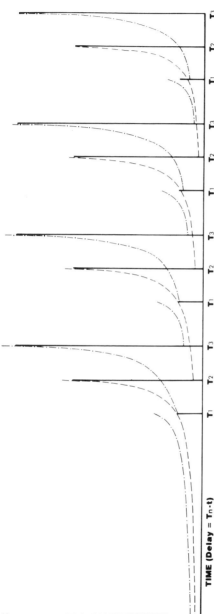

C

TIME (Delay = T_n-t)

Summed Reward Value

Figure 6.1. How rules can serve midrange interests: The discounted values of three rewards (13:70:100) such that (A) in a single choice, the first temporarily dominates the second; (B) at the beginning of a series of four choices, the first never dominates the second, but the second dominates the third; (C) only if the first "allies" with the third can it dominate the second before such a series. If our choosing either the first or the second reward ends the contest, the second will wind up chosen if and only if (1) it has fostered a personal rule and (2) the third has not allied with the first.

Their apparent proliferation in modern times may well be caused by an environment that is much more under our arbitrary control than the one in which the human race evolved, an environment that thus puts us more in danger from our own impulses than from external perils. That still other rule-based pathologies have not been described may be only because it is difficult to quantify their harm. The failure to "rise above a rule that has grown too narrow for the actual case" is at most a relative failure, usually combined with the mastery of an impulse that previously had done demonstrable harm. There are many people who have overcome youthful recklessness to the point that they avoid even worthwhile risks, others who have mastered their gullibility to the extent that they are maladaptively cynical, and others who have contained their whimsy within such comprehensive rules that they permit themselves only "things that make economic sense," despite the aesthetic losses of which Scitovsky and others have complained (Csikszentmihalyi, 1977; Lasch, 1984; Scitovsky, 1976). The desperation of such people is a quiet one, and so has gone unnamed in both diagnostic parlance and common speech.

In the longest run, such a person may find his spontaneous behavior without the rule to be less harmful than the rule – better to be fat than anorectic, vulnerable than alexithymic, fallibly human than rigidly perfect. Systems of self-government abiding strictly by Kantian principles may represent the "pharisaism" warned of by some Christian theologians, sellouts that the person can expect to regret (von Hildebrand & Jourdain, 1955, pp. 13–21). Despite such costs, people are apt to be dominated by series of rewards recruited through explicit rules, rather than by the richer but riskier prospects that subtler principles offer.

Because of the power of personal rules, a person's long-range interest is apt to be more threatened by sellouts than by addictions. A person with a practical knowledge of rules may adopt some compensatory principles, as England once established courts of equity to soften the rigidity of its courts of law, but these only partially solve the problem. For instance, a student may find that his attempts to control procrastination have led to such ambitious rules for doing homework that he allows himself no recreation, and thus is torn between evenings of grinding on one hand and the guilt that attends failure of his will on the other. If he realizes that his rules have become maladaptive, he may make a rule *limiting* the amount of homework he may do (e.g., no more than 2 hours no matter what) and thereby limit the danger homework was posing to his other goals. However, this is a stopgap measure at best, and the student may not even think of so bold and counterintuitive a step. He will then be open to "rescue" by social pressure for parties, the challenge of video games, or even a sudden realization that there is no point to staying in school. In like fashion, a person whose rules against anger have become impossibly confining needs to define some adequately frequent exceptions, lest he be overtaken by periodic urges to drink until he is no longer "himself" – naturally, even brutish rage expressed while he is not himself need not threaten the rules that govern him while he is sober. Accordingly, seasoned clinicians have learned to look behind complaints of addiction to see if they may be allied with a genuine long-range interest to get relief from overgrown rules.

The most stubborn sellouts cannot be controlled by the clever redrafting of concrete rules, but require a person to develop clear perceptions of the criteria actually necessary to realize his long-range interest. To meet such standards as "mutuality in relationships" or "toleration for ambiguity" may be impossible for the beginner; indeed, they may elude a person for a lifetime. Even when a person knows the inadequacy of concrete rules, he still may be unable to formulate rules that can adequately motivate giving up the midrange reward while being subtle enough not to harden his character.

Because the effectiveness of a rule gives it power not only against shorter-range interests but also against longer-range ones, a person may incur a long-range loss by adopting a concrete rule that serves midrange interests with great efficiency. A person trying to contain his anger may figure out that a particular nation or ethnic group can be linked by some line of association to his major frustrations, thus finding unopposable the argument that he should hate all members of that group. A smoker who is trying to quit may find that he is able to limit himself to smoking only at the end of meals, thus finding it *harder* to give up the habit altogether. A person drawn into psychotic confusion may realize in a flash that designing the perfect automobile would solve all his problems and thus discipline himself to give up all endeavors not related to that design. In such cases, the discovery of a partial solution endangers the possibility of finding a complete solution, the kind of point the Bolsheviks were always making against the Mensheviks.

Such a process might even allow an insightful person to impose a rule on someone else who does not want it. A child who notices another's tendency to be easily disgusted may chant "those aren't raisins, they're flies," and render his victim unable to eat his rice pudding, even though the latter knows perfectly well that the chant is a lie. What the first child did was propose a limited occasion for disgust that had not occurred to the other – but the tormentor would have had to know that his victim was extraordinarily concerned with dividing the clean from the unclean. Similarly, a person who knows that a man suffers feelings of guilt and also that he feels somewhat threatened by women might literally curse him with impotence: The curse would form a rule ("Do not get erections with women") that would let the man run from his fear of women and at the same time punish himself for whatever guilt he felt. Thus, it may be that witchcraft has not depended entirely on the credulity of its victims, but also on the witch's intuitions regarding their ambivalence; Golden (1977) gives modern examples.

Of course, the more benign the rule, the more receptive a person will be when someone suggests it. Hypnosis may have its more startling effects when the subject lets the operator suggest boundaries between two sides of an ambivalence, a process that when conducted with skill also seems like magic.[6]

---

[6] Jay Haley describes many examples in his account of hypnotherapist Milton Erickson's technique. For instance, he describes a patient who paced incessantly in Erickson's office. Erickson said,

> "Are you willing to cooperate with me by continuing to pace the floor as you are doing now?"
> The patient replied, "Willing? Good God, man! I've got to do it if I stay in the office."
> Erickson then asked the patient if he could participate in his pacing by partly directing it. The patient agreed, and Erickson suggested that the patient pace over here, and then pace back and forth over there, and so on. After a while, Erickson began to hesitate in his directions, and the patient began to pause in his pacing and wait for them. Then Erickson seated the patient in a chair where he continued to go into a trance. [Haley, 1963, p. 52]

6.4.5 Excessive coercion is attributed to outside forces

Recognition that a person's own rules can cause feelings of imprisonment is erratic, even among experts. Certainly warnings about this danger have sounded more poetic than scientific; there has been no concept that could place such a danger within a framework of reward and punishment, much less within the individual's common sense of his own motives. Coercion by an overwhelming motive is understandable when the source of motivation is a single, concrete stimulus, such as a hot radiator that compels the person who sits on it to jump off. When the motive is created by the concentration of a whole series of choices along a bright line, as when someone "cannot" break a perfect attendance record, people may well be at a loss to account for it. In that case, they are apt to discern external incentives.

When a person binds his behavior by personal rules to about the same extent that his neighbors do, the resulting compulsions are apt to be called his character: "That's how he is." Even at this low level of compulsion he may experience such commitments projectively, that is, as facts that are given by the environment. He may perceive his ordinary rule to seek or avoid a particular situation as the fact that the situation *is* good or bad (Ogden & Richards, 1930, pp. 124–125). The "facts" he responds to may have no ethical connotations at all; he may "know" certain objects to be dirty, unhealthy, or unlucky, even though his actual information about those objects is ambiguous. For instance, a person who fears drifting into procrastination may see his housekeeping behaviors as precedents that predict the extent of that drift; he may experience this perception as the belief that a cluttered house is a health hazard, a belief he embraces despite the absence of any objective evidence that tells him it is true. Likewise, if a person fears that he will be ostracized for excessive competitiveness, he may interpret his personal rule against it as a supernatural commandment (e.g., "Love your neighbor as yourself."). If a person fears that masturbation may reduce the importance of his human relationships, he may form the belief that it is physically unhealthful.

Such projective perceptions let a person account for whatever mixture of freedom and commitment he is experiencing. Although there is an ostensibly factual component that is seen as beyond his power to change, he still feels he has the option of "believing in" these facts or not, or, expressing the choice as an even more active one, to "make a leap of faith" or not (James, 1896/1967b). Once he has made the leap, he is still free to avoid whatever course the "facts" seem to dictate, at the expense of some kind of punishment. In reality, this punishment is the loss of the stake he bets against impulses, a loss that portends a more arduous task of impulse control in the future. However, he may explain his aversive feelings after losing a bet as punishment inflicted by a supernatural being, or as guilt, the natural consequence of violating a universal moral law; danger from impaired impulse control is perhaps most apt to be experienced through this stereotyped emotion. (In the presence of depression or obsessional disorder, feelings of guilt may arise without needing much occasion, and thus not always imply loss of a private side bet.) However, such a person may not feel wrong at all, but rather ill or contaminated. Society accepts a number of projective explanations as perfectly sane, perhaps because they seem to be the most expressive way to describe the experience of being bound by personal rules.[7]

If a person uses this kind of precommitment excessively, he may be disturbed to notice that he has bought freedom from impulses at the cost of rigid restraints on his behavior. He may try to will new

---

[7] Projection attributes one's own internal decision making to outside people or forces. It has heretofore been explained as a device to shift blame by reducing the projected motives or by making the person less aware of them (Fenichel, 1945, pp. 146–147; A. Freud, 1966, p. 122; Freud, 1920/1956k, p. 29; Hendrick, 1936), but research has found it not to have either consequence (Holmes, 1978). Instead, two rule-related mechanisms may be at work: (1) Projection often may represent the person's attempt to describe the experience of being bound by personal rules to criteria outside of his immediate control. A person who rules out angry conduct may attribute this avoidance to a belief that his parents strongly disapprove of anger; if this avoidance has become automatic and unquestionable, he might even develop the belief that a supernatural force is taking his anger away. (2) In addition, projection can be a process for hedging on such commitment: Personal rules create a motive to lower one's threshold for perceiving the criteria that permit the regulated behavior. The person who does not let himself initiate anger will be strongly motivated to detect signs of anger in others, so that he will have permission to "respond" with his own. His lowered threshold for perceiving anger will also be called projection. Many examples arise from hedging on rules for testing reality, the rationale for which will be given in section 8.4.3. Projection does excuse the person in part for violating his rule, just as orthodox theory says, but not by reducing either his motives or his awareness of them. Aside from direct perceptual distortions caused by psychotic processes, projection is apt to be greatest where behavior is most rigidly bound to rules, and represents both the person's awareness of this binding and his attempt to reclaim some of his lost autonomy (Melges & Freeman, 1975).

choices, but discover that no way of perceiving them frees him from the risk of a grave break with precedent. He will not be able to describe this inflexibility beyond saying that "something" makes him do things or stops him from doing things. If his overconcern with principle is general, he may be diagnosed as having a compulsive personality or obsessive-compulsive disorder.[8] At the extreme, compulsiveness sometimes resembles paranoid psychosis (Shapiro, 1965, pp. 104–107).

Special needs to resist particular kinds of temptations seem to produce the sellout-range character traits described in the preceding section – narrow concerns with thrift, sexual performance, emotional invulnerability, and so on.[9] Thus, the resort to personal rules may produce serious side effects, even conditions that are themselves called mental illnesses. Accordingly, the compulsive behaviors that are loosely called addictions appear not to be addictions in the sense I have used the term, but sellouts enforced by personal rules. As such, they are at least as destructive to the person's long-range interest, not to mention his sense of free will. "Compulsive hoarding can be just as weak-willed as impulsive spending" (Elster, 1989a, p. 37).

---

[8] Actual obsessive-compulsive disorder has an admixture of itch-range urges – to wash, to check, to perform groominglike behaviors – that seem to be coerced by guiltlike feelings even in the absence of any perception of having set an ominous precedent (Baer et al., 1990; Goldstein, 1985). It is as if the disease can short-circuit the usual process by which guilt is occasioned, perhaps by lowering the person's threshold for that emotion.

[9] Evidence is increasing that compulsive symptoms and many character traits are rooted in the sufferer's heredity (Carey & Gottesman, 1981; Robins & Regier, 1990) and mediated by his biology (Cloninger, 1987; Hollander et al., 1988). Such findings do not remove these traits from the realm of intertemporal conflict, but rather suggest mechanisms for their owner's exceptional readiness to feel out of control, or impoverished, or sexually inadequate, or emotionally vulnerable. These feelings create motives that presumably interact like all other motives in the person's comprehensive internal marketplace (see section 2.2).

7. Self-generated reward as the basic impulse-control problem

We have been discussing the problems of ambivalence that can be traced to the temporary-preference phenomenon: addictions and other unwelcome urges, including physical pain, as well as such entanglements as compulsions and rule-based sellouts that result from attempts to combat these urges. This is only a start. The curve by which delayed events are discounted should shape all motives, great and trivial, normal and abnormal, into the same kinds of patterns. The same puzzles should recur in many different guises, and the same solutions should be applicable.

Certainly there are many puzzles concerning the way people value goods that have not been solved thus far by any descendant of Bentham's felicific calculus (see section 1.2). Some of these puzzles will require merely the application of principles discussed thus far to goods as they are conventionally understood. I shall discuss two examples before taking up the nature of goods themselves: the artificial and sometimes inconsistent way people value money, and people's tendency to commit themselves more to poorly rewarded activities than to well-rewarded ones, which has been ascribed to "cognitive dissonance."

7.1 The consistent value of money depends on personal rules

Hyperboloid discount curves clearly do not persist from an individual's personal valuations into the realms of finance and trade. They would create a banking world far different from the one we know. With exponential curves, two bank accounts of the same type, begun at different times, but with the same deposit, will stay exactly proportional in value at all future times in the absence of new deposits. However, if the interest curve were more sharply bowed (e.g., hyperboloid), then their rates of accruing interest would differ depending on how long they had been in existence, and their balances would increasingly diverge. This is another way of saying that borrowers would have to offer ultra high interest to attract initial deposits, a phenomenon admittedly seen in the prizes and special interest rates offered new depositors at banks, but usually not a necessary feature of borrowing money. Actually, banking would almost cease if people could not make binding commitments to loan or deposit money well in advance of when they had it, because no one would be motivated to sacrifice present consumption to future gain.

This is a serious problem for temporary-preference theory, because interest rates on loans and investments are ultimately determined by the preferences of individual people for spending versus saving. If these rates are exponential in shape and relatively low, a major explanation is required if we are to go on believing that the individual's fundamental discount curve is hyperbolic and steep.

In a world of hyperbolic discounting, the value of an event rises and falls radically over time. Even goods that remain readily available change in value because of changes in the relevant hunger. Thus, the spontaneous value of lemonade goes down for the person who is not thirsty, and the value of a comedy record goes down when the person is tired of listening to comedy.

Obviously it would be costly for a person to make his choices on the basis of these spontaneous valuations. For instance, assume that he likes to go snowmobiling in the winter and sailing in the summer, that he is willing to pay only what each vehicle costs ($1,000 for a used model on which there is little annual depreciation) at the beginning of the season, and that he can sell each of them back to a dealer at the end of the season for 25 cents on the dollar. Then, every 6 months he will face the choice of getting $250 immediately versus saving $1,000 in 9 months, alternatives that equation (3.7) evaluates at $250 and $100, respectively.[1] If he actually sees this as an isolated instance, the matching law predicts that he will sell.

However, if he expects to face a similar choice twice each year for

---

[1] $V = A/[Z + \Gamma (T - t)]$, calculated in months, with the constants set to 1.0.

Table 7.1. *Present value of present and future choices*

	Future	
Present	Sell	Hold
Sell	250 + 167 = 417	250 + 489 = 739
Hold	100 + 167 = 267	100 + 489 = 589

roughly the next 20 years, the incentives he faces are the sum of 40 installments of $250 each (one immediate, the others discounted) versus the sum of 40 installments of $1,000 (each 9 months after the corresponding $250) [equation (5.2)]. The prisoner's dilemma he faces is shown in Table 7.1. He will hold his vehicles for next season if he believes that he must do so this time in order to continue doing so (i.e., if the upper right cell is not a credible outcome) and if he believes that he will continue to do so if he does so this time (i.e., if he does not see a great risk that the lower left outcome will occur).[2]

---

[2] Of course the period must be only *roughly* 20 years: A known endpoint would motivate defections in the final choice, and hence the one before it, etc.

If values are calculated on a daily basis, rather than monthly, a more complicated but ultimately similar picture results: The aggregate, discounted value of his pleasure for a given season on the first day of that season can be represented as concentrated at a point 16 days from the beginning (Appendix III). Equation (3.7) represents his incentives as follows:

$$V = A/(1 + 16) = 1,000$$

(Note that we are following the rule of thumb that $Z = 1.0$ of whatever time unit is the most convenient size.) If we solve for A, it is $17,000, the amount that the person's relevant pleasure for the entire season would be worth if it could be concentrated at a delay of zero; in this and most life situations, such an advance concentration would be impossible, but the peremptory craving created by certain drugs suggests that they may effect something close to it. This calculation would also suggest that his *spontaneous* valuation of immediate snowmobiling or sailing on a given day would be about $17,000/90 \cong 200.

When he has the chance to sell the vehicle, it would be about 9 months before it would deliver pleasure again:

$$V = 17,000/(1 + 317) = 53$$

where 317 is the 42-day virtual delay of 90 days of consumption beginning after 275 days (Appendix III). It is thus worth only about a fifth of the $250 he can get for it (or, strictly speaking, a fifth of whatever good he would buy with the money, the discounted value of which must be at least $250 at the time he buys it; for simplicity we shall assume that this good is worth $250 to him and is consumed immediately).

If he sees the transaction as a precedent, he must choose between 40 installments

As with the bedtime example in section 5.5 (Figure 5.4), the prisoner's-dilemma matrix summarizes the choices posed by summed hyperbolic discount curves, in this case, the value of enjoying $250 every spring versus $1,000 over the following winter (Figure 7.1); for simplicity, the summer–fall sailboat choices have been left out of the figure.

Seeing a transaction as a member of a larger category somewhat dampens the fluctuations in spontaneous value predicted by the matching law. However, even the person who does this in the preceding example will be indifferent between selling and holding at a selling price of $354 for a good that will be worth $1,000 to him in just 9 months. Although people sometimes may buy and sell according to discount rates of such magnitude – the effective rates in Hausman's study (1979) of air-conditioner purchases reached 89% (see section 3.2) – it is still much higher than would be called either normal or prudent. We must appeal to three additional factors to produce the stability with which economists are familiar:

First, cash pricing makes a wide variety of transactions conspicuously comparable and hence invites an encompassing personal rule about the value of money generally. Just as the person in the foregoing example achieved more constancy than he otherwise would by seeing his choices about the snowmobiles as related to his choices about the sailboats, so he will become more constant still if he sees each of his financial transactions as a precedent for all others. That is, if he sees what he spends for food, clothes, movie tickets, toys, postage stamps, and so forth, as examples of wasting or not wasting money, he will add thousands of examples to his interdependent set of choices, each flattening his effective discount curve by a greater or lesser amount. The ease of quantitatively evaluating and comparing all financial transactions lets the value of purchasable goods fluctuate much less over time than, say, the value of an angry outburst, or of a night's

---

of $250 and 40 installments of $17,000 that are each discounted for 275 + 42 days more than the corresponding $250:

$$V_{(sell)} = \Sigma_{i=0-39}250/(1 + 180i) = 255$$
$$V_{(hold)} = \Sigma_{i=0-39}17,000/(1 + 317 + 180i) = 327$$

If he expects to follow the precedent he sets with his current choice, he will be motivated not to sell the vehicle.

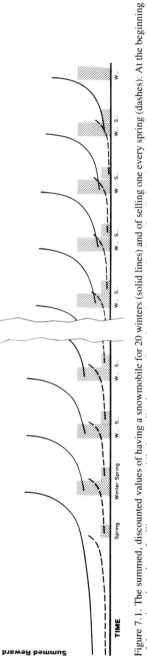

Figure 7.1. The summed, discounted values of having a snowmobile for 20 winters (solid lines) and of selling one every spring (dashes): At the beginning of the series, the value of selling a snowmobile immediately never rises above its summed values for all the winters.

sleep. Accordingly, it is unusual to see someone swayed by his immediate emotional comfort by only a tiny fraction more than by next year's comfort, but it is common to see him behave as if his immediate wealth is worth only a tiny fraction more than next year's.

Second, financial transactions tend to become rivalrous activities, which adds an additional stake to the goods involved in the transactions themselves. Unless the night owl robs his sleep so much that he falls asleep at work, his discomfort is unlikely to become the basis for invidious distinctions between himself and his fellow citizens. However, in buying and selling he is not choosing simply in parallel with his neighbors, but in competition with them. If some of them are prudent enough to buy his snowmobile every spring for $500 and sell it back to him every fall for $1,000, they soon will be richer than he, and their rewards in terms of power over him, not to mention prestige, will be added to the goods that originally seemed to be at stake. Of course, rivalry also can make people rash, but if the relevant choices are perceived in series of precedents, they will further increase the motivation for deferral of gratification. It may be the need to defend at least rough comparability with one's peers that makes a credit-card rate of 20% the indifference point for consumer interest, instead of 200%. Conversely, it may be the relative invisibility of Pacific-rim economic growth to American consumers that lets the latter continue to indulge in a 20% rate rather than setting a still lower one, despite the consequent transfer of wealth overseas.[3]

Of course, a society often makes nonfinancial activities a basis of competition as well. Where people gain an advantage by staying hungry to attain stylish slimness or by cultivating sexual indifference to increase their bargaining power with partners who are more readily aroused, the expectation of this advantage forms a stake for the personal rules governing these activities, just as it does for the rules governing the value of money, and sometimes it can motivate heroic acts of abstention. However, just as cash pricing makes the largest

---

[3] Agreeing upon what is to be a community's "normal" discount rate is a highly charged social process. Individuals or groups who accept a higher discount rate than the consensual one tend to be ostracized as shiftless, but they are apt to seem less threatening to other people than are individuals or groups who have achieved a lower rate, who often are accused of being misers and are persecuted, as in the pattern of Western anti-Semitism, or the attacks on Indians in Africa or the Chinese in Southeast Asia.

number of a person's choices comparable, so it engages the largest number of people in social competition.

Finally, a person can set up his personal rules so that investment decisions will not be weighed against his strongest temptations. As Shefrin and Thaler (1988) have recently pointed out, people assign their wealth to different "mental accounts," such as current income, current assets, and future income. These accounts seem to represent personal rules for how readily the money they govern may be used to satisfy immediate wants. In effect, a person finds lines like the river in Figure 5.5, selecting them where he thinks they will never demand so great an act of abstention that he will prefer to abandon them by spending money from the asset account ("breaking into capital"), or borrowing against future income.

People are apt to have a fourth account to the left of Shefrin and Thaler's three: a category for comparatively small windfalls, such as gifts or prizes, or money earned under exceptional circumstances, like the pay for Ainslie and Haendel's subjects (see section 3.2). Such money is beyond the protection of rules, as Thaler (1990) reported noticing personally when it was suggested to him that he spend $300 in football winnings evenly over his expected lifetime. Only in this account are a person's valuations of single choices apt to obey the matching law for single cases [equation (3.7)].

Actually, a person may have any number of accounts in which valuation is governed by some kind of personal rule. At the extreme are disciplines like Shefrin and Thaler's asset account, in which expenditures must maximize long-range income and thus are weighed by the standards of the investment market. For most people, such deferral of gratification is possible only because of other accounts, designated perhaps by source ("current income"), perhaps by use ("food," "supplies," "entertainment"), that are meant to satisfy day-to-day wants. Under the rules of such accounts, the person no longer weighs all expenditures against his strictest discount rate. Rather, he tests expenditures from such accounts only by rules for the prices of particular goods (a "fair price" for air conditioners or glasses of beer), which are apt to imply a somewhat steeper discount rate than that for the asset money. Skillful designation of income as "investment" versus "spending" money (or the even less protected "found money") may permit a person to accept bank discount rates on some of his money, while still appeasing temptations that might overwhelm a monolithic rule. Thus, an individual may evaluate goods in compartments, requiring investment rationality in one, abandoning himself to the matching law in another, and probably following intermediate rules in still others.

Acting in his long-range interest, he looks for chances to shift any sums that cannot buy much additional reward in the near future across the line into the asset account. Infrequent wages help this process: Income that arrives in large lumps, such as a biweekly paycheck, will produce rapidly diminishing returns if spent all in a few hours (Prelec, 1989). The person thus has an opportunity to protect some of his income by dividing it between spending money and savings while much of the reward that could be realized through spending is still distant.

The person's short-range interests will then succeed only insofar as they find rationales to put money in more lax accounts. In Shaw's *Pygmalion*, the ne'er-do-well Alfred P. Doolittle asks Professor Higgins for £5 to spend on "one good spree for myself and the missus." The professor is charmed by Doolittle's hedonism and offers him £10, but Doolittle refuses: "Ten pounds is a lot of money: it makes a man feel prudent like; and then goodbye to happiness" (1916/1951, p. 50). Most rationalizations to permit immediate consumption are less costly, but still may erode a person's will to maintain an account governed by conventional prudence, sometimes leading to a spendthrift syndrome.

The overall effect of applying personal rules to the accountancy of money is that spontaneous desire is tamed. For most people in modern society, money ceases to be a simple means to immediate ends, valued when we need it for a specific purchase, but not otherwise. Instead, it is assigned value according to an extensive set of personal rules designed to maximize objective income as far as possible in the face of shifting spontaneous preferences. Most valuations are made not only or even mainly according to a hunger, but according to the precedents they will set. However, the realm of rational market behavior thus created – and the realms of less "objective" but still somewhat consistent consummatory behaviors that border it – should not be confused with the realm of spontaneous preference. They are special cases within the universal matching law, much as Newtonian physics is a special case of relativistic physics.

7.1.1 The artificiality of spending decisions

Personal rules dampen swings in a person's valuation of money, but, as they do with other behaviors, they introduce a characteristic artificiality into the choice-making process. Their failure to make financial behavior simply objective can be seen in occasional examples in which a chance for a tiny gain is valued beyond what would be expected, apparently because it preserves a precedent. Some people will not allow themselves to pass a penny in the street without picking it up, or put more postage than necessary on a letter to avoid searching for the right stamps, or be short-changed in any amount by a clerk or vending machine, or buy gasoline at a convenient service station when the price at an out-of-the-way station is 1 or 2 cents lower.

Many decisions that most people would regard as simple value comparisons are demonstrably arbitrary. A person who does not buy a melon because "the price is too high" does not weigh the cost against his hunger; even an exorbitantly priced melon would not put a significant dent in most people's incomes. Rather, he notices that the price is higher than the prices he usually sees, and he judges that the purchase would violate his principles of thrift. If he does buy the melon, it is apt to be under some provision that limits the effect of the purchase as a precedent, such as perceiving his spontaneous urge to eat this melon as a relatively infrequent craving, or seeing the dealer as a connoisseur who is apt to be offering especially good melons for sale, or finding some unique circumstance in the current situation, such as the fact that he is visiting a strange city. Alternatively, he may give up the idea of buying melons, even though the "exorbitant" cost would represent a smaller portion of his income than melon prices did 10 years earlier, when he bought them often; he gives them up not because he has weighed his appetite against the cost but because they are now expensive "for melons."

Even in the case of a more peremptory appetite, say cigarettes for a smoker, a person may temporarily do without cigarettes that are "too expensive," even though they are not too expensive in terms of what he would eventually pay to service his appetite. If cigarettes were outlawed or became scarce, as they did in wartime internment camps in the 1940s, he might readily pay the equivalent, as measured by his effort, of 10 or 100 times that price (Radford, 1945). The factor determining his resistance may be largely the second of the three leveling factors described earlier – a rule not to let anyone take advantage of him. Thaler (1985) asked two groups of economically sophisticated subjects to imagine that they had been lying on a hot beach, and each had to tell a friend who was going to bring him a beer how much he was willing to pay; if the friend was said to be going to "a fancy resort hotel," they named a price almost twice as high as that named if he was going to "a small, run-down grocery store." The beers themselves would have been the same; the difference was only in the apparent "fairness" of the price considering the nature of the vendor.

Those were not spontaneous choices, but were made because money "shouldn't be wasted." A violation of that rule will undermine a person's long-term interests with respect to money in general and thus will have much greater importance than would the loss of the single economic opportunity that was literally at stake. If a person perceives himself to have wasted money, that perception in itself may actually increase his future tendency to waste money in more significant ways. Of course, a person who is afraid of his impulses or unwise in his choices of rules may carry this concern to an inefficient extreme and become a miser, in the same way that anorectics starve themselves to death for fear of seeing themselves give in to their hunger.

The few data that are relevant to the childhood origins of rules for maintaining value are difficult to interpret. Children confuse normative rules with laws of nature, and they confuse the loss of such rules' intended benefits with the innate punishments for disregarding natural laws (Piaget, 1932/1965). Confronted with a simple operant schedule, children as young as 2.5 years look for general principles of responding, thus growing out of the apparently spontaneous, sensation-based pattern that infants share with lower animals (Bentall, Lowe, & Beasty, 1985). By the age of 6 years these principles have taken on a rigidity that prevents some adaptations to changing schedules of reward, such as the sacrifice of greater size to obtain a still greater rate (Sonuga-Barke, Lea, & Webley, 1989); it is not clear whether this failure to use information as well as a pigeon does is a consequence of the child's controls on spontaneous swings of motivation or is simply the side effect of moderate sophistication in evaluating the options that he more usually faces. Whatever the mechanism, this rigidity has abated in some individuals, but not others, by the age of 12 years (Sonuga-Barke et al., 1989).

Depending as they do on bright lines, personal rules that mediate between a person's motives to spend and save may dictate radically different valuations of money when he moves across one of these lines. For instance, he may exert great effort to avoid incurring small expenses if these are called "penalties" for late payment, but he may carelessly incur greater losses simply by not promptly depositing money in the bank. He may work harder to avoid paying "too much" for an article than he would to earn the relevant amount of money to begin with, and he may pay more for an item if it is to be a gift than if it were for his own use. The first two cases reflect greater aversion to a conspicuous lapse than to equally costly behaviors that cross no bright line; the last is an example of a loophole.

Rule-governed mental accounts for self-control are discernible behind many of the inconsistencies that Kahneman and Tversky (1979, 1984) ascribe to shifting perceptual "frames." For instance, those authors found that subjects were more averse to losing a given amount of money than to not gaining the same amount. But rules to avoid losses are more readily enforceable than rules requiring gains, and more necessary in view of the fact that a person has only a finite amount of money to lose before suffering privation; just as some military commanders have tried to go by a rule never to retreat, many people seem to commit themselves to hold on to what they have, even when they must pay for that inflexibility. The natural consequence is a greater aversion to a loss than to a missed opportunity to gain the same amount. Furthermore, because a loss that violates a personal rule has substantial importance regardless of the size of the loss, a gamble that offers the chance to avoid facing a loss will be worth more than an outcome of the same "objective" value (probability × amount) that entails a certain loss.

The same authors reported most people as saying that they would not pay to replace a lost theater ticket, but they would buy the ticket initially even if they had just lost the equivalent amount of money

(Tversky & Kahneman, 1981). The circumstance of having lost the first ticket would make it difficult to avoid counting the cost of both tickets as the price for admission, which would be "too high" as long as other people were getting in for half that amount. On the other hand, there is no reason that one should have to count lost money as part of the cost of his next contemplated purchase. Thaler's "mental accounts" and Tversky and Kahneman's "frames" are not environmental givens, except that the environment furnishes the variety of stimuli that are more or less serviceable as the boundaries of these accounts. The actual adoption of such boundaries is a motivated behavior, like the adoption of criteria for any personal rule. A long-range interest in evaluating money consistently fights with a short-range interest in imminent pleasure, in this case seeing the show, whatever the cost. For the majority of subjects, the lost ticket gave the battle to the long-range interest, because the person would not risk perceiving himself to have paid double the admission price. However, the lost money does not provoke a conflict of interests, and no precedent is at issue unless a person has a rule to punish himself for accidents involving money.

Another example: Most subjects report that they would be willing to travel 20 min to save $5 on a $15 purchase, but not to save the same amount on a $125 purchase (Kahneman & Tversky, 1984). This is another anomaly for economic man, because a person who wanted unambivalently to maximize his wealth would set an hourly value on his time and make both choices in the same direction. But a person whose long-range interest in wealth would generally require him to spend 20 min to save $5 could safely give in to a short-range interest in convenience if and only if he could count on the adequate rarity of such exceptions. A rule that would grant an exception only when the difference in prices would be a small proportion of the purchase price would thus be acceptable.[4] However, once a person thus complicates his internal bargaining, he is prone to further anomalies. For instance, a car buyer might accept a succession of accessories, each as a negligible proportion of the car's price, but then reject the total

---

[4] A more complex internal bargaining situation might even make such a rule necessary for a person's longest-range interest. If a sellout-range interest in moneymaking required maximal savings regardless of effort, only proportional valuations would spare the person from endless demands on his time.

price as a substantial absolute expense, a pattern that has been found experimentally and offered as an example of intransitive preferences (Tversky, 1969). A recent author has argued that such a phenomenon is inconsistent with the economic explanation of behavior generally (Schwartz, 1986) (see section 2.2), but it only demonstrates the artificiality of people's rules for valuing money.

Where conflicting rules may apply to a purchase, either short- or long-range interests may use attention control to protect one rule from being modified for consistency with another. That is, where a person's rules are permissive, he is apt to avoid noticing seemingly applicable rules from more strictly regulated areas – household shopping rules when on vacation, workplace cost-effectiveness rules for time allocation when hunting collectibles, and so forth. It would spoil the fun of a book collector to calculate whether or not dealing in the same books would pay for his time. To prevent that, he may direct his attention so as to avoid direct comparisons between certain activities. In the extreme, such precautions make some areas "sacred" or "taboo," in Mary Douglas's sense (1966), and thus contribute to the appearance of incommensurability that Schwartz, Taylor, and others have taken to be a fundamental property of motivation (see section 2.2).

Where a long-term interest has created rules, we should expect to see short-term interests negotiating loopholes on the basis of "just this once," and the rules establishing the value of money are no exception. All transactions are unique in some respect; conversely, all can be compared to at least one category of other transactions. Determining the proper context of evaluation becomes a complex problem in internal law.

It is an old trick of sellers to compare the prices of their products with their prospective buyers' appetites, rather than with the going market prices. Another is to make the sale unique: a dish that is not served elsewhere, a personality "backing up" the product that overshadows the product itself, a product tied to a special occasion. Entrepreneurs dealing in contests seem to find that they can further appeal to people's short-term interests by offering specific, extravagant prizes, such as sports cars and vacations, rather than money, which a winning entrant might feel he would have to spend sensibly designating the prize in this way seems to be enough to create the desired exception, even though the winner can sell the item or take cash instead under the rules of the contest. It is also well known that people on vacations will buy things they would not ordinarily buy, just as they have "shipboard romances" with people they otherwise would not consider as partners.

Merchants often find that they can profit by allying with a customer's short-term interests and providing those interests the bargaining points they need. If a person rewards himself especially for finding bargains, he may become the willing prey of a merchandiser who sells inferior goods "marked down"; this person evades his rule for thrift by claiming that he has found a bargain and thus, acting in his short-term interest, is perfectly willing to pay the penalty of getting inferior goods. Similarly, a person may use different rules of scrutiny for different price categories, which he divides by the natural bright lines of round figures; the merchant who marks his goods down to the next lower price ending in 99 or 95 invites the person's short-term interest to plead a lower price category against the long-term interest's rules for thrift, without really having created the illusion that the merchandise is substantially cheaper.

When a person accumulates more money than is necessary to satisfy his visceral needs, he must confront another of its properties: It is a natural counter in gamelike activities. He may perceive himself to be earning money simply as a means to various ends, but if those ends are basically games ("process" rewards), they are in competition for his attention with the activity of earning (or saving) money per se. The nature of this competition will be clearer shortly, after we have discussed the rationale of gamelike rewards. It is enough to note here that this role for money further diminishes the importance of the goods that are the ostensible reason for earning it.

These examples of a continuing struggle between spending and saving suggest that the value of money is not established simply by a mental substitution of a dollar amount for the goods to which a person is attracted, but rather by the personal legislation of a systematic discipline that requires the person to act "as if" the money had a certain value, legislation that is modified by a variable amount of evasion. Specifically, an individual must rule as to what exponential discount rate he will accept for his most protected category of wealth – such as Shefrin and Thaler's "future income" (1988). The rate achieved by the most future-oriented segment of a society will be that society's "rational" discount rate, after allowing for uncertainty and the prospect of inflation. A rule establishing this discount rate will not be adopted by everyone and will not apply to all of the transactions of the people who do adopt it. Outside of its limited protection, the value of money ceases to be anything like a scalar quantity, but rather becomes the arbiter of an intricate set of internal conflicts. No wonder people seem irrational to an observer who thinks they are simply trying to maximize income.

7.2 Rules to prevent vacillation are seen in "cognitive dissonance"

Just as we have seen that other kinds of commitments produce projective perceptions (see section 6.4.5), the personal rules that establish a relatively steady value for money create the projective experience that worth inheres in money. A similar but less systematic valuation process seems to have been reproduced in many experiments by Festinger and his followers in the 1950s and 1960s (Abelson et al., 1968; Festinger, 1957): Human subjects' attitudes toward a marginally interesting task were elicited both before it was assigned to them and somewhat afterward. The lower the apparent reward for the task, the more the subjects increased their professed valuation of it from the first measurement to the second. Festinger explained this seemingly irrational outcome as subjects' attempt to reduce "cognitive dissonance" between their perceptions that they were doing the task and that they were poorly rewarded for it. Such a concept implies a discrete motivational system for cognitions, a "field theory" like the interaction of electrostatic charges envisioned by Kurt Lewin (1951). The cognitive-dissonance phenomenon seemed unexplainable in behavioral terms, but given the need for precommitting devices to influence future behavior, an explanation is not difficult.

We need only note that there is a fundamental cost to ambivalence, namely, the extent to which it undermines those goals that require consistent choices if they are to be obtained. When a person is deciding between two movies, he is not seeing either of them, and when he is doing a task only halfheartedly, he may accomplish no more than if he did not do it at all. I may only half want to jump over the ditch ahead of me, but if I only half jump over it, I shall be worse off than if I had chosen decisively either to jump or not to jump.

In such situations a person needs rules governing his valuations of the alternatives, for much the same reason that he needs rules making his valuation of money consistent: If he signs up for activities and then quits them, or buys goods and then turns them in, he will realize less reward than if he had bound himself to stick to his choices in the absence of strong reasons to change them. Spontaneous choice-making will reduce his income. But his attitudes represent just such rules. He undertakes to behave "as if" they were his spontaneous motives. They must, of course, be systematic, lest short-range motives (doubt, boredom, other momentary urges toward vacillation) evade them. And they must be stronger or more fundamental the more the person expects that his spontaneous valuation of the expected reward will prove inadequate at some moments. The cognitive-dissonance effect is the way that rules for consistent valuation manifest them-selves; such rules cover financial decisions but go well beyond them. The dissonance is not the clash of mental fields, but only a realistic apprehensiveness about the effects of ambivalence.

7.3 Most rewards are not limited by environmental events

Two unexplained facts of behavior that were described in chapter 1 will require a still closer look at the basic process of motivation: that a good's rewarding power depends on attitudes that may be unrelated to the good's physical effect, often called tastes; and that people assign rewarding power to goods that have only trivial physical effects, a process not commonly discussed, which psychoanalysts call cathexis. I shall argue that these phenomena are related and that they subsume other particular puzzles: the tendency for the value of goods to "wear off," despite a person's increasing skill at consuming them; the ap-parent tendency of some goods to defeat any direct attempt to obtain them; and the readiness of some values to change sign, from positive to negative or vice versa, on the basis of slight changes in the valued objects. All these patterns are predicted by the actions of highly bowed discount curves on ordinary motives. They represent different aspects of one fundamental constraint on an organism's capacity to be rewarded, a constraint that comes not from some environmental scarcity but, paradoxically, from the ready availability of reward.

7.3.1 Tastes and appetites

In section 4.2 I proposed that a temporary-preference model can account for the partial control that people seem to have over the experience of aversion: that aversive mental processes are rewarding both more intensely and more briefly than the processes with which they interfere. Aversion is then a form of seduction, typically made available by external circumstances, but chosen by a person in an open bidding process, not imposed on him. That is, despite the physical nature of many painful events, they do not induce aversive experiences except through choice in the marketplace. Where they act as keys that fit a perceptual lock, what is unlocked is the opportunity for pain, not the experience of pain itself.

Conventional reward theory needs a similar revision. In its original form it depicts drives as negative events that an organism can escape insofar as he finds antidotes, called rewards, that will "reduce" the drives. This venerable model is "hydraulic," in that it depicts drives as accumulating like water behind internal dams, requiring the organism to search the environment for the right wrench to open any given outflow tap. When he stays in a state of high drive, he is assumed to have been unable to find the appropriate reward, which therefore must be something outside of his control. Such a model depicts an intuitively acceptable, well-balanced game that an organism can be seen to play against the world, but two of its assumptions are contradicted by observation: (1) that drive is necessarily aversive and (2) that reward depends on external stimuli. The former problem has now been somewhat understood, so that few authors still depict drive as a negative force; but the latter has not.

1. In the hydraulic account of motivation, which used to be accepted by psychoanalysts and behaviorists alike, drives arose in individuals by an autonomous process that was uninfluenced by reward; those drives motivated a person to "discharge" or "reduce" them (Freud, 1920/1956k; Hull, 1943); some analysts, like Compton (1983), still

speak that way.[5] Drives were seen as aversive events, except that authors did not examine the implication that subjects should thus avoid drives in advance, an observation rarely made with drives other than pain. The value of a drive per se (for hunger, sex, exploration, etc.) was not considered until recently.

When that value was finally studied, it was generally found to be positive. For instance, intracranial stimulation that induces drives is generally rewarding in moderate amounts (Beyra, 1976). It has also been found that given a drive, a subject may be motivated to perform activities that never lead to the reduction of that drive. For instance, male rats will work for the chance to copulate with a receptive female even if the copulation is always interrupted before ejaculation (Sheffield, Wulff, & Barker, 1951). Similarly, rats with esophageal diversions that prevent what they eat from entering their stomachs continue to sham-feed despite the nonoccurrence of satiety, and they continue to do so after many similar trials (Geary & Smith, 1982). The concept of drive is still meaningful, but it should be redefined, in light of such studies, as the capacity to be rewarded in a particular modality. The buildup of this capacity may or may not be aversive, and reward sometimes may occur without its dissipation.

2. It is logically possible to do away with the concept of drive as hydraulic pressure and still keep the notion of storage tanks for fluid, with rewards as specific wrenches that fit the taps: What is stored and tapped is then the organism's supply of potential reward, and its actualization still can depend on specific releasing stimuli that occur with limited frequency in the environment. That is what conventional theory would require.

Conventional theory also takes account of the fact that an organism's capacity to be rewarded by these stimuli often is modified by learned factors called tastes. The associated occurrence of other rewards or punishments is thought, in effect, to change the shape of the tap and thus change the range of wrench shapes that can turn it. In that model those stimuli that become the objects of tastes must at least predict the unlocking of reward if they initially lack direct rewarding ability themselves. If a person develops a taste for golf or

---

[5] In the authorized English translation, Freud's term *Trieb* is controversially rendered as "instinct" – see Strachey's note (Freud, 1895/1956a, pp. xxiv–xxv).

the smell of liquor, it is because those things have predicted reward; if he develops a distaste for them, it is because they have predicted nonreward or aversion. Thus, the conventional concept of tastes stays close to the concrete model of wrenches and taps.

It is true that tastes often are formed because the consumption of their objects has led directly to rewarding or unrewarding consequences, a process that usually is described in terms of classical conditioning or the equivalent operant concept, visceral learning (Atnip, 1977; Garb & Stunkard, 1974; Garcia, Hankins, & Rusiniak, 1974; Hearst, 1975). However, it is equally true that tastes affect and are affected by the conflict between the person's longer- and shorter-range interests. Tastes for temporarily preferred activities threaten the person's abstinence from them. People facing this threat sometimes lose their tastes for even physiologically rewarding goods like foods and sexual objects. The loss of taste would not follow from a personal rule against consuming these objects; simply forbidding an activity does not change its power to reward and therefore need not reduce its appeal to taste. Where a taste is eliminated, either of two additional circumstances must be present: avoidance of appetite, or complete success of the relevant rule.

Many activities require a preparatory process in order to be fully rewarding, sometimes in order to be rewarding at all. A person must get into the right mood to enjoy an evening of farce, or an argument, or a square dance. Even for concrete rewards – especially for concrete rewards – a process of "appetizing" is important. "Appetite" is sometimes used as a synonym for "taste," but "taste" does not also denote this transient state of readiness to be rewarded, as in, "his appetite was aroused." Appetite, in this second sense, is a behavior in its own right, much like an emotion, and is thus presumably subject to differential reward. It is related to taste in a way that may account for changes of taste in the service of self-control:

Where the rewarding power of an activity depends on a preparatory appetite, the need to arouse that appetite imposes a delay between choice and reward. Such a delay is apt to keep the activity from being overwhelmingly tempting, as long as the appetite has not been aroused. In that case, a person can supplement his personal rules with a form of emotion control: early avoidance of the appetite. At a moment when a person can initiate an appetite for a short-range reward, that reward may be sufficiently distant that his knowledge of its consequences will deter the appetite. The person simply will not "work up" the appetite and thus may maintain his long-range preference. If he regularly inhibits appetites for a particular activity, he will be said not to have a taste for it. He can thus restrict his tastes to only some of the activities that could be rewarded by the underlying drive.

The other factor that may eliminate an apparent taste is complete obedience to a rule against the relevant behavior. If that rule is strong enough to convince a person that there is no likelihood that he will indulge in the activity, that fact will motivate him not to keep considering it as an option. He will stop imagining its rewards and will avoid initiating a futile appetite for it, unless something in the appetitive process itself is sufficiently rewarding to repay the effort. A reformed smoker who is sure that he will not smoke again usually will stop thinking about cigarettes and eventually will report that he has lost his craving for them or even become disgusted by them, but a person may find it rewarding to fantasize a sexual adventure that he is equally sure he will not undertake.

Where an appetite is rewarding in its own right, a person may need an additional rule prohibiting not only the consumption of a particular class of rewards but also the preparatory process that makes the forbidden activity rewarding, lest entertaining the appetite make the latency of reward for that activity too short for it to be resisted. That is, simple foresight may not suffice to inhibit appetites that are tempting in themselves; personal rules may be necessary. Insofar as those rules succeed, the person's taste will have changed by the first mechanism, avoidance of appetite. Of course, if his rule against the consummatory activity is weak enough that this activity sometimes occurs, the appetite for it will be rewarded, which is also apt to occur even if this appetite is not rewarding in its own right.

Thus, the application of self-control tactics to either consummatory activities or appetites for them may affect the experience of taste. It is not difficult to find examples of tastes that have been edited down in the service of self-control from what their underlying drives originally made possible. For instance, all societies regard some sources of reward as taboo or unclean, and their members have effectively lost their capacity to be rewarded by those sources (Douglas, 1966).

Contact with a taboo object has even been used as a punishment. People in modern society usually rule out dogs or other pets as food, and members of the nuclear family as sexual objects, although both are biologically able to deliver the relevant rewards. The dangers attached to them are clearly of the moral sort. However, the rules against using them in these ways are experienced as lack of desire for them, or even as disgust at the idea of using them in such ways, rather than as restraints against a desire; the tastes themselves have changed.

As Lazarus (1972) has argued in the case of one group of negative tastes – the phobias – the attempt to trace all tastes to simple pairings of their objects with reward or punishment strains credibility (see section 1.2.1); for evidence confirming this view, see Murray and Foote (1979). Lazarus distinguished those phobias formed by contiguous punishment and those formed by ideational processes, a distinction reaffirmed by Wolpe (1981). An example of the latter would be an a priori deduction that an object was unclean or taboo, in which case classical conditioning clearly would founder as an explanation. Although tastes are experienced as beyond the control of the will, they nevertheless must be regarded as motivated processes that can sometimes shift because they exemplify a larger principle of impulse control.

It has long been a psychoanalytic tenet that people regulate their appetites and thus form tastes with a view to augmenting their impulse control (Salzman, 1965). The concept of personal rules governing the generation of appetites seems to coincide with the psychoanalytic concept of "bound cathexis." Such cathexis, perhaps better translated as "importance," is given to an object by a person, but thereafter inheres in the object in an inertial way, so that it cannot be withdrawn easily (Freud, 1916–1917/1956i, pp. 348, 422). For example, a man who perceives sexual activity with women to be a trap may forbid himself a sexual appetite in the presence of women. However, if he notices a line that divides some less dangerous sexual activity from the sexual activity he fears, he will be motivated by the whole force of his sexual drive to seek that criterion (Fenichel, 1945, p. 330; Freud, 1938/1956q, pp. 202–203). Such a criterion might be the presence of women's underwear, or prepubescent girls, or boys, or some situation in which women seem less threatening, such as exhibitionism. The criterion he adopts for permitting a sexual appetite will be the hinge of a personal rule, the stake for which will be all that he had expected to lose if he had succumbed to his original sexual impulse. That stake can be described as the energy with which the criterion is cathected (Freud, 1923/1956l, pp. 42–47). The common perception of this situation will be that he has a taste for the sexual stimuli on the permissible side of the criterion.

It is not obvious why personal rules sometimes permit the generation of appetites for temporarily preferred rewards, producing the experience of a desire opposed by either a deliberate rule or a compulsion, and sometimes forbid the appetite itself, producing the experience of indifference or revulsion. Why, for instance, do some people remain attracted to sexual experiences they have forbidden to themselves, whereas others cease generating such sexual appetites or even generate disgust? Perhaps forbidding an appetite itself produces greater safety against the impulse, but at the expense of some harmless reward that cannot be consumed in the absence of the appetite. Thus, ruling out an appetite will be a stronger but potentially more costly defense than simply ruling out its corresponding consummatory behavior.

7.3.2 The perils of self-reward

In the case of appetite, we have seen how the actions of physiological rewards may be modified by factors totally unrelated to their physiology. Even so, it would be possible to believe that reward is limited by the availability of specific, scarce stimuli. But even this seemingly fundamental constraint on an organism's freedom of opportunity fails to withstand ordinary scrutiny. I shall argue that the presence of such ostensible releasing stimuli often is inadequate to produce rewards, and also unnecessary. In the weak form, this hypothesis states that "process" or gamelike rewards, especially emotions, are within a person's power to give himself at any time and thus must be limited by some principle other than the scarcity of environmental releasers. In the strong form, the hypothesis states that all rewards have this property, even those that seem to depend on a concrete physical process like the ingestion of a substance.

As noted in section 1.3.4, few of the drives that are important in modern life require a physical stimulus for their gratification. Certainly the vast catalog of gamelike[6] or "process" rewards are self-generated in this sense. In these cases, at least, it is physically possible to short-circuit the "normal" dependence of rewards on external events. But if that is the case, why would people ever develop needs for external objects (food, drink, warmth, and other tissue-need satisfiers possibly excepted)? Furthermore, because the development of nontissue needs depends on the reward obtainable by satisfying them, why would not the best objects be universally available ones like stones or chairs? As Csikszentmihalyi discovered in the course of his extensive investigation of gamelike activities, "almost any object or any experience is potentially enjoyable" (1977, p. x). Why do people ever give importance to objects outside of their grasp, in preference to total involvement in rewarding themselves? What would happen if someone decided to become self-sufficient, and to reward himself without regard to environmental input? The basic question is why those tastes that are not innately bound to a physical substrate – the tastes that Freud (1923/1956l) would have attributed to the "neutralized energy" directed by the ego – require any object at all.

This is a difficulty for both behavioral and psychodynamic theory. The behavior therapists who have taken notice of people's ability to reward themselves mentally seem to have no construct to account for why this self-reward does not become an all-absorbing behavior (Rachlin, 1974), thereby undermining the activity that seems to have been the most important product of human evolution, social interaction (Caporael, 1987). Freud said that producing satisfaction by means of hallucination, although possible, would lead to "exhaustion" (1900/1956b, p. 598). Thus, he implied that such short-circuiting of the usual paths to reward would be limited by some intrinsic cost, but he said no more about the nature of that cost. He later reaffirmed that "insofar as the ego is auto-erotic, it has no need of the external world" (1915/1956g, p. 135). He said that such autoeroticism was limited by the "instincts of self-preservation." But literal self-

---

[6] Or "playlike," if we use Karl Groos's definition of play: "activity performed for its own sake" (1901/1976, p. 77). Csikszentmihalyi makes a word of that definition – "autotelic" – then exchanges it for an adjective/noun from his subjects' speech: "flow" (1977, p. 36). However, his subsequent use of "flow" is restricted to activities that are not only autotelic but also intensely rewarding.

preservation requires little effort in modern society and does not seem to be the motive that induces people to give up hallucinations or fantasies. In fact, young children gradually reduce their fantasy lives not because their parents and teachers beat them into line but because their fantasies become relatively less satisfying and fail to compete with other forms of play. Likewise, although hypnotists have found that "hallucinations involving any one of the senses can be produced, as in dreams, by appropriate suggestion," people who have learned autohypnosis show little tendency to withdraw into the fantasies that accompany it (Kroger, 1963, pp. 18, 85).

There have been further observations concerning two kinds of psychiatric patients who try to bring their sources of reward into their own hands and withdraw their investments in risky activities: Schizoid characters feel threatened by social give-and-take and often contrive to live entirely in their rooms, or in a shack in the woods. Insofar as they succeed in doing that, their solitary activities mysteriously become stale, and often they fall prey to worries, fears, or rituals. At a higher level of functioning, narcissistic characters choose their activities and companions so that continual success is a foregone conclusion. They, too, report a mysterious reduction in satisfaction that cannot be accounted for by any confrontation with reality; on the contrary, their problem is that they have managed to get their reality to obey them almost as well as their fantasies do. Thus, the harshness of reality does not seem to be the factor that limits arbitrary self-reward. It looks more as though self-reward, indulged in ad libitum, becomes unsatisfactory for that reason itself.

The staleness of reward reported by self-absorbed people makes one think of habituation or fatigue. Any neuronal process, if repeated frequently over a short period of time, will lose vigor. For instance, if a person stares at a solid color for any period of time, the visual pigment that subtends that color will be depleted, so that if he then stares at a neutral screen he will see the complementary color. Data on the generality of this phenomenon in psychophysiology were summarized by Solomon (1980), who proposed an increasing recruitment of antagonistic processes as an explanation; but the simple fatigue of the process in question should account for its decreasing ability to hold off its competitors. If the physiology of reward is not an exception, then repeated attempts to invoke a given kind of reward should produce diminishing returns. Even self-reward should be expected to satiate.

Furthermore, satiation does not seem to be simply proportional to the amount of rewarding activity that has occurred. A person will get more or less aggregate satisfaction from a given opportunity for reward (i.e., drive) depending on how he consumes the reward. Rapid consumption of a reward tends to entail an even more rapid satiation of a person's capacity to be rewarded in that modality, so that some of the drive is wasted. It is easy to think of examples where this model seems to hold true. To go from the more concrete to the less: Filling up with food too rapidly spoils the pleasure of a meal; premature ejaculation reduces the pleasure available from sexual intercourse; looking ahead to the outcome of a mystery story wastes the suspense that has been built up; coming to the punch line too fast reduces the effectiveness of a joke; and people generally become bored with tasks that allow their minds to anticipate completion, that is, tasks that contain no elements of surprise or ambiguity (Douglas, 1966, p. 37; Empson, 1930). Such tasks seem to include all activities that are entirely under the control of the person's memory – all solitary intrapsychic activities once they have lost their novelty.

It seems that people often face a choice between rapid satisfaction of a drive, which dissipates the capacity of that drive to produce reward in the immediate future, and the slower, more productive satisfaction of that drive. They have an inevitable urge to consume rewards rapidly because this makes the peak intensity of rewarding effect occur earlier. Thus, a rapid tempo of consuming a reward is seductive but wasteful.

The temporary-preference model can apply not only to the choice of competing rewards, such as drink versus sobriety, but also to alternative rates of consuming a given reward. In the cases just listed, the disproportionate attractiveness of the immediate satisfaction of a drive makes a person momentarily prefer it to satisfaction of the same drive at a different tempo.

This situation is shown graphically in Figure 7.2. The solid lines depict two possible reward curves. The choice between intense, brief periods of reward and equally frequent, less intense, more prolonged periods of reward clearly poses the smaller-earlier versus larger-later reward problem. If the discounted value of each moment of consumption is calculated according to the matching law, equation (3.7), and those values are added together, and then the resulting values are plotted for each moment before consumption occurs, the curves (broken lines) favor the slower consumption of reward when the two consumption patterns are viewed at a distance, but temporarily favor the rapid, less productive consumption pattern when it is imminently available. Any highly bowed discount curves will generate the same result: Rapid consumption can be an impulse that threatens more efficient consumption patterns for the same reward.

Inefficient consumption would not matter if an organism had a limitless number of drives and they could be tapped without delay. Neither of those conditions seems to exist, however. We do not know how many appetites there are that can satiate separately – that is, sources of reward that can remain productive when other sources have fatigued, as when one is hungry but not thirsty. If we had such information, we would be able to count the number of separate drives it would define (Herrnstein, 1977).[7] However, we can infer that the number must be small from the fact that appetite is so widely regarded as a precious commodity: People not uncommonly work up an appetite for dinner, boast of an appetite for sex, complain of a jaded appetite for entertainment, and so on. Among gamelike activities, one factor analysis has suggested that there are only five kinds of satisfaction – warm interpersonal experiences, risk (or "vertigo"), problem solving, competition, and new creation (Csikszentmihalyi, 1977, p. 27) – although there might be separately satiating activities within these categories. Furthermore, it seems that to indulge an appetite requires a relatively unrewarding setting-up period: A person must change his interests, "settle down" to the new task, or "get in the mood," and if his attention is distracted in the midst of this process, he must partially repeat it. Distractions have an aversive impact.

[7] In actuality, some drives may be only partially divided from others. Thus, under some circumstances, appetite for a particular kind of food seems to satiate temporarily, whereas that for a novel kind of food remains sharp (Rolls, Rolls, Rowe, et al., 1981); however, such findings may turn out to reflect several specific food drives that satiate entirely separately (Mook, 1988). The partial separation of drives has been little explored.

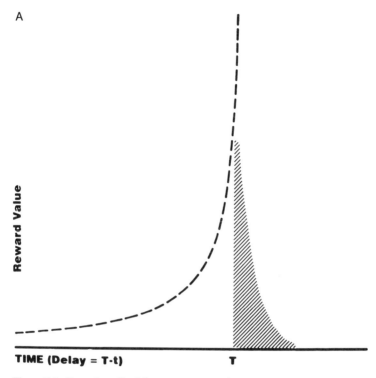

A

Reward Value

TIME (Delay = T-t)   **T**

Figure 7.2. Rewards realized from two consumption patterns (shaded areas) and their expected discounted values. A: A rapid, intense pattern. B: A slower pattern that produces a greater aggregate reward. C: The two patterns superimposed. The intense reward temporarily dominates the slower reward.

Apparently, switching to a new source of reward entails an unavoidable cost (i.e., some loss of reward actually realized). If that were not so, we would expect to see wide-ranging foraging among a number of sources of reward that would be scanned for "ripened" rewards. A person's behavior should be that observed in a pigeon on a concurrent variable-interval schedule without changeover delay: frequent alternation between alternatives to see if elapsing time has made more reward available on the other key (deVilliers, 1977, pp. 242–243). People would roam among television channels, literally and figuratively, as diminishing returns in the current choice made other alternatives marginally better; eating, drinking, making love, reading, and

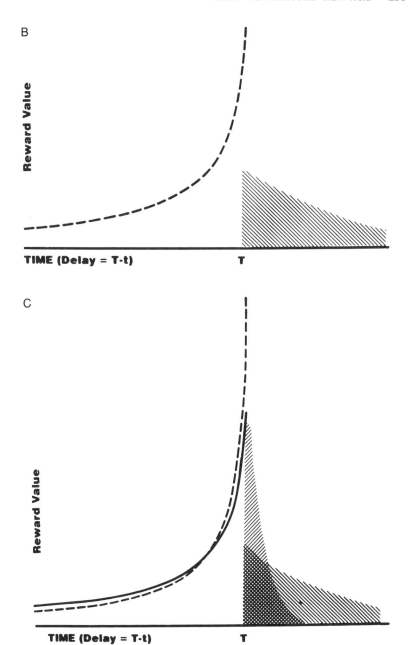

playing games would all be indulged in short bursts. Absence of such alternation implies a start-up cost (or changeover cost) in opting for reward.

In other words, the incentives faced by an individual who can self-reward at will in a given modality are much like those faced by movie companies that owned perennially favorite movies like *Gone with the Wind* and *Cinderella* before the market changes caused by videotape: A company could rerelease a movie at will, but its administrative costs would be repaid decreasingly because of the saturation of the audience, and so it would not pay to make the movie continuously available. Companies would release such movies only after several years had elapsed since the previous release, so as to allow sufficient interest to build up to repay the cost of distribution. The larger the cost of distribution, the more infrequent the release would be.

We might be able to infer the size of changeover costs from the frequency with which a person switches between particular activities, except that he might also be responding to the limited availability of drives. That is, the cost of satiating drives rapidly and switching to new ones includes not only the decrease in reward while new appetites are generated but also a decrease in the aggregate productivity of the set of all drives. A consumption pattern of rapid satiations followed by switches to new drives may be intensely rewarding, but only until no fresh drives are available. It will be in the person's long-range interest to conserve his drives.

7.4 Devices that limit self-reward will be valuable

In modalities in which a reward can be had simply by opting for it, subject only to the constraining slowness of the onset of the appetite and rapidity of satiation, a person will have a great long-term interest in finding precommitting devices that can prevent premature satiation. He will have such an interest even where reward requires a physical behavior or object, if that behavior or object is available at his will. It is not difficult to think of concrete devices that can serve that purpose: banquets with many courses that pace their consumption, eating lobsters or crabs out of the shell, retarding orgasm with anesthetic creams, and so forth. But even for physical behaviors, these mechanical devices are apt to be of limited availability and usefulness. Against the ultimate temptation, the availability of purely intrapsychic self- reward,[8] they will be of use only if they can reduce the potential reward from the drive itself (e.g., the effects of tranquilizers on angry fantasy). A broadly applicable device to prevent premature satiation must tie a person's self-reward behavior to the occurrence of events outside of his control, and it must use purely psychological ties.

But a personal rule is just such a device. A person can make a rule to congratulate himself only when he has finished a certain task, or when someone else congratulates him; he may allow himself to be elated only when a friend is, or only when he wins some kind of prize that is not too easy to get. He can make binding gambles. He can "invest" importance in a person, or a cause, or just a piece of entertainment, so that his self-reward is thereafter tied to the fate of his investment.

In behavioral terms, the competition between an impulse and a personal rule is a competition between two schedules of self-reward, one of which realizes less actual reward but at an earlier time than the other. A person rewarding himself on the more ascetic schedule will always have the option of abandoning that schedule and realizing more reward at an earlier time. He may even generate the cues for self-reward himself, as long as something limits the rate at which he can do so.[9] Even impulsive self- reward must depend on a cue, that is not always present, if it is to remain a robust alternative over time. However, a person himself can generate many such impulsively used cues, cues that permit rapid self-reward that is not so rapid as to produce total satiation. For instance, a person may reward himself every time he can reproduce an obsessional thought, a schedule that will be temporarily preferred in the itch range. The cues for slower,

---

[8] People sometimes use "self-reward" to mean only "self-congratulation," which is only one example of a reward not physically controlled by a releasing stimulus. I shall use "self-reward" to mean all reward that does not require such release. If no reward requires a releasing stimulus, a possibility I shall develop shortly, then all reward is self-reward, and I shall use the latter term only when I want to remind the reader of that property.

[9] If a person rewards himself continuously he will soon exhaust the drive on which the reward is based. That is, if he tries opting unconditionally for reward in a given modality, he will find that most of the time the drive will be satiated, and so the unconditional opting behavior will extinguish without being even temporarily preferred.

more productive self-rewards usually must come from the environment. For practical purposes, a person faces a choice of self-reward schedules between those that he can make pay off quickly and those that are largely outside of his control.

If a person does not bind his reward process to events outside of his control, he might be said to be withholding his "cathexis" from them and thus making the mistake of narcissism or introversion, as Freud used the terms (Freud, 1916–1917/1956i, pp. 374, 414–416), or autism. In doing so, he returns to the sterile omnipotence of infancy and acquires a species of Midas touch: His every appetite is gratified, but so quickly that the anticipation that is necessary to harvest full satisfaction from a drive never develops, and so briefly that he must repeat the process indefinitely. A person cannot rid himself of the opportunity for this kind of regression; it must be, like the old idea of original sin, a constant factor in his motivation. He can only control it, through the adoption of precommitting devices. This contingency might account for the guilt that attends autistic behaviors – masturbation has long been a prototype among nonpsychotic people – despite the liberalization of social attitudes toward them.

In this model of value, the availability of environmental rewards is not the limiting factor in the operation of a person's internal reinforcing mechanism. Rather, the limiting factor is the availability of discipline, that is, of means of restricting self-reward according to a pattern that makes the best use of the underlying drive. External objects are valued not because they can peremptorily bestow or withhold reward, but rather are valued insofar as they can serve as useful boundaries between a person's long-term interest in maximal aggregate reward and his short-term interest in immediate reward. If a personal rule can turn upon a particular situation in a way that permits a large amount of aggregate self-reward over time and is not particularly vulnerable to the competition of brief, intense self-reward patterns, that situation will be valued for the same reason that Schelling's battle commander valued the river (see section 5.6.1). The person will pay money to obtain it and to learn behaviors that will increase its availability.

An omnipotent organism has a shortage of scarcity; he needs objects that can maintain appetite if he is to get the greatest possible reward. This is what makes an organism who has an extensive capacity to reward himself take an interest in the outside world.

7.4.1 Surprise as the ultimate shield against wasteful self-reward

Effective pacing devices must somehow limit not only the consumption of rewarding stimuli but also the self-reward process itself. The rewards in gamelike activities are apt to be ideas or images – the resolution of a story or joke, a pattern of musical notes, or another person's response to one's own behavior – and hence readily reproducible from memory. Memory is poorly controlled by personal rules, perhaps because it is not entirely reward-dependent (Rescorla, 1988; Shiffrin & Schneider, 1977), perhaps because it operates as fast as the process of rule enforcement itself. Therefore, patterns of any self-reward that is occasioned by ideas or images will inevitably deteriorate with rehearsal, no matter how rewarding they once were, as learning causes earlier elements to evoke later ones and thus hasten the satiation of that modality of reward.

Thus, in modalities where picturing the outcome (or a range of outcomes) in advance reduces the appetite for it, ruling that one will reward oneself according to the outcome will not be sufficient to pace actual reward. Here a person must invest importance in relatively unpredictable outcomes, thereby committing himself to keep seeking novelty in the environment. For an experience to stay rewarding with repetition, it must contain an element of surprise, and the appetite for it must accordingly contain an element of suspense. To create such a circumstance, a person must have invested an unpredictable event with importance (must have "cultivated a taste" for it). For instance, for a person to keep a sense of excitement about hosting parties, he must undertake to keep a changing mix of personalities happy with one another and must tolerate the resulting anxiety about whether or not that will happen on a given occasion. For an actor to keep his performance "fresh," he must endow it with an importance that invites stage fright. To maximize his high from gambling, a person must bet significant portions of his disposable income.

Readiness to be rewarded by an unpredictable event is usually, perhaps always, an aversive state. People ask not to be kept in suspense, and they are always tempted to end it either by hastening the outcome or reducing its importance. In the short run, the return from one more replay of an increasingly familiar pattern is apt to be greater than that for striking out into doubtful territory. Unless a person is alert to the danger of a primrose path (a schedule whereby the greater reward in a current choice leads subsequently to poorer choices; see section 2.4.3), he may even believe it wiser to stay with predictable experiences as they become progressively ritualized. Even if he knows that value of surprise, it will take effort to keep inviting fresh suspense as the old is resolved.

Temporary-preference theory thus supports recent suggestions that surprise is the basis of aesthetic value (Berlyne, 1974; Scitovsky, 1976) and justifies some doctrines of the philosophy of existence that have otherwise seemed mystical: "The world is ambiguous . . . [this] is the reward for being human because it adds challenge, variety and opportunity to existence" (Herzberg, 1965, p. 62). Furthermore, "as long as man is an ambiguous creature he can never banish anxiety; what he can do instead is to use anxiety as an eternal spring for growth into new dimensions of thought and trust" (Becker, 1973, p. 92). Insofar as an organism is capable of rewarding himself, surprise will be the only commodity that can be scarce.

It is not clear why nature should have selected pacing devices for self-reward as the goods that organisms will value, rather than a turnkey system of reward that must literally be controlled from the outside. We do know that lower animals are not entirely dominated by concrete rewards. Hungry monkeys have been observed to prefer exploration tasks to tasks that would produce food, and even in animals like rats the power of visceral rewards such as food and sexual activity is modified by factors like variety, which are wholly unnecessary to the physical consumption of those rewards (Dewsbury, 1981; Fisher, 1962; Walker & King, 1962; Wilson, Kuehn, & Beach, 1963).[10] It may be that the problem of motivation is analogous to those problems of mechanical invention in which the most direct solution has

---

[10] In the short run, such need for novelty can be accounted for by the simple habituation of a repeated neuronal process (Rolls, Burton, & Mora, 1976), but that will not account for a loss of an object's rewarding power that endures after there has been time for recovery.

been found to be too rigid – where the device that works in practice is engineered to allow slippage among its parts. Perhaps the design of rewarding stimuli as pacing devices rather than as absolute determinants of realized reward permits the most flexible adaptation to the environment.

For instance, such a mechanism may motivate maximal environmental exploration over a wide range of success rates, both by naive youngsters and by experienced problem-solvers. If internal reward were strictly proportional to the amount of some external stimulus, a proportion sufficient to shape behavior in a beginner might lead more advanced problem-solvers to rest on their laurels. But instead, as an organism becomes increasingly skilled in an activity, the reward that such activity generates increases only at first, and then decreases again because of his increasing speed at achieving the criteria for self-reward.

> The paradox is that it is just those achievements which are most solid, which work best, and which continue to work that excite and reward us least. The price of skill is the loss of the experience of value – and of the zest for living. [Tomkins, 1978, p. 212]

As long as games of tic-tac-toe dole out wins and losses in a pattern that repays the cost of paying attention to the game, a child will value them. When the range of possible outcomes is so familiar that he anticipates them all at the outset of the game, it ceases to be a useful pacing device for self-reward and is no longer valued. To go on with this method of disciplining reward, the child must take up checkers, and perhaps chess in turn. Similarly, when a daydream or a joke becomes familiar, the mind leaps ahead to the ending, dissipating the suspense and poorly repaying the cost of attending to it in the first place. A person must search for new daydreams or new jokes, or undertake an activity even less under his control, such as a challenging relationship with another person. To remain useful as a pacing device, the activity must either (1) change so that it remains novel (golf on new courses, new foods, new sexual partners, new tunes, and, as the style in which the tunes are produced becomes increasingly familiar, new styles of tunes) or (2) be intricate or subtle enough to defy total comprehension – this is the quality a work of art must have to save it from the obsolescence of fashion (Empson, 1930).

7.4.2 Premature satiation spoils the direct path to some rewards

Many apparently rewarding experiences cannot be produced by direct effort. The preceding chapter mentioned some states that usually occur as by-products, such as sleep, laughter, contentment, and dignity, and that are lost by "trying" to attain them, states well defined and discussed at length by Elster (1981). Such states may be highly valued, but it seems paradoxical to count them as operant rewards when they lack behaviors to reward.

Some such states cannot be achieved directly because the activity of trying to do so leads the person too close to temptations that undermine the ultimate goal. For instance, Frank (1988, pp. 71–95) has argued that one cannot maintain a reputation for honesty simply through prudent care for appearances (i.e., without actually being honest), because such a project is compatible with cheating where apprehension seems unlikely; without ruling out cheating, a person will be tempted to try it often enough that he will sometimes be caught. A similar argument could be made for dignity – that a narrow concern for dignity leads a person to neglect the less obvious behaviors that are necessary to sustain it in the long run. In fact, Frank's logic can explain why people have found a perceived helplessness to be of use in pursuing such diverse goals as sobriety, nuclear peace, and the salvation of their souls (see section 6.3). If a person is dissuaded from "applying" willpower, he can only look for evidence that fate will grant him what he desires; because much of that evidence depends on behaviors that are in fact effective in producing his goal, such an assessment of the situation creates a private side bet that is resistant to hedging.

But this logic can also be applied to acts of consumption that are subject to premature satiation. Where a person can obtain a reward just by trying to, increasingly masterful exercise of his skill is apt to attenuate the reward through premature satiation. If he could make himself laugh, or make himself content, he probably would keep himself satiated in those modalities. In doing so he would make them trivial as sources of reward, unless he found it practical to bind their consumption to pacing devices. Flexing one's leg is a powerful reward to someone who has been tied up or splinted, but it is insignificant to people who can move freely, because direct action harvests the potential pleasure as soon as the least bit has built up. However, unlike the case of dramatic suspense, building up appetite for free movement apparently is not worth the effort. If it were, we would see examples of physical confinement used as pacing devices, in the same way that saunas seem to build up potential reward by temporarily depriving people of comfortable temperatures.

It may be that a "by-product" reward is noticed as a reward precisely because there is both a direct route to it that offers no protection from wasteful consumption patterns and another route that contains some natural impediment to getting the reward by direct action. The reward will motivate behavior to obtain it, but insofar as ostensible "tries" to obtain it are counterproductive (trying to sleep is arousing, trying to be dignified is ludicrous), they will pose the same problem that other temporary preferences pose to other long-term interests. To obtain the by-product reward, the person will have to take the second route, that is, precommit himself not to try to seize it directly. He may even have to be unaware that the behavior he finally adopts is a means to get that reward (the precommitting device of attention control discussed in section 5.3.2). Thus, although a person probably will not undermine his wish for emotional catharsis if he buys a joke book, he may find no conscious strategy that brings contentment. The only way to defeat his tendency to make selfish grabs at contentment may be to tell himself that virtue is its own reward, keeping in the distant back of his mind the idea that virtue may also be rewarded by contentment. This situation is not an exception to the usual laws of operant reward, only another impulse-control problem.

7.5 Even physiological rewards may operate by pacing self-reward

The failure of ad libitum self-reward to repay an activity's setup costs may also be a limiting factor, perhaps *the* limiting factor, for reward in modalities that seem to require a physical substrate, such as eating, drug euphoria, and pain. That is, all reward may be self-reward, in that a person may be able to generate it without input from the environment. This is the strong form of the self-reward hypothesis. The evidence for it is only suggestive, but is worth examining.

Physical events that ostensibly control a person's experience of reward have been found not to do so on close examination. The effects of intoxicating substances, for instance, can regularly be produced by placebos. Even experienced drinkers cannot tell if certain mixed drinks contain alcohol (Maisto et al., 1977), and the pattern of "intoxication" they experience has been shown to be determined by their culture's arbitrary beliefs about the effects of alcohol (Critchlow, 1986). Smokers in one study could not detect the presence of nicotine, rating no change in satisfaction and less than a 25% change in tobacco "strength" after smoking more than 200 nicotine-free cigarettes (Goldfarb, Jarvik, & Glick, 1970). Some heroin addicts cannot tell whether a substance they have injected is heroin or just a saline solution (Ternes, O'Brien, & Grabowski, 1979). Eventually a placebo supports the behavior of intoxication less well than would the active agent, but in the meantime the person generates that behavior without the active agent. Conversely, a person who uses an intoxicating substance for the first time may not experience the "high"; he may notice no effect at all. He must actively learn the emotional activities that will be supported by the drug (Becker, 1963, pp. 41–58). Intoxicants are neither necessary nor sufficient to produce the rewards associated with them.

Turnkey control of reward by an external stimulus may not occur even in the case of hunger. Rats that are raised in a relatively satiated state, with food always present, and are then food-deprived learn poorly how to satisfy their hunger by rapid eating when food is intermittently made available (Ghent, 1957); this finding suggests that the connection between eating and the satisfaction of hunger is more tenuous than we usually think. In fact, we have long had some indication that this satisfaction is a psychological event rather than a physiological event; in parametric experiments, a food reward has its effect at the moment of consumption, even though the sugar acids that apparently mediate satiety to most foods[11] do not appear in the

---

[11] Satiation to glucose may occur in the mouth, but it is well documented that

bloodstream until considerably later (Oomura, 1988). However, although we know that the reward value of tasting a food *can* be modified by learning (Booth, Lee, & McAleavey, 1976), research is lacking on whether or not it *must* be created by learning, that is, by association with the satisfaction of physiological needs. Until we see whether or not animals that are tube-fed from birth learn to sham-feed (to eat food that is then diverted away from their stomachs), we shall not know if the taste of food itself has the power to reward, without its predicting the appearance of plasma nutrients.[12] But such reservations do not apply to hypnotic rewards. Hypnosis, which never actually fools the subject (Hilgard, 1977), and may even be self-induced, can occasion "physical" pain or pleasure (Weitzenhoffer, 1953, pp. 130–137). It would be difficult to call hypnotic rewards conditioned; but if not, they must be self-rewards. Significantly, the experiences that "fantasy-prone personalities" can generate with near-hallucinatory vividness are not restricted to the gamelike rewards, but include warmth and cold, the taste of food, and copulation – sometimes leading to orgasm by fantasy alone, as in 75% of Wilson and Barber's subjects (1983).

The complex relationship between pain stimuli and pain behaviors has already been reviewed (see sections 4.1.4 and 4.2). What it illustrates for the present argument is that pain stimuli are neither

---

satiation to other foods occurs no earlier than the stomach (Mook, 1988). Of course, it is possible that a turnkey reward receptor exists at a different site than that of satiation.

[12] The ability of stimuli to occasion reward when they are not innately connected to a central reward mechanism usually has been explained through classical conditioning. By association with an innate process like the actions of nutrients or a drug dissolved in plasma on a brain reward center, tasting food or alcohol or feeling a needle is said to take on the ability to produce reward even if those are not innate releasing stimuli. Stimuli such as the sight of food or preparations for intoxication would be less rewarding only because they would be less than perfectly associated with subsequent "hard" rewards. In the procedural sense, this hypothesis is often true. Many appetites for foods and intoxicating substances are learned through the proper kind of pairing with the active substance. But learning by pairing seems to occur only for information, not for the kinds of emotional responses involved in reward, as was described in chapter 2 (Brown & Herrnstein, 1975, pp. 159–160; Rescorla, 1988). If these rewards require a physical key, then the sight and, possibly, the taste of food and intoxicants may provide information that this key will eventually reach the lock, but such stimuli should not be able to operate the lock themselves. Conversely, if the reward does not require the substance, information that the substance is coming may be an excellent cue by which to pace self-reward in the modality, as we shall see.

necessary nor sufficient for pain behavior. Where an opportunity (i.e., drive) for pain exists, an organism who is not used to it responds in a disorganized fashion, rather than with stereotyped pain behavior [as with Thompson and Melzack's isolation-reared dogs (1956)], and an organism who additionally perceives a sudden stimulus that does not predict a pain stimulus will nevertheless use it as an occasion for a "conditioned" response, the familiar phenomenon of pseudoconditioning (Hineline, 1981) or "backward conditioning" (Spetch, Wilkie, & Pinel, 1981).

Thus, our existing knowledge contains hints that an organism's repertoire of self-rewards may include concrete rewards, that is, those rewards that are conventionally held to demand a physiological stimulus.

7.5.1 A mechanism for concrete reward

We know that an adequate physical stimulus is not sufficient to release reward if the organism does not have a taste for it (see section 7.3.1), and we have just seen that such a stimulus may not always be necessary to release reward. We should thus ask if physical rewards may function in the same way as gamelike rewards, not as obligatory releasers but as opportunities for an organism to limit ad libitum self-reward.

Such a possibility might seem to require that the effect of goods on the success of self-reward be based entirely on their aesthetic properties as pacing devices. Food, say, would assuage hunger no better than a work of art, assuming that they suggested the same rhythm of self-reward. Of course, that could not be true. Although there may be no reward that is unlocked by a tangible good as by a key, some modalities clearly require the specific physical effects of some goods to govern self-reward patterns if those patterns are to be successful over any length of time. That is, a substance seems to be necessary to regulate self-reward in certain modalities – to prevent its deterioration into an unproductive or even aversive activity:

Eating can be vividly imagined, or experienced through hypnotic suggestion, but insofar as such behavior is not accompanied by real food that is really absorbed, a person will be motivated to repeat the process indefinitely, because only real food will reduce the drive.

Likewise, a sleeper who responds to a full bladder by dreaming that he is urinating must do so repeatedly, because urination remains rewarding as long as his bladder remains full. To eat without satiation might at first glance seem to be hedonic heaven, a perfect reward-generating activity; but the urge for immediate reward will cause this fantasy to occur more often and reach consummation more rapidly, and so it will evolve into an itchlike, obsessional pattern that is aversive from the perspective of distance.[13]

Added to the aversiveness of such deteriorated fantasy will be an urge to entertain hunger pangs and other pains, which will be made available by the fasting body and advertised by pain sensations, so that it will become difficult to avoid the pain behavior by controlling attention. Preparatory activity (i.e., appetite) may make such pangs worse if the hunger drive is not soon reduced. Schelling (1986, p. 192) has pointed out that a gourmet may derive much of his satisfaction from a fine meal during his anticipation of it. The gourmet clearly does this by means of self-reward, because the ostensible rewards have not been delivered yet; but if he generates the anticipation and then does not get the meal, he almost certainly will have made himself worse off by it. Indeed, if that were not the case, no doubt there would be more fantasy and fiction about food, and more attempts to "fool" oneself about prospective food, similar to what we see for prospective wealth (e.g., lotteries) or fame (e.g., vanity presses and talent searches). In Mischel's experiments on waiting for preferred foods, the children who seemed to generate appetites ("hot thoughts") for their goal rendered themselves less able to wait than those who did not (Mischel & Moore, 1980) (see section 5.3.3), as if the appetite without the food added an element of aversion; Grosch and Neuringer (1981) found the same effect in pigeons.

Because of both the deterioration of fantasy and the difficulty of resisting actual pain, a starving person or starvation dieter will take his attention away from the whole modality as best he can; he will

---

[13] This is the same pattern described earlier for premature satiation, except that what satiates cannot be the hunger drive itself, for food and the idea of food continue to be rewarding. The limiting factor must be some temporary refractoriness of the fantasy process. Even the most glorious of images cannot hold the attention continuously, but must be recalled repeatedly, indicating the existence of a brief form of satiety at this level.

be greatly inconvenienced by the sight or smell of unavailable food, which will urge upon him the only possible hunger-based rewards in his situation: fantasies and pangs. The same factors can be discerned in the case of intoxicating substances. With repeated ingestion, alcohol supports the belief that one has been drinking, and a consequent "intoxicated" self-reward pattern, better than does a placebo, and tobacco supports a nicotine high better than does cornsilk. This is not just because exploration will show the person that under the placebo his perception of the signs of intoxication is under his arbitrary control; the real intoxicant will also inhibit the drives for certain competing behaviors, such as the urge to emit the pain behavior of alcohol withdrawal.

A withdrawing alcoholic who believes that he is drinking alcohol, but is not, still may avoid withdrawal pain as long as he does not not notice its availability; however, any exploration will show him that such pain behavior is actually available. The amphetamine user can experience a rush with a placebo, which is not surprising in light of examples in which beliefs have caused a similar rush, such as the intense high experienced by men in battle when they believe that their lives are on the line. Like the self-reward made available by hunger, a drug reward may well be physically accessible without the drug, but protected from casual access by the availability of shorter-range urges. Rather than develop the state of arousal needed for a drugless high of the amphetamine type, for instance, a person will be tempted to relax his vigilance, calm his fears, and seek rewards of an easier kind. Some people may have the discipline to generate such a high by a means that does not involve physical commitment (e.g., by using fiction), but most will require more of a commitment, such as the actual danger of parachute jumping (Epstein, 1967). Premature comfort will be a temporary preference in the itch range with respect to the longer-range preference for this kind of high – of addiction range in the case of drugs, probably of still longer range in thrill-seeking sports. Urges for such comfort are inhibited by amphetamine drugs and made futile by actual danger, but they tend to be overwhelming if they must be resisted arbitrarily.

Thus, a person uses rewarding stimuli in two ways: as pacing criteria for self-reward, and as direct means of inhibiting short-range urges that can be a nuisance to the self-reward process in some modalities.

Concrete rewards may not operate the reward mechanism in turnkey fashion, but probably are turnkeys for modifying the underlying drive.

Placebo reward is as "real" as that occasioned by an active agent. It will select the behaviors it follows with the same force and will be discounted in the same hyperbolic curves. For instance, a person who gets high from a fake cocktail will have the same euphoria as a person who gets high from a real one. However, in concrete modalities, placebos tend to become poor occasions for self-reward, which is the property that sets concrete modalities apart from gamelike ones.

Thus, according to the strong form of the self-reward hypothesis, what defines gamelike or process rewards is the property of not needing regulation by physiological stimuli. The processes with the greatest potential for pacing self-reward by themselves have been found and exploited as genres of fiction: romantic (including sexual) feeling, anger, fright, humor, disgust, melancholy, pity, competitiveness. Those rewards that are preferred only briefly in the absence of the relevant physiological stimulus are notably absent from song and story. Consider eating, for instance; the infrequent writer who has ignored this property has only demonstrated it the more, as in Gilbert and Sullivan's occasional tedious songs about the pleasures of food. Many other body functions fail as vicarious activities, such as thirst, elimination, actual pain, and possibly sleep, although the enjoyment of a lullaby arguably may be a case of vicarious sleep.

A hungry person who thinks of food may thereby prepare himself to notice painful pangs or may actually excite such pangs, just as a sexually deprived person sometimes finds it dysphoric to fantasize about sex. The difference is that a vicarious pacing device, such as a story, will not be able to modify the pangs of hunger so as to make them pleasurable in the longer run, whereas that may well be possible for feelings of sexual longing. Finding pacing devices that will increase the long-range productiveness of self-reward in modalities where this is possible is the familiar process of sublimation.

7.5.2 How the prospect of concrete rewards governs appetites for them

A person's estimation that he is apt to reward himself in a given modality will in turn motivate any behaviors that will increase reward effectiveness in that modality. He will try to "work up an appetite" in the form of sexual anticipation, of drug craving or actual withdrawal symptoms for the addict, or of food hunger leading to salivation. However, he may soon regret that preparatory behavior if it is not followed by a reward process that leads to satiety, that is, if it stirs up itch- or pain-range urges that interfere with longer-range reward and are well inhibited only by satiety. In situations where he knows that satiety will not occur, either because the necessary physiological stimuli are not available or because of a credible personal rule against the behavior that could lead to it, he usually will not engage in the preparatory behavior. Thus, craving for cigarettes is said not to arise either when the smoker knows that there is no way to get them or when he knows for sure that he will not allow himself to smoke them, as when an orthodox Jew forbids himself cigarettes on the sabbath (Schachter et al., 1977, p. 39). Similarly, starving people report that they stop "having" an appetite: "[After 3 days of fasting,] instead of an eagerness for food, there was almost an indifference toward food, despite the persistent hunger call of the empty stomach" (Carlson, 1916, pp. 134–138).

The "conditioned" cravings that have been observed for addictive substances (Childress, McLellan, & O'Brien, 1986) and food (Weingarten, 1985) will not fit the pattern of classical conditioning, even if classical conditioning were a distinct type of motivation (see section 2.3.2): The "unconditioned stimulus," namely, the substance, satisfies craving, whereas the supposed conditioned stimuli in these situations have the opposite effect. Such cravings are better understood as goal-directed preparatory behaviors.

As was noted in section 7.3.1, preparatory behaviors themselves often produce rewards, which may be preferred in the itch range, even if the person does not expect satiety. Indeed, these behaviors may simply be examples of self-reward without consumption of the physiological stimulus, an activity that, we have just speculated, will not become itchlike until some time has elapsed without any consumption. This will mean that to "anticipate" or "savor" food or alcohol or sex or play is to reward oneself in the relevant modality before the pacing stimuli are present (Loewenstein, 1987), an activity that may help to optimize aggregate reward if these stimuli subsequently appear. If they do not appear, the activity will turn itchlike in the case of food and alcohol, and possibly sex, a prospect that may or may not sufficiently motivate a person to avoid the savoring activity in circumstances where the pacing stimuli are unlikely to appear. In the case of play, and possibly sex, the savoring is merely a daydream, preference for which need not be temporary even if no concrete stimulus follows. Where indulgence in a reward is prohibited by a person's personal rules and the savoring activity stands any chance of motivating him to break his rules, the balance of motivation is especially apt to tip toward savoring.

7.6 The self-reward hypothesis accounts for the imperceptibility of the stimuli necessary for reward

An indirect mechanism of action for concrete rewards, such as that just outlined, would also account for people's unreliability in identifying the active elements in these rewards. Because placebos can produce rewards even in these modalities, we should not be surprised to find that people attribute rewarding properties to stimuli that do not physically contribute to the process of reward. Although people develop strong opinions about what does and does not reward them, these opinions do not seem to be direct observations, but theories arrived at indirectly. Smokers, for instance, have numerous theories about what the rewarding elements of smoking are, such as handling the cigarette, sociability, and force of habit (Ikard, Green, & Horn, 1969; Spielberger, 1986), but in view of the fact that inhaled nicotine is necessary for smoking behavior in the long run (Jarvik, 1970; Schachter et al., 1977), these self-reports miss the mark. As has been mentioned, smokers cannot report radical changes in the nicotine levels of their cigarettes in the short run (Goldfarb et al., 1970), though their actual smoking behavior usually is reduced somewhat by additional nicotine intake (Jarvik et al., 1978; Kozlowski, Jarvik, & Gritz, 1975; Kumar et al., 1977). They seem not to perceive the rewarding element directly, but to be casting about for a reason why they experience a strong desire to smoke.

We can state this conclusion another way: Although the value of a rewarding substance must somehow be to support a certain kind of reward, nevertheless when people are asked what is necessary for reward, they cannot reliably identify the elements demonstrated by controlled research. Indeed, reward per se does not seem to be identifiable. Even a direct reward to an animal by intracranial stimulation will have no behavioral effect unless it is labeled by a simultaneous stimulus or happens immediately after a physical behavior (Hawkins & Pliskoff, 1964). It is as if a person seeking reward gropes for a handle in the dark with a hand that lacks sensory nerve function, and must guess by indirect cues whether or not he has grasped it. He can test his guesses only by his affective experience over time, which will reflect how productive his self-reward process has been. Whatever has uniquely accompanied the experience becomes his name for and theory of the handle, even if that unique feature is only a chance accompaniment of his behavior. Thus, if a person is able to self-reward more effectively when under the influence of nicotine, he may believe that puffing smoke or fiddling with his cigarette, or any of a number of behaviors coincident with nicotine intake, is "giving him pleasure."[14]

Because a person actually rewards himself not according to the ingestion of the rewarding substance but according to his theory of what effectively rewards him, his theory confirms itself in the short run, even if it sometimes leads him to grasp the wrong handle. He opts for reward where he thinks doing so will be effective, and if the relevant drive has not been satiated, he will thereby realize actual reward, even though this particular cue for opting is not supported by an active substance and thus will soon lose its usefulness. His theory is unlikely to be disproved even when the active ingredient is absent, but as exploration shows him that competing itch- or pain-range rewards are still available, the handle will seem to become less and less effective, leading to the familiar decay of a placebo.

In summary, an organism's rewards are self-generated, necessarily so in the case of gamelike rewards, and quite possibly even in the case of concrete rewards. Self-reward is not independent of environmental events, which act directly on the drives that make reward possible and also offer criteria for pacing the self-reward process. However, an organism cannot determine immediately which pacing

---

[14]Again, Freud may have been prescient: "An instinct can never be an object of consciousness, only the idea that represents the instinct can" (1914/1956f, p. 177).

criteria are most effective, because most pacing devices tend to work in the short run. Thus, the incentive effect of external events is buffered by the organism's power to reward himself arbitrarily, and his theories of what actually constrains his experience of reward will be idiosyncratic to the point of superstition.

8 The demon at the calliope

8.1 A mechanical model demonstrates the limits of self-reward

It is no surprise that self-reward is normally limited by constraints. Absence of such limits would produce a lethal autism, which we may glimpse in the self-stimulation of the brain-damaged child, the endless bar-pressing of the rat that stimulates its septal brain area, and the driven repetition of the "crack"-inhaler. However, it is difficult to picture constraints that do not depend on a scarcity of rewarding stimuli. The incentive to safeguard available drives from premature satiation is just another product of the matching law, but the behaviors it engenders will be subtler than finding food or escaping pain. The kinds of mathematical functions that behavioral psychologists and economists have always used to account for consumption choices are radically transformed when drive levels, rather than the availability of consumption goods, are what limit effective reward.

I shall summarize the self-reward hypothesis with an illustration, making reference to both the classical economic tradition, as elaborated, for example, by Becker and Murphy (1988) to handle apparent motivational conflict, and a mechanical model that may make the illustration easier to picture. This model comprises many specific factors that are not based on specific data, only the suggestions of ordinary experience; it is not meant to be the definitive model of reward, only one that is consistent with our existing knowledge of motivation, and that performs in the predicted ways when programmed on a computer (details available on request):

A person[1] is assumed to maximize his aggregate expected dis-

---

[1] The problem of an unbridled ability to reward oneself is largely a human problem, probably for reasons relating to intelligence, which greatly expands the subject's ca-

counted reward at the time of each choice, an assumption also made by economists, who call this quantity the utility of the choice (Page, 1968). The model holds that all mental processes except the "automatic" processing of attended-to stimuli (Shiffrin & Schneider, 1977) are behaviors, that is, that they depend on differential rewards. Economists make the same assumption for all behaviors they recognize as choices, although usually they have not dealt with purely mental processes.

To illustrate the innovations of the self-reward model, it will be useful to start with an existing economic theory. Becker and Murphy's model (1988) deals with the phenomena of psychological conflict more extensively than any other theory in economics (see section 3.3). This model makes the present utility of a good the integral of all its expected future utilities, discounted exponentially; each of these future utilities is a function of three factors: c, its utility without having been modified by a history of consumption; y, the utility of not choosing it, unmodified by a history of choosing it; and S, a "capital" factor by which the accumulated effects of the good's past consumption interact with c and y. The formula is

$$U(0) = \int_{0 \to \text{Death}} e^{\sigma d} u[y(d), c(d), S(d)] dd \qquad (8.1)$$

where d is delay ($T - t$ in my own equations), and σ is the discount rate.[2] Like the conventional economic models on which it is based, this approach assumes exponential discounting and thus has no other rationale for limiting utility than according to the physical availability of the good.

The alternative approach developed here is that people discount the value of future goods (rewards) hyperbolically and that such goods

pacity for vicarious reward (see chapter 7). It is unlikely that any qualitative difference in motivational principles is responsible for the absence of an important self-reward problem in lower animals. If intelligence is indeed the source of the problem, it is also the enabling factor for the most powerful solution: personal rules. Because we shall be concerned with organisms that have a high potential for arbitrary self-reward, I shall speak of people rather than organisms generally in this section.

[2] As was noted in chapter 2, increments in U will become infinitesimal long before the person's life expectancy, unless that expectancy is extremely short or σ is extremely small. This diminution defines, albeit vaguely, a time horizon, which is in effect the central principle of Becker and Murphy's theory of why people act in contradiction of their own future interests, and which for any practical purpose should replace "Death" as their limit to integration.

have no intrinsic dependence on stimuli – the strong form of the self-reward hypothesis: Access to reward is limited only by the exhaustion of its drive and by innate parameters relating latency, rate of satiation, and rate of recovery to the rate of emission of the behavior that obtains the reward. That is, all reward is assumed to be freely available in all modalities without innate releasing stimuli. The limitation of available drive is what keeps people from coining reward at will, a capacity that would lead to an explosive positive-feedback system of the reward process rewarding itself. The value of stimuli, beyond whatever turnkey effects they may have on drive, is to serve as criteria for personal rules that limit shortsighted induction of a reward (i.e., rules against self-reward patterns that waste available drive). Of course, this approach would have no rationale whatever if the discounting of future events were exponential.

The picoeconomic equation for computing expected value – the equivalent of the economists' utility – is similar to that of Becker and Murphy, except for the hyperbolic discount function. The value V of a choice at the time it is made is the integral of all rewards expected to follow it, discounted by equation (5.1) adapted for compatability with (8.1):

$$V(0) = \int_{0 \to H} r(d)/(Z + \Gamma \cdot d) \tag{8.2}$$

where H is the horizon at which further increments will be infinitesimal,[3] r is momentary realized reward, that is, effective activity in the person's reward center(s), d is delay of this reward, and Z and Γ are the constants in Mazur's equation (3.7), here taken to equal 1.0. The term r is not identical with self-reward: Self-reward is only the behavior that opts for r, which the person chooses insofar as he expects r to be available in the relevant modality. If this modality is satiated or otherwise blocked, self-reward behavior will not generate any r; it will not be "rewarded" and thus will be seen as a less valuable alternative in similar situations in the future.

---

[3] This notation simply acknowledges the practical limitation of foresight that also affects Becker and Murphy's model (see footnote 2). This limitation does not govern any important feature of motivational conflict. The difference in notation is not important for comparison of the models.

In the mechanical illustration, r (or consumption) is modeled by the variable loudness of a steam calliope.[4] Each separately satiable modality is a separate note, with its own separate boiler and controlled by its own key on a keyboard. Separately keyed boilers are competitive in that the "demon" can press only one key at a time.[5] That part of a person that evaluates choices is the player; the keyboard is freely accessible to the player at all times. The player cannot choose capriciously, but must value expected sounds (r's) strictly according to the matching law. Because the player has no motivation independent of this equation, he is not a whole personality, but a demon. The demon has all the person's cognition, perception, and memory, but instead of having motives he follows an instruction: Maximize the probable aggregate volume of future sounds, with each future sound discounted proportionately to its delay from the present moment. This is an obedient demon, like that of Maxwell or Planck, not to be confused with the whole-souled homunculus of the old vitalists. However, the person, and hence the demon, may come to the logical conclusion of this instruction slowly, or not at all: that the likelihoods of his future choices have strong implications for which of his current choices is best – Kreps and Wilson's "sequential" refinement of the Nash equilibrium (1982) – and that his current choice is apt to contribute to a reputation that will influence his expectations in future decisions (cf. Weigelt & Camerer, 1988).

Choice-making is thus divided into two components: a mechanism governing what reward is available and a mechanism that learns these contingencies of reward and chooses accordingly. Together, the calliope that models motivation and the demon that models cognitive and behavioral capacities describe the entire person (Figure 8.1). The reader with limited interest in the problems of modeling motivation may skip to section 8.1.1, which summarizes the mechanical model concisely.

The economists' momentary consumption, c, is broken down into three aspects: the behavior, opting for r; its hedonic effect, r; and its effect on future consumption (i.e., to what extent r is "consumed"

---

[4] I have learned that steam calliopes actually had only one loudness – extreme – but I have not been able to find another analogy as readily graspable, and thus I shall stay with my already nonstandard circus machine.
[5] Any limited number that would be a small proportion of the possible keys could be assumed equally well.

Figure 8.1. A mechanical model of self-reward: The choice-maker is constrained only to maximize expected loudness (reward), discounted according to the matching law.

in the sense of no longer being available). This last aspect would be a change in capital stock in an economist's model (S in the Becker–Murphy equation), although it is far from the only basis for such changes of stock.[6]

Opting (o) for r must maximize expected value according to equation (8.2):

$$o_i(t) = f[\text{expected } V_i(t)] = f[\text{past } V_i(t)] \tag{8.3}$$

where i is each separately satiable modality, and t is the time at which the opting is decided upon. The functions by which relevant choice points in the past are identified and a future expectation is derived

[6] The "learning by doing" on which Becker and Murphy focus is a longer-range, less easily reversible process; the learned satiation described in chapter 7 would be an example. Such a process is part of the demon, not the calliope. Even without considering the accumulated stock of such learning, there will be at least three changes in the calliope that will depend on past behavior and thus will represent capital-stock functions.

from them are imponderable in this model – they use the person's whole cognitive apparatus, speculation about which is beyond the scope of this book.[7] In the mechanical model, opting is key-pressing, which the demon is instructed to perform insofar as past presses have produced loud sounds in similar situations.

The hedonic effect of opting is momentary reward, r. This quantity depends on drive, D, in the relevant modality and, in most modalities, on an apparent factor of appetite, preparedness, or excitement, which will be designated E. Many modalities seem to become temporarily refractory to further reward without being satiated, leading to pauses, followed by renewed consumption: Examples include the pauses after a copulatory run in a rat, after some eating activity in many species, and after a period of hilarity for a person at a comedy. A temporary drive state, or phasic drive, $D_p \leq D$, will be inferred from such phenomena. Thus, realized reward is a function of opting, phasic drive, and excitement:

$$r(t) = f[o(t), D_p(t), E(t)] \tag{8.4}$$

In the calliope analogy, a key-press sends an electric current to a powerful heating coil in the wall of a boiler. If there is water in the boiler and the current is sufficient to make the water boil, steam will escape through a whistle, generating a "hoot" that will depend on the whistle's shape:

Momentary loudness = f(Steam flow) = f(Key-press, Boiler level, Heat)

with the functions expressed by both the shape of the whistle and the shape of the boiler. For instance, a narrow neck in the wired wall of the boiler might produce rapid boiling only when there was water at that level. Such a shape would model a modality of reward in which

---

[7] To avoid assumptions about the way people estimate the outcomes contingent upon their choices, a computer model must assume perfect knowledge of these outcomes. In real life this is impossible, if only because of people's limited computational powers: "If we really made $n(n - 1)/2$ pairwise comparisons for every n feasible options (even without allowing for the several consequences of varying likelihood involved in each), we would get nothing done at all" (Hollis, 1983, p. 248). Even a computer takes all night to do this. However, insofar as people's satisficing methods work well, they should approximate the computer's calculated state of knowledge, rather than some other state.

the latency to realized reward was less under conditions of high drive than under low drive.

Consumption could affect "consumption capital" in various ways. Three that seem to have some basis in behavioral observation or common experience will be part of the basic model:

In theory, the availability of reward in a modality might be independent of how much reward had been realized from this modality in the recent past; that is, nothing in the concept of reward requires it to consume the drive on which it is based. A phenomenon like pain might indeed seem insatiable, but I have argued that even pain must satiate temporarily (see section 4.2.3) – in the present terms, it must dissipate D_p if not D. Certainly, common speech verifies the reasonable prediction that an insatiable drive would be useless for an organism's survival: "Consumption" of a good expresses in the same breath the good's enjoyment and its exhaustion. However, enjoyment need not precisely parallel exhaustion; I have argued that it often does not (see section 7.3.2) and that the failure of enjoyment to keep pace with exhaustion at high rates of consumption can make such rates an impulse-control problem. Thus, whereas the momentary change in D_p is, like r, a function of current D_p and E, it is apt to be a *different* function of those quantities than r is. In addition, D_p sometimes may be dissipated by means other than the consumption of reward, as when amphetamine directly reduces the capacity to be rewarded by food.[8] Finally, D_p will tend to be restored as long as there is D. Thus, a momentary change in phasic drive is a function of opting for reward, of the current level of phasic drive, of the current level of excitation, of turnkey stimuli that dissipate phasic drive, and of the current level of total drive:

$$dD_p(t) = f[o(t), D_p(t), E(t), s(t), D(t)] \tag{8.5}$$

where s is the effect of any turnkey stimuli that dissipate drive.

In terms of the calliope, water loss in the form of steam does not necessarily parallel the amplitude of sound created by that steam. As the water in the boiler gets hotter and increases the rate of steam

---

[8] Drive may also be increased by direct turnkey stimulation, e.g., onset of a painful stimulus, but this need not be modeled separately from other kinds of increases, because none of these kinds depends on the demon's opting behaviors.

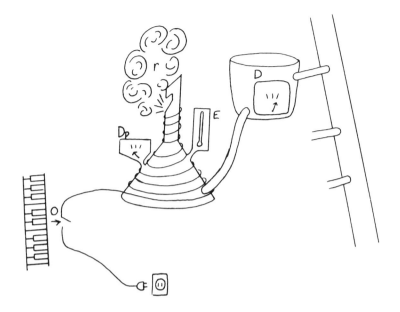

Figure 8.2. A boiler and whistle that model a single reward modality: A console key controls a heating coil around the boiler, which holds water D_p at heat E, produces sound r, and is refilled from reserve tank D.

flow, the hoot will get louder, but less than proportionately. Also, extrinsic factors may directly drain the boiler. The boiler refills from a more slowly filling reserve tank, which stores the water representing the rest of the drive, D. Thus, the momentary change in water level in the boiler is a function of key-presses, the existing water level, the heat level, extrinsic drainage, and the level of water in the reserve tank:

$$d(\text{Boiler level}) = f(\text{Steam flow, Drainage, Tank level})$$
$$= f(\text{Key-press, Boiler level, Heat, Drainage, Tank level})$$

with the functions expressed by whistle and boiler shapes, as before, by the turnkey operation of a drain valve, and by the diameters and locations of pipes leading from the tanks to the boilers (Figure 8.2).

The excitement factor, E, is generated by the person's opting (o) for r within the given modality, that is, by the demon's repeatedly pressing a key. Excitement must reach a threshold before it induces *r*. This threshold may be so low that it is reached immediately, as in many aversive modalities like fear and pain, or it may be high, creating a lag of unproductive time that will serve as an entry cost to a modality. The need to "get up steam" may be all that allows strategic self-control in process-reward modalities like sex and anger, which are not guarded by the threat of pain for arousing appetite in the absence of a drive-reducing substance (see section 7.3.1). For a modality that has both a significant heat threshold and negative acceleration of loudness as heat increases, a plot of loudness as a function of heat (in turn proportional to key-pressing) will be an S-curve (Figure 8.3A). A plot of loudness as a function of rate of steam loss will express the efficiency of a given heat level and will also be an S-curve (Figure 8.3B). An S-shaped curve of loudness defines an optimization task for the demon, a task made difficult by the fact that moves to the right will be disproportionately valued when they are immediately available.

By the happenstance of how nature has wired in the drive interactions, opting for *r* in one modality may not only increase *E* in that modality but also increase or inhibit *E* in another. The latter case – inhibiting *E* – is important in the self-reward model, for pains seem to act not just by occupying attention, but by "spoiling" other appetites (e.g., for food).[9] That activity in some drives may *enhance* others (e.g., pain increasing sexual excitement) is interesting but not vital for the self-reward model. Because one modality seems to affect another only when it becomes active – not, for instance, if a drive like pain is blocked by medication – the interactive effect probably should be represented as a function of the excitation, given the drive level of the interfering modality; this need not be the same function that determines its *r*, but in the absence of specific data I shall make it that for simplicity. For a given modality there may be many specific ways that activity in other modalities contributes to excitation:

[9] Another example (see section 7.3.2): If there are several partially separate hunger drives, satiating one will have some effect on the others (Rolls, Rolls, Rowe, et al., 1981).

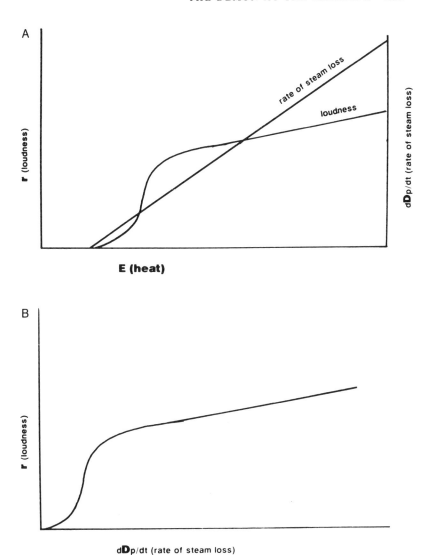

Figure 8.3. Hypothetical graphs modeling (A) rate of realized reward (loudness) and rate of satiation (steam loss) as functions of rate of opting for reward (heat) and (B) the relationship of realized reward to satiety. With an increasing rate of opting, reward does not keep pace with satiety.

$$dE(t) = f[o(t), r_i(t)]$$ (8.6)

where the r_i are reward activities in other modalities that act on the E of the given one. For the calliope, the momentary change in heat,

$$d(\text{Heat}) = f(\text{Key-press, Loudness of interacting boilers})$$

where the contribution of other boilers to the function is determined by specific wiring arrangements.

Finally, a person's capacity for reward (his wealth, for economists) is changed according to his intrinsic rate of drive regeneration (wages, or w) and his rate of satiation of drive (expenditure):

$$dD(t) = f[w(t), dD_p(t)]$$ (8.7)

where dD_p is ongoing consumption of available drive. Regeneration happens according to the nature of its modality – slowly for those drives like food and sex where the biologically most adaptive incidences of satiation are spaced apart by hours to days, but so rapidly for pains that the concept of a reserve tank adds nothing to the model, that is, $D_p = D$, and $dD_p = dD = w$, which is so high as to produce rapid replenishment of D_p. In terms of the calliope, the change of water level in a tank depends on outflow to the boiler and inflow to the tank from its pipe:

$$d(\text{Tank water}) = f(\text{Steam loss, Inflow})$$

These relationships are summarized in Table 8.1.

8.1.1 Summary using the calliope illustration

A keyboard representing a person's ability to opt freely for all possible rewards controls current flow to heating elements in the casings of an array of boilers – all the sources of reward that have evolved with the species (Figure 8.1). Each boiler fills from a pipe of characteristic size, representing the speed with which its drive recovers, and has its own whistle of characteristic size and shape, representing reward production as a function of attention to that modality and of the level of its drive. It is this property that determines efficiency – sound production per amount of steam lost – at the various possible rates of boiling and levels of water. Despite the water simile, this model

Table 8.1. *Summary of the demon at the calliope: equivalent economic, behavioral, and mechanical terms*

Economic	Behavioral	Mechanical
Utility	Value = aggregate discounted r	Aggregate discounted loudness
Consumption (1)	Opting = f (Past value → expected value)	Key-presses = f (Past loudness → Demon's expectation)
Consumption (2)	Reward = f (Opting, Phasic drive, Excitation)	Loudness = f (Opting, Boiler water, Heat)
Capital (1)	d (Phasic drive) = f (Opting, Phasic drive, Excitation, Turnkeys, Drive)	d (Boiler water) = f (Rate of steam loss, Turnkey valve effects, Tank water)
Capital (2)	d (Excitation) = f (Opting, Reward in alternatives)	d (Heat) = f (Key-presses, Loudness of alternatives)
Capital (3)	d (Drive) = f (Drive loss, Recovery)	d (Tank water) = f (Steam flow = Boiler loss, Inflow)

is not hydraulic in the sense of the old drive theorists (Hendrick, 1958, chs. 5 and 8), but economic. Here the water does not exert pressure, but accumulates as a good for possible consumption.

The immediate value of pressing a key will depend on how quickly a boiler can produce sound after presses on its key and on how many presses are required to initiate sounds. That is, discounted realized reward will depend on the latency of self-reward in a given modality when the person opts for it and on the reward's setup cost in attention. The latency is modeled as a function of the speed of heating of the thermal wiring and the diameter of the boiler – a narrower boiler heats more rapidly at a given flow of heat from its wall. Wiring that heats more slowly models drives in which appetite is aroused more slowly. Boilers are generally narrower at the top than the bottom, to reflect the observation that appetite is less quickly aroused at lower drive levels.

Water inflow to the tanks that model drives like hunger and sex must be slow, because restoration of maximal drive after complete satiation takes hours to days; for a drive like pain it will be rapid, because pain is not refractory for more than a fraction of a second. Turnkeys cannot affect key-pressing, but can control drainage valves on the boilers. Steam outflow depends on the rate of boiling, as does sound production, but the two are not determined by the same function: As boiling becomes more rapid, sound production increases less rapidly than steam loss, reflecting the wastefulness of rapidly consuming most rewards.

Thus, there are three factors that reduce sound production: keypress time spent bringing water to boil before sound is produced; inefficiently rapid boiling; and key-pressing that undermines heat delivery to other boilers. The first models appetitive activity before consumption can occur, which may determine the entry cost to some reward modalities. The second models premature satiation, and the third painlike activities.

8.1.2 Illustrations using the calliope model

A drive like that underlying hoarding, which does not require a turnkey stimulus, will look something like the apparatus in Figure 8.4. It never has a large heating surface (thus does not reach great productivity) and has few heating coils (thus does not rapidly become intense), but its narrow neck means a short latency. It has wide pipes to both the boiler and the reserve tank (thus short durations of both phasic satiation and exhaustion). Some widening from top to bottom reflects only moderate growth in intensity with prolonged heating. It does not inhibit other drives.

Sexual drive might differ from hoarding in having dense heating coils (thus potential for greater intensity), a wide base (thus the potential for great productivity), and a narrow pipe into the tank (thus slow recovery from exhaustion) (Figure 8.5). The narrow neck permits rapid excitation before the rest of the boiler is heated. A pattern of reward through fantasy may exploit only this part, while avoiding deeper excitation; such activity does not directly inhibit other drives, but may undermine them through competition.

Pain might differ from hoarding in having dense heating wires and being narrow for its entire height (thus reaching great intensity rapidly but satiating rapidly) (Figure 8.6). A wide supply pipe (rendering a tank meaningless) reflects rapid regeneration of drive and no long-term exhaustion, but it is opened only by a turnkey stimulus for pain (absent which there is no pain drive). Wires branch out from the heating coil to inhibit heating of coils in other drives.

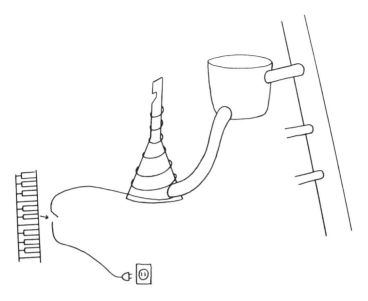

Figure 8.4. A reward system that might underlie hoarding.

The demon's task is not simple. He must take into account both the mechanical properties of the calliope and the choices that his own strict instructions will most likely require him to make in the future. However, his task is neither ambiguous nor indeterminate. The self-referential loop in his forecasting procedure is no more arcane than that of a transistor, the input to which consists partially of its own output. The demon himself has no motives, no urge or tendency to deviate from the letter of his instructions – the motivational process is modeled entirely by the calliope. His apparent subtlety in predicting his own future choices comes simply from his instructions, which tell him to use all available information in applying the matching law to his choices. I argued earlier that this kind of self-referential feedback loop is sufficient to produce the quality of free will (see section 6.3).

It is unnecessary to deal with the question of how many independently satiating drives there are, or whether or not there are subdrives. Subdrives would represent some kind of loculation within a drive, so that the capacity to be rewarded by one kind of process

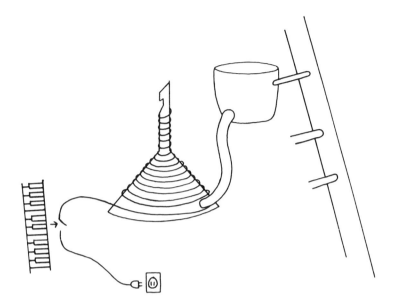

Figure 8.5. A mechanical model of sexual drive.

would be partially but not totally affected by a related process – for example, appetites for chocolate, fat, sugar, and so forth, within the hunger drive, which might depend partially but not entirely on the organism's general level of satiation by food. The answers to these questions would not change the nature of the model, and there is not adequate information to answer them one way or another.

8.1.3 Precommitments open to the demon

Because of his instructions to follow the matching law, the demon will press fast-acting keys exhaustively and wastefully unless he discovers how to use personal rules that hinge upon external cues to limit his key-pressing. Where such rules will increase his expected reward, his instructions call on him to adopt them, but also to find loopholes that will permit additional current consumption without losing the increase in expectation. External cues represent possible

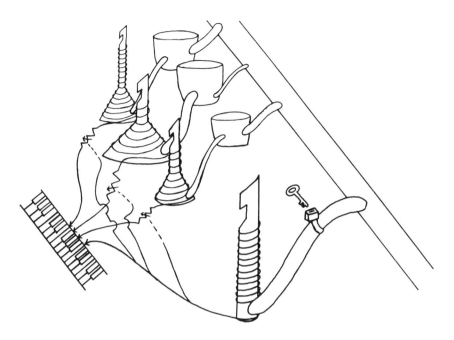

Figure 8.6. A mechanical model of pain.

sheet music, as it were, for his playing. They increase his ability to sustain loud sound. Even though at many points he would produce louder sound in the immediate future by pressing and holding a single key than by playing the next few notes of the music, still the expected discounted loudness of the whole piece may be greater at each point than the expected discounted loudness of spontaneous play. As long as he believes that he must stick strictly to the piece or expect to abandon it entirely, he is apt to stick with the music. The available sheets of music – external stimuli – thus form the criteria of personal rules, which the demon often adopts so as to maximize expected loudness under the matching law. To the whole person the stimulus pattern may be a dinner, or evidence that he will have dinner, or a story, or the events in a game, but to the demon they matter only as possible constraints on his playing the calliope. He chooses this music not to match the pattern of reality but to make a louder sound.

Besides binding his playing to sheet music, there are other methods by which the demon can constrain what delays and amplitudes of sound will be available to him in the near future, and thus increase his long-range productiveness. These methods model the effects on self-reward of drive interaction, perceptions, and extrinsic physical factors – the factors manipulated by the three forms of precommitment other than personal rules. Having dealt with personal rules already, we shall keep going in reverse order:

Control of emotion takes advantage of the interaction of drives. Activity in some boilers affects the heat level in others; their activity reduces or increases the delay necessary before self-reward can be realized in the other modalities. If the demon expects that the matching law will at some point require him to self-reward shortsightedly in a given modality, he may keep the latency for sound from that modality long – and thus decrease its value at the point when it must first be chosen – by not firing boilers that transmit heat to the boiler in question. Or he may fire boilers that will compete with that boiler over the necessary period of time. The constraints on this activity are, of course, those of the process it models: emotion control. Nature has made only certain interactions available, and activity meant to influence the attractiveness of other modalities may or may not be richly productive in its own right.

Attention control is the processing of information in such a way that cues as to the availability of reward in a target modality are not noticed. This itself is a behavior, and its choice is subject to the matching law; there are occasions when this behavior is the demon's best hope of increasing the latency of an impulsive route to self-reward. He might avoid performing estimation tasks that would tell him how soon reward could be realized from the target modality. However, such behavior would give the demon blind spots.

Extrapsychic devices, even when available, may not solve the demon's precommitment problem. Having a person's jaws wired shut will reduce his opportunity to eat food, but not to self-reward in the food modality. He still must deal with the urge to spin fantasies about eating, which in the absence of the physical effects of ingested food will be an itchlike temptation. That is, the matching law may require the demon to play eating notes to the memory rather than to the current stimulus of food, even though such a pattern is aversive from any distance. In contrast, taking diet pills can lower the water level in the boiler for the moment, thus controlling the urge to self-reward in that modality at its root. However, such extrapsychic devices are apt to have innate defects, such as leading to a rebound enlargement of capacity for self-reward in the target modality when they are discontinued, or supporting an addictive pattern of self-reward in its own modality, in this case to the diet pills. It is the general availability of self-reward that makes extrapsychic commitment devices far less useful in practice than the naive therapist expects.

8.2 The crucial properties of pacing devices are aesthetic

Almost any source of varying facts can serve as a pacing device for self-reward. Even an unusual reading on an automobile odometer – 100000 or 77777.7, for instance – repays notice. A simple string of "ons" and "offs," like the rhythm of a single drum or even the ticking of a clock, sometimes can be experienced as rewarding. A person can simply reward himself whenever a unit of time has passed, as bored children used to do when school clocks clicked loudly every minute. But the facts must not be under the person's arbitrary control. It would not be rewarding to set a dial to 100000 or make a ticking sound oneself.

A monotonous event is not much of a pacing device, although it can be enriched by adding partial uncertainty as to its timing, as in a percussion rhythm. A simple rhythm is soon fully explored; subsequently, small but frequent increases for a clock or odometer will lead to such brief, insignificant reward that the recurring minor urge to repeat it will become an itch. It will persist only in the absence of richer patterns for self-reward. The chance to indulge in it may be a nuisance, and the person may turn the clock away or make a rule not to look at the odometer just to be rid of the repeated opportunity for brief reward. The competition between the self-reward response based on this cue and the self-reward responses based on the delayed cues will be the same as that between any impulse and a long-range interest. In either case, the actual choice will be determined by the greater aggregate prospect of actual reward, discounted according to the matching law, that the person faces at the moment of choice.

The less commonly a fact is encountered, the more it is apt to be valued, once a person has invested that particular domain of facts with importance. Simple rarity has no effect unless it has become the object of a taste. Almost all events are rare from one point of view or another. Thus, one bird may be no more interesting than another until a person becomes a bird-watcher, that is, until he lets a significant part of his self-reward depend on sighting birds. Thereafter, rarer birds will be occasions for more self-reward than less rare ones, and this will be true as long as he follows procedures that keep them rare. There would be no point in going to an aviary to increase his sightings; he might as well imagine the birds, or reward himself without regard to occasion. Similarly, an "original" painting will plummet in value, despite unchanged artistic features, if art collectors conclude that it is a "fake" and hence less rare (Bachrach, 1991).

As was mentioned in section 7.1, one use of money is as a counter in gamelike activities. Quite apart from what it can buy, money can be valuable as a pacer of self-reward. In effect it becomes like bird sightings or mountain peaks to climb, another object of collection. A person then tends to behave so as to maximize the aggregate reward realized from this pacing effect, rather than to maximize his actual income. Naturally, the rules of this activity still will call for him to maximize income (and minimize expense); otherwise the game would not be "real," but would be only one of any number of arbitrary activities, thus losing much of its value as a pacing device. However, "maximize income" is a very general rule and is susceptible to hedging. For instance, a person may congratulate himself on how much money he saves by recycling glass or using food-store coupons so long as he can evade the intuition that, audited strictly, the activity would not pay for his time.

This example of cheating on rules for realistic money-making is trivial, but some are not. Even professional investors are prone to it and must be cautioned against it in business schools: For instance, a person who has made a bad investment might be obliged by his rules for valuing money to reduce his rate of self-reward, but if he regards that investment as part of a larger investment that still stands a chance, he can defer this duty or evade it altogether (Arkes & Blumer, 1985). Thus, protecting his sunk cost, although objectively less adaptive (Northcraft & Wolf, 1984; Staw, 1981), will be in his best short-term interest. Where there can be no way to count the sunk cost as apt to be made good by a subsequent gain – as when a person has simply lost a theater ticket and would have to count that as a dead loss even if he bought another ticket and enjoyed the show – there seems to be no urge to "protect" the sunk cost by investing more money (Tversky & Kahneman, 1981). There are many times that any person is motivated to "fool himself," as it is often called; properly, what he is doing is finding loopholes in his own personal rules on the basis of one short-term interest or another.

The fact that we assign value to money according to our own rules, rather than discerning value in money, is shown by the existence of exceptions: Where the pursuit of money would undermine other valued activities, a person requires himself not to value it. Money is not to be weighed against affairs of the heart, for instance, or to be counted as a reason to obey or disobey the law, or to be considered when seeking medical care.

Neither money-getting itself nor the activities money makes possible are the only efficient ways to pace self-reward. Indeed, there is much hoary wisdom saying that such activities are relatively poor at this in the long run (i.e., that they are apt to be sellouts). Thus, some people may value money extensively, and among these some will be better than others at playing a disciplined game that will maximize aggregate reward. Some people will not value money highly and will tend to earn only as much as they need for other ends. And some may change from one outlook to the other in the course of their lives.

8.2.1 Optimal rarity

Like the criteria for any rule, pacing cues will be most effective if they are clearly set apart from stimuli in the background. Suppose that a person tries rewarding himself according to a complex cue that in its commonest form occurs too frequently for efficient self-reward. If the properties of that cue vary continuously, with no demarcating line, it will be useless as a pacer of self-reward, because it will have the same problems as cueless self-reward. If the person can detect boundary lines between its common and uncommon states, it may become a highly useful pacing device, depending on how bright the lines are (see section 5.6.1) and how efficiently the pattern of self-reward it dictates exploits the relevant drive. For instance, people who save grocery coupons say that there are a few valuable coupons that obviously are "worth it," and others that clearly are not. The bulk of their effort goes into deciding whether or not to bother with those in the middle ground, and it is this effort that decides whether or not the activity as a whole is worthwhile.

A person may devote quite a bit of lawyerly effort to deciding when he will let himself call an event rare – witness the number of ways records can be set in sports statistics. This effort may or may not permit more overall reward from watching a sport, but it clearly reduces the impact of individual rare events; a record set in one of a thousand possible ways is less of an occasion than a record set in one of ten possible ways. Likewise, the more religious relics there are, or shrines, or days that are holy, the less the experiential impact of each. The person or the culture must select how many holy occasions there are on the basis of the same considerations they use to select the difficulty (number of winning outcomes) of games of solitaire.

The optimal rarity of a pacing cue depends to some extent on the potential yield of the relevant drive. If this yield is great and the person has selected a rare event to occasion it, he will be strongly motivated to reward himself also at lesser events that bear some intrinsic relationship to the rare event. Cues that predict the rare event might be such occasions; an observer might thus see them as secondary rewards based upon it, except that many such occasions have no predictive power whatsoever, as when someone "shakes the hand that shook the hand" of a celebrity.

The best rules for control of self-reward are partially responsive to a person's wishes. Totally responsive rules are no rules at all, and totally unresponsive rules often will happen to waste a good deal of possible reward. It follows that good criteria for rules compose a limited resource. Furthermore, different interests within individuals will favor rules of different responsiveness – the more short-term the interest, the more responsive the rules favored.

The selection of a pacing device may itself be influenced by interests of less than the longest range. Some pacing devices appeal to a mid-range interest against longer-range interests. For instance, events in fiction pace self-reward more slowly than those controlled by a person's fantasy, but faster than those in "real life"; pacing by fictional events may become a durable but suboptimal pattern of obtaining reward from the relevant drive(s). One or another kind of fast-return pacing often is tempting, despite its wastefulness. If a person is wealthy enough, he can eat only sirloin tips and desserts, but he will not thereby maximize the reward available from his hunger.

In the case of emotional or "process" drives, a person can always feed himself the equivalent of sirloin tips and desserts. However, "self-realization," the term by which Jon Elster summarizes "the deepest form of satisfaction," in its initial stages is "usually painful to some extent. It involves both pain and pleasure – with, moreover, the pain being an essential condition for the pleasure" (1990, p. 11). Instead of reading a book, a person may see the movie or read a synopsis, thus getting to the same ending, but with less satisfaction than if he had gone through the more painstaking development of the original. The children in *Peter Pan* ask Wendy to tell them not whole fairy tales, but only the endings. But the news that Cinderella lived happily ever after is not particularly satisfying unless one has developed a longing for that to happen. The development of this longing takes time and is relatively unrewarding. It would be especially difficult for children if they had to do it without guidelines (viz., a story); given the availability of a story, they still have to accept the suspense, that is, keep themselves from prematurely assuaging their longing by asking for the ending. An optimal self-reward pattern is threatened by the urge to produce reward more rapidly but less richly.

Over evolutionary periods of time, drives probably are shaped by natural selection, so that the objects that are most adaptive for the organism to seek have become the most effective pacing devices for the rewards based on those drives. However, in a rapidly changing world, that is not apt to be the case (Glantz & Pearce, 1989). Furthermore, among individuals, the choice of the most effective pacing devices may depend on the accumulated wisdom of the society, and this, too, is undermined by rapid change.

The amount of fast-return pacing for which people will opt will depend both on their access to fast pacing devices and on their wariness of those devices. In a society where densely caloric food is easily obtained and prepared and where the wisdom of time has not yet responded to this availability, people will tend to "graze," even though this style of eating undoubtedly reduces the total reward available from satisfying the hunger drive. Where communication technology has made fiction copiously available, stories must compete as to how fast they can reach moments of gratification; the "flip value" necessary to capture the mass market rises. Such changes may simply be signs that the relevant drives have become less important as sources of reward, but because the number of drives remains limited by nature, it is more likely that knowledge of how to speed the availability of reward has outdistanced knowledge about how to delay it. Recent developments in technology have served our short-term interests better than our long-term interests.

8.3 The main value of other people is to pace one's own self-reward

The behaviors of other people are particularly apt to be useful in pacing self-reward, because people can readily learn to cooperate in providing occasions at an optimal rate. For instance, if I have a friend who sometimes drops by and suggests that we take a coffee break during the workday, and if he does not come too rarely or too often, I am spared the need to regulate my breaks. If I have to decide arbitrarily when to take a break, I cannot take it whenever I feel ready, for fear that the sensation of readiness will come with increasing frequency and make me unable to complete any difficult task. Rather than take the chance of an arbitrary decision, I may go without breaks altogether. But if my rule merely says that I can have a break when my friend invites me, and if my friend is a "good" friend in this respect, my problem is solved.

Because most social rewards are emotional and thus are within the the individual's power to generate at will through imagination, even under the weak form of the self-reward hypothesis, the value of other people must be to occasion such rewards. A person who has invested importance in a somewhat unpredicatable human relationship rewards himself more efficiently than the narcissist, not because the latter is incapable of the full range of human feeling but because the narcissist retains too much arbitrary control over when he will generate the feeling. To reach their greatest intensity, feelings of pride, love (with or without the adjuvant of sex), rage, celebration, gloating, compassion, contempt, awe, and countless others must depend on being invited. Despairing of richer activities, a person is apt to be more rewarded by even the rancor or embarrassment occasioned by others' abuse of him than by any feeling generated autistically, and hence will seem unaccountably to be "a glutton for punishment" – one of the people Eric Berne described as playing games for "brown stamps" (1972, pp. 24–25); for many plausible examples of behaviors rewarded by ostensible punishments, see his original catalog of games (Berne, 1964).

When a person exchanges pacing stimuli with another person, usually he will be alert to evidence that his stimuli are important to the other person, lest the latter capriciously manipulate the exchange. Ordinary bargaining will tend to produce mutuality of investment in each other's pacing stimuli. A person's demand for evidence of the other's investment not only protects his own investment but also serves the other's needs: The latter must surrender his short-term control of what pacing stimuli he will use, and to the extent that he does so, he will be protected from his own greed for immediate self-reward. Mutual relationships, whether of friendship or enmity, will be good producers of the two properties needed for optimal self-reward: partially unpredictable stimuli and the commitment to reward oneself according to those stimuli.

Thus, a person's choices of emotional objects are apt to depend on how their behaviors let him pace self-reward. Insofar as they provide optimal challenges, he will "have feelings for" them and value them even if they are enemies, because even enemies can provide useful criteria for limiting premature self-reward. Conversely, a person is apt to avoid another when the other person interferes with his self-reward strategies. Another person's example is potentially a robust boundary between one's long- and short-range interests just because it is not arbitrary; it is especially compelling insofar as his circumstances are like one's own. If that boundary seems to encroach on the present domain of either a short- or long-range interest, that interest will motivate avoidance of the other person. In modern times, the fear of heterodox beliefs seems a benighted attitude, but that is because we expect people to achieve some distance from others' examples, not because those examples lack force. The damage done by a heresy can be real (see section 6.4.4) and is notoriously greatest when it arises in a kindred spirit.

Aversion to another person will be even stronger when that person's adherence to a personal rule leads him to "achieve" behaviors that one perceives as impulsive. For instance, a person who has been learning not to be provoked to anger will be disturbed by the behavior of another who is struggling to overcome timidity and assert himself.

Even the pacing provided by human behavior is subject to premature satiation. This is more apt to happen the more one can control either the pacing or one's investment in it. A person who reads a book or watches a videotape can stop, jump ahead or backward, or replace it, entirely at his whim. He may make sure that he never does any of these things once under way, but his awareness of his arbitrary control over the book or tape still will reduce its value as a pacing device. In a movie theater, he is more committed to watch straight through, and he is also in the company of real people who may react spontaneously to his behaviors, albeit only as fellow members of an audience: He risks embarrassment from laughing in the wrong place or sharing the sight of wishes that he disowns being enacted on the screen, but he also has the chance to get more occasions for his feelings. Thus, movies survive in competition with the cheaper and more convenient tapes. In a live theater, the performers, as well as his fellow audience members, may react to his behaviors, a step even closer to optimal responsiveness that justifies the much greater cost of tickets to live theater. But neither audience nor performers will give him much of their attention, making theater inferior to more mutual human transactions, except insofar as the performers can invite importance and resist anticipation through their art.

Many conventional roles besides being fellow audience members allow strangers to interrupt premature satiation in each other. However, this process may deteriorate, not only through lack of investment but also through erosion of the norms that keep these interactions surprising.

Finally, even supposedly mutual relationships can lose their ability to engender surprise. This may happen through a conspiracy to avoid surprise that is dictated by the members' short-range interests – for instance, by allowing the relationship to fall into ritual and become "old hat." Or it may happen through the acquiescence of one member to control by the other – in which case it is the *controlling* member who is lured into losing a source of surprise. At the extreme of this continuum, the victim in a sadomasochistic relationship usually does not lose interest in it, but the aggressor does (Benjamin, 1988). Among strangers, conventional roles that let people interrupt each other's premature satiation may deteriorate through a similar erosion of discipline. Thus, a bemused columnist recently wrote that

> with the entire population going crazy trying to think of new ways to shock jaded fellow citizens, there is no one left in the crucial job of being shocked. . . . Miss Manners proposes that some of us volunteer. [Martin, 1991]

In a society in which physiological rewards are plentiful, the values of goods will come to depend on their capacities to induce surprise. The richest source of this power is other people's responsiveness. Among people who might supply their responses, one's choices of those who are actually valued will depend on happenstances of investment, which may depend in turn on a number of accidental factors such as timing, fashion, or superficial resemblances to past acquaintances; but insofar as human responsiveness is not used in mutually demanding relationships, its power to surprise is apt to be used inefficiently. As communication technology makes the most artful spectator amusements plentiful, people increasingly attend to them, rather than investing in mutually demanding relationships. That is, passive attention to the world's best artists or athletes increasingly competes in the same league as having relationships, at least in terms of its immediate capacity to support self-reward; it supports self-reward less well in the long run because of the person's arbitrary control over his investment.

Where a person identifies spectator activity as competing with long-term relationships, he may prefer it only temporarily, in the addiction or sellout range. Thus, a person may feel guilty about the amount of time he spends watching television, or regret the energy he has spent being a fan, instead of cultivating friendships. However, the subtle nature of the competition is apt to leave undisturbed one's innocent, primrose-path evaluation of such activity as simply better than keeping company with the disappointing people in his community (see section 7.4.1). This misperception is especially likely because day-to-day personal interactions may become easier as they become less important; the less a person lets another hold his self-reward hostage, the less tense will be their negotiations with one another, and the friendlier they will appear. Thus, no relationship will seem to have been lost. Furthermore, the popularity of spectator activities in a community is apt to make its members more disappointing as significant emotional objects, because the attention they pay to these activities is withdrawn from each other; this makes peer responsiveness scarcer and harder to compete for, and thus a poorer prospect than passive entertainment.

This reasoning suggests the sinister likelihood that mass media impoverish a society in the same way as drugs and other addictions, although more subtly, by draining away more attention than they return. A strong personality in a local community draws inspiration from the attention paid him and returns it in the form of leadership. But a national celebrity cannot use more than a fraction of the attention paid him, and he can return only nondemanding performance, not a personal relationship. The art of this performance may nevertheless reduce the market for local leadership, as well as for peer and dependent relationships – with the availability of mass media, human attractiveness has increasingly become a winner-take-all market (Frank, 1990). Local masters are proletarianized, as it were, and the old, the inhibited, and the dull are driven from the responsiveness market altogether. They cannot compete even for each other's attention, and when they are not placated by mass media they must be dealt with by paid helpers.

8.4 The need to pace self-reward determines the equilibrium of fantasy and reality

The use of facts as pacing devices for self-reward creates short-term motivation to change one's perception of the facts. That is, fictions that are not too liberal in calling for self-reward may compete strongly with facts as pacing devices; to control the urge to authenticate such fictions as facts and to pace their reward accordingly, people must have some way of testing reality according to personal rules. Without such rules they will not maximize the reward they realize in the long run. Even with them, people face an ongoing temptation to find loopholes.

The interplay of external information with a person's self-rewarding behavior will be best illustrated by those behaviors that serve as their own rewards: the emotions. If a person has learned to arouse his appetite for anger when he hears insults, his response will be more vigorous if the cues meet the test of being real, and more still if they really apply to him. The same is true for fear, sexual arousal, or indeed any emotion. One can always make oneself emotional, if necessary by rehearsing a fantasy or a memory, but this emotion will not be as vivid as that occasioned by a fact.

Note that such a relationship makes no sense if reward is not something one does – if instead it is something that happens to one. The difference in vividness between imagination and present fact lies not in the stimulus properties of the present fact; a writer of fiction makes use almost entirely of his reader's imagination to create scenes that are emotionally evocative. What makes our usual imaginings paler than a story is neither a lack of detail nor a lack of sensory intensity, but the fact that they are being summoned at will. When we undertake to summon them only as directed by a storyteller, they become scarcer and hence more moving.

If we perceive the story to be "real," that one attribute makes it even more vivid. A belief about reality may be entirely projected, and it probably always depends somewhat on our having filled in blank spaces with our own personal memories. However, if our observation and logic are adequately disciplined, authentication as real by these two processes will greatly increase the story's capacity to occasion our emotions. A news story read as fact will be more vivid than one read as fiction, and part of the art of telling a ghost story is to suggest to the audience that it really happened.

The most vivid facts will be those we believe to be occurring right now. This is true even when we get little sensory information about them, as from a radio broadcast. Facts are no less true now than they will be when they are past, but they are rarer, for there is only one present moment, whereas there are many past ones. Many televised entertainments, such as ball games and quiz shows, rely entirely on being both real and live to attract an audience. If they are found to be fixed, the damage done is only to the audience's effort to see them as real, but the importance of this effort is demonstrated by the scandal that ensues. Furthermore, even a real game has much less value when rebroadcast, and this is true even when the audience does not know the outcome. It is likely that this drop in value comes from the perception that a rebroadcast is only one of many possible rebroadcasts; programs that are regularly shown a short time after they have been taped keep their value as being "live."

Thus, the operation called belief singles out one of the many available fantasies or fictions that are otherwise aesthetically equal[10] and thereby makes it a potent pacer of self-reward, quite apart from any information it may contain about impending events. The practical effect of belief is to regulate a particular modality of self-reward in accordance with the facts believed in. That is, if one believes that a drink contains alcohol, he performs the emotional and physiological behaviors that have succeeded in the presence of alcohol. As we have seen (section 7.5.1), this is not a case of falsely anticipating a reward, for these behaviors are themselves the object of drinking; rather, the belief in alcohol entails the belief that shorter-range rewards like fear or self-consciousness are unavailable, a belief that may keep the person from sampling them and from thereby undermining the desired emotional behaviors. Some examples follow:

If one believes that a drink contains poison, he is tempted to abandon his usual fear-controlling rules and surrender to panic. If he believes in the truth of a story, he allows himself to "get involved" in it, that is, to give it importance. If he believes that he is in the presence of an unseen listener, or a ghost, or a divine spirit, he lets himself have social feelings and may react to ambiguous stimuli with all the responsiveness he usually reserves for social communications. If he believes transvestite performers actually to be members of their ostensible sex, he will let himself have different emotional reactions than if he does not. If he believes that a relic actually belonged to a

---

[10] What the aesthetic theorist Benedetto Croce would call "intuitions," to which "the distinction between reality and non-reality is extraneous" (1909/1969, p. 3).

movie star or saint, he makes it the occasion for warm, personal feeling; if this feeling is sexual, his appetite for the object is called fetishism.

That belief somewhat depends on evidence is well known. "Make-believe" lacks the vividness of the belief that is not arbitrary. However, a person's power to shape his own beliefs is also well known – to believe he is in danger or not, or that he is liked or not, or that he is in the presence of a divine spirit or not, by a deliberate "leap of faith" when evidence is lacking or even when it is overwhelmingly contrary. Belief is clearly an active rather than a passive process, but the way evidence constrains this process has not been well explained. There is an obvious difference between daydreaming and a leap of faith, for instance, but it cannot be characterized in conventional terms.

8.4.1 Belief is an application of will

The quasi-voluntary nature of belief is well accounted for by the self-reward hypothesis, even in its weak form. This hypothesis states that, except for some direct effects on drive, stimuli are valuable mainly as cues by which to pace self-reward – elements to guide aesthetic behavior, rather than sources of reward in their own right. Even where stimuli furnish information about the availability of other stimuli, such information may be valued for its own pacing properties as well as for its usefulness in obtaining the other stimuli. But insofar as stimuli are occasions for self-reward, a person will have short-range interests in discerning their existence on the basis of flimsy evidence.

Many realities must be guessed at: "Can I expect to be a millionaire?" "Do people really like me?" "Is my missing spouse alive?" Some people cherish the belief that they have special talents or intelligence that in reality they probably do not have, or that their "ship will come in" when it shows no sign of doing so. People gamble in lotteries despite information that they are decreasing their expected wealth, and sometimes they deny facts of truly major importance, such as the death of a spouse, while otherwise not appearing insane. Because of the potential for such distortion and the damage it can do to personal rules for pacing reward, a person must create still other rules to police the process by which he identifies criteria for reward. The function of such rules is to define and protect the set of beliefs that he authenticates as real. Of course, these rules ultimately depend not on the accuracy of the resulting beliefs but on aggregate realized reward. It is the person's need for adequately rare pacing criteria that keeps this reward somewhat correlated with the beliefs' accuracy.

We do not think of ourselves as testing reality as we live from day to day. People seem to adjust their views of reality continuously rather than in discrete decisions, and when the process of forming beliefs demands particular effort, they see it as one of gathering information rather than controlling impulses. Thus, in common intuition, belief has more to do with perception than with motivation. It seems unmotivated, or, if motivated, then motivated by an intrinsic reward for perceiving the world correctly. Beliefs that are otherwise motivated are commonly looked upon as pathological. However, ever since the pragmatist philosophers there has been some acknowledgment that even normal beliefs may be motivated by their expected productiveness (James, 1907/1978).

Although it seems to be common wisdom that a person's natural aim is to perceive the world accurately, the self-reward hypothesis suggests that people use reality mainly for aesthetic purposes, that is, for entertainment, in the broad sense of the word. "It has always been difficult for Man to realize that his life is all an art," said Havelock Ellis (1929), who thought that this art was most related to dance. That is, a person's main concern in interpreting reality probably is how to pace his self-reward activity over time. If he sometimes values accuracy because it predicts actual facts, the value of those facts, in turn, is as pacing devices. Thus, the penalty for not being realistic is not a loss of access to reward, but rather defenselessness against the lure of inefficient self-reward patterns. We look to reality to call the figures of the dance, so that we shall not have to choose them arbitrarily. Just as the writer of comedies finds that jokes can be the enemy of long-range plot and character development, a person finds that distortions of reality may permit instant reward but will make his experiences vapid in the long run. In view of people's great ability to generate rewarding experiences at will, testing reality must be looked on not as an instinctive process but as a discipline that is adhered to for the sake of maximizing realized reward.

As Caporael (1987) has recently pointed out, the evolution of the human mind was shaped by the needs of "being social" – the epitome of a gamelike activity – rather than the needs of critical reasoning. Accordingly, testing reality is not so much like target shooting as like baseball, where the challenge to the runner is not accuracy in finding the base, but deciding how much of a lead he can take from his base without being thrown out by the pitcher. A person usually has a short-range interest in evading his own rules linking self-reward to facts and in concealing that evasion from the scrutiny that is based on his long-range interests. Once again the implications of a temporary-preference model of motivational conflict coincide with one of Freud's descriptions: A primary process motivated by immediate gain distorts objective reality and is imperfectly supplanted by a secondary process that tests reality objectively for the sake of maximizing long-term gain (1911/1956d). The resulting view of reality is not the view that would be obtained by a camera, or even by a scientist whose main motive was to be accurate; it is more like the view that would be compromised upon by a legislature, if such a body had reason to promulgate an official view of reality.

8.4.2 Leaps of faith are based on personal rules

I have argued that belief is imagination that has been edited by one's rules for testing reality. But these rules operate in the service of maximizing midrange or long-range reward, rather than in the service of achieving accuracy per se. A rule for testing reality sometimes may permit the greatest actual reward if it goes beyond a photographic faithfulness to facts and requires particular interpretations unsupported or even contradicted by the available evidence. For instance, some limited cognitive distortions that improve an individual's reported self-evaluation, sense of control, and "optimism" beyond what would be justified by his objective situation have recently been observed to be correlated with his happiness, personal effectiveness, and even physical health (Snyder & Higgins, 1988; Taylor & Brown, 1988). However, once one has left the uniqueness of the bare facts, the risk of deterioration into fantasy also becomes greater.[11]

Because testing reality ultimately depends on motivational support rather than accuracy, beliefs are sometimes crafted to extend well beyond the testable facts. Spontaneous perception, like spontaneous motivation, frequently is modified to suit longer-range interests. The only requirement is that the aggregate reward expected from this belief be great enough to motivate resistance to each urge to disbelieve, also counting any expected damage to the person's rules for testing reality. Such beliefs define some kinds of doubt as impulsive – hence faith as a virtue, and William James's "will to believe" (1896/ 1967b). Just as a person can make implicit rules to overcome impulsive behaviors, so someone who must get along with another may find himself with a selectively positive view of that person and an unaccountable discomfort when contrary evidence comes up; or a person who must not develop a romantic attachment to close blood relatives may become unable to perceive sexually attractive aspects in them. Thus, belief may operate as a precommitting device that incorporates two or even all three of the possible intrapsychic tactics (see chapter 4): It uses personal rules to forbid or require certain perceptions of reality and thereby in effect forbids or requires certain emotions as well.

Like all personal rules, a belief achieves its purpose only insofar as a person expects it to succeed; he can believe something only if he expects to go on believing it. To accept a belief and then abandon it, in the absence of a new justification, has the same effect as making any other personal rule and failing to observe it. Accordingly, a belief is strengthened by evidence that one is committed to it. This effect is especially visible where a belief is poorly supported by facts – not only where people embrace a particular religious tenet but also where a person believes that he will marry a movie star, or believes his gimcrack invention will fly, or believes he will end his troubles in suicide. To maintain those kinds of beliefs, people often must seek

---

[11] Compare the argument of Oliver Wendell Holmes, Sr., that telling the truth is more prudent than lying because there is only one truth, but many possible lies (1904, p. 116).

opportunities to see themselves behaving as if their beliefs were true, such as making a sacrifice to or for a god, writing a letter to the movie star, scheduling a demonstration of the aircraft,[12] or making a credible suicide attempt. Without such a chance to establish a credit rating, the person may lose his expectation that he will follow his rule in this case, and thus he may be forced to abandon his particular leap of faith.

This understanding of "belief" bridges what usually are regarded as separate meanings of the word, such as "believing in" miracles versus "believing in" exercise. At their roots, these types of believing are both products of will. External evidence may assist either process, just as natural boundary lines assist the making of rules and contracts, but both basically seek reward.

What makes a belief difficult to maintain are the occasions for short-range self-reward offered by its alternatives. We have discussed the case in which the drive that permits these short-term urges arises from an obvious physical process, such as hunger or alcohol withdrawal (chapter 7). Similar urges arise from short-range emotional rewards. Doubts are temptations to abandon the discipline of a particular belief. Thus, the urge to be self-conscious, a reward in the itch range of temporary preference, may be resistible as long as a person can maintain the belief that "people approve of me." He may still maintain the belief when people seem to be sniggering at him, but the urge to abandon it will be strong. Conversely, a person may protect himself from a felt vulnerability to others' influence by adopting the belief that "I am among enemies"; he will then find the others' friendliness to be irritating, as a paranoid patient typically does, because it tempts him to lapse from his belief.

Similarly, a person may use his belief in his safety to rule out his urge to panic. This belief, or at least the use of the belief to control panic, can be threatened by either of two events: a surge in his appetite for panic, such as can be induced in a panic-disordered patient by a lactic acid infusion (Rifkin & Siris, 1984); or information that he probably will not be able to maintain the belief, such as

---

[12] I recall primitive newsreel footage of a man at the turn of this century who invited the press to the first test of his personal flying machine, then confidently jumped off the Eiffel Tower to his death.

undeniable danger or the presence of a phobic object that previously had led to panic. The person may try to preserve part of his willed belief by making a loophole in his rule so as to permit him to feel endangered in the presence of particular signs of danger ("real" danger). But he may not succeed if no bright line exists (e.g., when a cancer-phobic has no way to prove he is healthy), and he sometimes does not want to try (e.g., on a cliffside path where the panic released by acknowledging real danger might increase that danger).

8.4.3 Hedges on testing reality

A person adopts the rule-governed perception of reality as a discipline to pace his self-reward because it is unique, and thus it resists hedging by his short-term interests' proposal of increasingly liberal schedules. Arbitrary schedules such as fantasies are much more vulnerable to such pressure. However, the value of even reality as a pacing principle for self-reward is threatened by its openness to interpretation: "Where all is real, nothing is real" – Croce (1909/1969). Within the rules for testing reality, as within other rules, usually there is scope for legal maneuver by short-range interests (i.e., hedging).

Hedging on rules for testing reality usually occurs in three ways: A person may find places where his rule is vague about when to recognize an occasion for self-reward; even where his rule is specific, he may avoid examining whether or not he complies with the rule; or he may retreat from the rule itself to a less demanding one, either as a practical step to save the credibility of his rules or as a means to further a midrange interest.

1. The world contains many cues about any subject, so that if a person has a wish to convince himself that a missing person is alive, or dead, or that he is talented or is being followed by the KGB, usually it is possible to make at least a minimal case for it: An expert can be found who has expressed a general opinion on a related subject that can be made to fit specifically, or an unusual coincidence sooner or later occurs, or one way of reading relevant statistics is supportive. But a person endangers the efficiency of his self-rewarding process by taking advantage of this potential. He generally maximizes his long-term gain by committing himself as rigidly as possible to inescapable interpretations. For instance, he may rule that he must test

reality by submitting his interpretations to social consensus, so that interpretations about what is real or not may come from a source that responds little to his motives. Thus, he may judge that, say, he has a good singing voice only if other people say he does.

However, there are major limits to the possibility of such commitments. For one thing, rules are insensitive to unlabeled variations in amount. Thus, a rule that turns on an amount, such as the degree of an enemy's hostility or the probability that a given event will occur, is wide open to hedging. Sometimes a self-reward strategy demands a fact that is unlikely ever to be "really" ascertained, for instance, whether or not I am welcome as a guest, whether or not my mate really loves me, or whether or not people find me faintly ridiculous. Sometimes the fact is simply not available at the moment: Does this pain in my stomach mean cancer? Did I leave the water running? Will I win the lottery? Facts that will become known only in the future are favorite targets for the maneuvers of shorter-range interests and will be discussed in more detail shortly.

2. A person can hedge his rules for testing reality by ignoring his own role in steering an interpretation one way or the other. That is, he may use attention control to create the perception that products of his behaviors are actually facts given by the environment. There are many ways in which people arrange to see their arbitrary perceptions as straightforward readings of reality. Where the real situations give scant occasion for self-reward, this arrangement may improve even their long-term productivity. However, the practice of seeing motivated events as unmotivated debases the value of reality as a pacing device generally and thus tends to reduce people's protection against their greed for short-range reward.

The Ouija board, an old divining tool become parlor game, was specifically designed to make that transition: Two operators put their hands on a planchet that moved over a board of possible answers, resulting (sometimes) in the perception by both operators that the planchet was externally guided.

The Ouija device has many variants: Each member of a group uses the others' status as independent judges to authenticate beliefs he shares with the group. Such devices create a conspiracy to "believe in" certain extensions of physical reality, phantom realities that maintain their realism only insofar as most of the conspirators accept them consistently most of the time. Thus, for a person who enjoys fantasies about rock musicians, the supposition that Elvis is alive probably can produce more satisfaction than the supposition that, say, Ricky Nelson is alive – even for a Nelson fan – because of the availability of other fans who are willing to trade belief-building behaviors about Elvis. Likewise, when circumstances generate an appetite for paranoid fantasy, people can convince each other that there is a local communist plot or a mysterious contagious disease (Kerchoff & Back, 1968). This strategy is also familiar in some religions, which construct whole other worlds and populate them with various specific creatures, while policing belief-sharing behavior by making heresy a crime.

Of course, a person can also fool himself without the collusion of others. In everyday life, people often misperceive the extent to which a "fact" depends on their interpretation. They assume that the ambiguous attitudes of others represent permission, rebellion, evasion, and so forth; countless examples have been described over the years as projection and transference. The actual determinant of belief is apt to be how well the perception limits indulgence in a short-range reward while still permitting some consumption of that reward. That is, if a belief calls for behavior that serves short- and long-range interests in a proportion that somewhat corresponds to their actual bargaining power, the person may adopt it for that reason alone. For instance, a medicine that is so noxious that it can be taken only in limited amounts has more placebo effect than a mild medicine, probably because the pain of taking it promises optimal pacing of cure fantasies. Likewise, people often believe that a task at work is worthwhile just because it is difficult.

A hypochondriac must decide whether or not to *be* sick by deciding whether or not he *is* sick through some method that does not appear arbitrary. He may look at his eyes in the mirror to see if they are bloodshot or swollen or there are signs of jaundice, and if the need to be sick is great that day, it will somehow let him perceive the telltale evidence of disease. However, it must not do so with such reliability that he catches himself *playing* sick.

Divination is the art of making but not recognizing assumptions, so that one's perceptions confirm one's feelings. Done delicately it may improve a person's access to his intuitions. Tea leaves or the entrails of sacrificed animals may be valued for generating an optimal amount of ambiguity, so that an operator who reads them according to ostensibly fixed rules can see his own intuitive conclusions as dictated by this regular reading. The same may be true of informal "tests" of friendship or loyalty, or of some psychological tests that purport to be projective only for the subject. But divination, too, is at risk of eroding a person's testing of reality by permitting too much arbitrary control.

3. Short-range interests may force a retreat from a belief, as when, after an instance of panic, a phobic person reduces the range of occasions he classifies as safe. Sellout-range interests may even create new but perverse rules, such as those for detecting enemies in the paranoid patient just mentioned. In both cases, such regression reduces the force of existing rules.

8.4.4 The projective experience of belief

Because people have to bind their self-reward behaviors to external objects, they naturally come to regard reward as inhering in those objects (see section 6.4.5). When the relevent rules succeed in maintaining a fairly unsatiated level of drive, the objects that are a person's criteria for self-reward will seem to be potent rewards, and he will be said to have a taste for those objects. A particular author's books, an object of collection, or even the presence of certain people may seem to reward him, just as a phobic object seems to punish. However, these motivational situations actually arise from the use of reality as a criterion for personal rules of self-reward.

The effect of belief is to increase investment in the believed fact and to discourage exploration of alternative patterns of self-reward. Insofar as the belief succeeds, it has the same effect as a concrete rewarding stimulus, such as the consumption of a substance. Consider two emotions: One is the feeling of joy at good news, the other the euphoria induced by cocaine. Both are feelings that are available in the person's repertoire – the cocaine-taker does not experience this euphoria for the first time when he first ingests cocaine. However, the feeling of joy is said to be natural, the feeling of well-being to be artificially caused by the cocaine.

Reports that the cocaine high and other drug highs can be duplicated with placebo have not changed this common view, possibly because people perceive that they cannot summon the euphoria at their whim. However, people's ability to summon joy at will is also limited. We really can do no more than imagine it without some "legitimate" occasion, namely, good news. The placebo that the cocaine-taker believes in will re-create euphoria, just as good news will occasion joy. Belief is what enables a person to reward himself most effectively in both cases. The result is that the occasion believed in will be experienced as intrinsically rewarding.

If a drug-taker knows that the "drug" he is given contains no active ingredient, he still may be able to use the ingestion ritual to get an actual high or relief from withdrawal (O'Brien, 1976), the way a person can use imagination or fiction to evoke joy. But in these latter cases, the compromise of a person's urge for premature satiation with his long-range or midrange interest in paced self-reward will be less stable. A ritual, or a story, or a fantasy is only one device among many, and a person knows that if he uses one he will soon use another, just as arbitrarily. Some of these pacing devices still may have value, even for his long-range interest, but not the value created by a well-followed rule for testing reality.

The point is that the radical self-reward model is consistent with our common knowledge of emotional rewards: The most effective self-reward is supported by a belief of some sort, and this belief is more durable if supported in turn by facts. The physiological consequences of such facts are not of moment-to-moment importance, even when these facts are psychoactive drugs. The fact of the drug is not necessary for the high, and the fact of the good news is not necessary for the joy. But the fact selects for a single belief, which otherwise would have a hard time holding its own against competing beliefs. The single belief, in turn, represents a rule for self-reward that, as long as it is maintained, prevents shorter-term programs of reward from being adopted. Hypnotic suggestions, placebo effects, and self-delusions have the same immediate effects as facts or the beliefs based on them, but differ from those in regard to stability.

What deteriorates with repetition is not necessarily the person's belief in the placebo. Instead, the rarity of the occasion for self-reward in that modality may be reduced. This, of course, is the basic limiting factor in self-reward. A person may generally be as ready to congratulate himself on being successful as on being well-liked, but when he has evidence of success he will lean toward the former, and when he has evidence of being liked, the latter. He may congratulate or otherwise reward himself in both cases, and in any number of others: when he has added an object to a collection, when he has made a purchase, when he has refrained from making a purchase, when he has enjoyed a meal, when he has stuck to his diet, and so on. But the more occasions he recognizes for self-reward, the less will be the value of each event. Likewise, as medical science has found repeatedly, the placebo effect of a newly discovered agent wanes as the agent becomes commonplace, without its actually having been proved ineffective. In deciding what occasions to recognize, he faces somewhat the same constraints as a nation deciding how much money to print: His potential wealth is limited by the productiveness of his drives, and if he uses them inefficiently, then through habituation he may realize even less actual reward, just as an inflated currency can cost a nation actual wealth.

8.5 Fantasy illustrates the role of reality

When one goes beyond belief and enters the realm of fantasy, anything is possible, and thus everything habituates. The rules of this realm are clearly distinguished from those of belief, and thus generally do not threaten them (Singer, 1966). In fact, the rules necessary for satisfactory fantasy indicate the value of reality.

If I reward myself in fantasy arbitrarily (i.e., without regard to events outside of my control), my fantasies will slide into premature satiation. At the very least I shall have to fantasize enemies to my imaginary goals, who operate according to inexorable rules to restrict my self-rewarding behavior. In fact, people who dwell extensively in fantasy are increasingly driven to paranoid scripts to maintain the vigor of their fantasies, a process well depicted in Hannah Green's *I Never Promised You a Rose Garden* (1964).

Even delusional people make use of others' behaviors to produce some element of surprise in their fictions: "If that man across from me looks at me with his head lowered, that will mean he is in league with my enemies." In that sense they are still motivated to test reality, even though they set up their tests to give themselves extensive arbitrary control. We would expect that the increase in arbitrary control would reduce their aggregate reward over time, but it may be that they are optimizing reward under the conditions imposed on them by a mental disease.

It is well known that daydreaming can be made more engaging, more durable, by committing oneself to a strict logic that limits the possible outcomes. True surprise is impossible, of course, and the person must continually change the scene on the basis of new experiences, stories told by someone else, and other outside impressions if the daydream is to maintain any vividness at all. Still, there are many portraits in fiction of people who have made fantasy as important as reality: Consider, as in the movies *The Secret Life of Walter Mitty*, *Morgan*, and *The Purple Rose of Cairo*. An articulate description of a person's investment in an alternative reality is Robert Coover's novel *The Universal Baseball Association, Inc., J. Henry Waugh, Proprietor* (1968). Here the protagonist experiences emotions so entirely according to a random-number-driven baseball fantasy that it becomes more important than the facts of his life. When a rare numerical outcome requires him to kill his favorite character, he faces the same personal crisis involving the temptation to bend his rule that another person would face after a real death, although in his case the rule is that establishing an alternative reality, rather than testing the one given by nature. Although the story has an obvious allegorical purpose, it is credible that such a character, an accountant who scrupulously observed his rule, could generate a commitment of such magnitude. People who have been studied while deeply involved in challenging creative activities or games seem to have come close to such commitment (Csikszentmihalyi, 1977, pp. 38–44). Insofar as a person can approach that kind of commitment, the impact of events in the fantasy will approach that of real events, lacking only the turnkey effects of some physiological rewards. Usually, however, people find the experience of daydreaming less involving than that of confronting reality, that is, of limiting their self-rewards by their rules of reality testing.[13] Alternative realities of this scope are rare.

---

[13] A small number of people are said to be able to spend much of their time engrossed in fantasy so vivid as to be actually hallucinatory, without impairing their ability to function in the world (Lynn & Rhue, 1988; Wilson & Barber, 1983). Such an ability might represent the extreme of a natural variability in how fast individuals' rewards in the relevant modalities satiate; however, its motivational constraints have not been explored.

I have been arguing that fictions created by someone else may serve to some extent as one's facts: A book or movie is apt to be preferable to one's own unrelieved company. A person usually is not conscious of investing importance in a movie, but the existence of this importance is shown in the case in which a movie becomes too punishing, and he withdraws his investment in its importance. He says to himself, "It's only a movie," and yet he is not discovering new information – he has never ducked when guns have been pointed toward the audience. Rather, he is announcing his disinvestment: "This movie shall no longer be important to me. I will no longer reward myself according to its vicissitudes."

A person can always abandon a pacing device and sometimes is forced to do so by the unusual strength of a short-term interest. However, when that happens, the long-term interest is somewhat undermined. The person who withdraws his investment during the scary part of the movie loses his chance to be rewarded by the parts that follow; to some extent he will lose his ability to keep his investment in subsequent movies when they tempt him to disinvest.

8.6 The testing of future realities is easily hedged

Insofar as beliefs are difficult to verify, they take on the quality of fantasies. Of course, people frequently make major choices on the basis of mere assumptions. A college student does not know the actual rewards of the possible careers for which he is preparing. A person who plans for retirement has never been old. People may even behave so as to obtain hypothetical rewards after they are dead. A person who behaves so as to increase his expectation of a distant reward thereby gives himself an occasion for current self-reward.

Recall that external events affect self-reward in two ways: by giving direct support to a self-reward pattern or its competitors through changes in drives and through the stimuli that predict those changes (section 7.5.1); and as a pattern by which to pace self-reward (sheet music for the demon, section 8.1.3). As the person expects the events to be delayed, their value decreases hyperbolically, except that insofar as he knows the sheet music, he still may use it currently to some extent for pacing self-reward. However much it is delayed, it will have a certain present value as fiction.

Some expectations are close to being fiction anyway ("When I graduate . . . when I retire . . . when I go to heaven . . . ") and thus become subject to the premature satiation that occurs when people reward themselves according to fictions. All expectations are potentially malleable. Insofar as an expectation rewards by providing a pattern for self-reward, its value will be greater the less malleable it actually is. If the process of expecting can be adequately limited by rules for forecasting the future, or even for projecting a future into an unknowable void, such as a life after death, it can become an effective discipline for self-reward. As an expectation is made rare by the person's rules for testing reality, its present value will rise. Some examples will illustrate how these factors affect the value of an expected event:

The comfort of lying on a beach in the Caribbean includes stimuli (warmth, breeze, smells, etc.) too complex to be entirely duplicated in fantasy, but as patterns for fantasy they still have value. This value is heightened if the person believes that he will really have a Caribbean vacation. The value will be greater if it is to begin in a week than if in a year, both because of the discount on the value it will have when present and because of the greater rarity of the immediate present than of the future; but its value probably will not be greater if it is to begin in 3 years than if in 6 years, because the discounted value of the actual event will be nil in both cases compared with its value as fiction-selected-by-reality.

Furthermore, its value as fiction may be greatest if it is not immediate, but somewhat delayed, so as to permit the fantasy process called savoring. For instance, people who were asked when they would rather have a kiss from a favorite movie star expressed preference for a delay of 3 days over no delay (Loewenstein, 1987). An event's usefulness as a basis for fiction does not decline by the same delay curve as reward occasioned by the event itself: Because the actual event marks the end of the fantasy, its fiction value is always greatest when it is not immediate; and because its scarcity is not greatly affected by differences among long delays, this value does not decline to zero, but reaches a level plateau for all distant delays.

Another case: The pain of a dread disease will have direct effects not reproduced by the idea of the disease. The discounted value of the pains themselves will be nil until shortly before they are available, but the values of alternative ("normal") rewards inhibited by the pain will be discounted over a longer time and will set, inversely, the discounted value of the anticipated disease. In addition to the discounted values of its expected rewards, the disease is apt to have some value as fiction, probably a nuisance value in the itch range of preferability. A person is drawn into imagining, "What would it be like to have this disease?" even if he would rather not think about it. This value, too, will be greater if the person thinks he really will get the disease. It probably will not be different if he expects the disease in 10 years or in 20, or for that matter as a punishment in hell after he dies.

The fiction value of a purely positive reward may also be negative, if the person is lured into entertaining it repetitively in an itchlike pattern. This is the child's pain of waiting until Christmas to open his presents, the "frustration" or "deprivation" (Hoch & Loewenstein, 1991) often hypothesized to be the aversive factor in delay. As we would expect from the plasticity of fiction, savoring and deprivation effects are complex and changeable – they have been explored best by George Loewenstein (1987).

It is not clear at what delay actual reward loses its practical value, that is, how long a reward can be delayed without being discounted into insignificance. Friedman (1963) says that the planning horizon for even rational investors does not exceed 3 years, and this seems to be as good an estimate as any. Beyond some such point, expected events are valuable only as fictions by which to pace current self-reward.

Much of this value will be determined by aesthetics, that is, by how good a pacing device the fiction is, and hence how "compelling." However, testing reality still will be a valuable discipline insofar as it selects one or a few expectations from the many that are imaginable. For the sake of legitimacy, one's rules for testing the distant future usually must be the same as those for testing the discountable future, perhaps including whatever discounting procedures one regards as realistic. Extending one's reality testing to the distant future may make it seem as if even long-delayed events have discounted value, but this value is apt to be purely conventional. That is, a person may be able to say that he prefers to receive $1,000 in 10 years rather than $500 in 8 years, and that report may be highly stable, but it probably means no more than if he were asked about that many Brownie points or units of an unfamiliar good. However, this does not mean that the person is unwilling to make important decisions on the basis of such a calculated preference; indeed, he is more likely to use the bank rate in calculating the value of distant goods than the value of nearer ones, because he will not have to overcome a spontaneous hyperbolic value function.

Events that have happened before are apt to be valued more than those that have not, both because a person makes this a factor in testing reality and because his memory of that happening provides a more complete text for the fiction. If the expected event has not happened before or has happened rarely, the person will have little basis for testing the accuracy of his expectation; and even when he has a good basis for predicting a distant event, that prediction may count for little against aesthetic factors – that is, how good a story the event makes. Hence the durability of myths based on little evidence, such as one's golden years of retirement, or the end of the world in nuclear war.

Some people develop a great investment in the future, just as some people invest in the past. To get pleasure from dwelling in either is a learnable skill. It hinges on a person's elaboration of his rules for testing reality in these time zones on the basis of the ambiguous evidence they usually provide, so as to let this evidence adequately discipline his self-reward.

For instance, it is possible to get pleasure by figuring out which pass Hannibal used to cross the Alps, as long as the person does not feel he has the arbitrary ability to pick one. It is unlikely that his choice could be decisively disproved, so he will have to commit himself to additional standards for justifying his belief: Can he say that the authors favoring his choice are superior to the others? Does he know a fact that has not been discovered before? Is his line of reasoning demonstrably more elegant? For the person's theory to affect his pacing of self-reward, it need not be accurate. It need only have the qualities that a good game of solitaire has: payoffs that are not too easy to obtain, and a single, undisputed formula for determining when they are to occur. Hence, perhaps, the propensity of societies over the ages to spin elaborate histories and sciences that added nothing to their people's predictive powers.

8.7 Rules for testing reality lead to some of the common emotions

Thus far I have spoken of emotions just as identifiable forms of intrinsically rewarded activity. Most authors identify about 10 such forms (e.g., excitement, joy, surprise, anguish, anger, disgust, contempt, fear, shame, and guilt) (Izard, 1972; Jorgensen, 1928; Mc-Dougall, 1923; Tomkins, 1962). They range in duration of preferability from the pain range (fear, anguish) through a midrange (anger, contempt) to emotions that either are unambivalently preferred or, as some philosophers, from the ancient Stoics (Zeller, 1870) to Sartre (1948) (see section 2.3.1), have believed, are sellouts (joy, excitement). These conspicuous emotions are stereotyped to the point that they can be recognized in facial photographs across cultures (Ekman & Friesen, 1986; Izard, 1971) and have sufficient innate momentum to be cultivated as precommitting devices (see section 5.3.3). At least some depend on elementary neurophysiological systems (Panksepp, 1982). However, there are many other motivational processes that are characteristic enough to be named as some kind of emotion but that lack corresponding stereotyped behaviors. "Emotion," after all, is a heterogeneous term, clearly narrower than its cognate, "motivation," but to an extent that has not been agreed upon. Essentially it seems to mean only some prominent motivation that is not based on a concrete reward, and/or the behavior so motivated:

> There are some basic classes of appraisals . . . that are associated with response patterns . . . the urge to produce [which] occurs in physiological, cognitive, phenomenal, and behavioral complexes. It would be a cluster of such components that constitutes an emotion. [Ortony & Turner, 1990, p. 329]

The "urges" named as several common emotions seem to reflect reward opportunities created by a person's rules for testing reality, rather than by an innate response pattern that can simply be summoned and ridden.

8.7.1 Hope

"Hope," for instance, is commonly used to refer both to an objective appraisal of future prospects as favorable and to self-deception that masquerades as such an appraisal. The latter process is sometimes called false hope, but the distinction is often vague, and the latter term may also be used for a realistic expectation that was in fact disappointed. In terms of the temporary-preference model, hope is self-reward paced by a person's testing of future reality. Insofar as his short-term interests interfere with the gathering of information predictive of future events or find loopholes in the rules governing reality testing, they can create hopes that are false in the sense that they are inflated. Because prediction of the future is an ambiguous process, a person has more opportunity to distort his perspective of it than in the case of present or past realities. Nevertheless, the more editing of information that is required, the more the person is creating a fiction, rather than perceiving an event outside of his control, and so the less useful his perception will be as a discipline for self-reward.

Rules depend on criteria and thus are naturally categorical. They respond to distinctions better than to quantities. In the area of testing future reality, they can assess possibility better than probability. There is a great gap between "impossible" and "possible but unlikely," and another between "likely" and "certain," but there is a broad, continuous category of "possible" between the "probable" and the "improbable" that lacks the internal boundaries needed for stable subdivision. This is true not only because evidence about the future is apt to be ambiguous but also because people's abilities to conceive relative probabilities may be fundamentally unstable. Differences among remote possibilities tend to be blurred, for instance, so that $1/1,000$ is seen as about equal to $1/1,000,000$, and the value of a loss is apt to be asymmetrical to that of a same-size gain. The irregularities of this process are not well understood, but they have been shown in some of the studies of Tversky and Kahneman (1981). The effect is that a person has a short-range interest in qualifying extravagant wishes as possible, however unlikely they may be. The long-range effect will be to cheapen the judgment of "possible," but at the moment it will give him permission for increased self-reward.

The systematic exploitation of these irregularities to maximize hope may be the art of gambling, an activity that has lacked a robust utilitarian explanation (Wagenaar, 1988, p. 3). Categorization as "possible" takes an event out of the highly habituated realm of fantasy and into a much fresher and more potent area. Thus, a person who has bought a lottery ticket can legitimately say it is possible that he will be a millionaire; the right to declare this seems to be worth much more for many people than the expected value of the bet, which is below the cash cost of the bet. Thus, the factor that makes gambling worthwhile probably is the service to the short-range interest in evading rules for testing future reality without breaking them. This phenomenon also works in favor of lower, itchlike processes, so that a person who perceives that he "possibly" has cancer may be more bothered by this than one would expect from the true odds. The same seems to hold true of mothers' fantasies of disaster for their children and other obsessional worries.

8.7.2 Regret

People usually are deterred from changing their perceptions of reality where they might be confronted by facts that are still boldly visible. Changing a testable fact is a sign of desperation, and it makes a bystander remarkably uncomfortable, as when a widowed person says that his spouse is out shopping, or a bankrupt shows up at the business that is no longer his, even though these people still undertake to treat all other apparent facts as true. The acceptance of any major alternative reality is something of a disaster to one's long-range interests, and yet sometimes it can be a sore temptation. The stronger the temptation, the more it will strain the person's will to test reality, and thus the more unpleasant it will be.

When the temptation actually prevails, it does not produce an identifiable emotion, except, in all likelihood, some uneasiness at having taken the perception of reality into one's arbitrary control. When it does not prevail, the person still has an urge to entertain the alternative version of events, as if trying to find a way that his rules will allow him to believe it. Such a lawyerly foray into denying the existence of the real fact (see section 6.4) is what Freud called "undoing" (1920/1956k, p. 119).

The closer the alternative event was to the actual event, the stronger the urge. At some point, the discomfort of this temptation is recognizable as regret. If the winning lottery number was completely different from one's own, that invites only mild regret. If it was one digit away, the regret is greater. If it was one digit away and the person just ahead in line had hesitated over buying that ticket, the regret is greater still. If one had actually let that person ahead of him in line, the regret is greatest; Kahneman and Tversky (1982) have demonstrated this systematically. The increase in dysphoria with the nearness of the miss does not make sense in conventional motivational theory, but it is what we would expect if a person is struggling with an urge to disbelieve the facts. Increasing nearness of the alternative version means a smaller and smaller change that a person will have to make in his belief, and hence a greater risk that he will do so.

By similar reasoning, "sins of commission" entail a greater risk of regret than do "sins of omission," because the former are specific acts that stand out from the status quo, whereas the latter compose the status quo. Among other things, this consideration probably creates the "endowment effect" that makes a person demand a higher price to part with one of his possessions than he would pay to buy the same possession (Thaler, 1980), or stay in the job he starts with rather than trying others (Kahneman & Tversky, 1984).

8.7.3 Guilt

Regret is not the same thing as guilt. Even though the lottery loser regrets his ticket purchase, he has not violated a personal rule in buying it. He has not even learned of a rule that could have made his chances better; he was just as likely to have obtained the winning ticket as to have lost it by letting someone ahead of him. But if a person perceives that he has violated a personal rule, he is in more complex trouble. He may regret the lapse, but if he obeys his rule for testing reality, he suffers from having disobeyed the rule he violated. He faces a decreased expectation of controlling his impulses if he acknowledges the lapse, but he faces damage to his rules for testing reality, and perhaps even greater long-term damage to impulse control, if he does not. This unpleasant quandary probably is guilt.

8.7.4 Envy

A particularly compelling alternative to reality arises when a person perceives a natural match between himself and someone who is enjoying better circumstances. Putting oneself in another's shoes may offer a single, distinct, and thus robust alternative to the perception of life in one's own shoes. This alternative perception of reality is experienced as envy. Again, its nature is shown by the fact that it is most intense not when the envied person is most prosperous, but when the perception is strongest that "it could have been me," as well documented by Elster (in press).

8.7.5 A converse of regret

A near miss of an especially bad outcome creates a different kind of temptation. The fantasy of the bad outcome that could have occurred, although unrewarding in the long run, may be extremely vivid and thus lure attention in the short run, leading to a vertiginous sense of horror and a morbid temptation to rehearse what could have happened. Again, the closer the awful possibility to the actual fact, the greater the nuisance of this temptation. There is no generally accepted name for this familiar and usually trivial emotion, which in some cases can form an important component of posttraumatic stress disorder.

8.7.6 The lure of false hope

An emotion created by the temptation to hope falsely is credible but not generally recognized. The future being untestable in any strict sense, false hope usually is less of a lapse than breaches of past and present reality testing, and it may not be resisted to the same degree. A temptation to hope falsely, if resisted, will correspond to the emotions of regret about the past and envy of the present.

8.7.7 Mirth

The emotion most elusive of explanation, mirth, also depends on testing reality. Psychologists and philosophers have had remarkable trouble accounting for mirth. Some time ago Max Eastman (1922) called it a philosophical sideshow. Recent research has shown that mirth can be explored as systematically as any other emotion. The age at which children can appreciate a joke is known, and the ability of people from diverse cultures to recognize laughter in the photograph of a face can be quantified (Izard, 1971). Mirthlike responses have even been identified in other mammals (McGhee, 1979, pp. 85–124). However, these findings do not lead us to an explanation, if by that we mean specifying the role of mirth in a person's motivational economy.

The most frequent explanation has been that mirth is a wish-fulfilling process (Eastman, 1922; Freud, 1905/1956c). This suggests that a person's rules for testing reality, which might be said to create wishes by limiting self-reward, are somehow involved. Without further elaboration, however, this theory does not explain how such a thing as a simple pun fulfills a wish. Even where a wish is evident in the mirth-provoking situation, wish fulfillment is only a partial explanation. How is this process of wish fulfillment different from daydreaming? And why does the closeness of a joking description to the literal description generate this particular emotion, instead of an emotion congruent with the theme of the joke (e.g., lust, avarice). Or, in accordance with what has just been argued, why does it not generate envy? It would also be difficult to say why surprise, an element more necessary to the joke than to ordinary fiction, assists in wish fulfillment.

I am not proposing that mirth is unrelated to wish fulfillment. However, it is not simply wish fulfillment. We need to consider both the primitive forms of mirth, which point back to its inborn basis, and the way that these forms may have been harnessed by higher processes.

The organizing principle of this emotion is the stereotyped central-nervous-system response – laughter – the innate stimulus for which seems to be pleasant surprise. It may be occasioned by a stimulus that has no cognitive meaning but that is an archetypical form of surprise: tickling. Tickling differs from simple touching, which does not provoke laughter, only by its unpredictability – one can touch oneself, but never tickle oneself. Laughter may also be occasioned by sudden good news or when anything leads to a burst of joy. These are the processes that are also seen in lower mammals. Thus, the need for surprise is not limited to jokes, but characterizes mirth in general.

Of course, it is not difficult to fantasize sudden good fortune. It might be expected that people would try to cultivate such an emotion, so as to increase its occurrence. But, like other self-rewarding processes, this fantasy will soon habituate unless it is limited to a relatively rare occasion that is kept rare by being outside of a person's voluntary grasp. Such occasions may be designated arbitrarily if the person will then stick consistently to this designation as a basis for future self-reward. Thus, a person may choose at will to become a stamp collector or bird-watcher, and if he consistently rewards himself according to the rules for success in those endeavors, he may laugh with glee at finding a rare stamp or bird. Similarly, he may cultivate competition with other people. Then another's bad fortune may be his good fortune, as in the ruin of an opponent – that was the paradigm of mirth for most of the authors who wrote about it before this century.

To evoke mirth, these events have to be surprises; a person is unlikely to laugh if his good fortune has been anticipated. If he has been able to rehearse the outcome in fantasy before allowing himself the greater satisfaction of perceiving it to be real, that activity will have had a habituating effect. Even a little habituation undermines mirth, as if only the sharpest change in expectations can call forth the stereotyped mirth response.

Neither tickling nor sudden good fortune is obviously related to the most familiar occasion for mirth: humor. How is humor involved? As we have noted, it has been described as wish fulfillment, and wishes are restrained by rules: "The most important function of humor is its power to release us from the many inhibitions and restrictions under which we live our daily lives" (Mindess, 1971). Such releases might certainly be examples of sudden good fortune, but how can humor create them?

If good fortune was simply an external event, a wish would be no more than the consciousness of a drive for such an event. However,

I have argued that a person makes his own good fortune through self-reward, and external events serve only as criteria by which personal rules discipline that self-reward. When one discovers a good loophole in his rules for testing reality that restrain self-reward, that find may also represent sudden good fortune. Such a loophole permits ample self-reward in the current case without setting a precedent that endangers the larger rule. It is a legal technicality that exempts the case at hand without reducing the person's expectation of long-term obedience to the rule. But finding such technicalities seems to be precisely the function of jokes.

In its simplest form, a joke seems to propose an exception to our accepted practices for describing the world, and craftily it leads us to the conclusion that up is down, or that facts obey rhymes, or that in some other way we are not obliged to reward ourselves according to the miserly rations given by the environment. It creates a brief holiday from reality and, if this holiday has not been counted on in advance, a burst of laughter.

In many specific cases our rules for testing reality support rules for conduct in turn: We must not get angry without "good reason" or harbor sexual wishes toward inappropriate people, and our enforcement of such rules for conduct depends on the reliable testing of reality. Those loopholes in testing reality that seem for a moment to free us from rules for conduct in turn have the augmented impact that Freud ascribed to "tendentious" jokes (1905/1956c, pp. 90–116). This brief release, long enough to be appreciated but not to be obeyed, has a time course similar to the spikes of reward I have postulated for pain (section 4.2.3), but because it does not inhibit other sources of reward, it is not aversive in the long run.

Obviously there is much more to be learned about humor, but it seems safe to say that part of its function is to stage limited raids on long-range interests, just as a lawyer may bring nuisance suits against a rigid organization without calling into question the goals of the organization. The general target of humor is the rule system we have set up to administer our self-rewards. Where this rule system has come to serve a sellout-range interest, short- and long-range interests may be allied, and the humor is apt to be the more robust.

Insofar as these alternative interpretations of reality do not threaten the integrity of this rule system, they will not be conflictual. But where a joke tempts a person to a broader disbelief in reality, the emotion becomes more ominous ("bitter"), passing through irony to frank envy or regret.

8.8 Summary

The matching law lets us imagine a mechanism by which external stimuli can support reward without turnkey control. Where reward is limited by its latency and the speed of satiation of its drive, external events will be important as occasions for reward, rather than as stimuli to release it. As cues predicting when self-reward will be effective in a given modality, external stimuli may govern any pattern of reward from pains to patterns that are unambivalently preferred; a person's long-range interest will be to invest in those stimuli that can serve as guidelines to prevent shortsighted patterns of self-reward. To resist decreases in effectiveness through anticipation, such stimuli must remain surprising.

This model permits the first economic hypotheses about the constraints on "testing reality" and on valuations of such process rewards as fiction, interpersonal relations, and some of the subtler emotions. An individual who is totally free to reward himself is still imprisoned by inflexible laws of motivation, accommodation to which will require a great share of his effort.

9. The texture of experience

Deeply bowed discount functions have led us from simple choice behavior to intricate strategies for ensuring the cooperation of future motivational states. Because this model also includes robust short-range motives to undermine such cooperation, the overall picture is one of negotiation among the diverse interests created by these discount functions. Before concluding, we should explore whether or not the line of deduction that led to this picture can clarify three other subjects: (1) What constitutes the mental processes that are experienced as the "self," and the "ego functions" that are ascribed to it? (2) How do rules grow and change with repeated use? (3) What consequences arise from the interaction of *inter*personal bargaining with the bargaining among successive motivational states?

9.1 The "self" is a community of interests

I have described how the longer-range interests forestall temporary preferences, a process that corresponds to the ego's function, as conceived by the psychoanalysts, of neutralizing instinctual energy (see section 6.1). Similarly, the tendency to form temporary preferences corresponds to the id; and perception of current choices as precedents, which leads to the phenomenon of willpower, fits Freud's concept of superego functioning. Even the experience of freedom of the will can be attributed to the recursive (transistorlike) properties of the self-prediction process (see section 6.3). However, there still remains the question of how successive motivational states evolve over long periods of time, achieving, or failing to achieve, the consistency that is called "identity" by psychoanalysts (Erikson, 1963) and "centeredness" by existentialists (May, 1967). That is, how can the bargaining of reward-based interests produce a sense of self?

According to Rollo May (1967), human selfhood has four characteristics: "[The person] seeks to preserve some center"; this "centeredness depends on his courage to affirm it"; he has the need "to participate in other beings"; and he is aware of these first three characteristics. It is the first, the desire to preserve a center per se, that needs to be accounted for. That it requires courage implies only that the process entails the defending of some kind of rule against some kind of challenge; the need for other people can be traced to their unique value as sources of surprise (see section 8.3); and the awareness, although self-referential, does not seem different in principle from other sorts of awareness.

The likely explanation comes from the very fact that there is no organ for producing ego functions – that a person's long-range interests are merely a population in an internal body politic. If these interests fail to maintain themselves, control of the person's decision making will pass to incompatible interests. For the person to avoid costly abandonments of the goals he generally values most, he must maintain an ego that represents a defensible "center" or common program that can prevent such abandonments.

There is certainly evidence of such an ego, one that is motivated to preserve itself specifically, as opposed to just preserving the person. Its activity is evident in situations where people sense impending changes of preferences between major alternatives. Individuals wrestling with serious temptations are apt to develop symptoms of being globally threatened, such as trouble in concentrating or going to sleep. Patients at imminent risk for lapsing into a dissociated personality or fugue state typically are anxious to the point of panic. The experience they fear is not punishment, but intense gratification (e.g., of angry or sexual urges), gratification that is the basis of incompatible interests. The experience would be pleasurable, but the alliance of long-range interests would be swept from power.

It is apt to be a motive to preserve some kind of self that makes most people value death negatively instead of neutrally, even though a view that death is nothingness would predict neutrality (aside from aversion to the visible pain of some particular deaths). Again, what a person tries to preserve is the integrity of some kind of center, rather than his general ability to behave: Many a person has been known to kill himself rather than become what he conceives as a different self (Bugental & Bugental, 1984).

It might be argued, by analogy to the natural selection of organisms, that those behaviors that include self-preservation will simply be selected for and eventually will prevail over those that do not. But, as in natural selection, such behaviors must have a mechanism for their self-preservation. Behaviors can survive only if differentially rewarded, and self-preservation per se seems to be rewarded only because of the need to avoid surrendering control. Any threat to the alliance of ego interests, even one unrelated to the choice at hand, may reduce the likelihood that the alliance will prevail and thus reduce the person's expectation of a whole range of long-term rewards. Member interests will be motivated to keep the alliance dominant at all times to preserve that expectation, much as bankers and brokers are motivated to preserve an equally intangible bargaining factor: business confidence.[1] Where an incompatible interest seems unstoppable, the ego interests' best move is to limit its damage to their personal rules, and hence its duration of dominance, by giving way, thus acquiescing in the creation of a vice district. However, if the alliance of interests is too narrow, the interests it has excluded may be extensive enough to support their own ego functions and remain dominant for days at a time – the "bad selves" of the multiple personality or binge drinker.

Insofar as the core alliance is tenuous, the ego may be said to be weak or split, as the psychoanalysts say, or to lack boundaries. This

---

[1] The behavior of stock markets is notoriously self-referential, and in one case, the market for closed-end mutual funds, almost exclusively so. Closed-end mutual funds are portfolios of stock to which nothing can be added or subtracted until the fund is liquidated. The striking, regular deviations of such a fund's price from the sum of the prices of its component stocks can be well accounted for only as speculation on speculation itself – other rational motives are lacking (Lee, Shleifer, & Thaler, 1990). Thus, the market for a fund has something of a "self," in the form of those characteristics that traders might expect to appeal to other traders, and this trading shows something like "free will": The behavior of the market for this fund is based upon the expectation of future changes in value, which is in turn based upon the current behavior of the market (see chapter 6). However, insofar as these traders can only buy and sell, rather than make side-transactions to manipulate value, the market will lack "ego functions."

does not mean that an organ is malfunctioning; rather, it is evidence that negotiations among important interests have broken down. Conversely, if an ego is "strong," then there is a set of interests that prevail consistently over time. The "self" may describe the person's awareness of the preservation process specifically, or of the set of interests it maintains. In the latter case it is analogous to the "national character" of a country, an observable thing, but something generated by regularities in the motives of its population, rather than willed by a single decision-maker.

9.2 The ego's job is to budget future motivation

Ego "functions" are then general behaviors that further an alliance of long-range interests.[2] Usually these behaviors either forestall rewards that might be temporarily preferred or find new sources of reward. These tasks are interdependent, for the more longer-range reward that can be found, the stronger will be its competition with short-range rewards. Forestalling temporarily preferred rewards means precommitment, which increases the leverage of a given amount of long-range motivation. Tactics for doing this were discussed earlier at some length; the ego is what performs the strategic planning for their use. The ego must also look for more sources of such motivation – both sources of appetite within the person's known tastes, and new tastes. This ongoing search is made necessary by the regular deterioration of current sources of reward, a process that will be described presently.

Given a knowledge of long-range reward sources and of precommitting devices to block short-range rewards, a person still must time the consumption of the former so as to adequately motivate the adoption of precommitting devices if he is to prevent his ego from falling from power on some occasions. That is, the continuity of his ego functions depends more on preventing expected long-range reward from ever dipping below a minimum than on increasing its average amount.

---

[2] Nonconflictual ego functions like sensory perception (Hartmann, 1958) are not considered here.

9.2.1 Finding reward

As was noted in section 7.6, the basic reward process may not be identifiable. That is, organisms may perform rewarded activities because over a long series of trials those activities become selected by the reward mechanism, not because they are consciously identified as rewarding. However, intelligent organisms apparently learn to hasten the exploration process. Trial and error can give information not only about the best circumstances for exploiting a given drive but also about regularities in these circumstances that can permit a systematic search for them. General behaviors that search for drive–reward combinations will thus come to be selected by the reward mechanism. For instance, a person who has discovered that cold sensations are pleasurable when he is hot may not only seek cold when he is hot but also find ways to make himself alternately hot and cold, such as a sauna. Likewise, a person may construct a fantasy or search for a book or go to an amusement park not to satisfy a current need but to generate needs that can be pleasurably satisfied.

These are examples of learning to work up appetites deliberately within known tastes. But a person may also invite new tastes, as when he tries an unknown style of cooking or art, or stays in an ambiguous personal relationship to see how his feelings will evolve. Adding the search for tastes to one's repertoire of behaviors represents a leap in learning analogous to Piaget's tertiary circular reaction (1937/1954): the regular search for causation once such searching has been found to be useful in general.

A deliberate search for reward may greatly increase the speed of learning, but like any shortcut past the slow, basic selection process, it has a cost: Lacking immediate feedback, a person will probe the possibilities of a new taste using hypotheses. He will try out rules of thumb ("I like cubist painters" or "I don't seem to like women who remind me of Aunt Jeanne") to categorize possible objects of his taste, and as long as those objects have adequate aesthetic properties, such trials will be self-confirming. A person who has declared that he loves his girlfriend, or boyfriend, or Picasso, or pasta, will reward himself according to his access to those objects. Within a wide range, this activity will pace reward well enough to sustain itself, and thus to confirm his declaration, but it may not be nearly the best activity available. This self-confirmation effect, added to the process that makes people overly confident of their current hypotheses to begin with (Einhorn & Hogarth, 1978; Oskamp, 1982), may introduce distortion into the conscious testing of a person's hypotheses about taste.

Further distortion may come from a person's wariness of forming any tastes that might become the basis of temporary preferences. As we have seen, tastes can somewhat be governed by personal rules (e.g., "I must never fall for a woman like Aunt Jeanne"; see section 7.3.1), and rules can serve interests in the sellout range as well as unambivalent preferences (see section 6.4.4). A person may thus reject, or fail to test, some hypotheses about reward that would in fact serve his long-range interests. Definition of tastes both by hypotheses and by personal rules may reduce aggregate reward when it bypasses the process through which reward spontaneously shapes tastes.

9.2.2 Budgeting reward

Ultimately, the task of avoiding temporary preferences depends on planning the availability of reward so as to adequately motivate this avoidance. Thus, the "highest" ego function may be to budget sources of likely rewards in such a way that incompatible interests will not become dominant. This is not simply a matter of maximizing overall rates of reward. A local, temporary failure of an expected source of reward could lead the currently dominant interest to fall from power. If a person lets himself get hungry enough, he may be motivated to sell his birthright for a mess of pottage; he may likewise be coerced by asphyxia, pain, or sexual desire. The budgeting process must also prevent extreme examples of dysphoria that are unrelated to obvious biological processes. The psychiatric patients labeled "borderline personalities" seem especially susceptible to such dysphorias, either from poor budgeting or from actual unevenness in their sources of reward – suddenly plummeting to emotional depths on the occasion of trivial social feedback – but to some degree the problem is universal.

The stricter a person's rule for self-reward, the more he runs the risk that the rule itself will fail for lack of adequate motivation and that a shorter-range interest will take over. A person who tries being overly ascetic is apt to be seduced. If he attempts too stringent a diet, he invites binging (Polivy & Herman, 1985), and if he tries to read too dry a book (or read a book too meticulously), he may put it down and read a magazine.

On the other hand, rules that are too lax lead to premature satiation, "jaded appetites," and thus also to eventual seduction by a succession of novelties that have little else to recommend them. They will cause a person to settle for hasty exploitation of the goods that are the objects of his tastes, followed by rapid loss of their reward-pacing ability. This pattern will lead the person into recurring disenchantment with these goods. Popular songs, media stars, and casual lovers are commonly "consumed" in this pattern. The new object, coming after a barren period and being exploited rapidly like the old one, will be richly rewarding at first and thus will be loved in its turn. The resulting succession of enthusiasms is familiar in English literature (Mr. Toad, Auntie Mame) and is the unrelieved life-style of the borderline personality, who intermittently finds the common personal rules for pacing self-reward to be intolerably strict.

On the basis of the limited motivation derivable from delayed rewards, the ego functions must arrange for motives much stronger than themselves to draw the person's successive choices steadily toward these rewards. If they fail even briefly to arrange such motives, the plan may stall and be diverted in another direction. Like herders who have to move an unruly group of animals to a destination by finding a succession of fresh pastures that will lead there, they not only must avoid immediate barren patches but also must keep from being led down routes that would become barren farther along.

9.3 Interests evolve over time

The task of budgeting is made even more difficult by the continual evolution of the reward-getting capacities of both the long- and short-range interests. That is, the natural overvaluation of imminent reward leads to continuous new learning on the basis of the short-range interests, which in turn requires adaptation by the long-range interests. The interaction of these two learning processes determines the evolution of the motivational structure that an observer will attribute to the person as a whole.

There are several consequences for personal rules: As learning by both interests progresses, a given personal rule can be expected to deteriorate by becoming both more rigid and less of an obstacle to promiscuous self-reward. Growth, occasioned by challenge from the environment, must continue if the rule is not to be increasingly compromised by the short-range interests. As rules become inflexible, they may even come to serve some interests that are too short-range to have formed rules themselves.

9.3.1 Factors that increase the rigidity of rules

Adoption of a rule entails some rigidity from the start, because the rule not only judges choices as precedents but also demands behaviors that can be clearly judged as following precedents or not, that is, behaviors that are more concrete than the person might have chosen spontaneously. Because of their need to dichotomize behaviors into good and bad, personal rules will tend to replace ambiguous behaviors with behaviors that are clearly classifiable. However, there are also three factors that tend to make rules become more rigid over time: accumulating history, increasing familiarity, and growing complexity:

1. Accumulating history. After a rule has been observed over a period of time, it stands out from other possible rules for that reason itself: It has become rare by virtue of its being a long-standing rule. Its criteria for conduct stand out and thus become bright lines because they are the only ones with a history. The rule is then called traditional. If a person has for many years taken just one drink on a certain occasion, he will be more able to be temperate on that occasion, and less able to be abstinent, than if he did not have that history. Like the traditional mores of a nation, a person's traditional rules will provide the most obvious resolutions for his motivational conflicts, even though his long-range interests might be able to find better criteria if the traditions did not exist. Of course, a rule that has become a clear hindrance to the long-range interests will be abandoned; but if it is merely inefficient, that is, if short-range interests have discovered a large array of loopholes and/or the rule continues to forbid reward that has become harmless, a traditional rule may survive where the same rule newly made would not.

For instance, if a teenager has long observed rules against being tempted into sexual activity, these rules may later serve as a pretext for fleeing social involvement. At first they served long-range social interests threatened by premature sex. Later, these same interests might best be served by less restrictive rules (e.g., just against promiscuity), and most people are able to make this modification; but if short-range interests created by fear of embarrassment, of vulnerability, or of other threats implied by romantic involvement are especially strong, they may be able to hold the long-range interests to the traditional boundary line. Such interests may be dominant in too short a time range to be the basis of their own rules, but still may find shelter in a vestigial rule and add their motivation to what the rule already has. This is an alliance of short-range and midrange interests (compare with that of short- and long-range interests in sections 5.3.3 and 6.4.4). Traditional rules form a body of internal common law, which may limit a person's freedom to formulate new personal rules.

2. Increasing familiarity. As a person gains more experience with a rule, he sees more decisions to which the rule applies, and which he must then see as precedents that either uphold or break the rule. Furthermore, if the rule's criteria are vague, the precedents he sets with his own current choices will tend to become criteria for future choices.

Thus, if a patient rules that he must pray every night for "the people I care for," he will tend to develop a more and more extensive list of these people as he notices omissions or makes judgment calls ruling in new categories of people who formerly were ambiguous in status. Furthermore, the growing sanctity of the rule deriving from its history of being followed will make omission a more significant hostile gesture toward possible candidates, thus also tending to swell the list. The prayer will become increasingly burdensome and may be abandoned, but it will not be simplified to its original form, because the person cannot unlearn the new ways he has learned to notice precedents.

Similarly, if a person rules that he must write in his diary every day, but has no clear criterion for how much he should write, he may feel that he is backsliding if he does not write at least as much today as he wrote yesterday. This spontaneous criterion puts a ratchet in his rule, permitting its demands to grow, but not to shrink. The ratchet effect is not apt to occur unless the person is vigilant in policing his rule; but where he is, it will readily create obsessional rituals.

In a similar way, the hoarder will see more things that come under his rules for saving, and the person concerned with his dignity or his integrity will see more situations as tests of these qualities.

A person's rules will most tend to ramify in this way when his choices are arbitrary rather than coerced by strong environmental incentives. His increased sensitivity to precedent will not necessarily make the rule more powerful. It may lead him to break the rule, or to direct his attention so as to avoid testing whether or not he is obeying it. However, if he is to uphold the rule and is aware of its detailed demands, he must become increasingly scrupulous.

Scrupulosity makes a rule inefficient by burdening it with missed opportunities for harmless reward. Over time, a person notices more and more ambiguities in his choices, and he gives up more and more reward, lest he look back upon a choice as a lapse. For example, a person might have a rule not to accumulate any social debt to other people. As he notices more and more ways in which his activities with a particular person could be seen as making him beholden, he may stop seeing that person, even though an observer might call the balance of obligations even. Likewise, a person who rules that he must keep a clean house may find more and more examples of things that could be cleaned, if nothing more compelling distracts his attention. If his house has rooms that he does not greatly need, he may even find himself staying out of them so as not to see things that need cleaning. Thus, dead limbs may be created on the branching tree of a person's personal rules. His activities must grow around them.

This kind of inefficiency is not unique to internal rules. An analogous process can be seen when the cumulative restraints that have gathered around civil-service hiring practices produce a highly rated but obviously incompetent applicant at the top of a particular job list. Such people are described as "closing down" the list, because agencies prefer to hire no one rather than hire the person who came to head the list drawn up according to such rules. In such a case the motives are clear; when the example arises from intrapsychic bargaining, the motives for closing down areas of functioning tend to be called irrational, if they are discerned at all.[3]

---

[3] The reader familiar with large organizations may have noticed that people who

3. Growing complexity. The inefficiencies that result from the preceding two factors might result in a change or abandonment of the rules in question were it not for a third factor: A person's estimate of what reward hinges on his rules is necessarily imperfect. For a rule governing a single, discrete behavior, some estimation is possible; the recovering alcoholic deciding about a drink usually has a good impression of the consequences of alcoholism and of sobriety. However, as rules broaden and become interdependent, it becomes impossible for a person to predict for sure what any given revision of a rule will do to his future observance of the rule itself, much less the reward he will realize in consequence; see Hardin (1984) on the difficulty of isolating the effects of a single choice on an interdependent system. If I rule that I must repay gifts, but not compliments, will it increase my compliance? If I rule that I need dust only until the room looks clean, as opposed to its leaving no smudge on a finger, will that become a loophole? Just what rewards depend on maintaining these rules, anyway? Because of the somewhat imponderable risk that he will subsequently see a current choice as an important precedent, a person is apt to be conservative in abandoning rules. He will bear their obvious inefficiencies rather than fly to others that have not been tested.

Rules by their nature advance the longer-range interests over the shorter-range ones, but because of these inefficiencies, the short-range interests often can find rules that will shelter them against their longer-range competitors. Research might even discover regularities in the properties of the midrange rules that seem to grow in the absence of strong external challenges. There is a striking parallel between such growth and the growth of large minority coalitions to seize wealth in nations that have avoided major disruptions for long periods. Mancur Olson (1982) has shown coalitions of a certain size to proliferate on the basis of their increasing the wealth of their members at the expense of the general population, despite the uni-

---

depend on personal rules excessively for their self-control are following the same decision-making principles that are seen in a bureaucracy. The predominant concern is a suspicion of spontaneous decision making, and its eradication through categorization of all choices as relevant to some rule. Conversely, bureaucracy can fairly be called an obsessional character disorder writ large, perhaps as an allegory, often, seemingly, as satire.

versal impoverishment and even national decline that the widespread adoption of this strategy causes. The dynamics of collective action among midrange interests within an individual may turn out to include some of the same rationales.

The only apparent antidote to these forms of deterioration in personal rules is to seek important new situations that will challenge one's self-control. Demanding jobs, unpredictable people, and other significant surprises keep one's choices from being made in detail according to an overly elaborate system of rules. But such measures are aversive in the short run and require either natural adversity or ego skills if a person is to adopt them.

9.3.2 Factors that decrease the productivity of rules

Just as there are factors that tend to make rules become more rigid with increasing use, there are factors that make them less productive, that is, that reduce the aggregate amount of reward to be realized from following the rule in question. Like the rigidity factors, these can lead to a situation in which a rule may eventually undermine a person's longest-range interests. Two factors are particularly important: (1) Means to distant ends can pace current reward without much regard to their actual efficacy in gaining the distant ends, creating the temptation for a self-reward practice that I shall call "counting coups." (2) Pacing stimuli become less surprising with repetition, making them less effective at controlling premature consumption, a process that I shall call "erosion of texture."

1. Counting coups. Behaviors that are chosen for reasons other than their own sake, that is, because they ration current self-reward, must be means to some future reward. Where the future reward is imminent, its discounted value selects which means the person will come to choose. Where the future reward is greatly delayed, it cannot effectively select for the means that will best obtain it; the person must set up intermediate goals, using his rules for testing reality to keep these goals related to the ultimate goal.

For instance, a student who wants to become an architect cannot make his day-to-day decisions according to how much they will help this career. He must invest importance in shorter-range goals, such as finishing college, or finishing a particular course in college, or doing well on a particular quiz in that course. In doing so, he makes these immediate goals pacers of self-reward, so that a good grade on the quiz will become an occasion for reward, and a poor grade will deny him that occasion.

All long-term projects are conducted by investing importance in intermediate goals. Economists have devoted much attention to the difficulties of long-term planning with imperfect information; in addition to such conventional obstacles as lack of skill, opportunity, or information, a recurrent threat to long-term projects is a person's motivation to set up intermediate goals according to how well they make current reward possible. Because these goals cannot be shaped by an actual success rate, they are restrained from becoming fantasy only by the person's rules for testing reality, and rules are always subject to hedging.

For instance, the student may be unable to detect a sharp line between courses that will help him become an architect and those that will not, so that he congratulates himself for "good grades" generally. To increase his rate of self-congratulation, he may then begin signing up for easier courses. Similarly, he may correctly perceive that making models of buildings will help him toward his goal, only to find that making models is such a good pacer of reward in its own right that he does it to the detriment of his course work, something he would have been able to curtail if he had not licensed it, as it were, to be an intermediate step toward his goal.

In general, means to distant ends tend to become increasingly important as ends in themselves. The intermediate goals that make for the most rewarding game will become institutionalized as a formal course of action for achieving a distant end, but may come to have no more than a ceremonial relationship to that end, just enough to satisfy a degenerated rule for testing reality. The Indians of the Great Plains fought bravely, but inefficiently, because they honored the striking of the first blow against an enemy, but gave little importance to the task of finishing him off. The resulting practice of "counting coups" rather than maximizing damage to the enemy put them at a disadvantage against soldiers who were trained to maximize obedience to orders. Individuals in our culture who give importance to inspiration rather than development of their ideas, winning a contract rather than fulfilling it, or getting grades rather than achieving a working knowledge of the subject can likewise be said to be counting coups.

The original end may be put off indefinitely, or even tacitly avoided if it threatens to materialize and spoil what has become a satisfying game. Thus, gamblers seeking a fortune, anglers who return annually to the same spot to pursue a particular grandfather fish, and enemies who cultivate pet targets for revenge may all throw away a victory if fate hands it to them.

Once the intermediate goals have become traditional, they can stand on their own as pacing devices, no longer needing a realistic connection with a distant goal to keep them from becoming arbitrary. Then the hoarder can go on collecting whatever his rules call for, the student can follow his rules for studying, and the socialite can maximize adherence to proper social form, whether or not they can believe that their behaviors will move them toward their original goals, and even if such behaviors are demonstrably counterproductive. In effect, a secondary reward can become temporarily preferred to its own primary reward!

As intermediate goals become ends in their own right, they become arbitrary, and thus tend to deteriorate as pacers of self-reward. "Getting there is half the fun" may sometimes be a sound long-range strategy for self-reward, but when getting there becomes most or all of the fun, it becomes hollow. Counting coups is a familiar activity for everyone, but when a person is caught doing it, he becomes the butt of humor, as does anyone obviously indulging in arbitrary self-reward. "The operation was a success," he is said to claim, "but the patient died."

Means transformed to ends do not lose all their value for limiting self-reward. Indeed, if they have the right aesthetic properties, they may remain efficient, becoming games that are entirely compatible with one's long-range goals. (Chess is said to have started as a way of planning actual battles.) However, they are more apt to become temporarily preferred activities in the addiction range or the sellout range. A person who ceases to "believe in" the value of jockeying for position in society, or in traffic, may still be lured into doing it time after time, as one may be lured into money-making schemes, righteous indignation, or the quest for honors. The rules maintaining these activities remain effective preventives of still shorter-range rewards, but they have in turn become a nuisance to the person's longest-range interests.

Of course, the interests served by coups find ways to defend the rules that permit the coups. As longer-range interests try to distinguish coups from valid intermediate goals, the midrange interests try to define goals that are indistinguishable from them – not necessarily useless to the final goal, but without more reference to it than is needed for verisimilitude. Like any free rider, coups survive insofar as they are difficult to identify as such. The most durable coups will be indispensable steps toward the distant goal that will function as coups rather than realistic signs of progress only because the midrange interests have invested them with too much importance: A person may gather materials past the point where he should move on to making the product, or keep running tests when he should act definitively. It is difficult for his long-range interests to rule out such activities, for no bright line separates them from activities that are necessary to the distant goal.

The midrange interests can use not only such legal maneuvers but also attention control to deflect examination of whether or not an intermediate goal is worthwhile; but the more that attention control is used to defend coups, the faster they will become wholly arbitrary.

Just as a bureaucracy that rewards employees according to rules will be inefficient at motivating them to seek its ultimate goals, so a person's longest-range interests will be served only partially by setting up immediate rewards based on intermediate goals. Any person has had days when he felt virtuous for performing above his standards, but actually accomplished little, and days when he made no definable progress, though knowing at some level that he had moved toward his larger goals. Sometimes a person is even conscious of choosing whether to look busy *just to himself* or to make progress, a choice that is unaccountable without recognizing the process of counting coups.

The reward-pacing or "game" value of an activity may simply supplement its value as a means to a distant end. This value will depend on the activity's rhythmic structure, not on its instrumental utility. The richest games are played for their own sake, and people may pay money for the opportunity. Poorer games may nevertheless be selected if they also serve as means to an end. For instance, a person might pay money for a Monopoly set, but would not pay money for a game in which the players pretended to save and trade in grocery coupons, collect trading stamps, or simply budget their money. However, if the person can classify these activities as "productive" in a way that stands up to his testing of reality, they may become more valuable than an arbitrary game like Monopoly. The person will increase the apparent rarity and hence the immediate value of the points he scores in a game by perceiving the game as a means to a valuable end.

Conversely, to ensure the moment-to-moment motivation for working toward a deferred goal, it is vital to a person's long-range interests to find some game value in the work. However, this supplementation of an activity's game value through its perceived productiveness is not without side effects. Once a game is classified as productive, it takes on an obligatory quality (see chapter 7). A person can stop playing Monopoly at his whim and do no violence to his personal rules. However, once he has undertaken to save coupons or stamps or to perform a particular budgeting task, he endangers rules either for self-control or for testing reality if he casually abandons the project. Worse, the increase in a game's value when it can be seen as productive exerts a corrupting influence on the person's rules for testing future reality, rules that already lack bright lines to defend them from evasion. That is, people often arrange to classify good gamelike activities as more productive than poor ones.

2. Erosion of texture. Although the growth of the practice of counting coups somewhat hampers the operation of rules, the main factor that makes them less efficient is the attenuation of the rewards on which they are based. Sometimes this occurs because of satiation of the underlying drive or a change in environmental opportunities, common processes that simply make the erstwhile rewards unrewarding (i.e., neutral). But in addition to these hazards, simple learning will cause these rewards to be accessed ever more rapidly (see section 7.4.1), a trend that will relentlessly constrict what aggregate self-reward can be realized. Increasingly skillful anticipation of how the situation can develop will both reduce the time until satiation occurs and prevent development of the appetite (suspense, doubt, curiosity, etc.)

that is needed for maximal reward to occur. As a result of this learning, the graph describing the reward realized from the activity loses aggregate area – not from the curve flattening out along the horizontal time axis, but from forming progressively thinner vertical spikes. Despite the small area under them, such spikes compete with other reward-getting activities and thus represent a nuisance to them similar to that caused by pains. Indeed, insofar as they interfere with other rewards, they take on the same form as the curves for pains and itches. They need not be very high to motivate premature consumption in the period before appetite has developed, for the reward that optimally paced consumption will produce in the near future is not great either.

To realize his long-range goals, a person must find sufficient compatible reward to prevent his domination by such spikes of incompatible reward at all times when he is free to choose. This process requires both adequate size and strategic placement of rewards, sufficient to keep alternatives from becoming too attractive. The most flexible method for this is making personal rules.

Turnkey effects aside, the fundamental quality that gives a good its value is its usefulness for pacing self-reward (see sections 7.4 and 8.3), a quality that could be called its "texture." This quality changes as learning bypasses stimuli that previously were barriers – that is, as surprise dissipates. Texture endures only insofar as it eludes anticipation, either through its novelty or through sufficient complexity or subtlety to prevent comprehension. Otherwise a previously effective pacing device may become useless or even an itch.

In other words, as a reward-consuming activity becomes increasingly familiar, it may pass from being an unambivalent pleasure or harmless operant into being aversive. A given activity tends to go from a longer to a shorter duration of preference as it is repeated over time. A child may at first embrace what adults find to be itchlike activities. He may sniff pepper to induce sneezing, or run in the cold to make his legs itch, or make up a game that requires him to count every telephone pole. But insofar as these activities stay rewarding, the reward becomes more and more short-term, so that he may come to avoid the opportunity to begin them. Likewise, a person may discover gambling or reckless driving or promiscuous sex with wholehearted joy, only later concluding that the chance to get such a reward has become a nuisance to him.

The same is often true for many activities of no great moral importance, even reading the daily news or comics. Of course, people sometimes read the paper because they need the information it contains, or feel that they need to be informed citizens, and so forth, and even the person who does it as a pastime is apt to give similar reasons for it; but the motivation may simply be the satisfaction of short-term curiosity, which is unsatisfying in the long run and may interfere with more valued activities, such as reading books, that require more sustained concentration (Feiffer, 1986). The same often may be true of doing crossword puzzles, eating snacks, or playing video games. The urge to check what time it is may also become an itch, and people have been known not to wear watches simply to control this activity. Likewise, a person on a boring automobile trip may resolve not to keep checking the odometer. These are examples of activities that start out being simply rewarding, but through familiarity and consequent premature satiation, they provide only a glimmer of reward as the person undertakes them. Looking forward or backward from a distance, the person often concludes that he would be better off without them.

Activities that come to be perceived as sellouts are even more apt to have been the person's highest goals at an earlier stage in his career. The person may have found that his initial ineptitude at getting money, power, popularity, and so forth made these activities optimally challenging, but that as he refined his skills these tasks lacked the subtlety to remain challenging over a period of years. This is especially apt to be the case when the activities have lost the discipline of being means to an end and have become coups.

Because of the many factors that determine whether or not long-range goals will deteriorate, the perceptions of what activities have become sellouts and what remain simply valuable differ widely among individuals. Some people always find that they function at their best in their trades or businesses, whereas others come to regard such activity as the narrow pursuit of money and try to find ways to minimize the energy they put into it. People divide similarly regarding such activities as competitive driving, making oneself glamorous, gaining power over others, finding bargains, having numerous sexual partners, and playing the predatory "games" cataloged by Eric Berne (1964).

The natural dissipation of goods' pacing ability creates major problems for the interests that have been based on them, particularly long-range interests. To be sure of self-preservation, it is not enough that these interests obtain what are currently their most rewarding objects; they must search for other objects to sustain them after learned premature satiation has spoiled their current objects. That is, the evolution of rules generally, and of texture especially, makes ego functions even more necessary for preventing the intermittent dominance of short-range rewards. This personal evolution selects for those interests that have become independent of any particular source of reward pacing – interests that could be described as having become "circular," in Piaget's sense of the word (1937/1954), because they are based on reward sources for which they continually prospect. The ego can be seen as the set of interests defined in that way, those that look for rewards upon which to be based and maintain themselves on the income, as it were, from this shifting portfolio.

The ego need not eventually abandon all pacing patterns that had once proved useful. It may continue to exploit a given source of reward, despite progressively learned premature satiation, if solution of the original task reveals other tasks that may serve as pacing devices. For instance, a player of a game progressively shifts his interest from tactical to strategic considerations as the tactical moves become "old hat" to him. As the structures that obstruct reward are increasingly nullified by learned shortcuts, structures that previously had been encountered too slowly to be valuable in this respect may emerge as useful pacing devices; the naked frame of a once finely woven texture may, through a shift of investment, serve as the texture of a larger frame. Games like tic-tac-toe, which have no complex strategic solutions, extinguish with learning. Others, like chess, involve strategies that can never simply be mastered and that may serve as durable pacing devices. Human relationships, too, must grow or be outgrown.

To restate this important consequence of learned satiation: Old sources of satisfaction must continue to be novel in some way or they will fail to restrain premature satiation. The texture of surprisingness can wear off an activity in the course of thorough exploration. It is as if familiarity causes a person to grow larger with respect to the environment in which the activity is conducted, in the sense that its barriers seem to become lower, or that he can take larger steps toward his goals. Great familiarity with an area will make it appear like a flat plain that can be traversed in a few strides, or, more literally, comprehended at a glance. "Growing larger" in this sense usually is accompanied by a short-range increase in reward, because what the simile portrays is the removal of obstacles to reward.[4]

Conversely, processes that inhibit exploration (such as attention control) leave the person "small" and keep the terrain that paces his reward mountainous, full of surprises. Even when this narrowing of attention comes from the impulse to avoid unpleasant information in the service of short-range interests (see sections 5.2.2 and 5.3.2), it may have a positive long-range aesthetic by-product. Hysterical defensive styles may be inefficient as means to deferred ends, but may well be better than compulsive styles in countering learned satiation. With no qualms about exploration, a person will tend to exhaust the ability of an environment to surprise him.

It is possible to find fresh texture by metaphorically shrinking rather than enlarging. That is, a person may obtain new pacing patterns within a given activity when fate or willpower restricts the availability of pacing stimuli, so that stimuli that previously had paid off too slowly to compete for his investment become choosable. As a person fails to encounter his accustomed occasions for self-reward, his highly unsatiated state will lead him to seize upon stimulus patterns that he had left unexplored. Thus, people sometimes become content with tasks that look totally frustrating to an observer, and a child who is

---

[4] A person can induce this kind of virtual enlargement not only by solving the puzzles intrinsic to the activity in question, but also by giving less importance to this activity. He may simply inhibit the early development of appetite for the events in this area, for instance, by the isolation of affect (see chapter 5). A narcissistic young patient once reported that he had learned to reduce the power of a risky world to hurt him by mentally "rising up in a balloon" so that its events seemed unimportant, but he later found that trick to be an addiction that made him feel empty. Likewise, a person may become much busier or emotionally involved elsewhere, and events in the area will lose their capacity to excite his attention; manic defenses against textures that have become aversive, as well as the "type-A" personal style (Friedman & Rosenman, 1974), rely on this process. In such cases, the enlargement is not compelled by a loss of texture in the available pacing stimuli, but is motivated by other reasons to disinvest in the activity.

never praised may find adequate social stimulation in criticism or even abuse. Hence also the proverbial enthusiasm of the prisoner in his cell for small changes in his routine, and the ecstasy of the religious ascetic. More mundanely, this probably is the hitherto puzzling process by which people increase their reported satisfactions by lowering their "aspiration levels" (Campbell, Converse, & Rodgers, 1976, pp. 471–508).[5] However, in the absence of great ego skill, people realizing reward at an initially lower rate will succumb to itches and addictions – alcohol, compulsions, repetitive fantasy – before the neglected stimuli can assume the necessary importance. A person pursuing an ascetic strategy deliberately must learn to ride out periods of low return while waiting for the spontaneous revision of his rules for self-reward, rather than search for new, more readily available occasions for self-reward. Ascetic strategies entail an especially large entry cost, and thus the long-range interests must employ great budgetary skill to motivate them.

Whenever a person's major long-range pacing devices lose their texture, he will be less able to resist impulsive consumption patterns. Addictions and itches will spring up like weeds, just as in the case in which his self-reward schedule is too strict. Insofar as he understands the problem of eroding texture, he will search for new and more challenging tasks or will find subtler rules for consumption so that the old tasks will remain optimally challenging and thus will not revert to a more short range rewarding pattern. This probably is the skill Freud referred to as "sublimation," although his concern was with the danger, not the learned satiability, of the original object; in both cases a person will solve his problem when he finds a self-reward pattern that exploits the drive without the negative long-range consequences of his original pattern. Becker and Murphy (1988) recognize the value of such a skill as "positive consumption capital." Such a skill allows a person to perceive a meal as a range of interacting flavors, rather than as simply a reducer of hunger, or to see another person as a subtle, unsolvable puzzle, rather than as simply an opponent or a means to some end. Given a person with adequate skill,

---

[5] Aspiration levels clearly are rules for self-reward, but are experienced projectively, i.e., as dictated by the environment, probably for the sake of feeling helpless in setting them. If a person saw himself deliberately tamper with his aspiration level, he would lose his expectation of having an important commitment against arbitrary self-reward.

some activities are sufficiently intricate that they never become predictable, thus remaining effective pacing devices for long periods of time. These are the patterns that come to be called art.

However, this solution is only relative; even art tends slowly to become predictable, and thus it becomes subject to fashion cycles (Lowe & Lowe, 1982). In painting, for instance, new aesthetic strategies regularly evolve from being inefficient because they have been poorly explored, through a stage of being maximally powerful, to becoming inefficient because they have become overly familiar (Martindale, 1986; Woelfflin, 1929, pp. 229–235). During this last stage, artists try to make up for this inefficiency by exaggerating its arousing features (e.g., through bizarre invention or intricacy of detail) before the style sinks into a period of total disuse from being thought hackneyed. It is only when a new generation has grown up relatively unfamiliar with the style that it may regain some value. Stages of artistic style represent, in part, a group effort to solve each artist's problem of keeping reward fresh. As the texture wears off a particular inspiration, his own or the group's, an artist is left with mere cleverness as a means to surprise. In poetry, for instance, internal rhymes or obscure allusions may increase (Basham, 1967, pp. 425–427), even to the point of writing in the form of palindromes or acrostics! The strictness of rules for composition offers at least rarity in the collector's sense, but cannot seriously impede learned satiation.

Toynbee cataloged many characteristics of disintegrating civilizations, but he traced them all to a disintegration in the "creative power in the souls of creative individuals" who would have inspired others to follow them: "The piper who has lost his cunning can no longer conjure the feet of the multitude into a dance" (1946, p. 245). Although Toynbee does not explain this loss of cunning, he depicts concomitant psychological changes that resemble some of the foregoing changes in rule-governed behavior: an increasing "mechanicalness," an inordinate concern with traditional forms, and a confusion of "stepping stones" with "pedestals," that is, means with ends (pp. 275–359). The idea that old tunes and old ways should lose something like texture, as I have just defined it, makes no sense in conventional utilitarian theory; thus, concepts like Toynbee's "nemesis of creativity," and the expression by many authors since Victorian times of an enervation that accompanies the systemization of modern life, have seemed somewhat mystical. However, the perverse urge to learn shortcuts to reward that is predicted by deeply concave discount curves can be expected to produce just such a phenomenon.

9.4 The evolution of rules affects the optimal budgeting of rewards

The five factors just discussed as governing the evolution of a person's rules are not necessarily an exhaustive list. They do not depend on particular rewards; the first four are predictable results of any personal rule formation in response to a deeply bowed discount function of delayed rewards, and the last is a predictable result of any situation in which reward is freely available intrapsychically. Three of these factors are results of learning: the increasing familiarity that leads a person to judge more choices as precedents, the discovery of coups that can effectively parasitize long-range rewards, and the discovery of faster routes to any given criterion for self-reward that cause the criterion to lose its effectiveness as a pacing device. One factor is the limit on a person's ability to learn and integrate information about his increasingly complex network of rules, which makes precedent-breaking behaviors seem especially risky; and one is simply his accumulation of a history of choices, which inevitably offers new bright lines that can be a force in his rule-making.

The evolution process has some consequences for optimal budgeting strategy that have not been obvious from our discussion thus far: (1) It may be more efficient to let learned satiation erode an impulse than to avoid the impulse by precommitment. (2) Often it will be necessary to turn to the lore of one's culture to predict how a given pacing strategy will evolve. (3) The most durable pacing strategies often will be those that elude precise definition in the form of rules.

9.4.1 Letting impulses satiate

Pacing devices that serve midrange interests may be prey to learned satiation, just like those that serve long-range interests. As a result, some distractions from a long-range task may be controlled with less effort if they are indulged than if they are forbidden. This situation is just an extension of the more obvious case of simple, unlearned satiation: A person with an urge to procrastinate by sharpening pencils or having a snack may find that simply obeying the urge may appease these appetites more cheaply than making rules against them, as long as fresh urges are not likely to appear in the situation.[6] For the case of learned satiation, this computation applies to the choice of allowing oneself (or, even more commonly, a dependent child) to fully indulge an impulse that can be expected to be outgrown – that is, to be killed by learned premature satiation – rather than control it and thereby delay or prevent the outgrowing of it.

Often it is difficult to know how an impulse will evolve: Outlawing it will preserve a process of which a person might otherwise tire, but on the other hand, failure to outlaw it may institutionalize it as a loophole. How does a person know that his child will outgrow excessive aggressiveness, or laziness, if he treats it tolerantly? Confronting such traits may make issues of them that will keep them alive longer than if they evolved spontaneously. But if they are allowed to evolve and do not die in that evolution, they become well defended by the precedents thus set. Likewise, how does a person know whether or not he will let himself become a habitual invalid if he shirks responsibility on days when he feels sick? If these holidays come from a limited and identifiable process such as migraine, he probably will not. If they are occasioned by an open-ended emotional response that he experiences as sickness, perhaps he will. But it may be difficult to tell which case he faces, and many people develop stoic attitudes toward illness just to be on the safe side.

9.4.2 Finding durable pacing devices

Recall that pacing devices oppose the vigorous urge toward premature consumption and that in the case of most rewards this opposition

---

[6] A person may even insist on doing these things before he begins the task, whether or not he has much appetite for them, just to prevent the appetite from arising later. Of course, totally ruling out such activities would do as well, but one cannot totally rule out eating, having adequate writing instruments and the like, and so may have to buy off the impulse. The decision whether or not to surrender to the impulse "just this once" is based on one's estimate of the cost of giving in to the impulse versus the cost of resisting it.

depends on the partial unpredictability of the stimulus patterns within the reward. The ego processes must allow for repeatedly obtained goals to lose much or all of this unpredictability (texture) over time. This loss and the growth of new tastes take place gradually, more like the growth of plants than the performance of behaviors, a situation that poses an information-gathering problem:

A person's way of predicting how a pacing device will evolve over time is limited at best – human subjects are poor at predicting the future behaviors of their tastes even for simple foods (Kahneman & Snell, 1990). Durable activities are those with texture under the texture, that is, those in which the original texture is worn away to reveal others just as rewarding; but this happy eventuality cannot be seen in advance. A pattern that will remain a good pacing device may start out grossly similar to one that will not. Just as it is difficult to tell if a new tool will wear well or a new computer utility will be helpful in one's own particular applications, an unfamiliar pacing pattern is a gamble.

It is pure luck when a durable pacing pattern happens to be sufficiently rewarding in its early stages to compete with more transient rewards. However, once discovered, such a pattern may become part of the lore of a community. Although those who transmit the lore may edit it to manipulate the recipient in their own interest (to make him obedient, pious, patriotic, etc.), he still may find it to be the best information available concerning the durability of possible investments. Conversely, the initial reward is not particularly apt to guide a person to the best long-term patterns. Thus, such patterns often must be sustained by the influence of the person's culture rather than by his own spontaneous preferences, until the progress of learned satiation reduces the power of their competitors. That is, the initial motivation often must come from purely external pressure, such as a parent who keeps a child at piano lessons until the child becomes skillful enough to love music for its own sake.[7]

However, pressure from an outside force may define a game in itself, which can prevent a person from learning the recommended

---

[7] James March has pointed out that perfect compliance with such guidance would impair the society's gathering of information on how various choices turn out, so that the "optimal sin" rate for a society is nonzero (1978, pp. 603–604).

game. To learn to satisfy a piano teacher is not quite the same thing as learning music. Understanding the nature of music may allow it to serve as a lifelong challenge; knowing a procedure for turning written notes into music will do little to retard learned satiation. Likewise, understanding the properties of altruism may introduce a person into a durably satisfying relationship with his community, but undertaking to satisfy a social demand for altruism will lead only to the competitive game of concealing his selfishness. The delicate task of teaching robust pacing devices, while not introducing the distraction of external demand, lies at the heart of socialization.

9.4.3 Avoiding overly concrete rules

Even with a good knowledge of what activities are apt to resist premature satiation in the long run, a person faces a budgetary problem in trying to adopt them. The necessary behaviors often are unrewarding at first; to get himself to perform them, he must convert the recipes his culture gives him for coping with learned satiation into personal rules. That is, he must define categories for the choices he actually faces in such a way that he will have adequate motivation to resist the impulsive choice from moment to moment. However, because rules become rigid and overinclusive and are weakened by evasions, insights about the most effective means for pacing reward often are distorted beyond usefulness when people try to convert them to personal rules.

The most important pacers of self-reward are the behaviors of other people. Interpersonal situations are generally subtle and open to interpretation. Indeed, they probably must remain this way if they are to stay effective as pacing criteria. A person may conclude from his observations that he is happiest when admired by others, or believe on authority that he should "turn the other cheek" if offended, but if he then makes rules that he must choose situations so as to maximize his admirability or that he must never express anger when offended, he will lose the flexibility he needs to make the best use of relationships. Rules of thumb may help him organize the complexity of human interaction, but when converted into principles of self-control, they fall prey to the cumulative distortions discussed earlier. What starts as a useful hint directing spontaneous, goal-directed behavior becomes ungainly when used as a personal rule.

Consider again the case of altruism. The suggestion that a person can get satisfaction by rewarding himself according to his empathic reading of another's feelings is frequently rediscovered. However difficult altruism has been for theoreticians of evolution (Trivers, 1971), it is evidently a successful method for maintaining the freshness of reward. However, it usually fails of adoption not through a person's ignorance but through his urges to interpret other people's behaviors as competitive. Such interpretations yield short-range gratification in the form of challenging races, or midrange gratification as a struggle to build wealth, power, fame, and so forth, by overcoming skilled competitors. Given this temptation, the information that altruism is a more durable strategy will mean little unless the person makes a rule such as "love other people as yourself." But the spirit of such a rule is unenforceable, and the concrete requirements a person is apt to add to make it enforceable are apt to wind up serving the original shorter-range goals, for instance in forms of competitive giving like potlatch, or the use of dutiful charity to belittle or control the recipient (e.g., Yezierska, 1925). Trying to police a rule requiring a subtle responsiveness only obscures the original insight further.

Given the tendency of personal rules to deteriorate and the limitations of the other impulse-controlling devices, it is difficult to know how a person can preserve his longest-range interest. The art seems to involve following the logic of rule formation to some extent, but avoiding concrete criteria. For instance, a former anorectic described to me how she managed to outgrow the highly effective rules that had organized her life around food intake: When she became aware of the constricting effect that those rules had, she began making decisions according to a simpler test: "How will I feel about it tomorrow?" That was also a rule – failure to sympathize with tomorrow's self would have been a lapse that would have made such sympathy more difficult in the future – and probably a highly vulnerable rule, given the impressionistic nature of the criterion. Nevertheless, that person used her recognition of its necessity to install it in place of a far more articulate system that had once been her main source of strength. Religions have recognized the value of this art, as when they warn of the "death of the spirit" that accompanies overreliance on the "pagan morality" of willpower (e.g., Davison, 1888, pp. 156–183); but it is not clear to what their suggested solutions refer in terms of motivation. Like the self-predictive process that probably underlies "free will" (see section 6.3), the course of optimal rule-making defies prediction from even the best knowledge of the circumstances. It represents another hiding place for the subtlety of the ego.

9.5 Internal bargaining interacts with external

Finally, we should note the obvious fact that the bargaining of an individual's successive motivational states often occurs within a context of bargaining among different individuals. I have hypothesized that motivational conflict is simple in principle – as simple as the prisoner's dilemma. However, as in interpersonal bargaining situations, internal conflicts are soon complicated by the appearance of many interests, by the recognition of many alternative solutions, and by the recollection of many past choices of varying salience to the current choice. Furthermore, interpersonal bargaining does not merely parallel the internal, but interacts with it. Not only do other people supply many goods that help one internal interest against another – pornography, fine art, gambling propositions, savings plans, alcohol, Antabuse – but as emotional objects they themselves influence the internal bargaining process and are sought or avoided or treated ambivalently for that reason. I seek out a friend because he helps me overcome my anger, I seek an enemy because he furnishes an occasion to indulge my anger, I join a protest group because it helps me harness and refine my anger, and so forth. Internal bargains are struck with an eye to influencing other people, and interpersonal negotiations are conducted so as to influence internal ones.

This interaction leads to two somewhat artificial conventions in our official beliefs about behavior: that all behaviors may be classified as voluntary or not, and that a person's voluntary behaviors spring from a single, ordered set of preferences. These beliefs do not closely match our spontaneous observations of each other, but are adopted so as to solve problems in interpersonal bargaining.

9.5.1 The voluntary/involuntary dichotomy

Most societies have recognized a category of urges that people "can't resist." Such urges are intense, rewarded with such immediacy once the person learns of them that he has no time to defend himself, and/ or recurring with such frequency that defense against them is impractical. Behaviors like panic, obsessional thinking, the emotions occasioned by pain, and others that are briefly preferred get classified as irresistible, even as reflexes. Conversely, strategic behaviors that are preferred for long periods, such as hoarding, self-aggrandizement, and embezzlement, are seen as deliberate, the full responsibility of the actor. Society has conspicuous difficulty in classifying the broad range of behaviors between these extremes, the ones preferred in the addiction range and often thought of as "weaknesses of the flesh." The idea that someone might be expected to rise above all such weaknesses violates not only common experience but also the teachings of the great religions. However, these behaviors clearly respond, at least partially, to efforts of will.

Western societies usually are intolerant of this ambiguity, forcing marginal examples into one category or the other. Indeed, they are somewhat committed to do so because of their efforts to help addicts' long-range interests by punishing addictive behaviors. Because punishment is a dichotomous decision, the behaviors that might be punished must be classified as either blameworthy or not, a decision that will depend in turn on whether they are seen as voluntary or not. This classification hinges in practice on these behaviors' likelihood of being deterred by the threat of blame or punishment. To optimize deterrence, societies must draw the line between behaviors that stand a substantial chance of being deterred and those that do not. Just as an individual tries to increase his resistance to marginal temptations by defining them as dangerous precedents, so a society tries to stiffen its members' resistance to addictive behaviors that are marginally resistible by outlawing those behaviors, in effect staking the credibility of its criminal-justice system on prosecuting each case that it encounters on the wrong side of the line.

This outlawry is thought of as a service to a majority of the society's members, because it adds additional pressure, perhaps a "swing vote" in the direction of resisting the temptation. But it has complicated effects. The assessment whether or not legal or other external sanctions are in the potential addict's long-range interest, or that of his society, usually involves a close call. There is evidence that they increase net deterrence for many people – alcoholism, as measured by cirrhosis deaths, declined during Prohibition in the United States (Fisher & Brougham, 1930; Merz, 1930/1968) – but they probably render the person they fail to deter worse off than he would have been without them. Furthermore, the failures may be partially determined by interactions of the external incentives with the potential addict's internal bargaining process. An external control may weaken his will, because it will deny him potential evidence of its sufficiency that he could have added to the stake against lapses (see section 5.7). In addition, a prohibition often creates a good gamelike activity in the evasion of it.

Nevertheless, societies and smaller groups repeatedly conspire to supplement their members' personal rules with external sanctions. Actual criminalization is directed only at addictions: gambling, some drugs (but not, in modern times, nicotine), some sexual perversions, and sometimes alcohol. However, a society may sanction hostility or derision for temporary preferences in all time ranges, despite the fact that the only victim is the subject himself: Misers and narcissists, overeaters and smokers, obsessional worriers and people prone to tics, and those who seem to have "unreasonably" low resistances to pain and panic are all apt to be blamed for these traits. This use of blame requires social agreement on a natural line between voluntary and involuntary, and the classification of these behaviors on the voluntary side of the line.

There is little argument about the existence of a line, but much about where it "really" lies in a given modality. Because people also use such a line for personal rules, the question whether a behavior should be called involuntary or not often is a sore one within an individual as well as between individuals. Some people, and perhaps all people at one time or another, expect their self-control to be better when the behaviors they fear are known as voluntary, leaving only those against which the will rarely succeeds in the involuntary category; Peele (1989) urges this attitude. Others would rather call marginally controllable behaviors diseases, using the rationale that the existence of the abnormally large temptation is itself beyond the control of the will, being perhaps hereditary or at least innate. The latter attitude can also be defended as supporting impulse control, because it implies an acknowledgment of helplessness against impulses that may move the subject to give temptation a wider berth (see section 5.6.1) and may also restore a modicum of the social support that was withdrawn when his behavior was seen as deliberate.

People divide readily into warring camps on the question when to call a particular kind of temptation irresistible. Alcoholism, to which some individuals seem innately much more susceptible than others, is seen as wicked by some, but as an externally imposed disaster by others. Moderately great pain involves the same situation: Those who react more than most people are labeled crybabies by some and victims by others. Interestingly, medieval writers ascribed what would now be thought of as symptoms of depression to the sin of "acedia," the giving in to a "bitterness of mind" that could have been resisted, although they also sometimes expressed the alternative view that it was a disease (Jackson, 1985). Such conflicts are consequences of the perceived need to draw a line where it "really" belongs, when both the degree of the natural urge and the degree of self-control skill are in fact continuously variable.

Furthermore, different societies or groups within societies agree upon different zones within which these conflicts of opinion are acceptable. Beyond them is an area where "everyone" calls behaviors voluntary, as well as another in which they agree that behaviors are involuntary. The locations of these zones must influence and be influenced by the work of that group (i.e., whatever difficult tasks it is geared up to do). What a member of a developed society would consider normal susceptibility to pain would have been seen as a moral flaw by the Mongols, the Plains Indians, and other stoic cultures that have existed from time to time, whereas those cultures accepted traits, such as lack of thrift, that are disapproved in ours. It could be argued that specialization in resisting different kinds of temptations has been a major consideration defining separate castes or orders within societies. For instance, the three estates that existed in Europe until modern times could be seen as arising from specialties in resisting fear (the nobility), pride and lust (the clergy), and spendthriftiness (the bourgeoisie), in that weakness toward each kind of temptation was seen as especially shameful in one estate, but tolerable in the other two. Those who lacked any self-control specialty were relegated to the plebeian remainder of the third estate.

Individuals, groups, and societies have drawn lines to outlaw different degrees of different temptations, but wherever they have drawn such lines they have believed them to be dictated by natural law. The common perception of a line between morally weak behaviors and behaviors that most people "can't help" has shielded from blame those people who engage in the latter and permitted the confident ostracism of those who habitually indulge in the former. The pico-economic view that there is no obvious place for such lines to be drawn, that both the durations and magnitudes of temporary preferences lie on continua, may itself have a role in these transactions – a negative one from the viewpoint of conventional morality. Lines drawn for pragmatic reasons invite redrawing, whereas lines given by some universal principle do not. To believe in the immutable necessity of a moral law probably adds something to one's will to obey it, at least if that will has not been broken by failures in the relevant area. Nevertheless, both the diversity of modern beliefs and the current ineffectiveness of means for restoring the power of failed wills suggest that society must increasingly deal with impulse control within the relativistic framework of bargaining theory.

9.5.2 The unity of the self

As we have discussed, a person in one motivational state may try various ways to impose his wishes on himself in future motivational states. However, this is rarely recognized as the process that makes his behavior consistent. People think of themselves as having a steady policy over time, and they regard it as an aberration when they depart from that policy (see section 3.6). A person is said to change his mind, as if that were the active process, rather than to passively let his mind change. He is said to have a unitary set of preferences, which are, however, subject to a number of exceptional processes like lapses, irrationality, seduction, passions, fugue episodes, and fragmentation of the personality. It seems to be more comfortable to argue from a theory of a single self that is subject to many flaws and complications than to say that successive motivational states are by their nature partially unrelated and can be brought together only to a moderate extent.

Like our belief in a natural division between voluntary and involuntary behaviors, the fiction of a unitary self may simplify bargaining among people and within a person. Although people often can elicit some sympathy when they excuse their actions by saying that they were not themselves, or "it was the alcohol talking," it would be maddening for others to deal on a regular basis with multiple selves within one body, especially when one of them could masquerade as another. Just as lawyers have found that they must treat the actions by all employees of a company as the actions of the company itself, so people hold a single entity responsible for all the moods and impulses expressed by a single body. Furthermore, they treat this legal fiction as a fact of nature. As with other projective explanations (see section 6.4.5), this perception may serve to prevent the hedging that inevitably attacks a mere rule.

Similarly, the long-range, or ego, processes within an individual that preserve a core of consistent goals probably find the norm of a unitary self to be a useful discipline. The fact that other people may punish deviations from that norm further motivates the discipline; conversely, the internal usefulness of this incentive moves the person to collude with others in maintaining the social threat of punishment. Again, perception of this norm as a natural law reduces tampering.

9.6 Psychological conclusions: The individual is a population of bargaining interests

The inconsistent and even self-defeating nature of human behavior is notorious. There still are theorists who try to account for this property as a defect in information processing: ignorance, misleading information from the environment, irrational cognition, and so on. It has often been asserted that the problem runs deeper, that there are stable entities within the individual that cause the inconsistency by fighting with one another: passion versus reason, id versus ego, conditioned behavior versus operant behavior, and so forth. However, no elementary principle has heretofore been identified as the basis upon which such entities might interact.

I have argued that the deeply bowed discount curves for delayed events described by Herrnstein and his school create conflicting interests within the individual and that these interests are stable; their conflicts are not resolved by the victory of one over another, because the interests are dominant at different times. The tendency to form temporary preferences predicted by this model accounts not only for the gross self-contradictions seen in addictive behaviors but also for much of the detailed interaction of impulse and defense mechanism described by Freud and his followers.

The clearest model for this interaction is Schelling's concept of limited warfare, which can be formally described by bargaining games, particularly the repeated prisoner's dilemma. Players of this game rely upon each other's current moves to predict their future moves; similarly, stable solutions to the intrapsychic bargaining problem require a person to perceive his current choices as precedents predicting his own most likely choices in similar future situations. He must use stimuli from the environment as boundary lines between those choices that he will count as examples of a given kind of situation and those that he will not. The cooperative solutions to this conflict among successive motivational states are personal rules that hinge upon such boundary lines, which may be experienced as direct physical effects of the stimuli themselves. The self-referential nature of this process can account variously for people's ability to resist external coercion and our experiences of impulsiveness, compulsiveness, or free will under various circumstances. This kind of bargaining, like other kinds, needs to be repeated only while the outcome is uncertain; where one choice or another has clearly won, that choice becomes second nature, and is usually experienced as reflexive or otherwise unmotivated.

With few additional assumptions, the model supplies parsimonious hypotheses about several other troublesome motivational paradoxes:

In the face of evidence that pain and other aversive emotions require an organism's active participation, conventional theories do not explain how aversive stimuli can seem to reward this participation while punishing the behaviors that led to it. But if we assume that temporary preferences can be extremely brief and can recur rapidly, we can understand pains as speeded-up versions of the temporary-preference cycle that is plainly visible in addictions and itches.

Consumption of many kinds of rewards depends on preparatory

behaviors called appetites, the regular habits of which are called tastes. The conventional understanding is that tastes are either innate or induced by classical conditioning, but I have argued that people's tastes often reflect their active control of their own appetites: sometimes by early avoidance; sometimes by such complete control of the corresponding consummatory behavior that the appetite extinguishes through nonreward; or, where the appetite is tempting in its own right, by personal rules. It is the requirements of impulse control that cause tastes to be restricted in the complicated ways that are familiar to clinicians.

Most of the rewards people seek when their physical needs have been met involve emotions that are within their arbitrary reach. If we assume that rapid consumption of available reward wastes the drive on which it is based, then deeply bowed discount curves predict that a person will tend to generate and resolve these emotions with the wasteful haste of daydreams unless he has tied them to external occasions by means of personal rules; there is sketchy evidence that *ad libitum* self-reward is possible even in modalities that usually require consumption of a substance like food or a drug. Insofar as self-reward is possible, external events, including human relationships, will be valued as pacing devices for reward, rather than as turnkeys that physically induce the reward process. Because attention is rewarded for skipping ahead in such pacing devices, those that remain valuable must remain surprising. This model accounts for several phenomena that have seemed irrational according to conventional theory, including subjects' inconsistent evaluation of money, the transience of fashions, and various ways in which well-learned self-control skills lose their edge with long use. Beyond preserving themselves to prevent the ascendancy of incompatible interests, the "ego" functions must plan for replacing the texture of surprise as it wears away from the person's important objects.

The fundamental insight of picoeconomics is that the mind bears less resemblance to a fact-gathering or puzzle-solving apparatus than to a population of foraging organisms. The foraging entities are interests that grow from rewards, just as populations of organisms grow on the basis of food sources. Like the variety of organisms that stably occupy a habitat, interests fill various motivational niches on the basis of their specific abilities to maintain and defend themselves there, which largely depend on the time courses of the rewards on which they are based.

9.7 Economic conclusions: Surprise is different from other goods

Economics has always recognized some effects of internal motivational change. Tastes are known to fluctuate, goods have been described that are medicinal in small doses but poisonous in large amounts, and "diminishing returns" is an old economic concept. But goods that remain attractive at times after they have been found to be poisonous represent a major difficulty for utilitarian theory. Even though Strotz (1956) pointed out a generation ago the need to evaluate a good strategically, that is, in the context of probable changes of preference over time, economic concepts have not grown in that direction. There has been almost no recognition that even purchasable goods are apt to be evaluated as the ends of limited internal interests, rather than as some continuous function of their quantity that can summarize their overall worth to the subject. The result is a growing catalog of choices that economists call anomalies. A closer look at internal motivational processes will be necessary to penetrate their mysteries.

Microscopic examination of economic processes, as of most things, does not reveal a miniature version of what has already been seen. Individuals' choices of goods are rooted not in the proportional rationality of economic man but in the intertemporal bargaining process made necessary by deeply bowed discount curves. The exponential discounting seen in rational markets is the solution to a bargaining problem: Where an individual has the skill at internal budgeting, he makes a rule to evaluate some or all kinds of goods *as if* they will lose value exponentially with delay (see section 7.1); and for at least some kinds of goods, this rule is adequately motivated by the increase in long-range reward it permits. Where he is in competition with other people, the individual encounters an additional incentive to adopt such a rule and to make the exponential discount rate it requires as low as he can stand: Other people who discount future goods less than he does will gradually become wealthier at his expense. Insofar as he is aware of this eventuality, the prospect of losing, or gaining, a competitive advantage will be added to the intrinsic incentives for the rule.

Thus, the most comprehensive interpersonal marketplace, that of finance, interacts with people's intrapsychic markets to produce a common, low exponential discount rate for some kinds of goods under some circumstances. This is the realm of conventional economics. It is not a contradiction of the deeply bowed discounting pattern described in this book, but rather represents a special case of it, just as Newtonian physics is a special case of relativistic physics.

However, like any rule, a person's rule for the consistent evaluation of purchasable goods shifts importance from his spontaneous liking of them to whether or not they offer concrete stimuli that are suitable as criteria for evaluation. Aspects like the ability to be weighed and counted will become more important than aspects like flavor or aesthetic appeal, although gross differences in the latter qualities still will have effects on prices. As long as the person's appetite for these goods remains relatively unsatiated, even crude rules for evaluating them may serve his long-range interests adequately. On the other hand, when the person has achieved extensive control over his supply of a good, rules to maximize its quantity probably will no longer serve his longest-range interest, although they may continue to serve interests in the sellout range. To be able to reward himself efficiently in that modality, he needs to adjust his perception of what is scarce. Appetite, rather than satisfaction, and surprise, rather than comprehension, are the factors that he will need to increase for optimal enjoyment. He will need to find goods that can husband these very *lacks* of things, and that also can provide enough short-range reward for him to select them in the first place.

This task somewhat conflicts with most of the obvious rules for maintaining the rational value of money, which in turn have determined the nature of conventional economics. If a person commits himself to take reward only when someone else is happy, that disturbs but does not destroy the hypothesis that he is an economic man; altruistic goods can be defined that behave more or less like other goods. But if the person detects a surfeit of a good – takes steps to restrain an ongoing wish to consume more of it so as to increase his enjoyment of it, or blocks his knowledge of it so as to be surprised by it – then he is no longer the economic man who has been familiar to us. Economics needs to adjust its concepts to handle the valuation of goods when those goods are still a necessary component of the reward process but are no longer the limiting factor.

9.8 Social conclusions: The pathology of leisure differs from that of scarcity

People in the developed world live in an environment vastly different from that in which our species evolved. The difference on which I have focused in this book is the great decrease in effort required to avoid the pains that dominated the lives of our ancestors: hunger, cold, and disease. As this task has become a smaller and smaller part of our motivation, motives that used to be restricted to brief windows of prosperity have grown to occupy the centers of our lives. Gamelike activities used to be tightly structured by the need to harness their motivation to the service of avoiding pains: Play rehearsed skills, social interaction took the form of cooperation for tasks, song in the form of chanteys paced labor, and so forth. Now that games have become our main occupations, their arbitrary nature has put us at the mercy of an inborn trait that apparently had not been problematic when motivation was driven by scarcity: the deeply bowed shape of our discount curves for delayed rewards.

Whatever their original adaptiveness may have been, deeply bowed discount curves prevent a farsighted organism like man from simply pursuing his greatest perceived long-range good. We must devote a fair proportion of our effort to forestalling our own temporary preferences for goods that are not in our long-range interest. As Goethe said, "every emancipation of the spirit is pernicious unless there is a corresponding growth of control" (quoted by Goodheart, 1968, p. 3). In the past, we were protected by the primitiveness of our technology. In an environment where the means to escape pains are scarce, the motivation to obtain such means usually will be enough to maintain precommitting tactics against short-range rewards. However, when deviations from this discipline cease to be punished severely and consistently, shorter-range interests will burgeon. Furthermore, increasing sophistication about this process will not necessarily arrest it, for this sophistication will serve short- as well as long-range interests. The science that invents Antabuse also invents "designer drugs," and the skill that formulates personal rules discovers loopholes. God and the devil stay neck and neck.

It would require another book to trace the histories of impulses and impulse controls through modern times. Roughly, the impulses seem to show continual growth, whereas the controls have become more cumbersome and less well motivated. As Toynbee noted more than 40 years ago, "[In modern Western society] there is no lack of evidence of *abandon* . . . on the other hand we may search in vain for a counter-resurgence of asceticism" (1946, vol. 1, p. 441). Easiest to trace are the addictive substances, which have progressed from one or two agents per society at the end of the Middle Ages (tobacco in parts of North America, coca in parts of South America, hemp in India, undistilled alcohol and opium in several regions), through the mutual exchange and refinement of these agents until the end of the nineteenth century, to the invention of major new agents, beginning with heroin just before the turn of this century (Austin, 1978). The pervasion of modern life with psychoactive drugs has been called "our modern antimiracle" (Cummings, 1979). It is more difficult to be sure of the nonsubstance impulses. New inventions may not have greatly increased the kick of gambling, but the amount of money spent on it seems to have grown dramatically over this century. The ancients may have known most of our sexual games, but again the investment of money and attention seems to have grown. Some other addictions, such as spending beyond one's means and risk-taking, are ancient, but many new ones have appeared, or at least have been recognized as addictions (see section 1.1).

Even taken together the identified addictions seriously injure only a minority, and it could be argued that they are the unfit of current evolution. But the qualities of "normal" activities have also changed progressively to make them objects of ambivalence. Entertainment is increasingly passive (creating "TV addicts"), dehumanized (creating video-game schizoids), and speeded up (leading even readers of books to complain of an insubstantial quality). Even passive entertainment by world experts competes successfully with mundane human relationships for a person's investment, and these relationships are increasingly expected to be transitory. I have argued that naive consumption of the wonders of hedonic technology has made the crowd lonely and the economy joyless; but naiveté does not mean that this consumption is unmotivated. When people discover the consequences of their consumption patterns and try to give them up, they often find that controls adequate to overcome the motivation for these patterns are not in their repertoires.

Indeed, the development of personal impulse controls seems to have peaked in the nineteenth century. Excepting some physical controls for specific applications (Antabuse, appetite suppressants, etc.), inventions in impulse control have occurred mainly in the exploration of will. In the seventeenth century the import of discussions about will shifted from the nature of its freedom to the nature of its strength. In practice, Puritanism seems to have led in the development of willpower, perhaps assisted by the device of defining all choices as predictors of whether one belonged in the category of the elect or the damned (see section 6.3). A major leap in understanding occurred when Kant's categorical imperative focused attention on the significance of choices as precedents, an approach that was developed and extolled by moral philosophers and then psychologists throughout the nineteenth century (see section 5.3.4). But the dangers of overprincipled choice were identified as early as the time of Kierkegaard. Around the end of World War I, educated people stopped talking of the will almost in unison, as if equating it with the *cran* ("guts") that military theorists had relied upon to impel millions of men to their deaths (Tuchman, 1962, p. 51).

Reliance upon willpower has been sporadically replaced by the theory, Marxian or Freudian or utopian, that enlightenment can render impulse controls unnecessary. Although a substantial tendency to see decisions in terms of personal rules persists, the members of developed societies have been subjected to a growth of institutional attempts to exploit their rule-following tendencies – laws, regulations, policies, codified procedures, the increasingly invasive threat of civil liability – modern theories of management have made this exploitation progressively fine-grained without increasing the usefulness of these rules to the targeted individuals. Thus we have grown profoundly suspicious of appeals to conscientiousness. Heroes of modern literature are much more apt to overcome the strictures of conventional morality than to overcome impulses (Goodheart, 1968). But in our disillusionment with the will, and in the absence of actual pain, there is not much to oppose the lure of cheapened life-styles.

Species do not evolve toward greater happiness, only toward more efficient motivation for the behaviors that have been correlated with survival and propagation. In fact, nature seems to use happiness as a lure to reward a successful effort only briefly before demanding new efforts (see the discussion of learned satiation in chapter 6). Instead of amassing a wealth of reward, an individual who has successfully met life's challenges is propelled toward increasingly subtle challenges; if he tries to rest on his laurels, he will be prey to an overgrowth of short-range preferences that eventually will spoil his success. Thus, our ancestors probably were kept adaptively engaged over their lifetimes. However, as humanity has solved the problems that shaped our reward structure, an individual's motives have ceased to develop in ways tested by evolution (Glantz & Pearce, 1989). The new challenges do not come from a demanding environment, but from the somewhat confusing properties of leisure, which in the past confronted so few people that it could have had little role in shaping the evolution of our motivational patterns.

Evolution will continue, of course; but the major limiting factor in modern reproduction is motivation. Henceforth, the people who leave the most surviving offspring will largely be those who are most motivated to do so (or least motivated not to do so), a trait that may not be particularly correlated with the skills of environmental mastery that our reward structure evolved to foster (Herrnstein, 1990). In the meantime, the people with those skills forage for new substrates upon which to apply them, driven by motives that are no less compelling for having outlived the selective pressure that shaped them. Realization that quests for wealth, power, fame, and personal pleasure may be evolutionary blind alleys is not apt to dampen enthusiasm for them. In the distant future, after another few hundred generations at leisure, the drives that shape people's tastes may be different, but for now these tastes have become irrelevant to natural selection.

At the same time, these tastes often have realized diminishing returns of reward. From what may have been the optimum returns as determined by evolution, competitive goods like power and fame reward fewer people, because they have become winner-take-all markets, and consumer goods reward less effectively because the goods' ready availability keeps people near their satiation points. Political science, like economics, needs to adjust to a world where people have enormously cheapened familiar rewards by the same mass production that cheapened bread and nails. We have only begun to understand the consequent loss of rewarding effect.

Appendix I: Glossary

In labeling picoeconomic concepts, I have chosen only common English words and have either used their usual meanings or made explicit analogy to those meanings. However, because my applications for them often are narrower than their usual meanings, the following specifications may be helpful. Italics denote terms that are defined elsewhere in this Glossary:

Addiction: An activity that alternates between being sought and being avoided, with a *cycle length* of hours to weeks. See section 4.1.1.

Aesthetic: Concerning effectiveness in producing or *pacing reward*, particularly in defending that effectiveness from the deterioration that often comes with familiarity. See *premature satiation, texture*. See section 8.2.

Ambivalence: Inability to make a stable choice between two alternatives despite familiarity with their consequences. See section 1.3.1.

Appetite: An activity that is preparatory to consuming a *reward*, often somewhat rewarding in its own right. See section 7.3.1.

Attention control: The restriction of information-gathering to strategically affect *interests* that might become dominant subsequently. One of the four possible devices for *precommitment*. See section 5.3.2.

Aversive: The quality of a situation that moves a subject to avoid or escape it. I have argued that aversion must attract a subject's involvement with a short-range *reward* component; otherwise he could simply ignore it. See section 4.2.

Bright line: A criterion for a *personal rule* that stands out from other possible criteria. See section 5.6.1.

Calliope: A steam-driven organ. In the mechanical model of decision making in chapter 8, the mechanisms by which a person *realizes reward*. See section 8.1.

Compulsion: A stable motive to choose alternatives that are not in one's longest-range *interest*. See section 6.4.

Cycle length: In a *temporary preference*, the usual time elapsing between successive shifts of preference in a given direction. See section 4.1.

Demon: An intelligent entity who must make choices on the basis of instructions, rather than from his own motivation; in the mechanical model of decision making in chapter 8, a whole person less his *reward* mechanisms, which are represented by a *calliope*. See section 8.1.

Discipline: A *personal rule* for *pacing self-reward*. Rules for testing reality are important examples. See section 7.4.

Drive: That capacity for *reward* in a given *modality* that satiates as reward is *realized* and recovers with time. See sections 7.4 and 8.1.

Extrapsychic commitment: Enlistment of means outside of one's mental control to strategically affect *interests* that might become dominant subsequently. One of the four possible devices for *precommitment*. See section 5.3.1.

Gamelike: Said of an activity, performed for its own sake; autotelic. See section 7.3.2.

Good: A rewarding situation or object. See sections 1.3.3 and 7.4.

Hedging: Finding rationales for evading *personal rules* without seeing oneself as breaking them. See section 5.7.

Hyperbolic discounting: Devaluation of delayed *rewards* proportionally to their delay, as described by any of the variants of Herrnstein's matching law. The shape of this discount curve is hyperbolic, as opposed to the exponential shape of conventional discount curves. See section 3.4.

Importance: Said of a situation, the extent to which a subject is committed to *reward* himself according to its vicissitudes. Importance is a loose equivalent of Freud's "cathexis" (original *Besetzung*). See section 7.4.

Impulse: *Temporary preference* for an alternative that is not preferred when seen at a distance. This is closer to Freud's usage than to the common connotation of a spontaneous choice or whim. See section 3.5.

Interest: The *reward* upon which a set of behaviors is based, or this set of behaviors itself. The term is useful only where a conflict between two or more alternative rewards fails to resolve because they are dominant at different times, thus creating a durable separation of interests. See section 3.8.

Investment: The process of attaching *importance* to a situation, i.e., committing oneself to *reward* oneself according to its course. See section 7.4.

Itch: An activity that is preferred only briefly and only when immediately available, perhaps a rapidly cycling addiction. See section 4.1.3.

Modality: Said of *reward*, a source that satiates independently of other modalities; a *drive* system. See section 7.3.

Occasion: As a verb, to signal a time when *opting* is likely to *realize* *reward*, thus perhaps seeming to reward directly; as a noun, a stimulus that provides such a signal. See section 8.2.

Opting: Opting for *reward* is performing whatever intrapsychic behavior *realizes* reward when the relevant *modality* is not satiated. See sections 7.4 and 8.1.

Pacing: Limiting one's *opting* for *reward* to adequately rare *occasions*, so as to increase the reward *realized* from a given *drive*. See section 7.4.

Pain: An event that can reward attention but not motor behavior, perhaps the repeated combination of an extremely brief reward followed by a longer period of obligatory nonreward. See section 4.2.

Personal rule: An individual's rule for behavior, when enforced by a *private side bet*. It differs from a *rule of thumb* in that its purpose is to strategically affect other *interests*. It is one of the four possible devices for *precommitment*. See section 5.3.4.

Precommitment: Constraint on one's future motivation or ability to choose. Precommitment is a strategic move by one *interest* to forestall the dominance of another interest. See section 5.2.

Premature satiation: Satiation of a *drive* faster than a subject would prefer if he chose at a distance, with consequent waste of potential *reward*. Premature satiation is an *impulse* that limits one's ability to *self-reward* optimally. See section 7.3.2.

Preparation of emotion: Cultivating or inhibiting an emotion to strategically affect *interests* that might become dominant subsequently. One of the four possible devices for precommitment. See section 5.3.3.

Primrose path: A deceptive schedule of *reward* by which choice of the greater reward in a current comparison leads to a reduction of the rewards offered in subsequent choices. Subjects may choose a primrose path to an extent beyond what would be caused by their *hyperbolic discounting* of the rewards, but only as long as they are ignorant of the deception. See section 2.4.2.

Private side bet: A side bet to commit one's own future behavior, where one's expectation of getting the benefits of consistent behavior in the desired direction forms the stake of the bet. A private side bet forms when an individual perceives a series of similar choices as each predicting the direction of the choices yet to come, i.e., as precedents. See *personal rule, public side bet.* See section 5.4.

Public side bet: A side bet to commit one's own future behavior, in which the stake is held by another party. See section 5.4.

Realize: Said of a *reward*, to actually obtain rewarding effect rather than just to *opt* for reward; to operate the reward mechanism. See section 8.1.

Responsiveness: Speaking of the subject's situation, the extent to which he can change it by his behavior. See section 8.2.1.

Reward: Any event that disposes the subject to emit more of a behavior that produces it. Logically, reward has two components – the neuronal process that generates this disposition, and the stimuli that lead to the neuronal process. I use "reward mechanism" to refer to the neuronal component specifically. See section 1.2.1.

Rule of thumb: A rule for improving task performance rather than committing future choice. Cf. *personal rule.* See section 9.2.1.

Self-reward: *Reward* that does not depend on a *turnkey* stimulus, thus possibly all reward. Because "reward" by itself commonly connotes a turnkey, I use "self-reward" where independence from such a stimulus should be kept in mind. See sections 7.3.2 and 7.5.

Sellout: An activity that is preferred for months or years at a time, despite an expectation that one will later avoid it. See section 4.1.2.

Specious: Speaking of a *reward*, one that is *temporarily preferred* to another. See Ainslie (1975).

Support: A concrete object supports *reward* if it helps *opting* to *realize* reward longer and/or inhibits competing, shorter-range rewards. For instance, a euphoriant drug supports the relevant reward, whereas a placebo does not, even though their immediate rewarding consequences may be identical. See section 7.3.

374   APPENDIX I

Taste: Learned readiness to be *rewarded* by a particular situation. See section 7.2.

Temporary preference: Preference that can be expected to change, especially where *hyperbolic discounting* of delayed goals will cause them to shift in relative value. See section 3.5.

Texture: The combination of stimulus properties and subject readiness that permits an object to *pace self-reward*. The subject's increasing familiarity with these stimuli causes the object to "lose" texture. See section 9.3.2.

Turnkey: Said of *rewarding* stimuli, the supposed property directly governing *reward mechanism*, subject only to satiation. See section 7.3.

Vice district: By analogy to neighborhoods where police openly give up enforcing vice laws, an area of behavior to which a person does not dare to apply his *personal rules* because of the likelihood of failure. See section 6.2.2.

Will: The power to forestall *temporary preferences* through *personal rules*. See section 5.4.

Appendix II

Values of a series of rewards, each of amount $= 1 =$ value at zero delay, at a moment before they are due; calculated according to equation (5.1); with any time units such that Z and Γ both equal 1.0.

Delay to first reward $= 0$
Value of first reward by itself $= 1$

Interval between rewards	Series of 10 rewards	Series of 100 rewards	Series of 1000 rewards
1	2.92	5.18	7.48
2	2.13	3.18	4.43
3	1.8	2.57	3.34
4	1.62	2.2	2.78
5	1.51	1.97	2.43
6	1.43	1.82	2.2
7	1.37	1.7	2.03
8	1.33	1.62	1.91
9	1.29	1.55	1.81
10	1.26	1.5	1.73
20	1.137	1.254	1.37
30	1.092	1.17	1.247
40	1.069	1.128	1.186
50	1.055	1.102	1.149
60	1.046	1.085	1.124
70	1.04	1.073	1.106
80	1.035	1.064	1.093
90	1.031	1.057	1.082
100	1.028	1.051	1.074

Delay to first reward = 1
Value of first reward by itself = 0.5

Interval between rewards	Series of 10 rewards	Series of 100 rewards	Series of 1000 rewards
1	2.01	4.19	6.48
2	1.46	2.59	3.74
3	1.21	1.97	2.74
4	1.06	1.64	2.21
5	0.97	1.43	1.89
6	0.9	1.28	1.67
7	0.85	1.18	1.51
8	0.81	1.1	1.39
9	0.78	1.04	1.29
10	0.75	0.98	1.21

Delay to first reward = 2
Value of first reward by itself = 0.33

Interval between rewards	Series of 10 rewards	Series of 100 rewards	Series of 1000 rewards
1	1.6	3.7	5.98
2	1.18	2.28	3.43
3	0.97	1.72	2.49
4	0.85	1.42	1.99
5	0.77	1.22	1.68
6	0.71	1.09	1.47
7	0.66	0.99	1.32
8	0.63	0.91	1.2
9	0.6	0.85	1.11
10	0.57	0.81	1.04

Delay to first reward = 3
Value of first reward by itself = 0.25

Interval between rewards	Series of 10 rewards	Series of 100 rewards	Series of 1000 rewards
1	1.34	3.38	5.65
2	1.00	2.09	3.243
3	0.83	1.58	2.34
4	0.73	1.29	1.87
5	0.65	1.11	1.57
6	0.6	0.98	1.37
7	0.56	0.89	1.22
8	0.53	0.82	1.1
9	0.5	0.76	1.01
10	0.48	0.71	0.94

Delay to first reward = 4
Value of first reward by itself = 0.2

Interval between rewards	Series of 10 rewards	Series of 100 rewards	Series of 1000 rewards
1	1.16	3.14	5.4
2	0.89	1.96	3.1
3	0.74	1.47	2.24
4	0.65	2.21	1.78
5	0.58	1.03	1.49
6	0.53	0.91	1.29
7	0.5	0.82	1.15
8	0.47	0.75	1.04
9	0.44	0.7	0.95
10	0.42	0.65	0.88

Delay to first reward = 5
Value of first reward by itself = 0.16

Interval between rewards	Series of 10 rewards	Series of 100 rewards	Series of 1000 rewards
1	1.03	2.95	5.2
2	0.8	1.85	2.99
3	0.67	1.39	2.16
4	0.59	1.14	1.71
5	0.53	0.98	1.43
6	0.48	0.86	1.24
7	0.45	0.77	1.1
8	0.42	0.71	0.99
9	0.4	0.65	0.91
10	0.38	0.61	0.84

Delay to first reward = 6
Value of first reward by itself = 0.14

Interval between rewards	Series of 10 rewards	Series of 100 rewards	Series of 1000 rewards
1	0.93	2.79	5.04
2	0.73	1.76	2.9
3	0.61	1.33	2.09
4	0.54	1.09	1.66
5	0.49	0.93	1.39
6	0.44	0.82	1.2
7	0.41	0.74	1.06
8	0.39	0.67	0.96
9	0.37	0.62	0.88
10	0.35	0.58	0.81

Delay to first reward = 7
Value of first reward by itself = 0.12

Interval between rewards	Series of 10 rewards	Series of 100 rewards	Series of 1000 rewards
1	0.84	2.66	4.89
2	0.67	1.69	2.82
3	0.57	1.28	2.04
4	0.5	1.04	1.62
5	0.45	0.89	1.35
6	0.41	0.79	1.17
7	0.38	0.71	1.03
8	0.36	0.64	0.93
9	0.34	0.59	0.85
10	0.32	0.55	0.78

Delay to first reward = 8
Value of first reward by itself = 0.11

Interval between rewards	Series of 10 rewards	Series of 100 rewards	Series of 1000 rewards
1	0.77	2.54	4.77
2	0.62	1.62	2.76
3	0.53	1.23	1.99
4	0.47	1.01	1.58
5	0.42	0.86	1.32
6	0.39	0.76	1.14
7	0.36	0.68	1.01
8	0.34	0.62	0.91
9	0.32	0.57	0.83
10	0.3	0.53	0.76

Delay to first reward = 9
Value of first reward by itself = 0.1

Interval between rewards	Series of 10 rewards	Series of 100 rewards	Series of 1000 rewards
1	0.71	2.44	4.66
2	0.58	1.57	2.7
3	0.5	1.19	1.95
4	0.44	0.98	1.55
5	0.4	0.83	1.29
6	0.37	0.73	1.12
7	0.34	0.66	0.99
8	0.32	0.6	0.89
9	0.3	0.55	0.81
10	0.29	0.51	0.74

Delay to first reward = 10
Value of first reward by itself = 0.09

Interval between rewards	Series of 10 rewards	Series of 100 rewards	Series of 1000 rewards
1	0.66	2.35	4.56
2	0.54	1.52	2.65
3	0.47	1.15	1.91
4	0.42	0.95	1.52
5	0.38	0.81	1.27
6	0.35	0.71	1.09
7	0.32	0.64	0.97
8	0.3	0.58	0.87
9	0.29	0.54	0.79
10	0.27	0.5	0.73

Delay to first reward = 60
Value of first reward by itself = 0.017

Interval between rewards	Series of 10 rewards	Series of 100 rewards	Series of 1000 rewards
1	0.15	0.97	2.86
2	0.14	0.73	1.76
3	0.13	0.59	1.31
4	0.12	0.51	1.05
5	0.12	0.45	0.89
6	0.11	0.40	0.77
7	0.11	0.36	0.68
8	0.10	0.33	0.61
9	0.10	0.31	0.56
10	0.10	0.29	0.51

Delay to first reward = 30
Value of first reward by itself = 0.03

Interval between rewards	Series of 10 rewards	Series of 100 rewards	Series of 1000 rewards
1	0.28	1.45	3.52
2	0.25	1.01	2.10
3	0.23	0.80	1.54
4	0.21	0.67	1.235
5	0.20	0.58	1.03
6	0.19	0.51	0.89
7	0.18	0.46	0.79
8	0.17	0.42	0.71
9	0.16	0.39	0.64
10	0.15	0.36	0.59

Delay to first reward = 90
Value of first reward by itself = 0.011

Interval between rewards	Series of 10 rewards	Series of 100 rewards	Series of 1000 rewards
1	0.10	0.74	2.48
2	0.10	0.58	1.57
3	0.09	0.49	1.18
4	0.09	0.42	0.95
5	0.08	0.37	0.81
6	0.08	0.34	0.70
7	0.08	0.31	0.62
8	0.08	0.29	0.56
9	0.07	0.27	0.51
10	0.07	0.25	0.47

Appendix III

Delay at which a single lump amount of reward would be valued the same as a series of rewards adding up to the same amount. For instance, 10 rewards of amount = 1, starting at delay = 0 and recurring every 0.1 unit of time, would be valued the same as one reward of amount = 10, occurring at delay = 0.391, according to equation (5.1). The same 10 rewards, starting at delay = 10, would be valued the same as one reward of amount = 10 at delay = 10.442. One thousand rewards of amount = 1, starting at delay = 0 and recurring every 0.1 unit of time, would have the same value as one reward of amount = 1000 at delay = 20.434.

Delay to first reward = 0
Value of first reward by itself = 1

Interval between rewards	Series of 10 rewards	Series of 100 rewards	Series of 1000 rewards
0.1	0.391	3.091	20.434
0.2	0.711	5.363	35.995
0.3	0.992	7.364	50.159
0.4	1.244	9.199	63.447
0.5	1.475	10.912	76.083
0.6	1.688	12.528	88.19
0.7	1.887	14.063	99.847
0.8	2.073	15.528	111.108
0.9	2.248	16.931	122.012
1.0	2.414	18.277	132.592

Delay to first reward $= 1$
Value of first reward by itself $= 0.5$

Interval between rewards	Series of 10 rewards	Series of 100 rewards	Series of 1000 rewards
0.1	1.415	4.516	24.274
0.2	1.782	7.182	41.868
0.3	2.115	9.545	57.896
0.4	2.423	11.726	72.99
0.5	2.712	13.777	87.415
0.6	2.984	15.729	101.318
0.7	3.243	.7.598	114.79
0.8	3.489	19.398	127.8959
0.9	3.724	21.138	140.675
1.0	3.95	22.824	153.167

Delay to first reward $= 2$
Value of first reward by itself $= 0.33$

Interval between rewards	Series of 10 rewards	Series of 100 rewards	Series of 1000 rewards
0.1	2.425	5.76	26.15
0.2	2.813	8.679	46.083
0.3	3.173	11.274	63.302
0.4	3.511	13.673	79.515
0.5	3.831	15.934	95.022
0.6	4.135	18.089	109.985
0.7	4.427	20.159	124.505
0.8	4.707	22.157	138.653
0.9	4.977	24.093	152.477
1.0	5.237	25.975	166.015

Delay to first reward $= 3$
Value of first reward by itself $= 0.25$

Interval between rewards	Series of 10 rewards	Series of 100 rewards	Series of 1000 rewards
0.1	3.431	6.925	29.579
0.2	3.831	10.032	49.549
0.3	4.208	12.801	67.678
0.4	4.565	15.365	84.736
0.5	4.905	17.783	101.049
0.6	5.231	20.091	116.793
0.7	5.545	22.309	132.079
0.8	5.847	24.452	146.98
0.9	6.14	26.532	161.55
1.0	6.425	28.555	175.83

Delay to first reward = 4
Value of first reward by itself = 0.2

Interval between rewards	Series of 10 rewards	Series of 100 rewards	Series of 1000 rewards
0.1	4.434	8.047	31.743
0.2	4.843	11.303	52.573
0.3	5.231	14.213	71.4514
0.4	5.601	16.91	89.202
0.5	5.956	19.456	106.17
0.6	6.298	21.887	122.545
0.7	6.628	24.225	138.445
0.8	6.947	26.485	153.947
0.9	7.258	28.679	169.11
1.0	7.559	30.815	183.975

Delay to first reward = 5
Value of first reward by itself = 0.17

Interval between rewards	Series of 10 rewards	Series of 100 rewards	Series of 1000 rewards
0.1	5.437	9.141	33.727
0.2	5.851	12.52	55.3
0.3	6.247	15.549	74.823
0.4	6.627	18.358	93.166
0.5	6.993	21.013	110.693
0.6	7.347	23.548	127.604
0.7	7.69	25.987	144.022
0.8	8.023	28.346	160.031
0.9	8.347	30.637	175.69
1.0	8.662	32.868	191.044

Delay to first reward = 6
Value of first reward by itself = 0.14

Interval between rewards	Series of 10 rewards	Series of 100 rewards	Series of 1000 rewards
0.1	6.438	10.216	35.581
0.2	6.858	13.699	57.811
0.3	7.26	16.83	77.905
0.4	7.647	19.738	96.769
0.5	8.022	22.486	114.787
0.6	8.385	25.112	132.167
0.7	8.738	27.639	149.038
0.8	9.082	30.084	165.488
0.9	9.417	32.459	181.578
1.0	9.744	34.773	197.317

Delay to first reward = 7
Value of first reward by itself = 0.12

Interval between rewards	Series of 10 rewards	Series of 100 rewards	Series of 1000 rewards
0.1	7.44	11.278	37.336
0.2	7.862	14.851	60.158
0.3	8.27	18.071	80.765
0.4	8.663	21.065	100.098
0.5	9.045	23.897	118.556
0.6	9.416	26.60	136.356
0.7	9.777	29.209	153.631
0.8	10.13	31.73	170.472
0.9	10.474	34.18	186.945
1.0	10.81	36.567	203.098

Delay to first reward = 8
Value of first reward by itself = 0.11

Interval between rewards	Series of 10 rewards	Series of 100 rewards	Series of 1000 rewards
0.1	8.441	12.33	39.012
0.2	8.866	15.981	62.375
0.3	9.277	19.28	83.45
0.4	9.676	22.352	103.21
0.5	10.064	25.259	122.068
0.6	10.441	28.038	140.249
0.7	10.809	30.714	157.891
0.8	11.169	33.305	175.088
0.9	11.521	35.822	191.907
1.0	11.865	38.275	208.398

Delay to first reward = 9
Value of first reward by itself = 0.1

Interval between rewards	Series of 10 rewards	Series of 100 rewards	Series of 1000 rewards
0.1	9.442	13.374	40.624
0.2	9.869	17.094	64.486
0.3	10.284	20.465	85.992
0.4	10.687	23.606	106.146
0.5	11.079	26.581	123.372
0.6	11.462	29.427	143.903
0.7	11.836	32.167	161.881
0.8	12.202	34.821	179.404
0.9	12.561	37.399	196.539
1.0	12.912	39.913	213.341

Delay to first reward = 10
Value of first reward by itself = 0.09

Interval between rewards	Series of 10 rewards	Series of 100 rewards	Series of 1000 rewards
0.1	10.442	14.413	42.182
0.2	10.872	18.194	66.508
0.3	11.289	21.629	88.415
0.4	11.696	24.834	108.935
0.5	12.092	27.872	127.504
0.6	12.48	30.778	147.359
0.7	12.859	33.578	165.649
0.8	13.231	36.289	183.472
0.9	13.595	38.924	200.901
1.0	13.952	41.494	217.988

Bibliography

Abelson, R. P., Aronson, E., McGuire, W. J., Newcomb, T. M., Rosenberg, M. J., & Tannenbaum, P. H. (1968). *Theories of cognitive consistency: a sourcebook.* New York: Rand McNally.

Adams, B. (1896). *The law of civilization and decay.* New York: Macmillan.

Ainslie, G. (1974). Impulse control in pigeons. *Journal of the Experimental Analysis of Behavior, 21,* 485–489.

(1975). Specious reward: a behavioral theory of impulsiveness and impulse control. *Psychological Bulletin, 82,* 463–496.

(1982) A behavioral economic approach to the defense mechanisms: Freud's energy theory revisited. *Social Science Information, 21,* 735–779.

(1984). Behavioral economics II: motivated, involuntary behavior. *Social Science Information, 23,* 247–274.

(1985). Rationality and the emotions: a picoeconomic approach. *Social Science Information, 24,* 355–374.

(1986a). Beyond microeconomics: conflict among interests in a multiple self as a determinant of value. In J. Elster (Ed.), *The multiple self.* Cambridge University Press.

(1986b). Manipulation: history and theory. In M. P. Nichols & T. J. Paolino, Jr. (Eds.), *Basic techniques of psychodynamic psychotherapy.* New York: Gardner Press.

(1987a). Self-reported tactics of impulse control. *International Journal of the Addictions, 22* (2), 167–179.

(1987b). Aversion with only one factor. In M. Commons, J. Mazur, A. Nevin, & H. Rachlin (Eds.), *Quantitative analysis of behavior: the effect of delay and of intervening events on reinforcement value* (Vol. 5). Hillsdale, NJ: Erlbaum.

(1988). Matching is the integrating framework. *Behavioral and Brain Sciences, 11* (4), 53–54.

(1989). *Internal self-control in pigeons.* Unpublished manuscript.

(1991). Derivation of "rational" economic behavior from hyperbolic discount curves, *American Economic Review, 81,* 134–40.

Ainslie, G., & Engel, B. T. (1974). Alteration of classically conditioned heart rate by operant reinforcement in monkeys. *Journal of Comparative and Physiological Psychology, 87*, 373–383.

Ainslie, G., & Haendel, V. (1983). The motives of the will. In E. Gottheil, K. Druley, T. Skodola, & H. Waxman (Eds.), *Etiology aspects of alcohol and drug abuse.* Springfield, IL: Charles C Thomas.

Ainslie, G., & Herrnstein, R. (1981). Preference reversal and delayed reinforcement. *Animal Learning and Behavior, 9*, 476–482.

Ainslie, G., Lyke, J. & Freeman, R. (in press). An experimental model of intertemporal conflict. In N. N. Commons, J. Mazur, J. Nevin, & H. Rachlin (Eds.), *Quantitative analysis of behavior: Vol. 10. Behavioral Economics.* Hillsdale, NJ: Erlbaum.

Alexander, F. (1963). The dynamics of psychotherapy in the light of learning theory. *American Journal of Psychiatry, 120*, 440–448.

Alford, G. S. (1980). Alcoholics Anonymous: an empirical outcome study. *Addictive Behaviors, 5*, 359–370.

Allen, C. (1969). *A textbook of psychosexual disorders.* London: Oxford University Press.

Allen, C. M. (1981). On the exponent in the "generalized" matching law. *Journal of the Experimental Analysis of Behavior, 35*, 125–127.

Allison, J. (1981). Economics and operant conditioning. In P. Harzen & M. D. Zeiler (Eds.), *Predictability, correlation, and contiguity.* New York: Wiley.

Alston, W. P. (1974). Can psychology do without private data? *Behaviorism, 1*, 71–102.

Anderson, L., & Alpert, M. (1974). Operant analysis of hallucination frequency in a hospitalized schizophrenic. *Journal of Behavior Therapy and Experimental Psychiatry, 5*, 13–18.

Andrade, C. (1954). *Sir Isaac Newton.* New York: Doubleday.

Annon, J. S., & Robinson, C. H. (1980). Sexual disorders. In A. E. Kazdin, A. S. Bellack, & M. Hersen (Eds.), *New perspectives in abnormal psychology* (pp. 325–352). London: Oxford University Press.

Anonymous (1980). *Overeaters Anonymous.* Torrance, CA: Overeaters Anonymous.

Appel, J. B. (1963). Aversive aspects of a schedule of positive reinforcement. *Journal of the Experimental Analysis of Behavior, 6*, 423–428.

Aquinas, T. (1948). *Summa Theologica* I–II 94, 2. In A. Pegis (Ed.), *Introduction to St. Thomas Aquinas.* New York: Modern Library.

Archer, W. (1888). *Masks or faces: a study in the psychology of acting.* London: Longman Group.

Arkes, H. R., & Blumer, C. (1985). The psychology of sunk cost. *Organizational Behavior and Human Decision Processes, 35*, 124–140.

Aronfreed, J. (1968). *Conduct and conscience.* New York: Academic Press.

Asch, S. S. (1971). Wrist scratching as a symptom of anhedonia: a predepressive state. *Psychoanalytic Quarterly, 40*, 603–617.

Ashton, T. (1948). *Industrial revolution: 1760–1830.* London: Oxford University Press.

Atkinson, J. W., & Birch, D. (1970). *The dynamics of action.* New York: Wiley.

Atnip, G. (1977). Stimulus and response-reinforcer contingencies in autoshaping, operant, classical and omission training procedures in rats. *Journal of the Experimental Analysis of Behavior, 28,* 59–69.

Austin, G. A. (1978). *Perspectives on the history of psychoactive substance abuse.* Rockville, MD: National Institute on Drug Abuse.

Axelrod, R. M. (1984). *The evolution of cooperation.* New York: Basic Books.

Azrin, N. H. (1961). Time-out from positive reinforcement. *Science, 133,* 382–383.

Azrin, N. H., Nunn, R., & Frantz-Renshaw, S. (1982). Habit reversal vs. negative practice of self-destructive oral habit (biting, chewing, or licking of lips, cheeks, tongue, or palate). *Journal of Behavior Therapy in Experimental Psychiatry, 13,* 49–54.

Bachrach, J. (1991). Duped! *Philadelphia Inquirer Magazine,* April 14, pp. 16–43.

Bach-y-Rita, G. (1974). Habitual violence and self-mutilation. *American Journal of Psychiatry, 131,* 1018–1020.

Baer, M. (1981). The imposition of structure on behavior and the demolition of behavioral structures. *Nebraska Symposium on Motivation, 29,* 217–254.

Baer, J. S., Kamarck, T., Lichtenstein, E., & Ransom, C. C., Jr. (1989). Prediction of smoking relapse: Analyses of temptations and transgressions after initial cessation. *Journal of Consulting and Clinical Psychology, 57,* 623–627.

Baer, L., Jenike, M. A., Ricciardi, J. N., Holland, A. D., Seymour R. J., Minichiello, W. E., & Buttolph, L. (1990). Standardized assessment of personality disorders in obsessive-compulsive disorder. *Archives of General Psychiatry, 47,* 626–630.

Bain, A. (1886). *The emotions and the will.* New York: Appleton. (Original work published 1859)

Bakan, D. (1968). *Disease, pain and sacrifice: toward a psychology of suffering.* Chicago: University of Chicago Press.

Bandura, A. (1986). *Social foundations of thought and action: a social cognitive theory.* Englewood Cliffs, NJ: Prentice-Hall.

Barnes, G. E., Brent, A. V., & Greaves, L. (1985). Characteristics affecting successful outcome in the cessation of smoking. *International Journal of the Addictions, 20,* 1429–1434.

Baron, J. (1988). Utility, exchange, and commensurability. *Journal of Thought, 23,* 111–131.

Barratt, E. S., & Patton, J. H. (1983). Impulsivity: cognitive, behavioral, and psychophysiological correlates. In M. Zuckerman (Ed.), *Biological Basis of Sensation Seeking, Impulsivity, and Anxiety*. Hillsdale, NJ: Erlbaum.

Bartlett, J. (1955). *Familiar quotations*. Boston: Little, Brown.

Basham, A. L. (1967). *The wonder that was India*. New York: Taplinger.

Baum, W. M. (1974). On two types of deviation from the matching law: bias and undermatching. *Journal of the Experimental Analysis of Behavior, 22*, 231–242.

——— (1979). Matching, undermatching, and overmatching in studies of choice. *Journal of the Experimental Analysis of Behavior, 32*, 269–281.

Baum, W., & Rachlin, H. (1969). Choice as time allocation. *Journal of the Experimental Analysis of Behavior, 12*, 861–874.

Baumeister, R. F. (1984). Choking under pressure: self-consciousness and paradoxical effects of incentives on skillful performance. *Journal of Personality and Social Psychology, 46*, 610–620.

——— (1990). Suicide as escape from self. *Psychological Review, 97*, 90–113.

Baumeister, R. F., & Scher, S. J. (1988). Self-defeating behavior patterns among normal individuals: review and analysis of common self-destructive tendencies. *Psychological Bulletin, 104*, 3–22.

Beard, G. M. (1881). *American neuroses*. New York: Arno.

Beck, A. T. (1976). *Cognitive therapy and the emotional disorders*. New York: International Universities Press.

Beck, A. T., & Emery, G. (1985). *Anxiety disorders and phobias: a cognitive perspective*. New York: Basic Books.

Becker, E. (1973). *The denial of death*. New York: Free Press.

Becker, G. (1976). *The economic approach to human behavior*. Chicago: University of Chicago Press.

Becker, G., & Murphy, K. (1988). A theory of rational addiction. *Journal of Political Economy, 96*, 675–700.

Becker, H. S. (1960). Notes on the concept of commitment. *American Journal of Sociology, 66*, 32–40.

——— (1963). *Outsiders*. New York: Free Press.

Beecher, H. (1959). *Measurement of subjective responses*. London: Oxford University Press.

Bellah, R. N., Madsen, R., Sullivan, W. M., Swidler, A., & Tipton, S. M. (1985). *Habits of the heart*. Berkeley: University of California Press.

Benjamin, A. C. (1966). Ideas of time in the history of philosophy. In J. T. Fraser (Ed.), *The voices of time*. New York: Braziller.

Benjamin, J. (1988). *The bonds of love*. New York: Pantheon.

Benjamin, L. T., & Perloff, R. (1983). E. L. Thorndike and the immediacy of reinforcement. *American Psychologist, 38*, 126.

Bennett, A. (1918). *Self and self-management*. New York: George H. Doran.

Bentall, R. P., Lowe, C. F., & Beasty, A. (1985). The role of verbal behavior in human learning II: developmental differences. *Journal of the Experimental Analysis of Behavior, 43*, 165–181.

Benzion, U., Rapoport, A., & Yagil, J. (1989). Discount rates inferred from decisions: an experimental study. *Management Science, 35*, 270–284.

Berlyne, D. E. (1971). *Aesthetics and psychobiology.* New York: Appleton-Century-Crofts.

——— (1974). *Studies in the new experimental aesthetics.* Washington, DC: Hemisphere.

Berne, E. (1961). *Transaction analysis in psychotherapy.* New York: Ballantine.

——— (1964). *Games people play.* New York: Grove Press.

——— (1972) *What do you say after you say hello?* New York: Grove Press.

Bernoulli, D. (1954). Exposition of a new theory on the measurement of risk. *Econometrica, 22*, 23–26. (Original work published 1738)

Beyra, M. (1976). On the relationship between brain-stimulation reward and motivational behavior. In A. Wauquier (ed.), *Brain-stimulation reward.* New York: American Elsevier.

Bialer, I. (1961). Conceptualization of success and failure in mentally retarded and normal children. *Journal of Personality, 29*, 303–320.

Bindra, D. (1974). A motivational view of learning, performance and behavior modification. *Psychological Review, 81*, 199–219.

Bjorkqvist, K., Ekman, K., & Lagerspetz, K. (1982). Bullies and victims: their ego picture, ideal ego picture and normative ego picture. *Scandinavian Journal of Psychology, 23*, 307–313.

Blachly, P. H. (1970). *Seduction: a conceptual model in the drug dependencies and other contagious ills.* Springfield, IL: Charles C Thomas.

Blessing, L. (1988). *A walk in the woods.* New York: New American Library.

Bloom, A. (1987). *The closing of the American mind.* New York: Simon & Schuster.

Boehme, R., Blakely, E., & Poling, A. (1986). Runway length as a determinant of self-control in rats. *Psychological Record, 36*, 285–288.

Bogen, J., & Moravcsik, J. (1982). Aristotle's forbidden sweets. *History and Philosophy, 20*, 111–127.

Booth, D. A., Lee, M., & McAleavey, C. (1976). Acquired sensory control of satiation in man. *British Journal of Psychology, 67*, 137–147.

Boring, E. G. (1950). *A history of experimental psychology.* New York: Appleton-Century-Crofts.

Brandt, R. B. (1967). Hedonism. In P. Edwards (Ed.), *The Encyclopedia of Philosophy.* New York: Macmillan.

Braudel, F. (1973). *Capitalism and material life.* New York: Harper & Row.

Brennan, G., & Tullock, G. (1982). An economic theory of military tactics: methodological individualism at war. *Journal of Economic Behavior and Organization, 3*, 225–242.

Breuer, J., & Freud, S. (1956). *Studies on hysteria*. in J. Strachey & A. Freud (Eds.), *The standard edition of the complete psychological works of Sigmund Freud, Vol. 2*. London: Hogarth. (Original work published 1895)

Broad, C. D. (1962). Determinism, indeterminism and libertarianism. In S. Morgenbesser & J. Walsh (Eds.), *Free will*, Englewood Cliffs, NJ: Prentice-Hall.

Broden, M., Hall, V., & Mitts, B. (1971). The effect of self-recording on the classroom behavior of two eighth grade students. *Journal of Applied Behavior Analysis, 4*, 191.

Brown, R., & Herrnstein, R. J. (1975). *Psychology*. Boston: Little, Brown.

Bruner, J. S., Goodnow, J. J., & Austin, G. A. (1956). *A study of thinking*. New York: Wiley.

Bugental, J. F. T., & Bugental, E. K. (1984). A fate worse than death: the fear of changing. *Psychotherapy, 21*, 543–549.

Bulfinch, T. (1948). *Bulfinch's mythology: the age of fable, or, stories of gods and heroes*. Garden City, NY: Doubleday.

Burckhardt, J. L. (1988). *Arabic proverbs*. London: Curzon.

Burnett, J. (1969). *A history of the cost of living*. Baltimore: Penguin Books.

Buskist, W. F., & Miller, H. L., Jr. (1981). Concurrent operant performance in humans: matching when food is the reinforcer. *Psychological Record, 31*, 95–100.

Camerer, C., & Weigelt, K. (1988). Experimental tests of a sequential equilibrium reputation model. *Econometrica, 56*, 1–36.

Cameron, O., Spence, M., & Drewery, J. (1978). Rate of onset of drunkenness: a preliminary study. *Journal of Studies on Alcohol, 39*, 517–524.

Campbell, A., Converse, P. E., & Rodgers, W. L. (1976). *The quality of American life: perceptions, evaluations, and satisfactions*. New York: Russell Sage.

Campbell, R., & Sowden, L., (Eds.). (1985). *Paradoxes of rationality and cooperation*. Vancouver: University of British Columbia.

Camus, A. (1955). An absurd reasoning. In *The myth of Sisyphus and other essays* (J. O'Brien, Trans.). New York: Random House.

Caporael, L. R. (1987). *Homo sapiens, Homo faber, Homo socians*: technology and the social animal. In W. Callebaut & R. Pinxten (Eds.), *Evolutionary epistemology: a multiparadigm program*. Dordrecht: Reidel.

Caporael, L. R., Dawes, R. M., Orbell, J. M., & van de Kragt, A. J. C. (1989). Selfishness examined: cooperation in the absence of egoistic incentives. *Behavioral and Brain Sciences, 12*, 683–739.

Cappell, H. (1975). An evaluation of tension models of alcohol consumption. In R. Gibbons, Y. Israel, H. Kalout, R. Popham, W. Schmidt, & R. Smout (Eds.), *Research advances in alcohol and drug problems* (Vol. 2). New York: Wiley.

Carden, M. L. (1969). *Oneida: utopian community to modern corporation.* Baltimore: Johns Hopkins University Press.

Carey, G., & Gottesman, H. (1981). Twin and family studies of anxiety, phobic, and obsessive-compulsive disorder. In D. F. Klein & J. Rabkin (Eds.), *Anxiety: new research and changing concepts.* New York: Raven.

Carlson, A. J. (1916). *The control of hunger in health and disease.* Chicago: University of Chicago Press.

Carnes, P. (1983). *The sexual addiction.* Minneapolis: Compcare.

Carr, A. (1974). Compulsive neurosis: a review of the literature. *Psychological Reports, 20,* 459–468.

Cautela, J. (1967). Covert sensitization. *Psychological Reports, 20,* 459–468.

Cautela, J., & Bennett, A. (1981). Covert conditioning. In R. J. Corsini (Ed.), *Handbook of innovative psychotherapies.* New York: Wiley.

Chance, S. (1989). Weenies anonymous. *Psychiatric Times,* June, 28–29.

Chevrier, J. O., & Delorme, A. (1980). Aesthetic preferences: influence of perceptual ability, age and complexity of stimulus. *Perception and Motor Skills, 50,* 839–849.

Childress, A. R., McLellan, A. T., & O'Brien, C. P. (1986). Nature and incidence of conditioned responses in a methadone population: a comparison of laboratory, clinic, and naturalistic settings. *National Institute on Drug Abuse: Research Monograph Series, 67,* 366–372.

Christensen-Szalanski, J. J. (1984). Discount functions and the measurement of patient's values. *Medical Decision Making, 4,* 47–58.

Christie, A. B. (1980). *Infectious diseases: epidemiology and clinical practice.* Edinburgh: Churchill Livingstone.

Chung, S., & Herrnstein, R. J. (1967). Choice and delay of reinforcement. *Journal of the Experimental Analysis of Behavior, 10,* 67–74.

Clairborn, W., Lewis, P., & Humble, S. (1972). Stimulus satiation and smoking: a revisit. *Journal of Clinical Psychology, 28,* 416–419.

Cloninger, C. R. (1987). A systematic method for clinical description and classification of personality variants. *Archives of General Psychiatry, 44,* 573–588.

Clum, G. A. (1989). Psychological interventions vs. drugs in the treatment of panic. *Behavior Therapy, 20,* 429–457.

Cohen, D. (1979). *J. B. Watson: the founder of behaviorism.* London: Routledge & Kegan Paul.

Compton, A. (1983). The current status of the psychoanalytic theory of instinctual drives *Psychoanalytic Quarterly, 52,* 402–426.

Conn, L. M., & Lion, J. R. (1983). Self-mutilation: a review. *Psychiatric Medicine, 1,* 21–34.

Coombs, C. H., & Avrunin, G. S. (1977). Single peaked functions and the theory of preference. *Psychological Review, 84,* 216–230.

Coover, R. (1968). *The Universal Baseball Association, Inc., J. Henry Waugh, Proprietor.* New York: Random House.

Corwin, N. (1983). *Trivializing America*. Secaucus, NJ: Lyle Stuart.

Craig, K., & Weiss, S. (1972). Verbal reports of pain without noxious stimulation. *Perceptual and Motor Skills, 34*, 943–948.

Crane, A. M. (1905). *Right and wrong thinking and their results*. Boston: Lathrop.

Crawford, M., & Masterson, F. A. (1982). Species-specific defense reactions and avoidance learning: an evaluative review. *Pavlovian Journal of Biological Science, 17*, 204–214.

Critchlow, B. (1986). The powers of John Barleycorn: beliefs about the effects of alcohol on social behavior. *American Psychologist, 41*, 751–764.

Croce, B. (1969). *Aesthetic – as science of expression and general linguistic* (D. Ainslie, Trans.). New York: Noonday. (Original work published 1909).

Cross, J. G. (1983). *A theory of adaptive economic behavior*. Cambridge University Press.

Cross, J. G. & Guyer, M. J. (1980). *Social traps*. Ann Arbor: University of Michigan Press.

Csikszentmihalyi, M. (1977). *Beyond boredom and anxiety*. San Francisco: Jossey-Bass.

Cummings, N. A. (1979). Turning bread into stones. Our modern antimiracle. *American Psychologist, 34*, 1119–1129.

Curry, S., Marlatt, A., & Gordon, J. R. (1987). Abstinence violation effect: validation of an attributional construct with smoking cessation. *Journal of Consulting and Clinical Psychology, 55*, 145–149.

Darwin, C. (1979). *The expressions of emotions in man and animals*. London: Julan Friedman. (Original work published 1872).

Davidson, D. (1980). *Essays on actions and events*. London: Oxford University Press.

(1983). Paradoxes of irrationality. In R. Wollheim & J. Hopkins (Eds.), *Philosophical essays on Freud*. Cambridge University Press.

Davison, W. (1888). *The Christian conscience*. London: Woolmer.

Dawkins, R. (1976). *The selfish gene*. London: Oxford University Press.

Day, W. F. (1969). Radical behaviorism in reconciliation with phenomenology. *Journal of the Experimental Analysis of Behavior, 12*, 315–328.

Deluty, M. Z., Whitehouse, W. G., Mellitz, M., & Hineline, P. N. (1983). Self-control and commitment involving aversive events. *Behavior Analysis Letters, 3*, 213–219.

Dennett, D. C. (1984). *Elbow room: the varieties of free will worth wanting*. Cambridge, MA: MIT Press.

deVilliers, P. (1977). Choice in concurrent schedules and a quantitative formulation of the law of effect. In W. Honig & J. Staddon (Eds.), *Handbook of operant behavior* (pp. 233–287). Englewood Cliffs, NJ: Prentice-Hall.

deVilliers, P., & Herrnstein, R. (1976). Toward a law of response strength. *Psychological Bulletin, 83*, 1131–1153.

Dewsbury, D. A. (1981). Effects of novelty on copulatory behavior: The Coolidge effect and related phenomena *Psychological Bulletin, 89*, 464–482.

Dobson, K. S., & Block, L. (1988) Historical and philosophical bases of the cognitive-behavioral therapies. In K. S. Dobson (Ed.), *Handbook of cognitive-behavioral therapies*. New York: Guilford.

Dollard, J., & Miller, N.E. (1950). *Personality and psychotherapy: an analysis in terms of learning, thinking and culture*. New York: McGraw-Hill.

Douglas, M. (1966). *Purity and danger: an analysis of concepts of pollution and taboo*. London: Routledge & Kegan Paul.

Dufty, W. (1975). *Sugar blues*. New York: Warner Books.

Dunaif-Hattis, J. (1984). *Doubling the brain: on the evolution of brain lateralization and its implications for language*. New York: Peter Lang Publishing.

Dweyer, P., & Renner, E. (1971). Self-punitive behavior: masochism or confusion? *Psychological Review, 78*, 333–337.

Eastman, M. (1922). *The sense of humor*. New York: Scribner.

Egger, M. D., & Miller, N. E. (1962). Secondary reinforcement in rats as a function of information value and reliability of the stimulus. *Journal of Experimental Psychology, 64*, 97–104.

Einhorn, H. J., & Hogarth, R. M. (1978). Confidence in judgment: persistence of the illusion of validity. *Psychological Review, 85*, 395–416.

Eisenberger, R. (1989). *Blue Monday: the loss of the work ethic in America*. New York: Paragon House.

Ekman, P., & Friesen, W. V. (1986). A new pan-cultural facial expression of emotion. *Motivation and Emotion, 10*, 159–168.

Ellenberger, H. F. (1958). A clinical introduction to psychiatric phenomenology and existential analysis. In R. May, E. Angel, & H. Ellenberger (Eds.), *Existence: a new division in psychiatry and psychology* (pp. 92–124). New York: Basic Books.

Ellis, A. (1976). The biological basis of human irrationality. *Journal of Individual Psychology, 32*, 145–168.

Ellis, A., & Grieger, R. (1977). *R.E.T.: handbook of rational-emotive therapy*. New York: Springer.

Ellis, A., & Sagrin, E. (Eds.). (1964). *Nymphomania – a study of the oversexed woman*. New York: Gilbert Press.

Ellis, H. (1929). *The dance of life*. New York: Random House.

Elster, J. (1979). *Ulysses and the sirens: studies in rationality and irrationality*. Cambridge University Press.

  (1981). States that are essentially by-products. *Social Science Information, 20*, 431–473. [Reprinted in Elster, J. (1983). *Sour grapes: studies in the subversion of rationality* (pp. 43–108). Cambridge University Press]

  (1989a). *Nuts and bolts for the social sciences*. Cambridge University Press.

(1989b). *The cement of society*. Cambridge University Press.

(1990). *Fullness and parsimony: notes on creativity in the arts*. Unpublished manuscript.

(in press). Envy in social life. In R. Zeckhauser (ed.), *Festschrift for Thomas Schelling*. Cambridge, MA: MIT Press.

Empson, W. (1930). *Seven types of ambiguity*. London: New Directions.

Engel, K., & Williams, T. (1972). Effect of an ounce of vodka on alcoholics' desire for alcohol. *Quarterly Journal of Studies on Alcohol, 33*, 1099–1105.

Epstein, S. M. (1967). Toward a unified theory of anxiety in B. A. Maher (Ed.), *Progress in personality research* (Vol. 4). New York: Academic Press.

Erdelyi, M. H. (1974). A new look at the new look: perceptual defense and vigilance. *Psychological Review, 81*, 1–25.

Erikson, E. (1963). *Childhood and society* (2nd ed.). New York: Norton.

Estes, W. K. (1969a). New perspectives on some old issues in association theory. In N. J. Mackintosh & W. K. Honig (Eds.), *Fundamental issues in associative learning*, Halifax: Dalhousie University Press.

(1969b). Reinforcement in human learning. In J. Tapp (Ed.), *Reinforcement and behavior* (pp. 63–94). New York: Academic Press.

Evans, D. (1975). Moral weakness. *Philosophy, 50*, 295–310.

Evenson, R., Altman, H., Sletton, J., & Knowles, R. (1973). Factors in the description and grouping of alcoholics. *American Journal of Psychiatry, 130*, 49–54.

Eysenck, H. J. (Ed.). (1964). *Behavior therapy and the neuroses*. New York: Pergamon.

(1967). Single trial conditioning, neurosis and the Napalkov phenomenon. *Behavior Research and Therapy, 5*, 63–65.

(1977). *Crime and personality*. London: Routledge & Kegan Paul.

Fair, R. C. (1978). A theory of extramarital affairs. *Journal of Political Economy, 86*, 45–61.

Falk, J. (1977). Sweet abuse and the addiction model. In J. Weiffenback (Ed.), *Taste and development: the genesis of sweet preference* (DHEW NIH 77–1068). Washington, DC: U.S. Government Printing Office.

Fantino, E., & Abarca, N. (1985). Choice, optimal foraging, and the delay-reduction hypothesis. *Behavioral and Brain Sciences, 8*, 315–330.

Faught, E., Falgout, J., Nidiffer, D., & Dreifuss, F. E. (1986). Self-induced photosensitive absence seizures with ictal pleasure. *Archives of Neurology, 43*, 408–410.

Feiffer, J. (1986). [Cartoon]. *Village Voice*, September 23, p. 4.

Fenichel, O. (1945). *The psychoanalytic theory of neuroses*. New York: Norton.

Festinger, L. (1957). *A theory of cognitive dissonance*. Evanston, IL: Row, Peterson.

Fields, W. C. (n.d.). The temperance lecture. Proscenium Records.

Fingarette, H. (1979). Feeling guilty. *American Philosophical Quarterly, 16*, 159–164.

Fisher, A. (1962). Effects of stimulus variation on sexual satiation in the male rat. *Journal of Comparative and Physiological Psychology, 55*, 614–620.

Fisher, I., & Brougham, H. B. (1930). *The "noble experiment."* New York: Alcohol Information Committee.

Fiske, S. T. (1989). Examining the role of intent: toward understanding its role in stereotyping and prejudice. In J. S. Uleman & J. A. Bargh (Eds.), *Unintended thought*. New York: Guilford.

Fodor, J. A. (1985). Precis of the modularity of mind. *Behavioral and Brain Sciences, 8*, 1–42.

Fordyce, W. E. (1978). Learning processes in pain. In R. A. Sternbach (Ed.), *The psychology of pain*. New York: Raven.

Fordyce, W. E., & Steger, J. C. (1979). Chronic pain. In O. F. Pomerleau & J. P. Brady (Eds.), *Behavioral medicine: theory and practice* (pp. 125–154). Baltimore: Williams & Wilkins.

Fowler, H. (1967). Satiation and curiosity: constructs for a drive and incentive-motivational theory of motive. In K. Spence & J. Spence (Eds.), *Psychology of learning and motivation* (Vol. 1). New York: Academic Press.

Frank, J. (1984). Therapeutic components of all psychotherapies. In J. M. Myers (Ed.), *Cures by psychotherapy: what effects change*. New York: Praeger.

Frank, R. H. (1988). *Passions within reason*. New York: Norton.

——— (1990). *Collaborative research on winner-take-all markets*. Working paper BEDR 90–06, Johnson Graduate School of Management, Cornell University, Ithaca, NY.

Freedman, J. (1965). Long term behavioral effects of cognitive dissonance. *Journal of Experimental and Social Psychology, 1*, 145–155.

Freeman, A., & Leaf, R. C. (1989). Cognitive therapy applied to personality disorders. In A. Freeman, K. M. Simon, L. E. Beutler, & H. Arkowitz (Eds.), *Comprehensive handbook of cognitive therapy*. New York: Plenum.

Fremouw, W. J., & Brown, J. P. (1980). The reactivity of addictive behaviors to self-monitoring: a functional analysis. *Addictive Behaviors, 5*, 209–217.

Freud, A. (1966). *The ego and the mechanisms of defense*. New York: International Universities Press.

Freud, S. (1956a). *Project for a scientific psychology*. In J. Strachey & A. Freud (Eds.), *The standard edition of the complete psychological works of Sigmund Freud* (Vol. 1). London: Hogarth. (Original work published 1895)

——— (1956b). *The interpretation of dreams*. In J. Strachey & A. Freud (Eds.),

The standard edition of the complete psychological works of Sigmund Freud (Vols. 4–5). London: Hogarth. (Original work published 1900)

(1956c). *Jokes and their relation to the unconscious.* In J. Strachey & A. Freud (Eds.), *The standard edition of the complete psychological works of Sigmund Freud* (Vol. 8). London: Hogarth. (Original work published 1905)

(1956d). *Formulations on the two principles of mental functioning.* In J. Strachey & A. Freud (Eds.), *The standard edition of the complete psychological works of Sigmund Freud* (Vol. 12). London: Hogarth. (Original work published 1911)

(1956e). *Totem and taboo.* In J. Strachey & A. Freud (Eds.), *The standard edition of the complete psychological works of Sigmund Freud* (Vol. 13). London: Hogarth. (Original work published 1913)

(1956f). *On the history of the psychoanalytic movement.* In J. Strachey & A. Freud (Eds.), *The standard edition of the complete psychological works of Sigmund Freud* (Vol. 14). London: Hogarth. (Original work published 1914)

(1956g). *Instincts and their vicissitudes.* In J. Strachey & A. Freud (Eds.), *The standard edition of the complete psychological works of Sigmund Freud* (Vol. 14). London: Hogarth. (Original work published 1915)

(1956h). *Repression.* In J. Strachey & A. Freud (Eds.), *The standard edition of the complete psychological works of Sigmund Freud* (Vol. 15). London: Hogarth. (Original work published 1915)

(1956i). *Introductory lectures on psycho-analysis.* In J. Strachey & A. Freud (Eds.), *The standard edition of the complete psychological works of Sigmund Freud* (Vol. 16). London: Hogarth. (Original work published 1916–1917)

(1956j). *From the history of an infantile neurosis.* In J. Strachey & A. Freud (Eds.), *The standard edition of the complete psychological works of Sigmund Freud* (Vol. 17). London: Hogarth. (Original work published 1918)

(1956k). *Beyond the pleasure principle.* In J. Strachey & A. Freud (Eds.), *The standard edition of the complete psychological works of Sigmund Freud* (Vol. 18). London: Hogarth. (Original work published 1920)

(1956l). *The ego and the id.* In J. Strachey & A. Freud (Eds.), *The standard edition of the complete psychological works of Sigmund Freud* (Vol. 19). London: Hogarth. (Original work published 1923)

(1956m). *The economic problem of masochism.* In J. Strachey & A. Freud (Eds.), *The standard edition of the complete psychological works of Sigmund Freud* (Vol. 19). London: Hogarth. (Original work published 1924)

(1956n). *Inhibitions, symptoms, and anxiety.* In J. Strachey & A. Freud (Eds.), *The standard edition of the complete psychological works of Sig-*

mund Freud (Vol. 20). London: Hogarth. (Original work published 1926)

(1956o). *Civilization and its discontents.* In J. Strachey & A. Freud (Eds.), *The standard edition of the complete psychological works of Sigmund Freud* (Vol. 21). London: Hogarth. (Original work published 1930)

(1956p). *New introductory lectures on psychoanalysis.* In J. Strachey & A. Freud (Eds.), *The standard edition of the complete psychological works of Sigmund Freud* (Vol. 22). London: Hogarth. (Original work published 1933)

(1956q). *An outline of psychoanalysis.* In J. Strachey & A. Freud (Eds.), *The standard edition of the complete psychological works of Sigmund Freud* (Vol. 23). London: Hogarth. (Original work published 1938)

Friedman, M. (1963). The concept of horizon in the permanent income hypothesis. In C. F. Christ et al. (Eds.), *Measurement in economics: studies in mathematical economics and econometrics.* Stanford: Stanford University Press.

(1973). Roofs or ceilings. In P. Samuelson (Ed.), *Readings in economics* (7th ed.) (pp. 35–36). New York: McGraw-Hill.

Friedman, M., & Rosenman, R. H. (1974). *Type A behavior and your heart.* Greenwich, CT: Fawcett Publications.

Fuller, R. K., & Roth, H. P. (1979). Disulfiram for the treatment of alcoholism. *Annals of Internal Medicine, 90,* 901–904.

Galbraith, G. C., Cooper, L. M., & London, P. (1972). Hypnotic susceptibility and the sensory evoked response. *Journal of the Experimental Analysis of Behavior, 80,* 509–514.

Galen (1963). *Galen on the passions and error of the soul* (P. W. Harkins, Trans.). Columbus: Ohio State University Press.

Gambrill, E. (1977). *Handbook of assessment, intervention, and evaluation.* San Francisco: Jossey-Bass.

Garb, J., & Stunkard, A. (1974). Taste aversions in man. *American Journal of Psychiatry, 131,* 1204–1207.

Garcia, J., Hankins, W., & Rusiniak, K. (1974). Behavioral regulation on the milieu interne in man and rat. *Science, 185,* 824–831.

Gately, D. (1980). Individual discount rates and the purchase and utilization of energy-using durables: comment. *Bell Journal of Economics, 11,* 373–374.

Gay, M., Blager, F., Bartsch, L., Emery, C., Rosenstiel-Gross, A. & Spears, J. (1987). Psychogenic habit cough: review and case reports. *Journal of Clinical Psychiatry, 48,* 483–486.

Geary, N., & Smith, G. P. (1982). Pancreatic glucagon fails to inhibit sham feeding in the rat. *Peptides, 1,* 163–166.

Gedo, J., & Goldberg, A. (1973). *Models of the mind: a psychoanalytic theory.* Chicago: University of Chicago Press.

Gerall, A. A., & Obrist, P. A. (1962). Classical conditioning of the pupillary dilation response of normal and curarized cats. *Journal of Experimental Psychology, 50*, 261–263.

Gerall, A. A., Sampson, P. B., & Gertrude, L. B. (1957). Classical conditioning of human pupillary dilation. *Journal of Experimental Psychology, 54*, 467–474.

Ghent, L. (1957). Some effects of deprivation on eating and drinking behavior. *Journal of Clinical and Physiological Psychology, 50*, 172–176.

Gibbon, J. (1977). Scalar expectancy theory and Weber's law in animal timing. *Psychological Review, 84*, 279–325.

Gibbs, J. P., & Martin, W. T. (1964). *Status integration and suicide: a sociological study*. Eugene: University of Oregon.

Gilbert, R. M. (1972). Variation and selection of behavior. In R. M. Gilbert & J. R. Millenson (Eds.), *Reinforcement: behavioral analyses*. New York: Academic Press.

(1976). Caffeine as a drug of abuse. In R. J. Gibbons, Y. Israel, & R. E. Kalant (Eds.), *Research advances in alcohol and drug problems*. New York: Plenum.

Giovachinni, P. L. (1975). *Psychoanalysis of character disorders*. New York: Aronson.

Gjesme, T. (1983). On the concept of future time orientation: considerations of some functions' and measurements' implications. *International Journal of Psychology, 18*, 443–461.

Glantz, K., & Pearce, J. (1989). *Exiles from Eden: psychotherapy from an evolutionary perspective*. New York: Norton.

Glatt, M., & Cook, C. (1987). Pathological spending as a form of psychological dependence. *British Journal of Addiction, 82*, 1257–1258.

Gleser, G., & Ihilevich, D. (1969). An objective instrument for measuring defense mechanisms. *Journal of Consulting and Clinical Psychology, 33*, 51–60.

Golden, K. M. (1977). Voodoo in Africa and the United States. *American Journal of Psychiatry, 134*, 1425–1427.

Goldfarb, T. L., Jarvik, M. E., & Glick, S. D. (1970). Cigarette nicotine content as a determinant of human smoking behavior. *Psychopharmacologia Berlin, 17*, 89–93.

Goldiamond, I. (1965). Self-control procedures in personal behavior problems. *Psychological Reports, 17*, 851–868.

Goldstein, W. N. (1985). Obsessive-compulsive behavior, DSM-III, and a psychodynamic classification of psychopathology. *American Journal of Psychotherapy, 39*, 346–359.

Goodheart, E. (1968). *The cult of the ego: the self in modern literature*. Chicago: University of Chicago Press.

Granda, A. M., & Hammack, J. T. (1961). Operant behavior during sleep. *Science, 133*, 1485–1486.

Green, H. (1964). *I never promised you a rose garden*. New York: Holt, Rinehart & Winston.

Green, L., Fisher, E. B., Jr., Perlow, S., & Sherman, L. (1981). Preference reversal and self-control: choice as a function of reward amount and delay. *Behavior Analysis Letters, 1*, 43–51.

Green, L., & Snyderman, M. (1980). Choice between rewards differing in amount and delay: toward a choice model of self-control. *Journal of the Experimental Analysis of Behavior, 34*, 135–147.

Greene, H., & Jones, C. (1974). *Diary of a food addict*. New York: Grossett & Dunlap.

Grether, D. M., & Plott, C. R. (1979). Economic theory of choice and the preference reversal phenomenon. *American Economic Review, 69*, 623–638.

Groos, K. (1976). The play of man: teasing and love play. In J. S. Bruner, A. Jolly, & K. Sylva (Eds.), *Play: its role in development and evolution* (pp. 68–83). New York: Basic Books.

Grosch, J., & Neuringer, A. (1981). Self-control in pigeons under the Mischel paradigm. *Journal of the Experimental Analysis of Behavior, 35*, 3–21.

Haan, N. (1963). Proposed model of ego functioning: coping and defense mechanisms in relationship to IQ change. *Psychological Monographs, 77*, 571.

Haley, J. (1963). *Strategies of psychotherapy*. New York: Grune & Stratton.

Halpern, H. M. (1982). *How to break your addiction to a person*. New York: Bantam Books.

Hare, R. M. (1963). *Freedom and reason*. London: Oxford University Press.

Hardin, R. (1984). Difficulties in the notion of economic rationality. *Social Science Information, 23*, 453–467.

Harlow, H. (1973). *Learning to love*. New York: Ballantine.

Hartmann, H. (1958). *Ego psychology and the problem of adaptation*. New York: International Universities Press.

Hatcher, R. (1973). Insight and self-observation. *Journal of the American Psychoanalytic Association, 21*, 337–398.

Hatterer, L. (1980). *The pleasure addicts*. New York: A. S. Barnes & Co.

Hausman, J. A. (1979). Individual discount rates and the purchase and utilization of energy-using durables. *Bell Journal of Economics, 10*, 33–54.

Hawkins, T. D., & Pliskoff, S. S. (1964). Brain stimulation intensity, rate of self-stimulation, and reinforcement strength: an analysis through chaining. *Journal of the Experimental Analysis of Behavior, 7*, 285–288.

Hayes, S. C., Kapust, J., Leonard, S. R., & Rosenfarb, I. (1981). Escape from freedom: choosing not to choose in pigeons. *Journal of the Experimental Analysis of Behavior, 36*, 1–7.

Hearst, E. (1975). The classical-instrumental distinction reflexes, voluntary behavior, and categories of associative learning. In W. Estes (Ed.),

Handbook of learning and cognitive processes (Vol. 2). New York: Erlbaum.

Hebb, D. O. (1955). Drives and the conceptual nervous system. *Psychological Review, 62*, 243–254.

Hendin, H. (1975). *The age of sensation.* New York: Norton.

Hendrick, I. (1936). Ego development and certain character problems. *Psychoanalytic Quarterly, 5*, 320–346.

(1958). *Facts and theories of psychoanalysis*, New York: Knopf.

Henry, J. (1963). *Culture against man.* New York: Random House.

Herrnstein, R. (1961). Relative and absolute strengths of response as a function of frequency of reinforcement. *Journal of the Experimental Analysis of Behavior, 4*, 267–272.

(1969). Method and theory in the study of avoidance. *Psychological Review, 76*, 49–69.

(1977). The evolution of behaviorism. *American Psychologist, 32*, 593–603.

(1981). Self control as response strength. In E. Szabadi & C. F. Lowe (Eds.), *Quantification of steady-state operant behavior.* Amsterdam: Elsevier/North Holland.

(1990). Changes in birth rate lower society's IQ. *Newsday*, September 9, 1990.

Herrnstein, R. J., Loewenstein, G., Prelec, D., & Vaughan, W., Jr. (1988). *Utility maximization and melioration: internalities in individual behavior.* Unpublished manuscript.

Herrnstein, R. J., & Prelec, D. (1991). Melioration: a theory of distributed choice. *Journal of Economic Perspectives, 5*.

Herrnstein, R. J., & Vaughan, W., Jr. (1980). Melioration and behavioral allocation. In J. E. R. Staddon (Ed.), *Limits to action.* New York: Academic Press.

Herzberg, F. (1965). *Work and the nature of man.* Cleveland: World Publishing.

Hilgard, E. (1977). *Divided consciousness, multiple controls, and human thought and action.* New York: Wiley.

Hilgard, E. R., & Hilgard, J. R. (1975). *Hypnosis in the relief of pain.* Los Altos, CA: William Kaufman.

Hineline, P. (1977). Negative reinforcement and avoidance. In W. Honig & J. Staddon (Eds.), *Handbook of operant behavior* (pp. 364–414). Englewood Cliffs, NJ: Prentice-Hall.

(1981). The several roles of stimuli in negative reinforcement. In P. Harzem & M. D. Zeiler (Eds.), *Advances in the experimental analysis of behavior: Vol. 2. Predictability, correlation, and contiguity.* New York: Wiley.

Hirschman, A. (1977). *The passions and the interests.* Princeton, NJ: Princeton University Press.

Hoch, S. J., & Loewenstein, G. F. (1991). *A theory of impulse buying. Journal of Consumer Research, 17*: 492–507.

Hodgson, R., & Miller, P. (1982). *Selfwatching: addictions, habits, compulsions: what to do about them.* New York: Facts on File.

Holinger, P. C. (1979). Violent deaths among the young: recent trends in suicide, homicide, and accidents. *American Journal of Psychiatry, 136,* 1144–1147.

Hollander, E., Fay, M., Cohen, B., Campeas, R., Gorman, J. M., & Liebowitz, M. R. (1988). Serotonergic and noradrenergic sensitivity in obsessive compulsive disorder: behavioral findings. *American Journal of Psychiatry, 145,* 1015–1017.

Hollis, M. (1983). Rational preferences. *Philosophical Forum, 14,* 246–262.

Hollitscher, W. (1939). The concept of rationalization. *International Journal of Psychoanalysis, 20,* 330–332.

Holmes, D. (1978). Projection as a defense mechanism. *Psychological Bulletin, 85,* 677–688.

Holmes, O. W. (1904). *The autocrat of the breakfast table: every man his own Boswell.* Cambridge, MA: Riverside Press.

Holz, W., & Azrin, N. (1961). Discriminative properties of punishment. *Journal of the Experimental Analysis of Behavior, 4,* 225–232.

Homme, L. E. (1965). Perspectives in psychology: XXVI control of coverants, the operants of the mind. *Psychological Record, 15,* 501–511.

Hugdahl, K. (1981). The three-systems model of fear and emotion – a critical examination. *Behaviour Research and Therapy, 19,* 75–85.

Hull, C. L. (1943). *Principles of behavior.* New York: Appleton-Century-Crofts.

Hunt, J. M. (1963). Motivation inherent in information processing and action. In O. J. Harvey (Ed.), *Motivation and social interactions: cognitive determinants.* New York: Ronald Press.

Hunt, W., & Matarazzo, J. (1973). Three years later: recent developments in the experimental modifications of smoking behavior. *Journal of Abnormal Psychology, 81,* 107–114.

Hunter, I., & Davison, M. (1982). Independence of response force and reinforcement rate on concurrent variable-interval schedule performance. *Journal of the Experimental Analysis of Behavior, 37,* 183–197.

Ikard, F. F., Green, D. E., & Horn, D. H. (1969). Scale to differentiate between types of smoking as related to the management of affect. *International Journal of the Addictions, 4,* 649–659.

Ince, L. P., Greene, R. Y., Alba, A., & Zaretsky, H. H. (1984). Learned self-control of tinnitus through a matching-to-sample technique: a clinical investigation. *Journal of Behavioral Medicine, 7,* 355–365.

Izard, C. E. (1971). *The face of emotion.* New York: Appleton-Century-Crofts.

——— (1972). *Patterns of emotion: a new analysis of anxiety and depression.* New York: Academic Press.

Jackson, S. W. (1985). Acedia the sin and its relationship to sorrow and melancholia. In A. Kleinman & B. Good (eds.), *Culture and depression: studies in the anthropology and cross-cultural psychiatry of affect and disorder.* Berkeley: University of California Press.

James, W. (1890). *Principles of psychology.* New York: Holt.

——— (1967a). The dilemma of determinism. In J. McDermott (Ed.), *The writings of William James.* Chicago: University of Chicago Press. (Original work published 1884)

——— (1967b). The will to believe. In J. McDermott (Ed.), *The writings of William James.* Chicago: University of Chicago Press. (Original work published 1896)

——— (1978). *Pragmatism and the meaning of truth.* Cambridge, MA: Harvard University Press. (Original work published 1907)

Janis, I. L. (1968). Stages in the decision-making process. In R. P. Abelson, E. Aronoson, W. J. McGuire, T. M. Newcomb, M. J. Rosenberg, & P. H. Tannenbaum (Eds.), *Theories of cognitive consistency: a sourcebook* (pp. 577–588). Chicago: Rand McNally.

Jarvik, M. E. (1970). The role of nicotine in the smoking habit. In W. A. Hunt (Ed.), *Learning mechanisms and smoking.* Chicago: Aldine.

Jarvik, M. E., Popek, P., Schneider, N. G., Baer-Weiss, V., & Gritz, E. R. (1978). Can cigarette size and nicotine content influence smoking and puffing rates? *Psychopharmacology, 58*, 303–306.

Jeavons, P., & Harding, G. (1975). *Photoreactive epilepsy: a review of the literature and a study of 460 patients.* London: Heinemann.

Jevons, W. S. (1911). *The theory of political economy.* London: Macmillan. (Original work published 1871)

Jones, I., & Barraclough, B. (1978). Auto-mutilation in animals and its relevance to self-injury in man. *Acta Psychiatrica Scandinavica, 58*, 40–47.

Jones, I., Congiu, L., Stevenson, J., Strauss, N., & Frei, D. (1979). A biological approach to two forms of human self-injury. *Journal of Nervous and Mental Disease, 167*, 74–78.

Jorgensen, C. (1928). A theory of the elements in the emotions. In M. Reymert (Ed.), *Feelings and emotions: the Wittenberg symposium.* Worcester, MA: Clark University.

Kabat, G. C., & Wynder, E. L. (1987). Determinants of quitting smoking. *American Journal of Public Health, 77*, 1301–1305.

Kagan, D. M. (1987). Addictive personality factors. *Journal of Psychology, 121*, 533–538.

Kagel, J. H., Battalio, R. C., & Green, L. (1983). Matching versus maximizing: comments on Prelec's paper. *Psychological Review, 90*, 380–384.

Kahneman, D. (1973). *Attention and effort*. Englewood Cliffs, NJ: Prentice-Hall.

Kahneman, D., Slovic, P., & Tversky, A. (Eds.). (1982). *Judgment under uncertainty: heuristics and biases*. Cambridge University Press.

Kahneman, D., & Snell, J. (1990). Predicting utility. In R. Hogarth (Ed.), *Insights in decision making: a tribute to Hillel J. Einhorn*. Chicago: University of Chicago Press.

Kahneman, D., & Tversky, A. (1979). Prospect theory: an analysis of decision under risk. *Econometrica, 47*, 263–291.

(1982). The simulation heuristic. In D. Kahneman, P. Slovic, & A. Tversky (Eds.), *Judgment under uncertainty: heuristics and biases*. Cambridge University Press.

(1984). Choices, values, and frames. *American Psychologist, 39*, 431–450.

Kammeier, M., Hoffman, H., & Toper, R. (1973). Personality characteristics of alcoholics as college freshman and at time of treatment. *Quarterly Journal of Studies on Alcohol, 34*, 390–399.

Kanfer, F. H. (1975). Self-management methods. In F. Kanfer & A. Goldstein (Eds.), *Helping people change*. Elmsford, NY: Pergamon.

Kanfer, F. H., & Karoly, P. (1972). Self-control: a behavioristic excursion into the lion's den. *Behavior Therapy, 3*, 398–416.

Kanfer, F. H., & Phillips, J. (1970). *Learning foundations of behavior therapy*. New York: Wiley.

Kant, I. (1959). *Foundations of the metaphysics of morals* (L. Beck, Trans.). New York: Bobbs-Merrill.

(1960). *Religion within the limits of reason alone* (T. Green & H. Hucken, Trans.) (pp. 15–49). New York: Harper & Row.

Kempf, E. J. (1920). *Psychopathology*. St. Louis: Mosby.

Kenen, R. H. (1986). Making agreements with oneself: prelude to social behavior. *Sociological Forum, 1*, 362–377.

Kenny, A. (1963). *Action, emotion, and will*. London: Humanities Press.

(1979). *Aristotle's theory of the will* (pp. 11–48). New Haven: Yale University Press.

Kerckhoff, A. C., & Back, K. W. (1968). *The June bug: a study of hysterical contagion*. New York: Appleton-Century-Crofts.

Kerr, W. (1962). *The decline of pleasure*. New York: Time Inc.

Killeen, P. (1972). The matching law. *Journal of the Experimental Analysis of Behavior, 17*, 489–495.

Kimble, G. (1961). *Hilgard and Marquis' conditioning and learning*. New York: Appleton-Century-Crofts.

Kimmel, H. (1974). Instrumental conditioning of autonomically mediated responses in human beings. *American Psychologist, 29*, 325–335.

King, G. R., & Logue, A. W. (1987). Choice in a self-control paradigm with human subjects: effects of changeover delay duration. *Learning and Motivation, 18*, 421–438.

Kiplinger, A. (1986). *The Kiplinger Washington letter, 63*, No. 17.

Klein, B., & Leffler, K. B. (1981). The role of market forces in assuring contractual performance. *Journal of Political Economy, 89*, 615–640.

Klein, G. S. (1954). Need and regulation. In M. Jones (Ed.), *Nebraska symposium on motivation* (Vol. 2). Lincoln: University of Nebraska Press.

Kobasa, S. C., & Maddi, S. R. (1983). Existential personality theory. In R. J. Corsini & A. J. Marsella (Eds.), *Personality theories, research and assessment*. Itasca, IL: Peacock Publishers.

Kohlberg, L. (1963). The development of children's orientations toward a moral order: I. Sequence in the development of moral thought. *Vita Humana, 6*, 11–33.

(1973). Continuities in childhood and adult moral development revisited. In P. B. Baltes & K. W. Schaie (Eds.), *Lifespan developmental psychology* (pp. 179–204). New York: Academic Press.

Kohut, H. (1977). *The restoration of the self*. New York: International Universities Press.

Koriat, A., Milkman, R., Averill, J. R., & Lazarus, R. S. (1972). The self-control of emotional reactions to a stressful film. *Journal of Personality, 40*, 601–619.

Kozlowski, L. T., Jarvik, M. E., & Gritz, E. R. (1975). Nicotine regulation and cigarette smoking. *Clinical Pharmacology and Therapeutics, 17*, 93–97.

Kramer, Y. (1977). Work compulsion – a psychoanalytic study. *Psychoanalytic Quarterly, 46*, 361–385.

Krebs, J. R. (1978). Optimal foraging: decision rules for predators. In J. R. Krebs & N. B. Davies (Eds.), *Behavioral ecology*. Sunderland, MA: Sinauer.

Kreps, D., & Wilson, R. (1982). Sequential equilibria. *Econometrica, 50*, 863–894.

Kroger, W. S. (1963). *Clinical and experimental hypnosis in medicine, dentistry and psychology*. Philadelphia: Lippincott.

Krueger, D. (1988). On compulsive shopping and spending: a psychodynamic inquiry. *American Journal of Psychotherapy, 42*, 574–584.

Kubey, R., & Csikszentmihalyi, M. (1990). *Television and the quality of life: how viewing shapes everyday experiences*. Hillsdale, NJ: Erlbaum.

Kumar, R., Cooke, E. C., Lader, M. H., & Russell, M. A. H. (1977). Is nicotine important in tobacco smoking? *Clinical Pharmacology and Therapeutics, 21*, 520–529.

Kummel, F. (1966). Time as succession and the problem of duration. In J. T. Fraser (Ed.), *The voices of time*. New York: Braziller.

Kurz, M., Spiegelman, R., & West, R. (1973). *The experimental horizon and the rate of time preference for the Seattle and Denver income maintenance experiments: a preliminary study.* Research Memorandum 21. Menlo Park, CA: SRI International.

Lachenicht, L. (1989, January). *Powers to do: commands, conflict, moral orders and indirect rationality in the analysis of procrastination.* Paper given at "Knowledge and Method Conference," Pretoria, HSRC, South Africa.

Landsberger, M. (1971). Consumer discount rate and the horizon: new evidence, *Journal of Political Economy, 79,* 1346–1359.

Langgard, H., & Smith, W. O. (1962). Self-induced water intoxication without predisposing illness. *New England Journal of Medicine, 266,* 378–381.

Lasch, C. (1979). *The culture of narcissism: American life in an age of diminishing expectations.* New York: Norton.

——— (1984). *The minimal self.* New York: Norton.

Latendresse, J. D. (1968). Masturbation and its relation to addiction. *Review of Existential Psychology and Psychiatry, 8,* 16–27.

Lay, C. H. (1987). A modal profile analysis of procrastinators: a search for types. *Personality and Individual Differences, 8,* 705–714.

Lazare, A., Klerman, G., & Armor, D. (1966). Oral, obsessive, and hysterical personality patterns: an investigation of psychoanalytic concepts by means of factor analysis. *Archives of General Psychiatry, 14,* 624–630.

——— (1968). Oral, obsessive, and hysterical personality patterns: replication of factor analysis in an independent sample. *Journal of Psychiatric Research, 7,* 275–290.

Lazarus, A. (1972). Phobias: broad-spectrum behavioral views. *Seminars in Psychiatry, 4,* 85–90.

Lazarus, R. (1975a). A cognitively oriented psychologist looks at biofeedback. *American Psychologist, 30,* 553–561.

——— (1975b). The self regulation of emotion. In L. Levi (Ed.), *Emotions, their parameters and measurement.* New York: Raven.

Lazarus, R. J. (1989). Constructs of the mind in mental health and psychotherapy. In A. Freeman, K. M. Simon, L. E. Beutler, & H. Arkowitz (eds.), *Comprehensive handbook of cognitive therapy.* New York: Plenum.

Lea, S. E. G. (1977). *Delayed gratification in normal adults: a questionnaire study.* Unpublished manuscript.

——— (1979). Foraging and reinforcement schedules in the pigeon. *Animal Behavior, 27,* 875–886.

Lea, S. E. G., & Dow, S. M. (1984). The integration of reinforcements over time. *Annals of the New York Academy of Sciences, 423,* 269–277.

Lea, S. E. G., & Roper, T. J. (1977). Demand for food on fixed ration schedules as a function of the quality of currently available reinforcement. *Journal of the Experimental Analysis of Behavior, 27,* 371–380.

Lee, C. M. C., Shleifer, A., & Thaler, R. H. (1990). Anomalies: closed-end mutual funds. *Journal of Economic Perspectives, 4,* 153–164.

Lehman, P. (1973). The decline and fall of conscience. In C. E. Nelson (Ed.), *Conscience: theological and psychological perspectives* (pp. 28–45). New York: Newman.

Leibenstein, H. (1976). *Beyond economic man: a new foundation for microeconomics.* Cambridge, MA: Harvard University Press.

Lepper, M. R. (1981). Social control processes, attributions of motivation, and the internalization of social values. In E. T. Higgins, D. N. Ruble, & W. W. Hartup (Eds.), *Social cognition and social behavior: developmental perspectives.* San Francisco: Jossey-Bass.

Levinson, H. (1975). *The great jackass fallacy.* Cambridge, MA: Harvard University Press.

Lewin, K. (1951). *Field theory in the social sciences.* New York: Harper & Brothers.

Lichtenstein, E., & Danaher, B. G. (1976). Modification of smoking behavior: a critical analysis of theory, research and practice. In M. Hersen, R. M. Eisler, & P. M. Miller (Eds.), *Progress in behavior modification* (Vol. 3, pp. 70–132). New York: Academic Press.

Lichtenstein, S., & Slovic, P. (1971). Reversal of preferences between bids and choices in gambling decisions. *Journal of Experimental Psychology, 89,* 46–55.

Licklider, J. C. R. (1959). On psychophysiological models. in W. A. Rosenbluth (Ed.), *Sensory communication,* Cambridge, MA: MIT Press.

Lieberman, D. A. (1979). Behaviorism and the mind: a (limited) call for a return to introspection. *American Psychologist, 34,* 319–333.

Linder, S. (1970). *The harried leisure class.* New York: Columbia University Press.

Lindner, R. (1955). *The fifty minute hour.* New York: Holt, Rinehart & Winston.

Loevinger, J. (1976). *Ego development.* San Francisco: Jossey-Bass.

Loewenstein, G. (1987). Anticipation and the valuation of delayed consumption. *Economic Journal, 97,* 666–685.

(1988). *The weighting of waiting: response mode effects in intertemporal choice.* Unpublished manuscript.

Loftus, G. (1985). Johannes Kepler's computer simulation about theory in psychology. *Behavior Research Methods, Instruments and Computers, 17,* 149–156.

Logan, F. A. (1965). Decision-making by rats: delay versus amount of reward. *Journal of Comparative and Physiological Psychology, 59*, 1–12.

Logue, A. W. (1983). Signal detection and matching: analyzing choice on concurrent variable-interval schedules. *Journal of the Experimental Analysis of Behavior, 39*, 107–127.

(1988). Research on self-control: an integrating framework. *Behavioral and Brain Sciences, 11*, 665–709.

Logue, A. W., & Chavarro, A. (1987). The effect on choice of absolute and relative values of reinforcer delay, amount and frequency. *Journal of Experimental Psychology: Animal Behavior Processes, 13*, 280–291.

Logue, A. W., Chavarro, A., Rachlin, H., & Reeder, R. W. (1988). Impulsiveness in pigeons living in the experimental chamber. *Animal Learning and Behavior, 16*, 31–39.

Logue, A. W., & Mazur, J. E. (1981). Maintenance of self-control acquired through a fading process: follow-up on Mazur and Logue (1978). *Behaviour Analysis Letters, 1*, 131–137.

Logue, A. W., Peña-Correal, T. E., Rodriguez, M. L., & Kabela, E. (1986). Self-control in adult humans: variations in positive reinforcer amount and delay. *Journal of the Experimental Analysis of Behavior, 46*, 113–127.

Logue, A. W., Rodriguez, M. L., Peña-Correal, T. E., & Mauro, B. C. (1984). Choice in a self-control paradigm: quantification of experience-based differences. *Journal of the Experimental Analysis of Behavior, 41*, 53–67.

Longstreth, L. (1971). A cognitive interpretation of secondary reinforcement. *Nebraska Symposium on Motivation, 19*, 33–80.

Lotka, A. (1957). *Elements of mathematical biology*. New York: Dover.

Low, A. (1976). *Mental health through will training*. West Hanover, MA: Christopher.

Lowe, J. W. G., Lowe, E. D. (1982). Cultural pattern and process: a study of stylistic change in women's dress. *American Anthropologist, 84*, 521–544.

Lynn, S. J., & Rhue, J. W. (1988). Fantasy proneness: hypnosis, developmental antecedents, and psychopathology. *American Psychologist, 43*, 35–44.

Macaulay, S. (1963). Non-contractual relations in business: a preliminary study. *American Sociological Review, 28*, 55–67.

McCarley, R., & Hobson, J. A. (1977). The neurobiological origins of the psychoanalytic dream theory. *American Journal of Psychiatry, 134*, 1211–1221.

McConaghy, N., Armstrong, M., & Blaszczyski, A. (1981). Controlled comparison of aversion therapy and covert sensitization in compulsive homosexuality. *Behavior Research and Therapy, 19*, 425–434.

McConaghy, N., & Barr, R. (1973). Classical avoidance and backward conditioning therapy of homosexuality. *British Journal of Psychiatry, 122*, 151–162.

McDiarmid, C. G., & Rilling, M. E. (1965). Reinforcement delay and reinforcement rate as determinants of schedule preference. *Psychonomic Science, 2*, 195–196.

McDougall, W. (1923). *Outline of psychology*. New York: Scribners.

McGhee, P. E. (1979). *Humor: its origin and development*. San Francisco: Freeman.

Mackintosh, N. J. (1974). *The psychology of animal learning*. London: Academic Press.

McNally, R. J., & Steketee, G. S. (1985). The etiology and maintenance of severe animal phobias. *Behavior Research and Therapy, 23*, 431–435.

Maisto, S., Lauerman, R., & Adesso, V. (1977). A comparison of two experimental studies of the role of cognitive factors in alcoholics' drinking. *Journal of Studies on Alcohol, 38*, 145–149.

Maital, S., & Maital, S. (1977). Time preference, delay of gratification and the intergenerational transmission of economic inequality: a behavioral theory of income distribution. In O. C. Aschenfelter & W. E. Oates (Eds.), *Essays in labor market analysis*. New York: Wiley.

March, J. G. (1978). Bounded rationality, ambiguity, and the engineering of choice. *Bell Journal of Economics, 9*, 587–610.

Marin, P. (1975). The new narcissism. *Harper's*, October.

Mark, V., Erwin, F., & Yakovlev, P. (1963). Stereotactic thalamotomy. *Archives of Neurology, 8*, 528–538.

Marks, I. (1976). Psychopharmacology: the use of drugs combined with psychological treatment. In R. Spitzer & D. Klein (Eds.), *Evaluation of psychological therapies: behavior therapies, drug therapies and their interactions*. Baltimore: Johns Hopkins University Press.

Marlatt, G. A., & Gordon, J. R. (1980). Determinants of relapse: implications for the maintenance of behavior change. In P. O. Davidson & S. M. Davidson (Eds.), *Behavioral medicine: changing health lifestyles* (pp. 410–452). Elmsford, NY: Pergamon.

Marshall, A. (1921). *Industry and trade*. London: Macmillan.

Martin, J. (1991). A shortage of shock sparks plea for more. *Philadelphia Inquirer*, February 3, p. 3-I.

Martindale, C. (1986). The evolution of Italian painting: a quantitative investigation of trends in style and content from the late Gothic to the Rococo period. *Leonardo, 19*, 217–222.

Maslow, A. (1968). *Toward a psychology of being*. New York: Van Nostrand. (1970). *Motivation and personality*. New York: Harper.

Mawhinney, T. C. (1982). Maximizing versus matching in people versus pigeons. *Psychological Reports, 50*, 267–281.

May, R. (1958). The origins of the existential movement in psychology. In R. May, E. Angel, & H. F. Ellenberger (Eds.), *Existence: a new dimension in psychiatry and psychology* (pp. 3–36). New York: Basic Books.

——— (1967). *Psychology and the human dilemma.* Princeton, NJ: Van Nostrand.

Maynard Smith, J. (1978). Optimization theory in evolution. *Annual Review of Ecology and Systematics, 9,* 31–56.

——— (1982). *Evolution and the theory of games.* Cambridge University Press.

Mazur, J. E. (1986). Choice between single and multiple delayed reinforcers. *Journal of the Experimental Analysis of Behavior, 46,* 67–77.

——— (1987). An adjusting procedure for studying delayed reinforcement. In M. L. Commons, J. E. Mazur, J. A. Nevin, & H. Rachlin (Eds.), *Quantitative analyses of behavior. V: The effect of delay and of intervening events on reinforcement value.* Hillsdale, NJ: Erlbaum.

Mazur, J. E., & Logue, A. W. (1978). Choice in a self-control paradigm: effects of a fading procedure. *Journal of the Experimental Analysis of Behavior, 30,* 11–17.

Mele, A. R. (1987). *Irrationality: an essay on akrasia, self-deception, and self-control.* London: Oxford University Press.

Melges, F., & Freeman, A. (1975). Persecutory delusions: a cybernetic model. *American Journal of Psychiatry, 132,* 1038–1044.

Melzack, R. (1973). *The puzzle of pain.* New York: Basic Books.

Melzack, R., & Casey, K. L. (1970). The affective dimension of pain. In M. B. Arnold (Ed.), *Feelings and emotions* (pp. 55–68). New York: Academic Press.

Melzack, R., Weisz, A. Z., & Sprague, L. T. (1963). Strategems for controlling pain: contributions of auditory stimulation and suggestion. *Experimental Neurology, 8,* 239–247.

Mendelson, J., & Chorover, S. L. (1965). Lateral hypothalamic stimulation in satiated rats: T-maze learning for food. *Science, 149,* 559–561.

Menninger, K. (1963). *The vital balance.* New York: Viking.

Merz, C. (1968). *The Dry Decade.* Seattle: University of Washington. (Original work published 1930)

Meyer, R. (1981, May). *Conditioning factors in alcoholism.* Paper presented to the American Psychiatric Association.

Michell, G. F., Mebane, A. H., & Billings, C. K. (1989). Effect of Bupropion on chocolate craving. *American Journal of Psychiatry, 146,* 119–120.

Milgram, S. (1974). *Obedience to authority.* New York: Harper & Row.

Mill, J. S. (1871). *Utilitarianism.* London: Routledge.

Millar, A., & Navarick, D. J. (1984). Self-control and choice in humans: effects of video game playing as a positive reinforcer. *Learning and Motivation, 15,* 203–218.

Miller, D. T., & Karniol, R. (1976). The role of rewards in externally and self-imposed delay of gratification. *Journal of Personality and Social Psychology, 33*, 594–599.

Miller, I. (1969). The Don Juan character. *Medical Aspects of Human Sexuality, 3*, 43–48.

Miller, N. (1969). Learning of visceral and glandular responses. *Science, 163*, 434–445.

Miller, N., & Dollard, J. (1941). *Social learning and imitation*. New Haven: Yale University Press.

Mindess, H. (1971). *Laughter and liberation*. Los Angeles: Nash.

Mischel, H. N., & Mischel, W. (1983). The development of children's knowledge of self-control strategies. *Child Development, 54*, 603–619.

Mischel, W. (1981). Metacognition and the rules of delay. In J. Flavell & L. Ross (Eds.), *Cognitive social development: frontiers and possible futures*. Cambridge University Press.

Mischel, W., & Baker, N. (1975). Cognitive appraisals and transformations in delay behavior. *Journal of Personality and Social Psychology, 31*, 254–261.

Mischel, W., & Ebbeson, E. (1970). Attention in delay of gratification. *Journal of Personality and Social Psychology, 16*, 329–337.

Mischel, W., Ebbeson, E., & Zeiss, A. (1972). Cognitive and attentional mechanisms in delay of gratification. *Journal of Personality and Social Psychology, 21*, 204–218.

Mischel, W., & Moore, B. (1980). The role of ideation in voluntary delay for symbolically-presented rewards. *Cognitive Therapy and Research, 4*, 211–221.

Mischel, W., Shoda, Y., & Rodriguez, M. L. (1989). Delay of gratification in children. *Science, 244*, 933–938.

Mischel, W., & Staub, E. (1965). Effects of expectancy on working and waiting for larger rewards. *Journal of Personality and Social Psychology, 2*, 625–633.

Mitchell, J. (1978). *Price determination and prices policy*. London: Allen & Unwin.

Modaresi, H. A. (1989). Reinforcement versus species-specific defense reactions as determinants of avoidance barpressing. *Journal of Experimental Psychology: Animal Behavior Processes, 15*, 65–74.

Mook, D. G. (1988). The organization of satiety. *Appetite, 11*, 27–39.

Moray, N. (1969). *Attention: selective processes in vision and hearing*. London: Hutchinson.

Mowrer, O. H. (1947). On the dual nature of learning: a re-interpretation of "conditioning" and "problem solving." *Harvard Educational Review, 17*, 102–148.

Munro, J. (1979). Clinical aspects of the treatment of obesity of drugs: a review. *International Journal of Obesity, 3*, 171–180.

Murray, E. J., & Foote, F. (1979). The origins of fear of snakes. *Behavior Research and Therapy, 17*, 489–493.

Myers, D. L., & Myers, L. E. (1977). Undermatching: a reappraisal of performance on concurrent variable-interval schedules of reinforcement. *Journal of the Experimental Analysis of Behavior, 27*, 203–214.

Navarick, D. J. (1982). Negative reinforcement and choice in humans. *Learning and Motivation, 13*, 361–377.

Navarick, D., & Fantino, E. (1976). Self-control and general models of choice. *Journal of Experimental Psychology: Animal Behavior Processes, 2*, 75–87.

Nelson, M. C. (1984). Introduction. In M. C. Nelson & M. Eigen (Eds.), *Evil: self and culture*. New York: Human Sciences.

Nemiah, J. C. (1977). Alexithymia: theoretical considerations. *Psychotherapy and Psychosomatics, 28*, 199–206.

Neuringer, A. (1967). Effects of reinforcement magnitude on choice and rate of responding. *Journal of the Experimental Analysis of Behavior, 10*, 417–424.

Nisan, M., & Koriat, A. (1977). Children's actual choices and their conception of the wise choice in a delay of gratification situation. *Child Development, 48*, 488–494.

(1984). The effect of cognitive restructuring on delay of gratification. *Child Development, 55*, 492–503.

Nordau, M. (1886). *The conventional lies of our civilization*. Chicago: Laird & Lee.

Northcraft, G. B., & Wolf, G. (1984). Dollars, sense, and sunk costs: a life cycle model of resource allocation decisions. *Academy of Management Review, 9*, 225–234.

Nurco, D. N., & Makofsky, A. (1981). The self-help movement and narcotic addicts. *American Journal of Drug and Alcohol Abuse, 8*, 139–151.

O'Banion, D., Armstrong, B. K., & Ellis, J. (1980). Conquered urge as a means of self-control. *Addictive Behaviors, 5*, 101–106.

O'Brien, C. P. (1976). Experimental analysis of conditioning factors in human narcotic addiction. *Pharmacological Reviews, 27*, 533–543.

Ogden, C., & Richards, I. (1930). *The meaning of meaning*. New York: Harcourt, Brace.

Ohman, A., Dimberg, U., & Ost, L. (1985). Animal and social phobias: biological constraints on learned fear responses. In S. Rice & R. Bootzin (Eds.), *Theoretical issues in behavior therapy*. New York: Academic Press.

Olds, M., & Fobes, J. (1981). The central basis of motivation: intracranial self-stimulation studies. *Annual Review of Psychology, 32*, 523–574.

Olson, M. (1982). *The rise and decline of nations*. New Haven: Yale University Press.

Olson, M., & Bailey, M. (1981). Positive time preference. *Journal of Political Economy, 89*, 1–25.

Oomura, Y. (1988). Chemical and neuronal control of feeding motivation. *Physiology and Behavior, 44*, 555–560.

Orne, M. T., Sheehan, P. W., & Evans, F. J. (1968). Occurrence of post-hypnotic behavior outside the experimental setting. *Journal of Personality and Social Psychology, 9*, 189–196.

Ortony, A., & Turner, T. J. (1990). What's basic about basic emotions? *Psychological Review, 97*, 315–331.

O'Shaughnessy, B. (1956). The limits of the will. *Philosophical Review, 65*, 443–490.

Oskamp, S. (1982). Overconfidence in case-study judgments. In D. Kahneman, P. Slovic, & A. Tversky (Eds.), *Judgment under uncertainty: heuristics and biases*. Cambridge University Press.

Overbeck, T. J. (1976). The workaholic. *Psychology, 13*, 36–42.

Packard, V. (1972). *A nation of strangers*. New York: David McKay.

Page, A. N. (1968). *Utility theory: a book of readings*. New York: Wiley.

Panksepp, J. (1982). Toward a general psychobiological theory of emotions. *Behavioral and Brain Sciences, 5*, 407–467.

Pao, P. (1969). The syndrome of delicate self-cutting. *British Journal of Medical Psychology, 42*, 195–206.

Parfit, D. (1984). *Reasons and persons*. London: Oxford University Press.

Paxton, R. (1981). Deposit contracts with smokers: varying frequency and amount of repayments. *Behavior Research and Therapy, 19*, 117–123.

Pears, D. (1984). *Motivated irrationality*. London: Oxford University Press.

Peele, S. (1989). *Diseasing of America: addiction treatment out of control*. Lexington, MA: Lexington Books.

Peele, S., & Brodsky, A. (1975). *Love and addiction*. New York: Taplinger Publishing.

Perris, C. (1988). The foundations of cognitive psychotherapy and its standing in relation to other psychotherapies. In C. Perris, I. M. Blackburn, & H. Perris (Eds.), *Cognitive therapy: theory and practice*. London: Springer-Verlag.

Perry, W. G. (1981). Cognition and ethical growth: the making of meaning. In A. Chicering (Ed.), *The modern American college*. San Francisco: Jossey-Bass.

Peterson, C., & Seligman, M. E. P. (1984). Causal explanations as a risk factor for depression: theory and evidence. *Psychological Review, 91*, 347–374.

Philips, A. (1984). Brain reward circuitry: a case for separate systems. *Brain Research Bulletin, 12*, 195–201.

Philips, H., & Jahanshahi, M. (1985). Chronic pain: an experimental analysis of the effects of exposure. *Behavioural Research and Therapy, 23*, 281–290.

Piaget, J. (1954). *Construction of reality in the child* (M. Cook, Trans.). New York: Basic Books. (Original work published 1937)

(1965). *The moral judgment of the child.* New York: Free Press. (Original work published 1932)

(1967). *Six psychological studies* (A. Tenzer, Trans., D. Elkind, Ed.). New York: Random House. (Original work published 1964)

Pigou, A. C. (1920). *The economics of welfare.* London: Macmillan.

Plagens, P., Miller, M., Foote, D., & Yoffe, E. (1991). Violence in our culture. *Newsweek,* April 1, pp. 46–52.

Plato. (1961). *Phaedo* (H. Tredennick, Trans.). In E. Hamilton & H. Cairns (Eds.), *Plato, the collected dialogues.* Princeton: Princeton University Press.

Platt, J. (1973). Social traps. *American Psychologist, 28*, 641–651.

Polivy, J., & Herman, C. P. (1985). Dieting and binging: a causal analysis. *American Psychologist, 40*, 193–201.

Polking, K. (1990). *Writing a to z.* Cincinnati: Writers' Digest.

Prelec, D. (1983). The empirical claims of maximization theory: a reply to Rachlin and to Kagel, Battalio, and Greene. *Psychological Review, 90*, 385–389.

(1984). The assumptions underlying the generalized matching law. *Journal of the Experimental Analysis of Behavior, 41*, 101–107.

(1989). *Decreasing impatience: definition and consequences.* Harvard Business School Working Paper 90–015.

Premack, D. (1959). Toward empirical behavior laws. I: Positive reinforcement. *Psychological Review, 66*, 219–234.

Pribram, K., & Gill, M. (1976). *Freud's "project" reassessed.* New York: Basic Books.

Prokasy, W. (1965). *Classical conditioning.* New York: Appleton.

Prokasy, W. F. (1984). Acquisition of skeletal conditioned responses in Pavlovian conditioning. *Psychophysiology, 21*, 1–13.

Putnam, F. W. (1989). *Diagnosis and treatment of multiple personality disorder.* New York: Guilford.

Quattrone, G., & Tversky, A. (1986). Self-deception and the voters' illusion. In J. Elster (Ed.), *The multiple self.* Cambridge University Press.

Rachlin, H. (1970). *Introduction to modern behaviorism.* San Francisco: Freeman.

(1974). Self-control. *Behaviorism, 2*, 94–107.

(1983). How to decide between matching and maximizing: reply to Prelec. *Psychological Review, 90*, 376–379.

(1985). Pain and behavior. *Behavior and Brain Sciences, 8*, 43–83.

Rachlin, H., Battalio, R., Kagel, J., & Green, L. (1981). Maximization theory in behavioral psychology. *Behavioral and Brain Sciences, 4*, 371–419.

Rachlin, H., & Green, L. (1972). Commitment, choice, and self-control. *Journal of Experimental Analysis Behavior, 17*, 15–22.

Rachlin, H., Green, L., Kagel, J. H., & Battalio, R. C. (1976). Economic demand and psychological studies of choice. In G. Bower (Ed.), *The psychology of learning and motivation* (Vol. 10). New York: Academic Press.

Rachlin, H., Logue, A. W., Gibbon, J., & Frankel, M. (1986). Cognition and behavior in studies of choice. *Psychological Review, 93*, 33–45.

Radford, R. A. (1945). The economic organization of a P.O.W. camp. *Economica, 12*, 189–201.

Ragotzy, S. P., Blakely, E., & Poling, A. (1988). Self-control in mentally retarded adolescents: choice as a function of amount and delay of reinforcement. *Journal of the Experimental Analysis of Behavior, 49*, 191–199.

Raiffa, H. (1982). *The art and science of negotiations*. Cambridge, MA: Harvard University Press.

Rangell, L. (1968). The scope of intrapsychic conflict: microscopic and macroscopic considerations. *Psychoanalytic Study of the Child, 18*, 75–102.

Rapaport, D. (1950). On the psychoanalytic theory of thinking. *International Journal of Psychoanalysis, 31*, 161–170.

(1959). A historical survey of psychoanalytic ego psychology. *Psychological Issues, 1*, 5–17.

(1960). *The structure of psychoanalytic theory*. New York: International Universities Press.

Rapaport, E. (1973). Explaining moral weakness. *Philosophical Studies, 24*, 174–182.

Raynor, J. O. (1969). Future orientation and motivation of immediate activity. *Psychological Review, 76*, 606–610.

Renner, K. E. (1964). *Delay of reinforcement: a historical review. Psychological Bulletin, 61*, 341–361.

Rescorla, R. A. (1988). Pavlovian conditioning: it's not what you think it is. *American Psychologist, 43*, 151–160.

Ricoeur, P. (1971). Guilt, ethics, and religion. In J. Meta (Ed.), *Moral evil under challenge*. New York: Herder & Herder.

Riesman, D., Denney, R., & Glazer, N. (1950). *The lonely crowd: a study of the changing American character*. New Haven: Yale University Press.

Rifkin A., & Siris, S. (1984). Sodium lactate response as a model for panic disorders. *Trends in Neurosciences, 7*, 188–189.

Robins, L. N., & Regier, D. A. (1990). *Psychiatric disorders in America*. New York: Free Press.

Robinson, J. P., Converse, P. E., & Szalai, A. (1972). Everyday life in twelve countries. In A. Szalai (Ed.), *The use of time*. The Hague: Mouton.

Rodriguez, M. L., & Logue, A. W. (1988). Adjusting delay to reinforcement: comparing choice in pigeons and humans. *Journal of Experimental Psychology: Animal Behavior Processes, 14*, 105–117.

Rolls, B. J., Rolls, E. T., Rowe, E. A., et al. (1981). Sensory specific satiety in man. *Physiology and Behavior, 27*, 137–142.

Rolls, E. T., Burton, M. J., & Mora, F. (1976). Hypothalamic neuronal responses associated with the sight of food. *Brain Research, 111*, 53–66.

Rosenberg, M. L., Smith, J. C., Davidson, L. E., & Conn, J. M. (1987). The emergence of youth suicide: an epidemiologic analysis and public health perspective. *Annual Review of Public Health, 8*, 417–440.

Rotter, J. (1982). *Development and application of social learning theory*. New York: Praeger.

Rousseau, J. J. (1959). *Emile* (B. Foxley, Trans.). New York: Dutton.

Ruderman, H., Levine, M., & McMahon, J. (1986). Energy-efficiency choice in the purchase of residential appliances. In W. Kempton & M. Neiman (Eds.), *Energy efficiency: perspectives on individual behavior*. Washington, DC: American Council for an Energy Efficient Economy.

Russ, N. W., Sturgis, E. T., Malcolm, R. J., & Williams, L. (1988). Abuse of caffeine in substance abusers. *Journal of Clinical Psychiatry, 49*, 457.

Russell, J. M. (1978). Saying, feeling, and self-deception. *Behaviorism, 6*, 27–43.

Russell, T., & Thaler, R. (1985). The relevance of quasi rationality in competitive markets. *American Economic Review, 75*, 1071–1082.

Ryle, G. (1949). *The concept of mind*. London: Hutchinson.

Salzman, L. (1965). Obsessions phobias. *Contemporary Psychoanalysis, 2*, 1–25.

Samuelson, P. A. (1937). A note on measurement of utility. *Review of Economic Studies, 4*, 155–161.

Sandler, J., & Joffe, W. (1965). Notes on obsessional manifestations in children. *Psychoanalytic Study of the Child, 20*, 425–438.

Sartre, J. P. (1948). *The emotions*. (B. Frechtmen, Trans.). New York: Philosophical Library.

Schacht, R. (1971). *Alienation*. Garden City, NY: Doubleday (Anchor Books).

Schachter, S., Silverstein, B., & Perlick, D. (1977). Psychological and pharmacological explanations of smoking under stress. *Journal of Experimental Psychology: General, 106*, 31–40.

Schalling, D., Erdman, G., & Asberg, M. (1983). Impulsive cognitive style and inability to tolerate boredom: psychobiological studies of temperamental vulnerability. In M. Zuckerman (Ed.), *Biological bases of sensation seeking, impulsivity and anxiety*. Hillsdale, NJ: Erlbaum.

Schelling, T. C. (1960). *The strategy of conflict.* Cambridge, MA: Harvard University Press.

(1967). Economics and criminal enterprises. *Public Interest, 7,* 61–78.

(1978). *Micromotives and macrobehavior.* New York: Norton.

(1986). The mind as a consuming organ. In J. Elster (Ed.), *The multiple self.* Cambridge University Press.

Schenck, J. (1954). The hypnoanalysis of phobic reactions. In L. Lelson (Ed.), *Experimental hypnosis* (pp. 465–476). New York: Macmillan.

Schoemaker, P. J. (1982). The expected utility model: its variants, purposes, evidence and limitations. *Journal of Economic Literature, 20,* 529–563.

Schoenfeld, E. (1979). *Jealousy.* New York: Pinnacle Books.

Schuman, M., Gitlin, M. J., & Fairbanks, L. (1987). Sweets, chocolate, and atypical depressive traits. *Journal of Nervous and Mental Disease, 175,* 491–495.

Schur, M. (1972). *Freud: living and dying.* New York: International Universities Press.

Schwartz, B. (1986). *The battle for human nature: science, morality and modern life.* New York: Norton.

Schwartz, B., & Williams, D. R. (1972). The role of the response-reinforcer contingency in negative automaintenance. *Journal of Experimental Animal Behavior, 17,* 351–357.

Schwartz, G. (1975). Biofeedback, self-regulation and the patterning of physiological processes. *Scientific American, 63,* 314–324.

Schwartz, J. C., Schrager, J. B., & Lyons, A. E. (1983). Delay of gratification by preschoolers: evidence for the validity of the choice paradigm. *Child Development, 54,* 620–625.

Schweitzer, J. B., & Sulzer-Azaroff, B. (1988). Self-control: teaching tolerance for delay in impulsive children. *Journal of the Experimental Analysis of Behavior, 50,* 173–186.

Scitovsky, T. (1976). *The joyless economy: an inquiry into human satisfaction and consumer dissatisfaction.* London: Oxford University Press.

Scodel, A. (1964). Inspirational group therapy: a study of Gamblers Anonymous. *American Journal of Psychotherapy, 18,* 111–125.

Scola, D. (1984). The hemispheric specialization of the human brain and its applications to psychoanalytic principles. *Jefferson Journal of Psychiatry, 2,* 2–11.

Sears, R. R., Maccoby, E. E., & Levin, H. (1957). *Patterns of child rearing.* Evanston, IL: Row, Peterson.

Seligman, M. E. (1971). Phobias and preparedness. *Behavior Therapy, 2,* 307–320.

Semrad, E., Grinspoon, L., & Feinberg, S. (1973). Development of an ego profile scale. *Archives of General Psychiatry, 28,* 70–77.

Senault, J. F. (1649). *The use of passions.* (Henry, earl of Monmouth, Trans.). London: Printed for J. L. and Humphrey Moseley.

Shapiro, D. (1965). *Neurotic styles*. New York: Basic Books.

Shaw, G. B. (1951). *Pygmalion*. Baltimore: Penguin. (Original work published 1916)

Sheffield, F., Wulff, J., & Barker, R. (1951). Reward value of copulation without sex drive reduction. *Journal of Comparative and Physiological Psychology, 44*, 3–8.

Shefrin, H., & Thaler, R. (1978). *An economic theory of self-control*. National Bureau of Economic Research Working Paper No. 208, Stanford, CA.

(1988). The behavioral life-cycle hypothesis. *Economic Inquiry, 26*, 609–643.

Shevrin, H., & Dickman, S. (1980). The psychological unconscious: a necessary assumption for all psychological theory? *American Psychologist, 35*, 421–434.

Shiffrin, R. M., & Schneider, W. (1977). Controlled and automatic human information processing: II. Perceptual learning, automatic attending, and a general theory. *Psychological Review, 84*, 127–190.

Shull, R., Spear, D., & Bryson, A. (1981). Delay or rate of food delivery as a determiner of response rate. *Journal of the Experimental Analysis of Behavior, 35*, 129–143.

Siegal, S. (1983). Classical conditioning, drug tolerance, and drug dependence. In R. Smart, F. Glaser, Y. Israel, H. Kalant, R. Popham, & W. Schmidt (Eds.), *Research advances in alcohol and drug problems* (Vol. 1). New York: Plenum.

Silberberg, A., Hamilton, B., Ziriax, J. M., & Casey, J. (1978). The structure of choice. *Journal of Experimental Psychology: Animal Behavioral Processes, 4*, 368–398.

Silberberg, A., & Ziriax, J. (1982). The interchangeover time as a molecular dependent variable in concurrent schedules. In M. Commons, R. Herrnstein, & H. Rachlin (Eds.), *Quantitative analyses of behavior: Vol. 2. Matching and maximizing accounts*. Cambridge, MA: Ballinger.

(1985). Molecular maximizing characterizes choice on Vaughan's (1981) procedure. *Journal of the Experimental Analysis of Behavior, 43*, 83–96.

Simon, H. (1983). *Reason in human affairs*. Stanford: Stanford University Press.

Simon, H. A. (1955). A behavioral model of rational choice. *Quarterly Journal of Economics, 69*, 99–118.

Simonton, D. K. (1990). *Psychology, science, and history*. New Haven: Yale University Press.

Singer, J. L. (1966). *The inner world of daydreaming*. New York: Harper & Row.

Sjoback, H. (1973). *The psychoanalytic theory of the defense processes*. London: Wiley.

Sjoberg, L., & Johnson, T. (1978). Trying to give up smoking: a study of volitional breakdowns. *Addictive Behaviors, 3*, 149–167.

Skinner, B. F. (1948a). Superstition in the pigeon. *Journal of Experimental Psychology, 38*, 168–172.

——— (1948b). *Walden two*. New York: Macmillan.

——— (1953). *Science and human behavior*. New York: Free Press.

——— (1981). Selection by consequences. *Science, 213*, 501–504.

Smith, J. W. (1982). Aversive conditioning hospitals. In E. Kaufman & E. Pattison (Eds.), *The American encyclopedic handbook of alcoholism*. New York: Gardner.

Smith, K. (1954). Conditioning as an artifact. *Psychological Review, 61*, 217–225.

Smith, W. O., & Clark, M. L. (1980). Self-induced water intoxication in schizophrenic patients. *American Journal of Psychiatry, 137*, 1055–1060.

Smith-Rosenberg, C. (1972). The hysterical woman: sex roles and role conflict in nineteenth century America. *Social Research, 39*, 652–678.

Snyder, C. R., & Higgins, R. L. (1988). Excuses: their effective role in the negotiation of reality. *Psychological Bulletin, 104*, 23–35.

Snyderman, M. (1983). Optimal prey selection: partial selection, delay of reinforcement and self-control. *Behavioral Analysis Letters, 3*, 131–147.

Solnick, J., Kannenberg, C., Eckerman, D., & Waller, M. (1980). An experimental analysis of impulsivity and impulse control in humans. *Learning and Motivation, 2*, 61–77; review, 217–225.

Solomon, R. C. (1975). *The passions*. Notre Dame, IN: Notre Dame University Press.

Solomon, R. L. (1980). The opponent process theory of acquired motivation: the costs of pleasure and the benefits of pain. *American Psychologist, 35*, 691–712.

Solomon, R. L., & Wynne, L. (1954). Traumatic avoidance learning: the principles of anxiety conservation and partial irreversibility. *Psychological Review, 61*, 353–385.

Sonuga-Barke, E. J. S., Lea, S. E. G., & Webley, P. (1989). Children's choice: sensitivity to changes in reinforcer density. *Journal of the Experimental Analysis of Behavior, 51*, 185–197.

Spengler, O. (1926). *The decline of the west: form and actuality*. New York: Knopf.

Spetch, M. L., Wilkie, D. M., & Pinel, J. P. J. (1981). Backward conditioning: a reevaluation of the empirical evidence. *Psychological Bulletin, 89*, 163–175.

Spiegel, H., & Spiegel, D. (1978). *Trance and treatment: clinical uses of hypnosis*. New York: Basic Books.

Spielberger, C. D. (1986). Psychological determinants of smoking behavior. In R. D. Tollison (Ed.), *Smoking and society: toward a more balanced assessment*. Lexington, MA: Lexington Books.

Spiegel, H., & Spiegel, D. (1978). *Trance and treatment: clinical uses of hypnosis.* New York: Basic Books.

Spielberger, C. D. (1986). Psychological determinants of smoking behavior. In R. D. Tollison (Ed.), *Smoking and society: toward a more balanced assessment.* Lexington, MA: Lexington Books.

Springer, S., & Deutch, G. (1981). *Left brain, right brain.* San Francisco: Freeman.

Staddon, J. E. R., & Hinson, J. (1983). Optimization: a result or a mechanism. *Science, 221,* 976–977.

Staddon, J. E. R., & Motheral, S. (1978). On matching and maximizing in operant choice experiments. *Psychological Review, 85,* 436–444.

Staddon, J. E. R., & Simmelhag, V. L. (1971). The superstition experiment: a reexamination of its implications for the principles of adaptive behavior. *Psychological Review, 78,* 3–43.

Staw, B. M. (1981). The escalation of commitment to a course of action. *Academy of Management Review, 6,* 577–587.

Stearns, P. N. (1986). Historical analysis in the study of emotion. *Motivation and Emotion, 10,* 185–193.

Steiner, C. M. (1974). *Scripts people live.* New York: Grove Press.

Sternbach, R. A. (1968). *Pain: a psychophysiological analysis.* New York: Academic Press.

Stevenson, B. (1967). *The home book of quotations, classical and modern.* New York: Dodd, Mead.

Stevenson, M. K. (1986). A discounting model for decisions with delayed positive or negative outcomes. *Journal of Experimental Psychology: General, 115,* 131–154.

Stigler, G., & Becker, G. (1977). De gustibus non est disputandum. *American Economic Review, 67,* 76–90.

Strickland, B. R. (1972). Delay of gratification as a function of race of the experimenter. *Journal of Personality and Social Psychology, 22,* 108–112.

Strotz, R. H. (1956). Myopia and inconsistency in dynamic utility maximization. *Review of Economic Studies, 23,* 166–180.

Stuart, R., & Davis, B. (1972). *Slim chance in a fat world.* Champaign, IL: Research Press.

Stunkard, A. J., d'Aquili, E., Fox, S., & Filion, R. D. L. (1972). Influence of social class on obesity and thinness in children. *Journal of the American Medical Association, 22,* 579–584.

Sully, J. (1884). *Outlines of psychology.* New York: Appleton.

Sutton-Smith, B. (1971). Play, games and controls. In J. P. Scott & S. F. Scott (Eds.), *Social control and social change.* Chicago: University of Chicago Press.

Tait, R., & Silver, R. C. (1989). Coming to terms with major negative life events. In J. S. Uleman & J. A. Bargh (Eds.), *Unintended thought.* New York: Guilford.

Tapp, J. T. (Ed.). (1969). *Reinforcement and behavior*. New York: Academic Press.

Taylor, C. (1982). The diversity of goods. In A. Sen & B. Williams (Eds.), *Utilitarianism and beyond*. Cambridge University Press.

Taylor, M. (1975). *Anarchy and cooperation*. London: Wiley.

Taylor, S. E., & Brown, J. D. (1988). Illusion and well-being: a social psychological perspective on mental health. *Psychological Bulletin, 103*, 193–210.

Telser, L. G. (1980). A theory of self-enforcing agreements. *Journal of Business, 53*, 27–45.

Ternes, J., O'Brien, C., & Grabowski, J. (1979). *Conditioned drug responses to naturalistic stimuli. In Proceedings of the 41st Annual Meeting of the Committee on Problems of Drug Dependence* (NIDA Research Monograph 27).

Thaler, R. (1980). Toward a positive theory of consumer choice. *Journal of Economic and Behavior Organization, 1*, 39–60.

(1981). Some empirical evidence on dynamic inconsistency. *Economic Letters, 8*, 201–207.

(1985). Mental accounting and consumer choice. *Marketing Science, 4*, 199–214.

(1990). Anomalies: saving, fungibility, and mental accounts. *Journal of Economic Perspectives, 4*, 193–205.

Thaler, R., & Shefrin, H. (1981). An economic theory of self-control. *Journal of Political Economy, 89*, 392–406.

Thompson, F. (1973). *Lark rise to Candleford*. London: Penguin. (Original work published 1939)

Thompson, W. R., & Melzack, R. (1956). Early environment. *Scientific American, 194*, 38–42.

Thoresen, C., & Mahoney, M. (1974). *Behavioral self-control*. New York: Holt, Rinehart & Winston.

Thorndike, E. J. (1905). *The elements of psychology*. New York: Seiler.

(1935). *The psychology of wants, interests, and attitudes*. New York: Appleton-Century.

Thurber, J. (1942). The secret life of Walter Mitty. In *My World and Welcome to It*. New York: Harcourt & Brace.

Tiffany, S. T. (1990). A cognitive model of drug urges and drug-use behavior: role of automatic and nonautomatic processes. *Psychological Review, 97*, 147–168.

Timberlake, W. (1980). A molar equilibrium theory of learned performance. In G. Bower (ed.), (Vol. 14, New York: Academic Press, pp. 1–58). *The psychology of learning and motivation* (Vol. 14, pp. 1–58). New York: Academic Press.

Titchener, E. B. (1910). *An outline of psychology*. New York: Macmillan.

Toda, M. (1980). Emotion and decision making. *Acta Psychologica, 45*, 133–155.

Todorov, J. C., de Oliveira Castro, J., Hanna, E. S., de Sa, M. C. N., & de Queiroz Barreto, M. (1983). Choice, experience, and the generalized matching law. *Journal of the Experimental Analysis of Behavior, 40*, 90–111.

Toland, A., & O'Neill, P. (1983). A test of prospect theory. *Journal of Economic Behavior and Organization, 4*, 53–56.

Tolman, E. (1932). *Purposive behavior in animals and man*. New York: Century.

Tomkins, S. S. (1962). *Affect, imagery, consciousness*. New York: Springer. (1978). Script theory: differential magnification of affects. *Nebraska Symposium on Motivation, 26*, 201–236.

Toynbee, A. J. (1946). *A study of history*. London: Oxford University Press.

Trachtenberg, P. (1988). *The Casanova complex: compulsive lovers and their women*. New York: Pocket Books.

Treit, D., Spetch, M. L., & Deutsch, J. A. (1983). Variety in the flavor of food enhances eating in the rat: a controlled demonstration. *Physiology and Behavior, 30*, 207–211.

Trivers, R. (1971). The evolution of reciprocal altruism. *Quarterly Review of Biology, 46*, 35–57.

Tuchman, B. W. (1962). *The guns of August*. New York: Dell.

Tulving, E. (1985). How many memory systems are there? *American Psychologist, 40*, 385–398.

Tversky, A. (1969). Intransitivity of preferences. *Psychological Review, 76*, 31–48.

Tversky, A., & Kahneman, D. (1981). Framing decisions and the psychology of choice. *Science, 211*, 453–458.

Tversky, A., & Thaler, R. H. (1990). Anomalies: preference reversals. *Journal of Economic Perspectives, 4*, 201–211.

Twain, M. (1899). Following the equator. In *The complete works of Mark Twain* (Vol. 13, pp. 9–10). New York: Harper & Brothers.

Twitchell, J. B. (1985). *Dreadful pleasures: an anatomy of modern horror*. London: Oxford University Press.

Vaillant, G. (1971). Theoretical hierarchy of adaptive ego mechanisms. *Archives of General Psychiatry, 24*, 107–118. (1976). Natural history of male psychological health: V. The relationship of choice of ego mechanism of defense to adult adjustment. *Archives of General Psychiatry, 33*, 53–54. (1980). Natural history of male psychological health: VIII. Antecedents of alcoholism and "orality." *American Journal of Psychiatry, 137*, 181–186.

Vallacher, R. R., & Wegner, D. M. (1985). *A theory of action identification*. Hillsdale, NJ: Erlbaum.

Vaughan, W., Jr. (1981). Melioration, matching and maximization. *Journal of the Experimental Analysis of Behavior, 36*, 141–149.

Vaughan, W., Jr., & Herrnstein, R. J. (1987). Stability, melioration, and natural selection. In L. Green & J. H. Kagel (Eds.), *Advances in behavioral economics* (Vol. 1, pp. 185–215). Norwood, NJ: Ablex.

Veblen, T. (1931). *The theory of the leisure class.* New York: Random House. (Original work published 1899)

von Hildebrand, D., & Jourdain, A. (1955). *True morality and its counterfeits.* New York: David McKay.

Wachtel, P. (1977). *Psychoanalysis and behavior therapy: toward an integration.* New York: Basic Books.

Waelder, R. (1960). *Basic theory of psychoanalysis.* New York: International Universities Press.

Wagenaar, W. A. (1988). *Paradoxes of gambling behaviour.* Hove, UK: Erlbaum.

Walker, W., & King, W. (1962). Effects of stimulus novelty on gnawing and eating by rats. *Journal of Comparative and Physiological Psychology, 55*, 838–842.

Wall, P. (1977). Pain and the peripheral neuropathies: mechanisms and therapies. In E. S. Goldensohn & S. H. Appel (Eds.), *Scientific approaches to clinical neurology* (Vol. 2, pp. 1942–1958). Philadelphia: Lea & Febiger.

Walls, R. T., & Smith, T. S. (1970). Development of preference for delayed reinforcement in disadvantaged children. *Journal of Educational Psychology, 61*, 118–123.

Watson, J. B. (1919). *Psychology from the standpoint of a behaviorist.* Philadelphia: Lippincott.

(1924). *Behaviorism.* New York: People's Institute Publishing.

Wearden, J. H. (1980). Undermatching on concurrent variable-interval schedules and the power law. *Journal of the Experimental Analysis of Behavior, 33*, 149–152.

(1983). Undermatching and overmatching as deviations from the matching law. *Journal of the Experimental Analysis of Behavior, 40*, 332–340.

Wearden, J. H., & Burgess, I. S. (1982). Matching since Baum (1979). *Journal of the Experimental Analysis of Behavior, 38*, 339–348.

Weber, M. (1958). *The Protestant ethic and the spirit of capitalism.* New York: Scribner. (Original work published 1904)

Weigelt, K., & Camerer, C. (1988). Reputation and corporate strategy: a review of recent theory and applications. *Strategic Management Journal, 9*, 443–454.

Weingarten, H. P. (1985). Stimulus control of eating: implications for a two-factor theory of hunger. *Appetite, 6*, 387–401.

Weitzenhoffer, A. M. (1953). *Hypnotism: an objective study in suggestibility.* New York, Wiley.

Wheelis, (1956). Will and psychoanalysis. *Journal of the American Psychoanalytic Association, 4,* 285–307.

Whipple, W. R. & Fantino, E. (1980). Key-peck durations under behavioral contrast and differential reinforcement. *Journal of the Experimental Analysis of Behavior, 34,* 167–176.

White, R., & Gilliland, R. (1975). *Elements of psychopathology: the mechanisms of defense.* New York: Grune & Stratton.

Wiens, A. N., & Menustik, C. E. (1983). Treatment outcome and patient characteristics in an aversion therapy program for alcoholism. *American Psychologist, 38,* 1089–1096.

Wilde, O. (1989). *An Ideal Husband.* London: Oxford University Press. (Original work published 1895)

Williams, B. (1973). A critique of utilitarianism. In J. C. C. Smart & B. Williams (Eds.), *Utilitarianism: for and against.* Cambridge University Press.

Williams, D. R., & Williams, H. (1969). Automaintenance in the pigeon: sustained pecking despite contingent non-reinforcement. *Journal of the Experimental Analysis of Behavior, 12,* 511–520.

Williams, J. M. G., Watts, F., MacLeod, C., & Mathews, A. (1988). *Cognitive psychology and emotional disorders.* New York: Wiley.

Willis, S. E. (1967). Sexual promiscuity as a symptom of personal and cultural anxiety. *Medical Aspects of Human Sexuality, 1,* 16–23.

Wilson, D. S. (1980). *The natural selection of populations and communities.* Menlo Park, CA: Benjamin/Cummings.

Wilson, E. O. (1975). *Sociobiology.* Cambridge, MA: Harvard University Press.

Wilson, J., Kuehn, R., & Beach, F. (1963). Modification in the sexual behavior of male rats by changing the stimulus female. *Journal of Comparative and Physiological Psychology, 56,* 636–644.

Wilson, J. Q., & Herrnstein, R. J. (1985). *Crime and human nature.* New York: Simon & Schuster.

Wilson, R. (1983). A review of self-control treatments for aggressive behavior. *Behavioral Disorders, 9,* 131–140.

Wilson, S. C., & Barber, T. X. (1983). The fantasy-prone personality: implications for understanding imagery, hypnosis, and parapsychological phenomena. In A. A. Sheikh (Ed.), *Imagery: current theory, research, and application.* New York: Wiley.

Wilson, T. G. (1978). Alcoholism and aversion therapy: issues, ethics and evidence. In G. A. Marlatt & P. E. Nathan (Eds.), *Behavioral approaches to alcoholism.* New Brunswick, NJ: Rutgers Center on Alcohol Studies.

Winston, G. C. (1980). Addiction and backsliding: a theory of compulsive consumption. *Journal of Economic and Behavior Organization, 1,* 295–324.

Wissler, C. (1921). The sun dance of the Blackfoot Indians. *American Museum of Natural History, Anthropology Papers, 16*, 223–270.

Woelfflin, H. (1929). *Principles of art history*. New York: Dover.

Wolberg, L. (1948). *Medical hypnosis*. New York: Grune & Stratton.

Wolpe, J. (1981). The dichotomy between classical conditioned and cognitively learned anxiety. *Journal of Behavior Therapy and Experimental Psychiatry, 12*, 35–42.

Wolpe, J., Groves, G., & Fisher, S. (1980). Treatment of narcotic addiction by inhibition of craving: contending with a cherished habit. *Comprehensive Psychiatry, 21*, 308–316.

Wyckoff, L. (1959). Toward a quantitative theory of secondary reinforcement. *Psychological Review, 66*, 68–78.

Yalom, I., Houts, P., Zimberg, S., & Rand, K. (1967). Prediction of improvement in group therapy: an exploratory study. *Archives of General Psychiatry, 17*, 159–168.

Yates, B. T., & Mischel, W. (1979). Young children's preferred attentional strategies for delaying gratification. *Journal of Personality and Social Psychology, 37*, 286–300.

Yezierska, A. (1925). *Bread givers*. New York: Persea.

Young, P. T. (1972). *Emotion in man and animal*. Huntington, NY: Robert Krieger.

Zajonc, R. B. (1980). Feeling and thinking: perferences need no inferences. *American Psychologist, 35*, 151–175.

Zborowski, M. (1969). *People in pain*. San Francisco: Jossey-Bass.

Zeller, E. (1870). *The Stoics, Epicureans, and Skeptics* (O. J. Reichel, Trans.). London: Longmans.

Zimmerman, J., & Ferster, C. B. (1964). Some notes on time-out from reinforcement. *Journal of the Experimental Analysis of Behavior, 7*, 13–19.

Zuckerman, M. (Ed.). (1983). *Biological basis of sensation seeking, impulsivity, and anxiety*. Hillsdale, NJ: Erlbaum.

Name index

Subject index